The Dissolution of the Monasteries in England and Wales

Studies in the Archaeology of Medieval Europe

Series Editor: Neil Christie, University of Leicester

Founding Editor: John Schofield

Conceived by John Schofield, this series has as its aim to bring together the results of an ever expanding archaeological resource to explore the diverse—but often interconnected—landscapes, places, materials, people and expressions of Europe across the first half of the second millennium AD. These volumes are not just syntheses, however. Written by experts in their field, they bring together old and new studies of town and country, industry and trade, houses and beliefs, but challenge these data to ask much more fully of the character and evolution of the medieval past and heritage. These volumes can be thus introductions, they can inform specialists in their field, they can broaden our vision across a wider geographical stage, and they can stimulate new work and new thinking.

PUBLISHED

Castles and Landscape: Power, Community and Fortification in Medieval England
O.H. Creighton

London 1100-1600: The Archaeology of a Capital City
John Schofield

Medieval Towns: The Archaeology of British Towns in their European Setting
John Schofield and Alan Vince

The Archaeology of Medieval Spain, 1100-1500
Magdalena Valor and Avelino Gutiérrez

The Archaeology of Prague and the Medieval Czech Lands, 1100-1600
Jan Klápště

The German Ocean: Medieval Europe Around the North Sea
Brian Ayers

FORTHCOMING

Medieval Visby and Gotland: The History and Archaeology of a Baltic Metropolis in its Context
Anders Andrén

Rome, 1000-1527 AD: Archaeology and History
Roberto Meneghini and Riccardo Santangeli Valenzani

The Archaeology and Architecture of Monastic Ireland, 1100-1600
Tadhg O'Keeffe

The Archaeology of Medieval Sicily: Cultures, Social Structures, Economies
Alessandra Molinari

The Archaeology of Stari Bar: The Evolution, Dissolution and Reinvention of an Adriatic Town
Sauro Gelichi

The Dissolution of the Monasteries in England and Wales

Hugh Willmott

SHEFFIELD UK   BRISTOL CT

Published by Equinox Publishing Ltd.

UK: Office 415, The Workstation, 15 Paternoster Row, Sheffield, South Yorkshire S1 2BX

USA: ISD, 70 Enterprise Drive, Bristol, CT 06010

www.equinoxpub.com

First published 2020
First printing in paperback with corrections 2022

© Hugh Willmott 2020

All rights reserved. No part of this publication may be reproduced or transmitted in any form or by any means, electronic or mechanical, including photocopying, recording or any information storage or retrieval system, without prior permission in writing from the publishers.

British Library Cataloguing-in-Publication Data

A catalogue record for this book is available from the British Library.

ISBN 978 1 78179 954 3 (hardback)
ISBN 978 1 78179 955 0 (ePDF)
ISBN 978 1 80050 163 8 (paper)

Library of Congress Cataloging-in-Publication Data

Names: Willmott, Hugh (Hugh B.), author.
Title: The dissolution of the monasteries in England and Wales / Hugh Willmott.
Description: Bristol, CT : Equinox Publishing Ltd., 2020. | Series: Studies in the archaeology of medieval Europe | Includes bibliographical references and index.

Summary: "This book provides a timely and original overview of the Dissolution of the Monasteries and its longer term affects on the social and physical landscape of England and Wales during the decades that followed. Whilst primarily focusing on archaeological material, the book also encompasses a range of diverse historical sources. It is aimed at students and scholars seeking an introduction to the main debates surrounding the Dissolution, as well as providing original in-depth case studies to illustrate these" — Provided by publisher.

Identifiers: LCCN 2020005920 (print) | LCCN 2020005921 (ebook) |
ISBN 978 1 78179 954 3 (hardback) ISBN 978 1 80050 163 8 paper) ISBN 978 1 78179 955 0 (ebook)
Subjects: LCSH: England—Church history—16th century. | Wales—Church history—16th century. | Monasteries—England—History—16th century. | Monasteries—Wales—History—16th century.
Classification: LCC BR757 .W48 2020 (print) | LCC BR757 (ePDF) | DDC 271.00942/09031—dc23
LC record available at https://lccn.loc.gov/2020005920
LC ebook record available at https://lccn.loc.gov/2020005921

Typeset and edited by Queenston Publishing, Hamilton, Ontario, Canada

This book is dedicated to my wife Neya for accepting my absence whilst on fieldwork, and my son Dominik who has probably spent far too much of his life rummaging on archaeological spoil heaps than is healthy for an eight-year-old boy

Contents

	List of Figures	ix
	List of Tables	xii
	Acknowledgements	xiii
1.	Introduction	1
2.	Monastic England and Wales at the Dissolution	9
3.	The Destruction and Asset Stripping of the Religious Houses	21
4.	The Dispersal and Acquisition of Monastic Property	47
5.	Avenues for Common Opportunity	71
6.	The Conversion to Domestic Use	99
7.	New Landscapes of Leisure	135
8.	Concluding Remarks	159
	Notes	165
	Bibliography	183
	Index	197

List of Figures

1.1	"King Henry and the Monasteries" Treasure No. 87 12 September 1964.	2
1.2	Cardinal Francis Gasquet and Dom David Knowles.	3
1.3	The gatehouse of Monk Bretton Priory before and after the removal of all roof and timberwork by P. K. Baillie Reynolds.	6
2.1	Plan of the church and cloister, Castle Acre Priory.	13
2.2	The rood screen, St Alban's Abbey.	14
2.3	The gatehouse, Thornton Abbey.	15
2.4	Plan of Watton Priory.	15
2.5	Plan of Mount Grace Priory.	16
2.6	Title page, *Valor Ecclesiasticus* 1535.	17
3.1	The eagle lectern, Newstead Abbey.	22
3.2	Lead ingot from Kenilworth Abbey, now in St Nicholas church.	24
3.3	Lead furnace, Northampton Greyfriars.	26
3.4	Lead hearth, Sopwell Priory.	27
3.5	Lead hearth, Thornton Abbey.	28
3.6	Reverberatory furnace, Keynsham Abbey.	30
3.7	Interior of the lime kiln, Thornton Abbey.	34
3.8	Disturbed tomb of John Ripon, Fountains Abbey.	35
3.9	Distribution and numbers of book fittings found by metal detecting in Norfolk, data from the Portable Antiquities Scheme.	38
3.10	Pews and panelling, Radbourne church.	43
3.11	Translated window glass from Dale Abbey, St Matthew's Church, Morley.	44
3.12	Tomb slab of Sir Henry Sacheverell, St Matthew's Church, Morley.	45
3.13	Stone mortar from Dale Abbey, St Matthew's Church, Morley.	46
4.1	Memorial brass to Sir John Tregonwell, Milton Abbey church.	56
4.2	Lands held in Norfolk by Thomas Howard, Duke of Norfolk before and after the Dissolution.	60

4.3	Monastic land acquired by Charles Brandon, Duke of Suffolk in Lincolnshire.	62
4.4	Monastic land acquired by Robert Heneage in Lincolnshire.	63
4.5	Monastic land acquired by Thomas Heneage in Lincolnshire.	64
4.6	Monastic land acquired by Robert Tyrwhitt in Lincolnshire.	65
4.7	Tyrwhitt family tree.	66
5.1	St Andrew's church, Stogursey, former Benedictine priory.	74
5.2	Reduced church, Great Bricett Priory.	74
5.3	Binham Priory church.	75
5.4	Bridlington Priory church prior to restoration in the later 19th century.	76
5.5	St Helen's church, Bishopgate.	78
5.6	Interior of Beaulieu Abbey church, the former monastic refectory.	80
5.7	Chichester friary church, retained as a town hall.	82
5.8	Post-Dissolution division of the cloister, Bristol Blackfriars.	83
5.9	Post-Dissolution division of the precinct, Newcastle Blackfriars.	84
5.10	Post-Dissolution division of the cloister, Newcastle Blackfriars.	85
5.11	18th-century view of Ipswich Blackfriars.	86
5.12	18th-century plan of Ipswich Blackfriars.	87
5.13	18th-century view of London Greyfriars.	88
5.14	The Free Grammar School, Coventry Whitefriars.	89
5.15	Inkwells found at the Free Grammar School, Coventry Whitefriars.	90
5.16	Hospital of St John, Cirencester.	92
5.17	Pottery wasters from Holy Trinity, Aldgate.	94
5.18	Wine glass fragments from Verzelini's furnace at Holy Trinity, Aldgate.	95
5.19	Infirmary Hall, Canterbury Blackfriars.	96
5.20	18th-century view of Gloucester Blackfriars.	96
5.21	Plan of the post-dissolution brewery, Gloucester Greyfriars.	97
6.1	Inserted Tudor windows, Netley Abbey.	100
6.2	Early 19th-century view of Netley Abbey church.	101
6.3	Plan of Titchfield Abbey.	105
6.4	Plan of Leez Priory.	106
6.5	Plan of Netley Abbey.	108
6.6	Medieval window tracery surviving in the church, Netley Abbey.	109
6.7	Plan of Lacock Abbey.	110
6.8	View of Newstead Abbey.	111

List of Figures

6.9	19th-century view of Egglestone Abbey.	112
6.10	Tomb of Sir Ralph Bowes (d. 1512), Egglestone Abbey.	113
6.11	Plan of Cleeve Mansion.	114
6.12	Plan of Buckland Abbey.	116
6.13	Plan of Vale Royal Abbey.	118
6.14	View of Norton Priory.	119
6.15	Late 17th-century sketch of Kington Priory by John Aubrey.	120
6.16	Plan of Kington Priory.	120
6.17	Plan of Burnham Priory.	121
6.18	Plan of Cleeve Farm.	122
6.19	Plan of Denny Abbey.	123
6.20	The medieval prior's lodge with Tudor additions, Watton Priory.	124
6.21	Converted prior's lodge at Thetford Priory.	125
6.22	Post-suppression house plans at Sopwell Priory.	128
6.23	The division of the former precinct of the Austin Friars, London.	130
6.24	View of Winchester House, London.	131
6.25	Plan of the London Charterhouse.	132
6.26	The division of St Mary Spital, London.	133
7.1	Monastic garden at the Austin Friars, Hull.	136
7.2	Post-Dissolution gardens at Lewes Priory.	137
7.3	Gardens at Haughmond Abbey.	140
7.4	Detail showing the ruins of Barlings Abbey, with Stainfield Hall in the distance.	141
7.5	Gardens at Egglestone Abbey.	141
7.6	18th-century copy of a 16th-century plan of Audley End.	142
7.7	RCHME survey of Jervaulx Abbey.	143
7.8	Reconstructed gardens of Jervaulx Abbey.	144
7.9	Brandon's gardens at Barlings Abbey.	146
7.10	View of Barlings Abbey and Brandon's house.	146
7.11	Stukeley's 18th-century survey of Kirkstead Abbey.	147
7.12	Brandon's gardens at Kirkstead Abbey.	147
7.13	Earthwork survey of the inner precinct at Thornton Abbey.	150
7.14	Resistivity survey of the inner precinct at Thornton Abbey.	150
7.15	The gatehouse at Thornton Abbey.	151
7.16	Division of the precinct at Thornton Abbey.	151

7.17	Garden plan of Thornton Abbey.	153
7.18	Cobble path of the formal garden, with gravel in fills.	153
7.19	The bakehouse at Thornton Abbey.	154
7.20	Plan by John Thorpe for a house for Sir Vincent Skinner at Thornton College.	156
7.21	Excavation of the foundation trench of Skinner's "house."	157
7.22	The "Abbot's Lodge" (originally the guesthouse) at Thornton Abbey.	158

LIST OF TABLES

2.1	Summary of religious orders and numbers of houses at the Dissolution.	10
4.1	Summary of grantees and land.	56
4.2	Summary of John Bellow and John Broxholme's Lincolnshire acquisitions.	68

Acknowledgements

I am very grateful to a range of people who have provided me access to, or pointed me in the right direction of, information used in this book: Caroline Atkins, Debbie Barnes (Assistant Curator of Human History, Colchester and Ipswich Museum Service), Keith Cunliffe (Collections Manager West Suffolk County Council), Adam Daubney (former Lincolnshire Finds Liaison Officer, The Portable Antiquities Scheme), Adrian James (former Assistant Librarian, Society of Antiquaries of London), Antony Lee (former curator at The Collection, Lincoln), Keith Miller (Inspector of Ancient Monuments, English Heritage), Tim Pestell (Senior Curator, Norwich Castle Museum and Art Gallery), Sian Rees, (former Inspector of Ancient Monuments, CADW), David Stocker, and Kristian Strutt (Experimental Officer, University of Southampton).

I owe much to the scholars who have written on the topic for the last century or more; I suspect many would not be happy with some of my conclusions, but their influence is still undeniably there. In particular, I am indebted to Glyn Coppack who has provided no end of support, advice, and access to his unpublished research. He was also, unwittingly, the person who first got me thinking about the Dissolution and its long-lasting impact. Likewise, stimulating conversations with Emilia Jamroziak have really helped hone my historical understanding of monasticism, and occasionally provided a grounded reality to my archaeological naivety. One of the great joys of working in a university is the opportunity to supervise a vibrant and diverse range of doctoral students. A number of these have written theses on monastic topics and have undoubtedly influenced my thinking, in particular Francesca Breeden, Sam Bromage, Martin Huggon, Emma Hook, Charlotte Howsam and Peter Townend.

Finally, I am grateful to Francesca Breeden, Martin Huggon, Duncan Wright and the anonymous referee for providing much useful comment on earlier versions of the text. Needless to say, all errors remain my own.

— 1 —

INTRODUCTION

It is a story repeatedly told, to generations of children and adults alike, and why would it not be? It has all the elements of a good yarn: a capricious and tyrannical king, innocent and pious monks, untold riches and often ancient relics, and of course the rather two-dimensional supporting cast of greedy courtiers and speculators hoping to make quick fortunes out of the suffering of the dispossessed. As well as being a regular staple of children's magazines (Figure 1.1), the Dissolution of the Monasteries is a narrative so well known it has provided fertile territory over the years for novelists such as Prescott and Mantel,[1] even leading one *Times Literary Supplement* reviewer to boldly declare, in a review of a book that dared to suggest somewhat otherwise, that "Henry's abolition of monastic life was a smash-and-grab raid on the wealth of the Church."[2]

Lest it be thought that such emotional sentiments were restricted to the literary sphere, established academics have been prone to resort to similar language. For example, the architectural historian Sir Howard Colvin was moved to state in the opening sentence of an essay on the topic, "The Dissolution of the Monasteries was the greatest single act of vandalism in English, and perhaps European history" and that this was undertaken by "a grasping and tyrannical king, and effected through…ruthless, cynical and philistine men."[3]

That the Dissolution, which of course was more than just merely a historical event, should stir such strong feelings even amongst usually placid academic circles should be of no surprise. In 1937 Geoffrey Baskerville was caused to note "the history of the suppression of the monasteries lends itself to more misrepresentation than any other event in our annals." He went on to characterize a polarized debate between two points of view, the "scavenging party" who believed in the necessary and inevitable march of historical progress, and the "merry Englanders" who possessed a sentimental and often ill-informed view of the monasteries.[4] This dichotomy of opinion appears time and again in the academic literature. Describing reformation studies more widely as an "academic industry," Marsh perceived a division of opinion based more upon religious sectarian lines, explicitly pitting the views of contemporary Protestant historians including Arthur Dickens against Catholics such as John Scarisbrick and Christopher Haigh.[5] It might be argued that Marsh's thinking was perhaps influenced by his long career working in Northern Ireland, and undoubtedly many reformation historians such as Eamon Duffy do not fit easily into either religious camp. However, he makes an important point;

Figure 1.1 "King Henry and the Monasteries" *Treasure* No. 87 12 September 1964 (© Look and Learn History Picture Library).

it is impossible to divorce historical interpretation from personal, theological and innate academic bias. Whether Colvin's denouncement of the actions of his perceived "philistine men" of the 16th century was a result of his personal spiritual beliefs or derived from his professional career as an architectural historian, is immaterial. An act such as the Dissolution of the Monasteries inevitably divides opinion based upon belief, something that has occurred since the event itself in the 1530s.

The Dissolution likewise polarized contemporary opinion. While those who perhaps encouraged and benefited from the closure of the monasteries are mostly silent historically, those who felt aggrieved were certainly not. As early as 1589, Francis Trigge, a Protestant cleric, felt confident enough to criticize the closure of the monasteries stating "many do lament the pulling down of the abbayes."[6] The motivation to regret the closure of the monasteries could sometimes result from unusual circumstances. The antiquarian Sir Henry Spelman, on acquiring the leases of the two monastic houses at Blackborough and Wormegay in 1594, was immediately plunged into a 30-year litigation battle.[7] The experience profoundly affected Spelman and he came to see the resulting legal wrangle as divine retribution, leading him to declare he had "discerned the infelicity of meddling with consecrated places."[8] A committed historian, he did not leave the matter there but chose to meticulously research the fate of all those who had sought to profit from former monastic lands. He inevitably concluded that it had not fared well either for them or their relatives, most of whom seemed to befall a bewildering array of unpleasant fates.[9] Incidentally, Spelman lived to the ripe age of 78, despite being convinced he had evoked God's displeasure.[10]

The notion that the fate of the monasteries, their buildings, and land held long-lasting implications for centuries to come has been picked up by modern historians, and Margaret Aston in particular. In her influential 1973 essay, she argued powerfully that the destruction of the monasteries and the creation of visible, lasting ruins inspired generations of not just poets and literary figures to reflect upon the past, but also historians too. Certainly, this nostalgia for a long-vanished era inspired some of the earliest historical studies into English monasticism and its suppression, perhaps not unsurprisingly from those engaged in holy orders.

One of the earliest "modern" historians of the Dissolution was Francis Gasquet, a Roman Catholic priest at Downside who was subsequently elevated to cardinal (Figure 1.2). His two-

Introduction

Figure 1.2 Cardinal Francis Gasquet (left) and Dom David Knowles (right) (© National Portrait Gallery).

volume study of the Dissolution, published in 1888, was the first work of its kind to explore the history of the suppression using the detailed record of the Court of Augmentations.[11] Gasquet's abilities as a meticulous historian have faced repeated criticism since his own lifetime, but whatever the errors contained within, his work was indeed ground breaking.[12] However, in his preface he openly acknowledges his potential bias and desire to tell the other side of the story when he stated;

> My sympathies are naturally engaged…if I have insisted more on the facts which tell in favour of the monasteries than on those which tell against them, it is because the latter are well known and have been repeated, improved on and emphasised for three centuries and a half, whilst that there is anything to say on the other hand for the monks, has been little recognized even by those who would be naturally predisposed in their favour.[13]

His work was intended to redress a perceived Protestant bias in previous histories, and to give voice to the monks he felt had been silenced in the 16th century.

Any academic work on English monasticism inevitably stands on the shoulders of its greatest historical father, David Knowles (Figure 1.2). A junior contemporary of Gasquet, he was also a monk at Downside where he was a teacher and later an acknowledged medieval scholar.[14] A far more formidable academic than Gasquet, Knowles' works on the monastic and religious orders in England were meticulously researched and written in an engaging narrative style.[15] However, despite taking a more balanced historical stance, there is inevitably a nostalgic and rather romantic tone to his work, and regret that the monastic way of life had been extinguished was clearly felt by this modern Benedictine historian. He certainly knew how to utilize a theatrical turn of phrase to add poignancy to his message; when discussing the initial closures of 1536 he dramatically stated: "as soon as the rumour of suppression had spread, and before the act had passed, the air was thick with wings making for the carrion."[16]

If many of the surviving contemporary accounts and early historical studies by the Catholic churchmen Gasquet and Knowles present just traditionalist "merry Englander" side of the story, how might the opposing view be discerned? Secular historians such as Youings and Woodward have certainly succeeded in providing more dispassionate accounts, principally by presenting readers with a range of primary sources to interrogate themselves. Despite this, Woodward still seems not to have been able to resist subtitling his book "a scholarly reassessment of one of the greatest acts of expropriation in all English history," which perhaps belies his actual views of events.[17]

Perhaps the simplest way to judge the popularity of the Dissolution within 16th-century England, as Ethan Shagan points out, is to ask would the Dissolution, with the massive and sacrilegious destruction of all the monasteries over such a short period, have been able to take place without some level of popular support?[18] Clearly popular "revolts" against the start of the Dissolution in 1536, the so-called Pilgrimage of Grace in Yorkshire and the Lincolnshire Rising (of which more is said below), show that there were pockets of real resistance. However, outside of these areas in the north, the populace did not march and on the whole monasteries acquiesced quietly, leading Shagan to suggest that historians have tended to assume that "the spoil of monasteries was a wholly profane and expedient response" to the Dissolution, even if it was "intrinsically unpopular."[19]

Ben Lowe has echoed this sentiment more generally, again stating that where there was resistance to the Reformation, this was rarely violent and was extremely limited. He further suggests that those who went along with the Reformation did so with "neither quiet acquiescence nor loud evangelical zeal," and perhaps the same could be especially said with regard to the closure of the monasteries which, unlike the parish church, could be seen to be mainly tangential to the majority of people's everyday lives.[20] That having been said, the specific issue of the Dissolution is potentially a more troubling narrative for historians wanting to tread such a moderate line, simply due to its blatantly destructive nature. Whilst the broader Reformation resulted in some initial, but limited physical changes to the fabric of everyday worship, it was nothing on the scale of the Dissolution. Perhaps for this reason, as Shagan has observed, the Dissolution is conspicuous by its virtual absence in the over-arching studies of the English Reformation by Eamon Duffy and Christopher Haigh.[21]

Where perhaps some historians have shied away from discussions of the Dissolution due to its uncompromising and challenging nature, George Bernard has recently presented a challenging reappraisal.[22] Although firmly in the "revisionist camp" and intentionally unsentimental and uncompromising in approach, he nonetheless provides a balance to the equally loaded accounts of those such as Knowles. Rather than stemming from a developed "master plan" that sought to enrich the crown from the start, he sees the Dissolution as emanating from Henry VIII's desire to assert authority over the religious, and a fundamental desire to reform monasticism along Erasmian lines. He points out that the Dissolution evolved as the political situation unfolded, especially after the rebellions of 1536, and notes that the paying of pensions to the former religious would have removed much of the short term financial gain, massively reducing the perceived windfall of riches. Whilst this view helps provide some welcome balance, it would be rash to entirely recast the roles played by the king and his principal advisors; as is demonstrated later in this book, the annual incomes of the former monastic houses that paid for the pensions of the religious were only one tangible asset that the crown took control of. Nevertheless, Bernard provides a useful counterpoint in an attempt to move away from the established narrative of political greed and personal avarice.

The motivation behind this book

As just outlined, the motives of those behind the Dissolution, and the desirability of their actions is a highly charged and well-worn discussion, and in this book I have no intention of getting embroiled in these entrenched debates. What I want to do is move the focus on to what the *physical* consequences of the Dissolution were, particularly from an archaeological perspective, and here I have been subject to two different influences. The first was as an avid visitor to the ruins of former monastic sites, usually those under the care of English Heritage. I was repeatedly struck that the information presented through signboards and on-site displays almost exclusively focused on the each site's history between the 12th and 15th centuries, yet said very little about the events that had created the very ruins being observed. The associated site guidebooks inevitably followed a similar theme, providing just a slight elaboration in a final paragraph concerning the date of closure, and more often than not followed by hint of an unexplained afterlife, along the lines of so-and-so purchased the site and turned it into a mansion.

My second inspiration came from a rereading about ten years ago of Glyn Coppack's 1990 *English Heritage Book of Abbeys and Priories,* when looking for material to include in a new undergraduate lecture on the monasteries. I was moved by the fact that Coppack intentionally chose to end his synthesis with this particular final sentence:

> One of the most important (*future research questions*) is, simply, to discover what happened to our monasteries and their estates after they ceased to be corporations of piety and workshops of prayer.[23]

What happened during the afterlife of so many monastic sites struck me as being the most fundamental of research questions, and one that I did not feel had been addressed in the decades following the publication of Coppack's book.

This is not to say that archaeologists had failed to write about the impact and aftermath of the Dissolution. In 1984 Colin Platt devoted a short section of his book on abbeys and priories to the Dissolution, although most of this followed the established historical narrative, simply illustrated with images of now roofless buildings. Indeed, his account almost entirely focused on the documented destruction of buildings, and at times was infused with the partisan language of earlier debates; he describes the Dissolution in rather martial terms, it being "a full scale assault" on the monasteries and even in one rather unjustified and inappropriate instance, in my opinion, a "holocaust."[24]

The 1990s saw two key overviews of monastic archaeology, the previously mentioned volume by Coppack and two years later, in 1992, a book by Patrick Greene.[25] Although aimed at slightly differing audiences, and thus providing somewhat different emphases, these followed a similar thematic format, with final brief chapters focusing on the Dissolution. Both these accounts benefitted greatly from the extensive use of archaeological evidence and especially drew on each author's first-hand knowledge and experience as dedicated excavators of monastic sites. As introductory guides to the archaeology of monasticism in England, these are still the best volumes available to the student. However, despite this, their treatments of the Dissolution are both perhaps, necessarily, brief due to the encompassing nature of each work. Furthermore, both still tend to focus on the immediate impact of the event as evidenced archaeologically, at the expense of looking at what happened on many sites for decades or even centuries after the 1530s.

What is surprising has been the reluctance of archaeologists to write more holistic works covering the period or to engage with the Dissolution at all, perhaps echoing apparent discomfort of some reformation historians to do the same. At the end of the last century overviews of the medieval archaeology of England by both Clarke and Steane omit almost any mention of it.[26] Perhaps these authors felt the Dissolution somehow fell outside of their rigid periodization, but it is also lacking from post-medieval syntheses. The earliest of these, by David Crossley in 1990, mentions the Dissolution in just one brief paragraph, although given the entire chapter on church archaeology spans only eight pages (as opposed to the 168 devoted to industrial topics), this is probably the result of his own biases in trying to set the agenda for what was then a new and emerging discipline.[27] Perhaps more unexpected is the total absence of the Dissolution in Matthew Johnson's *An Archaeology of Capitalism*; in Marxian terms, to my mind at least, there can be little more fitting a topic for such a work than the appropriation of communally held land and resources by an emerging and opportunistic elite.[28]

Where a more comprehensive archaeology of the Dissolution can be found is in the myriad of more specific thematic works and within individual excavations and site-specific studies in particular. Here, perhaps, taking a more detailed and longer-term overview of what happened after is thought appropriate and, crucially, manageable. Coppack's surveys of the Cistercian and Carthusian orders (the latter with Mick Aston) both contain informative sections on the effects the Dissolution had on these two very different orders.[29] Some excellent and detailed case studies can be found in a range of excavation reports, such as the comprehensive publication on the seminal excavations at Norton Priory, Cheshire.[30] One issue that seems to pervade much of this detailed archaeological work subconsciously is the almost implicit assumption that the Dissolution, and what followed, was an inevitable process, almost possessed of its own agency; crucially people often appear to be absent in the discussions of asset stripping, the desire to create private residences and the like. This is, in part I suspect, due to archaeologists' nervousness, or unwillingness, to engage with historical sources and to place individuals at the heart of their narratives.

There are, of course, some notable exceptions. Paul Everson and David Stocker in their interpretation of the transformation of Barlings Abbey, Lincolnshire after its suppression place the character of Charles Brandon, Duke of Suffolk and the new master of Barlings at the centre of their interpretation.[31] This explicitly biographical approach is one that Alan Bryson and myself took in our examination of the post-Dissolution archaeology of Monk Bretton Priory, South Yorkshire.[32] Here we closely linked the noticeable changes at the site to the individual owners and their needs, from

Figure 1.3 The gatehouse of Monk Bretton Priory before and after the removal of all roof and timberwork by P.K. Baillie Reynolds (© Barnsley Archives, Author).

the lawyer and Cromwellian commissioner William Blithman to the Earl of Shrewsbury and other gentry families. We finally focused on P. K. Baillie Reynolds, the 20th-century Inspector of Ancient Monuments whose orders for Ministry of Works workmen to strip away later "additions" did more to mutilate and transform the site than any Tudor grandee (Figure 1.3).

The scope of this work

Despite the wealth of evidence excavated since the 19th century, covered in a range of more general surveys and a vast number of individual site reports, to date, there has not been a book focusing specifically on the archaeology of the Dissolution of the Monasteries, and this volume is an attempt to redress this imbalance. What follows is a personal synthesis; undoubtedly others would approach the topic differently, or place their emphases in other areas. I certainly have not been able to fit reference to every published work into this book, nor would it be desirable to do so. However, I have included references to what I think are the key themes and studies.

I have tried to guide the narrative in two ways, in part to avoid a disjointed site-by-site discussion and to provide a greater textual coherency. The first is along broad chronological lines in the ordering of the chapters and topics. The Dissolution, in both the historical and the archaeological literature, is often presented as a 1530s' "flash in the pan" that saw the religious evicted, the houses pulled down, and the land sold off. However, while the entire round of suppression was indeed extremely rapid, the aftermath continued for the remainder of the 16th century and beyond. As a result, I have chosen to order the text to reflect the sequence of events; starting with the asset stripping of sites, before moving onto the expected and unexpected opportunities monastic sites provided, through to the sale and acquisition of land. I then go on to examine what are in part the practical questions of why, and then how, new owners of monastic sites chose to convert cloister to country house, before examining the broader transformation of precinct into constructed leisured landscapes, some of which endure to this day. I acknowledge there are some overlaps between these themes, which should not be considered entirely in isolation. For instance, the monastic precincts in towns were more usually subject to entrepreneurial redevelopment than conversion into gardens, and the physical destruction of monastic fabric benefited not just the crown financially but provided civic authorities with needed building materials to improve harbours and town defences.

My second aim has been to try and put the people of Tudor England back into the narrative of the Dissolution, as far as is possible. By this I do not mean the key players, the King and Cromwell, whose roles are well known if contested, but those that took a direct and personal hand in the destruction and then rebuilding of monastic buildings and landscapes. Some, of course, are familiar members of the aristocracy, the dukes of Norfolk and Suffolk both play their parts, but also the more obscure members of the gentry who acquired and, often unlike those further up the social scale, actually lived in the transformed monastic properties. Can we see patterns emerging in what they chose to do? Likewise, albeit at a more institutional level, can we detect differing responses amongst civic authorities and urban communities in how former monastic possessions were dealt with? It is, of course, a potentially tricky path for an archaeologist, albeit a historical one, to tread. However, I think it essential to make the attempt; just as the lead from the church roofs did not melt themselves down for the benefit of the king, houses, gardens, civic buildings and new parish churches did not just spontaneously appear out of the ruins, but were constructed by individuals and communities to serve their specific needs.

In a book like this, any such biographical approach is inevitably focused and has been in large directed by my own research, or those of other scholars I have found pertinent. Readers will see repeated references to the Tyrwhitts of Lincolnshire, but it could equally be the Stanhopes or Byrons of Nottinghamshire, and while the burgesses of Newcastle feature prominently, it could equally have been those of Hull, Southampton or Leicester. Whichever actors are focused upon the broad narrative remains the same.

In adopting this approach I hope I have provided a contextualized analysis of the Dissolution, that starts to move beyond the polarized arguments of the past, and one that most importantly of all demonstrates the values of an archaeologically informed treatment of the topic.

A note on the illustrations

A large number of plans are reproduced throughout this book, and the majority have been redrawn from original published illustrations. I have deliberately simplified these as much of the fine architectural detail or nuanced phasing is not relevant to the discussion presented here. In these plans pre-Dissolution walls that were retained and reused after the suppression are shown in solid black, those demolished as bounded plain boxes and any new work that was added is in grey.

— 2 —

MONASTIC ENGLAND AND WALES AT THE DISSOLUTION

Given today's increasingly secular world, the extent to which religious activity was *physically* engrained within everyday life at the start of the 16th century cannot be underestimated. In addition to the ubiquitous parish church, other religious institutions, and monastic houses in particular, were present in every town and throughout the countryside. By the time of the Dissolution, Knowles and Hadcock have estimated that there were between 825 and 831 monastic houses in England and Wales, and whilst such a precise figure might be subject to some questioning, it provides a good insight into the dominating presence these institutions must have had upon the consciousness of all, lord and peasant alike.[1] To these "closed" monastic houses should be added the hospitals, also run along religious lines, and although harder to estimate in number due to the incomplete survival of contemporary documentation, a conservative estimate would suggest there were at least 600 of these still in operation at the Dissolution.[2] In total, perhaps 10,000 men and women were in religious orders, in addition to the countless secular priests serving in the parishes and colleges across the country. To this figure should also be added the lay brethren, servants and other employees who worked for the religious, perhaps some 30,000 people by the time of the Dissolution.

Monastic life had its origins in the eremitic tradition of the early Christian desert fathers in Egypt,[3] and by around AD 600 there were a number of influences that shaped an evolving insular monastic tradition in Britain, including missionaries from Ireland and Continental Europe, as well as a persisting Romano-British tradition of Christian practice.[4] How many monasteries were present in late Anglo-Saxon England is uncertain; Knowles and Hadcock estimated around 60, but this is a highly speculative figure. Furthermore, it is increasingly apparent that it is hard to identify what actually constituted a monastery in this period, especially in the absence of corroborating historical sources.[5] However, what is certain is that with the arrival of the new Norman lords following the defeat of the Saxons at the Battle of Hastings, there was a staggering increase in the number of foundations made during the late 11th and 12th centuries.

Ordering the world

At first glance, there was a bewildering array of different monastic orders across medieval Europe. Despite this, there was much that united these groups in both ritual practice, and the ways they organized the monastic world around them. Almost all followed the Rule of Saint Benedict, or later revisions of it, and at the most basic level, all monasteries consisted of communities of the religious partaking in a life of structured prayer and study, while living in common.

The majority of those living in monastic communities, perhaps as much as 80%, were male,[6] and can be divided into three general types: monks, canons regular, and friars (see Table 2.1). Monks were individuals who had taken the holy vows to live a life of poverty, chastity, and obedience to their order. When the Rule of Saint Benedict was formulated in the 6th century, the vast majority of monks were not ordained so could not undertake certain rituals, such as the performing of the Mass, but by the 12th century increasing numbers were also priests, but this was not an automatic progression. The most common and oldest order of monks were the Benedictines (sometimes known as the Black Monks due to the colour of their habit), who traced their origin back to the 6th century and Saint Benedict himself, and lived in independent priories or abbeys.[7] Other monks belonged to orders that followed a reformed version of the rule of Saint Benedict, which was thought by them to have become too lax, and were structured more hierarchically with a central "motherhouse" and a succession of dependant, usually later, foundations. The largest of these orders were the Cistercians, founded by Robert of Molesme the first abbot of Cîteaux in France at the end of the 11th century, and who by the Dissolution had 76 houses across England and Wales.[8] Another important reformed order were the Cluniacs. Although the order dated back to the 10th century following the foundation of the motherhouse at Cluny, by the Dissolution they were in possession of just 27 houses.[9] The final small, but particularly significant for this study, reformed order were the Carthusians. Traditionally thought to have been formed by Saint Bruno in the foothills of the Alps in the 1080s, more recent work suggests that Guigues de St-Romain was actually their founder. They sought to recreate the hermitic lifestyle of the early desert fathers, so while the monks still lived their life communally, most of their time was spent in physical and spiritual isolation.[10]

The second category of male monastic was the canon regular. The chief difference between the canon and the monk was that the former was an ordained priest and able to perform the Mass. However, unlike the secular canon or priest, canons regular also

Table 2.1 Summary of religious orders and numbers of houses at the Dissolution (data extracted from Knowles and Hadcock 1953, 359–366)

Order	Minimum Number of Houses
Benedictine	133
Cluniac	27
Cistercian	76
Carthusian	9
Augustinian	171
Premonstratensian (Norbertine)	32
Gilbertine	24
Friaries	187
Military Orders	35
Female Houses	137
Total	831

lived a communal life under vows, rather than independently attached to a church. The Augustinians, whose name derived from the saint's rule that they followed, were the largest of the canonical orders in England and Wales, with 171 independent houses. Other orders of canons regular included the Premonstratensians (or Norbertines) and the Gilbertines, the latter being the only monastic order that could be claimed to be uniquely "English."[11]

The third major category of male monastic was the friar. The friar was a member of one of the mendicant orders introduced into England and Wales in the 13th century. More evangelical in mission, rather than being confined to the cloister the mendicant orders sought to provide more charitable care to the communities around them, and were therefore generally located within, or in close proximity to, towns. They also eschewed the community's accumulation of wealth, so generally held little property outside of the immediate precinct and relied much more heavily on charity themselves. Four main orders of friars were introduced, the Carmelites (White Friars), the Franciscan (Grey Friars), the Dominicans (Black Friars), and Augustinians (Austin Friars).[12]

Other male communities were quasi-monastic in nature, and the military orders in particular. Originating in the 12th-century Holy Land, orders such as the Hospitallers and Templars were formed to provide charity and protect pilgrims visiting the holy sites.[13] Whilst they also established quite a large number of houses, known as preceptories, in England and Wales, those of the Templars were all suppressed in the early 14th century, and by the Dissolution only around 35 Hospitaller houses were present.[14]

It was not just males who lived in monastic communities, female houses, or nunneries, were present throughout England and Wales, albeit in lesser numbers; by the time of the Dissolution it is estimated that there were around 137.[15] During the first few centuries of occupation some nunneries appeared to have also housed a number of male canons, so were not strictly "single sex." For example, at Swine, despite the house being ruled by a prioress, the presence of brethren as well as nuns was recorded several times during the 14th century.[16] Furthermore, unlike their male counterparts, it is often hard to tell to which order most nunneries belonged. Many claimed to be Benedictine, Cistercian, Cluniac or Augustinian, amongst others, but certainly, amongst the more hierarchical orders, there was a reluctance for the motherhouse to accept this supposed allegiance, which could be quite fluid through time.[17] Some nunneries even claimed to be allied to the mendicant orders, such as the Dominican and Franciscan sisters, but unlike their male counterparts, they lived a more traditional cloistered existence.[18] One further phenomenon was the double house, a more formal mixed-sex community of males and females living together on one site, albeit under strictly separated conditions. In England, this included eleven Gilbertine monasteries and a single Bridgettine house at Syon.[19]

It is important to remember that all monastic communities relied on additional labour to enable the day-to-day running of the house, and this could take two forms, lay brethren and paid servants. Lay brethren, or *conversi*, adopted a semi-monastic lifestyle, and without taking the final vows, lived in close proximity to the religious, being housed in the precinct and worshipping in the monastic church. The Cistercians and Carthusians made particularly extensive use of lay brethren, who in the former's case lived in the west range of cloister. In earlier Carthusian charterhouses, up to and including the foundation of Beauvale in 1343, the lay brethren occupied a separate "lower house" of cells, although in later foundations they seem to have been housed in the main complex. Other orders, such as the Benedictines and Augustinians, seem to have chosen to employ paid servants, or *mercenarii*,[20] and these were not usually accommodated in the inner precinct.

The topography of belief

Even the smallest monastery consisted of a wide range of buildings both in stone and timber, and it is well beyond the scope and purpose of this work to provide a comprehensive review of the varied archaeological evidence for these. However, following a monastery's suppression, it was these very buildings that were the focus of asset stripping and conversion to secular use, while the wider precinct was sometimes transformed into landscaped gardens. Consequently, to understand the changes that took place from the 1530s onwards, at least an impression of what was coming into the hands of their new owners is required.

Although all monasteries were superficially very different, most conformed to a broadly similar plan irrespective of their order or location, a pattern that came fossilized from the 10th century onward in continental Europe. Thus, an Italian Benedictine visiting a Cistercian or Augustinian house in Yorkshire would have been able to navigate their way through the main buildings and precinct with relative ease. The exceptions to this norm were the Gilbertine double house and the Carthusian charterhouse (see below), although in essence most of the elements of a more ordinary monastery were still present in these complexes, just reordered and a different emphasis given to the layout to fit the differing lifestyles of the inhabitants.

The heart of the monastery was the church; here the daily life of worship was focused. Given this, and of course its spiritual significance, the monastic church was the largest and most lavishly decorated of all buildings in the precinct. As a result, it was a key focus for those wishing to profit from the removal of valuable materials after the Dissolution, and being such a substantial structure, it could also be reused in new and sometimes innovative ways. In plan, the monastic church resembled that used by the parish, albeit on an often far grander scale. However, variations occurred, particularly between orders where liturgical practices may have been different, and dependent on whether other communities, such as lay brethren or the local parish, were also sharing the church for worship with the religious.[21]

This having been said, the majority of monastic churches can be divided into three broad zones defined by their architecture and use, and this can best be seen at a well-preserved site such as Castle Acre Priory (Figure 2.1). The principal of these was the presbytery occupying the east end, mirroring the area known as the chancel in an ordinary parish church. In the monastic church, the presbytery typically consisted of the sanctuary, the area immediately surrounding the high altar, and the choir, the stalls occupied by the religious during their daily services. Depending on the size of the community and the church, the choir might be confined to the east end of the church, but in some cases could extend further west into the crossing. This was an area flanked to the north and the south by the transepts that gave almost every monastic church its cruciform shape. The crossing usually sat beneath some form of central tower, even if this was simply a low construction or even just a peaked roof, and as a result the crossing was defined by four piers, or columns, that were the most substantial in the church and built to carry the additional weight of the tower above. The transepts to the north and south held further side chapels with their associated altars.

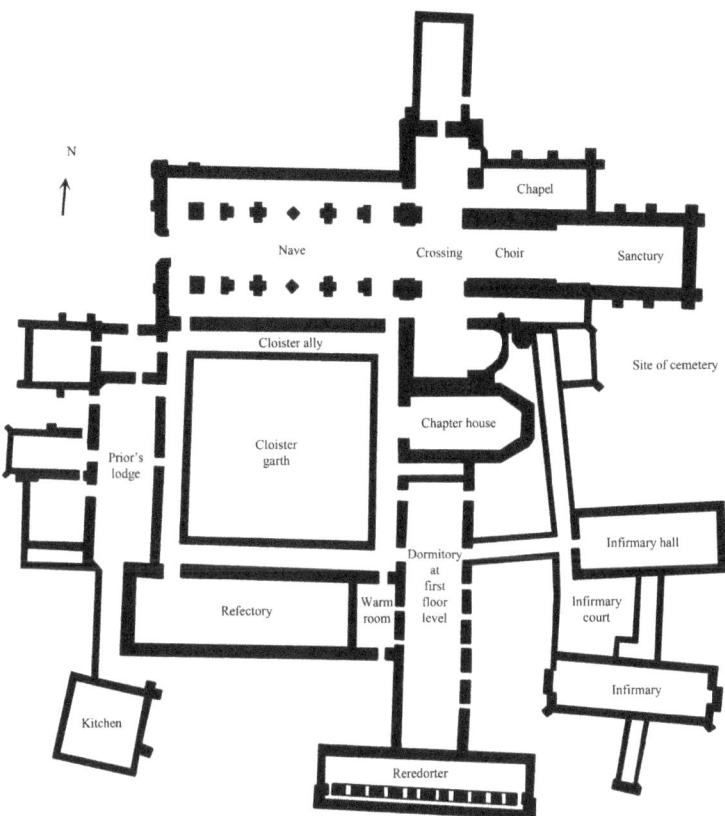

Figure 2.1 Plan of the church and cloister, Castle Acre Priory (after Raby and Baillie Reynolds 1952).

The western portion of the church, the nave, was physically, as well as symbolically, separated from the choir by the rood screen. Although this could have been made from timber, in most larger monastic churches this was an elaborate stone feature, highly decorated with statues and other painted scenes (Figure 2.2). The nave was usually aisled, and a pair of towers often flanked its western entrance. Sometimes used for parochial worship (see Chapter 5), by the end of the Middle Ages the nave's main function was for lay burial as well as being the last place visited during Sunday processions.

Whilst the church was the focus of spiritual life, the cloister was the heart of the domestic side of monastic life, as can be seen again in the layout of Castle Acre Priory (see Figure 2.1). The cloister garth, an open space surrounded by a covered walk way, or alley, was potentially an area for quiet contemplation, but also fulfilled the more functional role of being a corridor that linked all the key areas of the inner monastery. Usually lying to the south of the church, it was connected by at least one door that led directly into the nave. The east range of the cloister contained some of the most important buildings and the chapter house in particular. This chamber, entered at ground floor level, was where the community met, the business of the day was decided, and important visitors received. Consequently, it is no surprise that when Henry VIII's commissioners made their visitations (see below), as had the bishops before them, they were met in the chapter house. The remainder of the east range at ground floor level consisted of cellar ranges and sometimes a warming room with fireplace, one of the few heated areas of the monastery.

The first floor of the east range housed the dormitory or dorter. This had a night stair that connected directly into the monastic church at one end and at the other lay an often quite substantial latrine block, or reredorter. The reredorter was almost always flushed by a diverted watercourse, which had first passed through the central monastic kitchen to the west that served the monastic refectory or frater located in the south range. The refectory could be located

Figure 2.2   The rood screen, St Alban's Abbey (Author).

at ground or first-floor level and was orientated east-west, parallel to the church. A notable variation to this pattern can be seen at many Cistercian houses, particularly in their later phases, where the refectory was set perpendicular to the cloister, in part to incorporate a kitchen in the south range and in imitation of a rebuilt north-south refectory at the mother-house of Clairvaux.[22]

The western claustral range was the one that had the most varied function, and in some instances its role is far from clear. In a Cistercian house, where the lay brethren were also housed in the inner precinct, the west range served as the lay dormitory, sometimes with its own separate reredorter. In other orders, particularly in smaller houses, the west range served as the prior or abbot's lodging, and thus in this case the range was more specifically adapted for personal comfort, making it a particularly popular focus for later secular occupation.

To the east of the cloister lay the monastic infirmary, and although these could vary in complexity and layout, from a single simple building to a second fully-developed cloister, its function was to house not only the sick but also those religious for whom the rigours of communal living had become too great.[23] In many cases the infirmary was linked to the cloister, and even the church, by an enclosed corridor enabling the inhabitants' easy access to the key areas of the monastery, implying that they were still expected to participate in the daily rituals of religious life if at all possible.

Outside of the core claustral ranges, there were also other substantial stone buildings. In monasteries where the abbot or prior was not lodged in the west range, a separate house for the community's head would usually be found close to the frater or infirmary. Likewise, many monasteries who expected to host secular visitors regularly would have a guesthouse specifically for this purpose, where those of high status could be housed in some comfort; excavations of the guest house at Kirkstall Abbey revealed it to be a grand hall with separate kitchens, bakehouse and stable.[24] Both abbot's lodges and guesthouses, being domestic in focus, could easily be converted to secular use with the minimum of effort.

The wider monastic precinct contained a range of other domestic and agricultural buildings, far too numerous to list in detail, although even a modest sized house might be expected to have stables, a bakehouse, brewhouse, barns, byres, and a mill. However, while many of these could, and were, retained for their primary use in the immediate post-Dissolution period, they tended not to be the focus of later redevelopment and occupation. The exception to this was often the gatehouse, which could still retain its significance in the post-Dissolution period.

Gatehouses could be very substantial structures; in the case of Thornton Abbey, it was the largest single building in the precinct after the monastic church itself (Figure 2.3). However, the gatehouse was also a very functional building that could suit the purpose of the new owners of a site as well as it had done those who first built it.

There were two significant variations to this general pattern, the Gilbertine double house, and the Carthusian charterhouse. The Gilbertines, with their tradition of housing men and women on the same site, required a unique solution to keep the sexes strictly separated, and the house that has traditionally been seen as the exemplar of this is Watton Priory (Figure 2.4). Here, excavations early last century revealed a plan with a monastic church divided down the centre to separate canons and nuns on either side, with an adjoining cloister to the north for the female inmates.[25] The male inhabitants were housed in a separate detached cloister to the east, with a rather curious second chapel instead of a church. This odd and very disjointed arrangement has now been shown to be somewhat atypical.

Figure 2.3 The gatehouse, Thornton Abbey (Author).

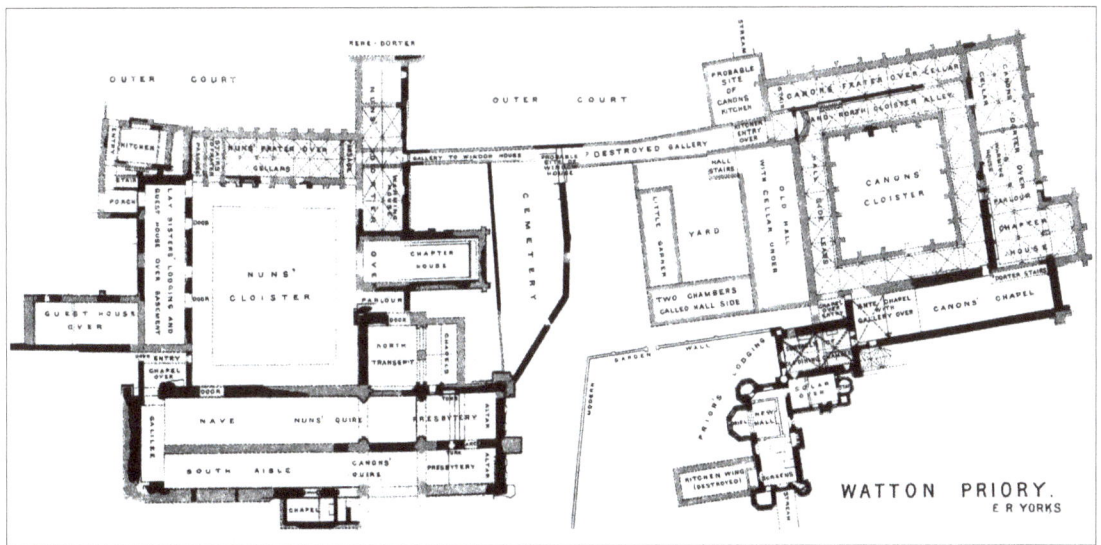

Figure 2.4 Plan of Watton Priory (© Royal Archaeological Institute).

A re-evaluation of the other Gilbertine double houses for which archaeological evidence survives, suggests the normal arrangement was for the two cloisters to lie to the north and the south of the monastic church so that the sexes had a parallel set of facilities both with easy access into the divided church.[26]

The other main variant, the Carthusian charterhouse, deviated from the standard plan even further, as exemplified by the most complete example in England, Mount Grace Priory (Figure 2.5). With their emphasis on personal isolation, instead of a shared dormitory and refectory, the monks were housed in individual cells arranged around a "great cloister." The church, in much-diminished form due to its reduced role within the order lay outside of the cloister, with further additional cells and ancillary buildings being housed in a second court. The evidence from Mount Grace only presents a partial picture, as it is now apparent that houses built before the middle of the 14th century had an "upper house" for the monks and a separate "lower house" that contained quarters for the lay brethren, mimicking the layout of the Alpine motherhouse at La Grande Chartreuse.[27]

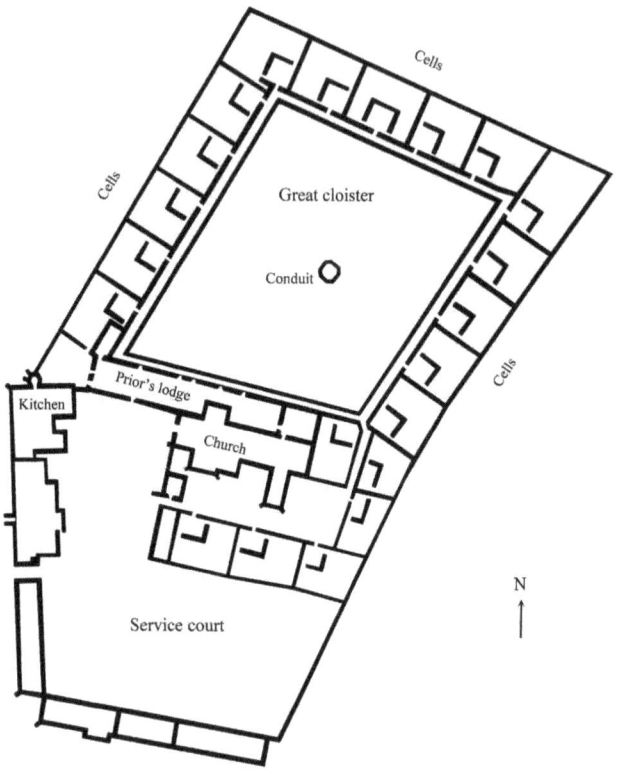

Figure 2.5 Plan of Mount Grace Priory (after Coppack and Aston 2002).

The process of Dissolution

Whilst the motivations and morality of the Dissolution are not the focus of this book, in order to understand its impact and aftermath, a brief exploration of the mechanics behind the suppression of the houses is needed. As has already been stated, the Dissolution was just one facet of the broader Henrican reformation, which had its origins earlier in the monarch's reign. However, the concept of monastic reform and closure was nothing new to the 1530s; there were earlier and well-established precedents.

From the end of the 13th century, following the wars with France, the crown frequently seized "alien priories," houses that were under the direct control of continental motherhouses. These properties and estates were usually transferred to other religious orders, but it was not unknown for them to stay permanently in lay hands.[28] In 1414 with the passing of the Act for the Suppression of the Alien Priories, parliament transferred the few remaining foreign houses into the hands of the king, although as in earlier years, these were usually redistributed amongst other religious organizations.

Occasional dissolutions of individual houses by church authorities were not unknown through the course of the 15th century, usually to provide incomes to fund newly established educational colleges. Thus, in 1484 William Waynflete, bishop of Winchester dissolved Selborne Priory to assist the foundation of Magdalen College, Oxford, while in 1496 John Alcock, bishop of Ely closed St Radegund Priory to help endow Jesus College, Cambridge.[29] With such closures setting a seemingly acceptable precedent for the restructuring of religious organizations for educational gain, it seems that Cardinal Wolsey had no qualms, and experienced few difficulties, gaining papal blessing to accelerate this process in the 1520s. He dissolved a total of 29 houses across England in order to support the foundation of two new colleges at Oxford (now Christ Church) and Ipswich.[30]

Monastic suppressions were part and parcel of reformation movements in nascent Protestant countries across Europe. In Denmark, the various mendicant orders were closed between 1528–1532, and as early as 1524 the Council of Zurich issued a decree suppressing all religious houses in Switzerland, diverting their incomes into secular educational establishments.[31] Consequently, by the time Henry VIII had decided to oversee a new wave of monastic closures in the 1530s, there was ample precedent for his actions from both Catholic and Protestant countries, and this probably helped inform the mechanism that would be implemented by Thomas Cromwell so effectively.

Following Henry VIII's split with Rome, the 1534 Act of the First Fruits and Tenths was passed. This act levied a 10% income tax on all church lands and offices that had formerly gone to the Pope and diverted this income to the crown.[32] In order to calculate the value of these taxable assets, between January and June 1535 commissioners were sent to examine the accounts of all religious institutions, including the monasteries, and their reports resulted in the compilation of the *Valor Ecclesiasticus* the same year (Figure 2.6). The commissioners who undertook such rapid, and on the whole accurate, valuations were usually members of the local gentry, mayors, and bishops who often held vested interests in the religious institutions being assessed. For instance, in Lincolnshire, the bishop and Mayor of Lincoln, as well as members of leading landholding families such as the Tyrwhitts, Heneages, and Skipwiths were all involved in the assessment.[33] Many of these commissioners were patrons of the religious houses they visited, and it is notable that many of them were to ultimately benefit from their closure (see Chapter 4).

At some point during 1535, and probably while this initial financial assessment was still being undertaken, the decision to close at least some of the less prosperous monasteries was

Figure 2.6   Title page, *Valor Ecclesiasticus* 1535 (© The National Archives).

made, and from the summer of that year until early in 1536, a second series of visitations of the monasteries was undertaken.[34] This time the visitations were undertaken by a small number of select agents of Cromwell, usually trained lawyers, and their remit was to report upon the state of the monasteries and how well they were being run. The precise purpose of these visitations has been debated, Knowles in his defence of the monasteries concluded that their "primary aim...was to extract damaging confessions."[35] However, these visitations were likely more than simply an attempt to affect a crude smear campaign, as Bernard has pointed out, since they were undertaken "reasonably and efficiently." Furthermore, he re-evaluates the frequent reporting of sexual crimes and that of "incontinence" in particular, noting that relatively few of these related to sodomy or inappropriate relations with the opposite sex, instead they referred to lesser "offences" such as masturbation, and that 90% of the religious questioned did not confess to breaking their vows of chastity in any way at all.[36] It should also be noted that some of the leading commissioners involved with the visitations of the monasteries, Legh, Layton, Tregonwell and Ap Rice, were at the same time inspecting the universities of Oxford and Cambridge. This suggests that there was a genuine desire to establish a picture of the real state of all religious institutions, and not just to tarnish the image of the monasteries.[37]

That being said, the picture painted by the commissioners was bleak. In the *Compendium Compertorum*, a collection of 142 visitation reports made by Drs Layton and Legh from northern England and East Anglia, many of the houses were said to have serious disciplinary issues, and the commissioners were also fastidious at recording "superstitions," usually relics said to hold miraculous properties.[38] This undoubtedly confirmed, if not created, the reforming intentions of the crown, which resulted in February 1536 of the passing of the Act for the Dissolution of the Lesser Monasteries. This act made provision for the enforced suppression of all houses whose annual incomes, assessed just a year previously, were below £200.[39] Of the 419 houses that were eligible for closure under the act, only 243 were actually dissolved in 1536.[40] The reasons for this were twofold. First, the monasteries had their patrons and supporters amongst the elite, and many of these petitioned Cromwell to spare individual houses from suppression, and although not always successful, a stay of closure could be granted upon the condition of payment of a suitable fee by the house. Second, and more significantly, upon the suppression of the monastery, those who wished to stay in holy orders were required to be transferred to a suitable alternative house, and those who wished to be released from their vows allotted a pension based upon their institution's income.[41] It seems that a very significant proportion of the religious was happy to continue in their vocation, and the numbers needing to be accommodated meant that it was not feasible to transfer them all to alternative institutions, thus preventing the potential closure of many houses.

If a monastery was to close, this was undertaken promptly under the terms of the act by crown agents, usually members of the local gentry, and the initial round of closures was swiftly achieved by the summer of 1536. The royal agents presented the head of the house with a copy of the suppression statute for the whole community to witness, examined the legal documentation of the house to establish its status and finally took formal possession of the monastery's seal in a symbolic final act of surrender.[42] Following the surrender and the departure of its former inhabitants, a survey of all sources of income was again taken, these often, but not always, tallied reasonably closely with those drawn up in the *Valor Ecclesiasticus*, and an inventory of all goods, possessions and monastic buildings compiled. Such documents, when they survive, provide an invaluable insight into the physical appearance of the monasteries at their point of closure, before they transferred into the direct ownership of the crown.

Whether the first round of closures was the full extent of what was initially intended, or whether it was just the first anticipated step towards total suppression of the monasteries is not our concern here. However, what changed the situation so rapidly was the series of revolts in northern England: the Lincolnshire Rising and the Pilgrimage of Grace in Yorkshire, in late 1536 to early 1537.[43] Whatever the complex motivations for these uprisings were, the closure of the lesser monasteries was undoubtedly a major contributory factor. Following the swift and brutal suppression of this unrest, that for a time seriously unsettled the authorities, it was clear a change in official policy had taken place in how the crown now intended to deal with the remaining monasteries.

Change when it came was piecemeal, but evolved rapidly. The first act was the immediate suppression of those monasteries that had taken part or were implicated in the revolts, soon moving onto closure of other unconnected houses. There was also a change in justification of this new official policy. Whereas before, suppression of the lesser houses had been rationalized as a mechanism to promote monastic reform, now the closure of the remaining monasteries was undertaken with the excuse that it was for the benefit of the religious themselves, as it "released" them from a lifestyle shackled by superstition. Certainly, in the later closures no more offers were made to transfer the affected inmates to alternative houses, all were pensioned off instead.[44] Whilst the closures in 1536 had been undertaken under the requirement of law, there was no legal basis for any of the later suppressions. These were done under negotiation, persuasion and ultimately coercion, in what Youings politely termed "induced" surrenders.[45] Those houses that failed to cooperate had their possessions forcibly seized and their occupants ejected with no provision of pensions, although actual instances of this were rare.[46] From the spring of 1538 onwards, it was now the turn of the friaries, who up until this point had remained unaffected, to be suppressed. These closures were largely undertaken under the supervision of Richard Ingworth, a former Dominican himself, and the last mendicant house closed in March 1539.[47]

In 1539 a second Act for the Dissolution of the Greater Monasteries was passed, but this statute, unlike its predecessor, did not make it legal for the crown to forcibly seize the remaining monasteries, merely for their abbots to surrender their houses voluntarily. Nonetheless, by the time of the act's passing, this was largely academic, as the majority of the remaining houses had already surrendered.[48] Even at this late date, influential individuals were petitioning the king in a forlorn attempt to prevent closures. In early 1540 the Duke of Norfolk was still trying to persuade the king to prevent the closure of Thetford Priory, as his father had been buried there in 1524 and the priory was a traditional place of family burial.[49] His efforts were to no avail as Thetford was suppressed on the 16th February, swiftly followed by the last remaining house, Waltham Abbey, on the 23rd March 1540.

It is probably worth noting that, while not within the specific remit of this book, the passing of the Second Act of Dissolution in 1539 was not the final culmination of this process of suppression and appropriation by the crown. In 1545 Henry VIII initiated the last, it might be said logical, phase of dissolution, this time focusing on the chantries and their associated religious communities. Established initially by individual wealthy patrons to provide intercessory prayers for the dead, many chantries in urban areas had grown into large and wealthy charitable organizations employing not just priests but lay officials such as wardens.[50] Few chantries were actually closed immediately, and it was only with the accession of Edward VI that a new act was passed and over 2,000 chantries across the country, and many of the remaining hospitals, were shut down in 1548.[51] The terms were similar to those for the monasteries, priests displaced would receive pensions, and assets used for charitable means, although the crown still benefited hugely from this fresh injection of income.[52]

As a result of these acts and suppressions, the face of religious life in England and Wales was irrevocably altered in just fourteen years. Every monastic house and chantry had closed, along with the vast majority of hospitals, and all that remained were the parish churches and cathedrals with their secular priests. While this probably seemed to be the brutal end of the story to those who had been evicted or lost their charitable support, it paved the way for a new dynamic phase of development to come.

— 3 —

The Destruction and Asset Stripping of the Religious Houses

Calculating the value of the monastic estates that passed to the crown between 1536–1540 is a complicated, and much argued, estimation to make. Savine suggested that the net income for 525 monasteries traceable through the *Valor Ecclesiasticus* to be around £136,360, although this is probably a significant underestimation of the total, given gaps in the available data.[1] Very crudely put, the real estate that passed to Henry could be estimated to be worth nearly three million pounds (if buyers could be found), based upon a standard price calculated at the traditional 20 years income. However, given that at the start of the Dissolution it was anticipated that Henry would retain or perhaps just lease most of this monastic property (see Chapter 4), the expected riches would not have been immediate and only accrued over time in the form of an additional annual income, albeit a generous one. Nonetheless, there was one instant source of revenue the crown could gather in: those aspects of the monasteries that were now redundant in their new secular contexts of use. The form that they were presented in varied between the different houses dependent on their size and wealth, but usually included the accumulated treasure, more mundane material culture and the recyclable building materials of the church and conventual buildings.

Removal of precious metals and plate

The most immediate source of wealth in all monastic houses were the precious metals that were either incorporated into the shrines and altar fittings of the church or the plate used for ecumenical and domestic purposes. Occasionally even large quantities of coinage were recorded as having been recovered. Given its value, such portable wealth was quickly removed and usually sent directly to the royal jewel house. Inevitably, there is very little archaeological evidence for such asset stripping; however, there is a considerable wealth of surviving historical sources that document the process.

Usually, the first focus of Cromwell's agents was the precious metals and stones incorporated within shrines, and the targeting of such structures was logical as not only could they contain materials of considerable value, it served as a very visible defacement of features now thought to be idolatrous. Although by no means did all monasteries possess richly adorned shrines, where they did occur, they could contain a significant quantity of material, even at a modest house. In the chapel at Caversham, a grange belonging to Notley Abbey, Dr London reported finding an image of Our Lady "thorowly platyd over with sylver" which he sent straight away to London sealed in a chest.[2] At a wealthier shrine, the rewards could be considerably higher. Cromwell's commissioners described the shrine of St Edmund at Bury as being "a riche shryne whiche was very comberous to deface," and 5,000 marks of silver and gold were removed in addition to a "riche crosse with emereddes...and sundry stones of great value." Despite this haul, the commissioners reported back to Cromwell that they had still left the church and abbot "very well ffurnesshed with plate of sylver."[3]

It was clearly realized by the religious that agents of the crown would target such portable wealth, and it is perhaps inevitable that attempts were made to conceal some items of obvious value. How often this took place undetected is uncertain, but the commissioners were very thorough in their searches. At Glastonbury Abbey, they reported the recovery of "bothe money and plate hyde and muryde up in wallis, vaulttis and other secrette placis."[4] Yet there were also disappointments, Pollard writing to Cromwell following a visit to the shrine of St Swithun at Winchester complained that in its construction "there was in it no pieces of gold, nor any ring, or true stone, but all great counterfeits."[5]

Figure 3.1 The eagle lectern, Newstead Abbey (Author).

Despite this, Pollard was still able to recover a cross of emeralds, two crosses of gold and two gold chalices, along with sundry silver valued at 2,000 marks. It was not just precious metals that the religious sought to conceal from the crown's agents, other objects thought to be of value or worthy of veneration were hidden. Perhaps the best-known example comes from Newstead Abbey where the canons concealed the altar candlesticks and the great brass eagle lectern in the priory pond.[6] These remained undiscovered until the 1770s when the pond was dredged, and they were finally recovered. The lectern was subsequently donated to Southwell Minster, where it remains in use today (Figure 3.1), although the whereabouts of the candlesticks are unknown.

Whilst not all monasteries possessed elaborate shrines such as that of Bury, even a small house would have owned a certain amount of silver or gilt plate. At Monk Bretton, a relatively modest Benedictine priory, two silver plated crosses, five silver chalices, a gilt pyx, two cruets, a great salt and various other tablewares were recovered, and weighed just over

18kg in total.⁷ Such sums, whilst on their own not immense, quickly mounted up as the visitations to the monasteries increased. An inventory drawn up by Master of the Jewels, Sir John Williams, records the gold and silver plate delivered into the king's custody from monastic institutions towards the end of the suppression between 1538–1540.⁸ The totals are as staggering as they are meticulous in their detail: gold plate 14,531 ¾oz, gilt plate 129,520oz, parcel gilt plate 73,774oz, parcel and white 4,341oz, silver plate 67,600 ¾oz. In total, and over just the two years recorded, 412kg of gold and 7,800kg of silver were harvested from the monasteries, with an additional £79,081 16s 4 ½d in coinage going straight into the royal purse.

Stripping of lead

Following the surrender of most houses, the first act of Cromwell's commissioners was to assess the quantity and value of the lead on the roofs, incorporated in the guttering and, where accessible the pipework, before ordering its removal and melting down. Always reserved for the crown, the stripping of lead from the monastic buildings served a dual purpose. As has often been observed, the lead was one of the most valuable material assets that could easily be removed.⁹ However, the removal of the lead was also a very effective mechanism to quickly render the buildings unusable, physically and symbolically, and did not require a large team of workers to do so.

The quantities recorded are, at times, enormous. At Rievaulx the lead was said to weigh in the region of 140 fothers, approximately the same weight in modern tonnes.¹⁰ At Jervaulx the total was 399½ fothers, with an estimated contemporary value of around £1,000, suggesting that lead could realize around £2 10s per tonne.¹¹ Whilst these were admittedly very large Cistercian houses, even a more modest Benedictine house such as Monk Bretton, South Yorkshire had an estimated total of 59 fothers of lead, which were removed for the king.¹²

Given the mass of lead roofing removed from many monasteries, it made sense that it was melted down on site into more manageable ingots before being transported away by the king's agents. Woodward suggested during the initial closures of the lesser houses, this was undertaken in a rather *ad hoc* fashion by local workmen in a rather inefficient two-stage process; first, the lead was melted in rough pits in the ground and then the residues left over from the process further refined to retrieve any residual lead.¹³ However, with the increasing number of later closures of the larger houses from 1537, Henry Johnson was commissioned on the 20 March to oversee the process in the North and construct more efficient furnaces. Johnson was well qualified for the task, a master gunner at the Tower of London who, a few years earlier, he had been made responsible for the melting and recasting of broken brass cannon.¹⁴ The professionalization of the process was not only the response to the growing quantity of lead needed to be processed; it meant that it could be undertaken with a much higher measure of accountability. Cromwell's agents, such as Pollard at Jervaulx, were ordered to melt the lead into "sows" and place the king's mark upon them.¹⁵

Ingots

One of the most striking pieces of evidence for the widespread practice of lead stripping is the rare find of surviving lead ingots. To date eight have been recovered, of which five still survive today. The best known is from Rievaulx, one of an original group of four found in 1920, the other three having been donated to York Minster and melted down to re-lead the Five Sisters window in the north transept.[16] When excavated, the four ingots were lying on the floor at the west end of the nave, covered by a contemporary collapse of fallen masonry, which presumably prevented their subsequent removal.[17]

The surviving ingot is "boat-shaped," with a flat upper surface and convex underside, and measures 113cm in length by 42cm wide, and is 18cm deep at its central point. Weighing around 450kg it seems to match the "half fodder" ingots Cromwell's agent Bellasis records casting at Jervaulx in November 1537.[18] The ingot is stamped on the top with a crowned rose in relief, and there is an angled hole in the top surface 10cm deep, presumably to enable the removal of the ingot from its mould with an iron tool.

An almost identical ingot survives from Kenilworth Abbey, Warwickshire, now reused as a makeshift seat in the local parish church. Discovered in 1888, it is also "boat-shaped," 132cm long, 39cm wide, having a maximum depth of 20cm and weighing 550kg (Figure 3.2).[19] The Kenilworth ingot also has an angled hole close to its centre for lifting and is stamped four times along its length. Over a century of wear and polishing since its discovery in the 19th century has made these marks more obscure, but instead of being a crowned rose, they appear to resemble a bow and arrow and perhaps are an early form of ordnance mark. This ingot is also marked in additional ways. Running down the length of its top and incised with a compass, are ten circles and a partial three quarter one. This has been suggested to represent the actual weight of the ingot, 10.75cwt.[20] Either side of these circles are a series of both smooth and striated groves, seemingly caused by a chisel or similarly sharp tool. Their purpose is uncertain, but it is possible that resulted from the intentional removal of small samples of lead, possibly as part of some testing procedure.

Two ingots, now housed in Bury St Edmunds and Ipswich museums, were discovered in 1835 during work on the site of Ixworth Priory, Suffolk. Slightly shorter and fatter (measuring 91cm x 43cm), they weighed 6.5cwt (33kg) and 7cwt (35.5kg) apiece.[21] These ingots were impressed with the royal stamp, consisting of crowned HR in a circle. Interesting, in a similar fashion to the ingot from Kenilworth, the weight of each pig was indicated using the appropriate number of incised rings on the upper surface.

The final example of an intact ingot comes from Haverfordwest Priory, Pembrokeshire, found in a similar circumstance to that from Rievaulx, covered by fallen masonry in the choir of the church.[22] Measuring 71cm long, 28cm wide and 10cm at its maximum depth, this is the smallest of the surviving ingots, but like that from Rievaulx, it was still impressed with the official rose and crown stamp.

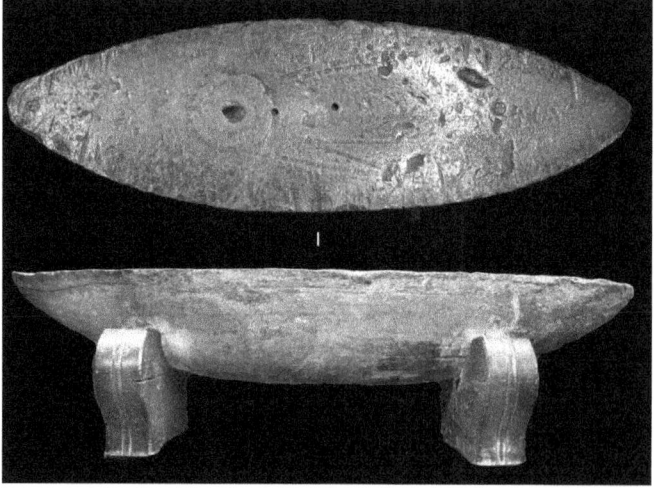

Figure 3.2 Lead ingot from Kenilworth Abbey, now in St Nicholas church (Author).

These surviving ingots are all indicative of the broader processes taking place immediately following the closure of monasteries across the country. Although they varied somewhat in size, they are identical in shape despite coming from very diverse locations geographically. As well as being similar in form, they are all marked with official stamps, even if these vary, and in the case of those from Kenilworth and Ixworth, there was an attempt to clearly mark the ingots with their weight. All this points to a centralized level of control, strict adherence to regulation, and a precise level of accountability throughout the whole process. As such, it mirrors the many accounts made by commissioners to Cromwell during the late 1530s valuing the lead from roofs and documenting its removal in great detail.

Lead melting and ingot casting

Whilst it is clear from these ingots that there was a reasonably consistent practice observed in the stripping of lead and its casting into ingots, the process by which this was achieved is somewhat less well understood. Occasional reports of melting furnaces are made in antiquarian reports, but these typically lack the detail required to reconstruct their form. During clearance at Fountains Abbey, it was reported that:

> ...part of a furnace the stalls, screens, and other fittings had apparently been used...to make fires for melting the lead; for here and there we found heaps of ashes nay, in the nave, part of the furnace where the operation had been conducted.[23]

A little more detail is given in the account of the excavation of Langley Abbey, Norfolk in 1921. Here, while excavating the presbytery, a "brick-built square furnace" was found at the location of the high altar, still containing a mass of charcoal, ash and molten led weighing over 30lbs.[24] A similar feature was encountered at the east end of the church at Muchelney Abbey in 1873, when a "fire-place...formed...of broken battlements for the purpose of melting lead" was found.[25] The accompanying plan shows it to be constructed from several moulded stones set on edge and measuring approximately 0.75 x 1m, with one open end and set in an oval pit measuring 1.5 x 3m. Finally, at Ixworth, in addition to the two lead ingots, the furnace used to cast them was said to have been uncovered;

> Below the level of the foundation was an excavation about 2 feet deep and 4 feet in diameter, apparently a fireplace for a furnace, the sides sloping inwardly and cemented all around. On the bottom, which was not cemented, were built two oblong lumps of stones and mortar, apparently to receive the bottom of the cauldron for melting lead, as there were remnants of lead and solder all around.[26]

More recent excavations at Northampton Greyfriars have provided better evidence for what could be a similar style of furnace to that encountered at Ixworth and elsewhere (Figure 3.3). Set within a larger circular cut within the floor of the church, the furnace was built from reused architectural stone and tiles. It was a roughly square structure, open on its eastern side to allow stoking and with a low central partition, presumably to support the melting vessel.[27] Inside was a layer of charcoal mixed with lead waste, the residue from its last firing.

A tile and brick furnace also appears to have been used at Sopwell Priory, Hertfordshire, built in the western portion of the nave and subsequently levelled when the post-Dissolution house was built on the site. What survived was a circular surface approximately 3m in diameter and made from reused tile edged with brick. Described as a "casting floor" in the original report, due to the presence of solidified lead in between some of the tiles, the size of the structure makes this unlikely, and it probably represents the base of a melting furnace. Significantly, of the same phase and immediately to the south of this structure was rectangular pit 30cm deep and 2.5m in diameter "filled with up to a foot of clayey sand, which also showed the effects of heat."[28] Although it is hard to say for certain, the description of this feature and its direct association to a probably brick-built furnace strongly suggests it was a casting pit for the ingots.

With the exception of the examples noted above, surviving furnaces are relatively scarce. However, several sites have provided further evidence for the casting of ingots. At Carmarthen Greyfriars, three hollows cut into the floor of the claustral range measuring 0.8 x 0.6m, 1.4 x 0.9m and 0.95 x 0.7m were suggested to be moulds to collect the run-off of molten lead from nearby small hearths, although the size and form of these would have produced much rougher ingots than those that have been found whole.[29] When the complete ingot was discovered at Haverfordwest, nearby in the nave floor, a tile-lined mould was also found which matched the shape of the lead pig exactly.[30]

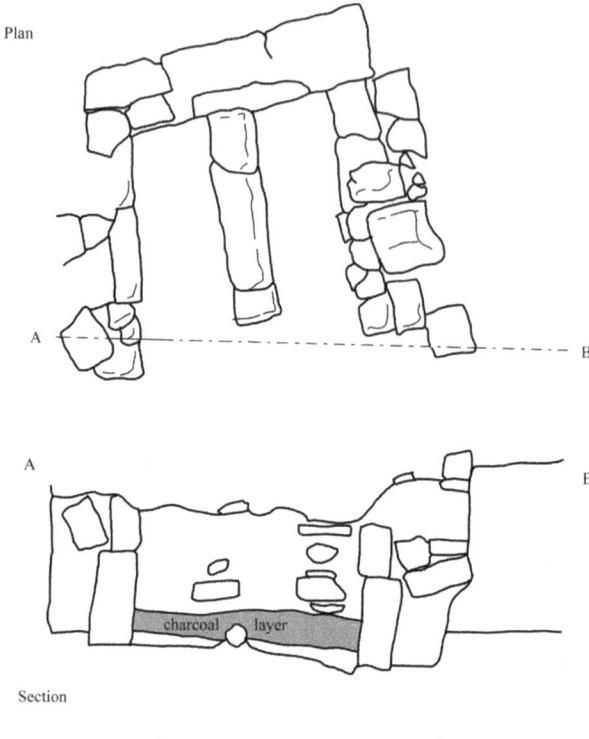

Figure 3.3 Lead furnace, Northampton Greyfriars (after Williams 1978).

What is striking is the consistent locations of these furnaces; all were in the church as indeed were all the ingots that had a precise find spot recorded. There were probably practical considerations for this placement of the furnace in the church. Such industrial structures likely functioned better when sheltered from the elements, and the church would have been the largest source of lead at most houses. However, there are good reasons why locating the melting operation in the church might have been less practical, not least the threat presented to the operation from falling debris whilst the roof itself was being dismantled. Indeed, in the cases of Rievaulx and Haverfordwest it was the reality of these dangers that preserved the ingots archaeologically. Given this, and the equally suitable range of locations around the cloister, not to mention the wider precinct, to establish the furnaces, some form of intentionality must have been at play. Perhaps Cromwell's agents chose the church as the most expendable building of the complex, having no clear secular function, but at Langley, the location of the furnace on the very site of the high altar must also have been a very conscious and symbolic act of desecration.

Small lead working hearths

Another common feature found on many sites are small circular bowl hearths, usually 1m or less in diameter, and associated with lead waste. It is often assumed in the face of little supporting evidence, for example at Thorney Abbey, that such structures were used during the Dissolution for cupellation, to extract naturally occurring silver from the lead, thus maximising the value of the recycled material.[31] However, such explanations are incredibly problematic and rather naive. Silver had been extracted from lead deposits in Britain from at least the 1st century AD, and late medieval writers such as Agricola outlined clearly the processes involved.[32] Such was the importance of lead as a primary source of silver in the Middle Ages, Blanchard has gone as far as to suggest that by the 12th century most lead in circulation in Britain was actually derived as the by-product from silver extraction.[33] Given this, it is inconceivable that the lead used in the construction of the monasteries would have still contained any appreciable traces of silver, as confirmed by the analysis of the window leads from Battle Abbey, which showed that they contained no measurable amounts of the precious element, and Cromwell's agents would have been well aware of this too.[34]

A typical example of such a hearth was found at Sopwell Priory (Figure 3.4).[35] Dug through the floor of the south range, a bowl-shaped depression 1m wide and 35cm deep was lined with a layer of yellow clay, into which were placed seven bricks in a circle to support the surviving fragments of an iron melting pot. Accumulated within the hearth was a thick layer of lead-rich ash and on the bottom a solidified cake of lead weighing 11kg. The first assumption of the excavators was that this was a cupellation hearth. However, chemical analysis of the ash revealed that there was a negligible quantity of phosphate present, which would be expected to be present as bone ash was used to absorb the lead oxide in the cupellation process.[36] Furthermore, comparative spectrographic analysis showed that lead from the hearth contained the same residual levels of silver as were found in window cames and pipework from the site.[37]

To complicate issues further, there are a few examples of where there is evidence for lead melting and more specialist metallurgical processes taking place on monastic sites prior to the Dissolution. At Tintern Abbey, a series of seven lead hearths were found in the former guest hall.[38]

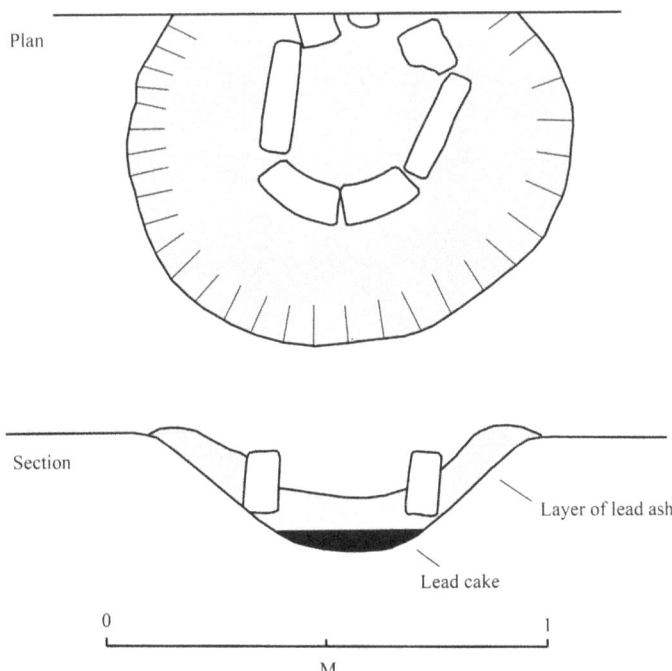

Figure 3.4 Lead hearth, Sopwell Priory (after Johnson 2006).

Several of these were inter-cutting, and their use seemed to have taken place over a more extended period. Indeed close dating of the structures indicated that these features predated the Dissolution, leading the excavator to suggest that they related to a period of repair of the monastic building in the final medieval phase.[39] At Carmarthen Greyfriars, a hearth containing 1.38kg of solidified lead as well as "white powder," was found in the infirmary. However, this too was dated to the pre-Dissolution period and again interpreted as belonging to a phase of repair rather than destruction.[40] The most conclusive evidence for more specialized metalworking comes from Norwich Greyfriars, where crucibles and litharge (lead oxide) cakes containing high levels of silver were recovered, but again these came from a pre-suppression context.[41] Given this evidence, it is entirely possible that other similar hearths, which have assumed to belong to the post-Dissolution period, have been misdated and in fact are late medieval in date.

These issues aside, many lead melting hearths, especially those found in more recent excavations, clearly do post-date the closure of the monastic house. Such an example was excavated at Thornton Abbey in 2012 by the author (Figure 3.5). Located in the courtyard of the inner precinct immediately to the west of the church, it was constructed from reused roof tile set into a mortar base and had been used to melt lead. However, the chronological context of this bowl hearth at Thornton is of particular note. Here, the hearth was cutting through a series of post-Dissolution layers containing redeposited monastic material culture, suggesting that it was probably built quite some time after the abbey had first closed. A similar situation can be seen at Beverley Blackfriars. Here excavations revealed three hearths cutting through Dissolution layers within the cloister, thereby dating to some time after the initial abandonment of the site and the stripping of its roofs by Cromwell's agents in 1539.[42] A further example is at Bordesley Abbey, where a lead melting hearth found in the south transept was constructed after the tiled floor had already been removed and was sealed shortly after use by the collapse of a section of wall masonry, which the excavators believed would have still been standing for some time after the Dissolution.[43] Even buildings outside of the cloister show evidence for this small-scale collection of lead. At Croxden Abbey, a small hearth was found in a vaulted hall and set into the flagged floor.[44] Almost certainly the abbot's lodge, this building evidently contained sufficient leaded window glass and possibly pipe work to merit the attention of those profiting from the recycling.

Given there is no evidence from any of these post-Dissolution hearths that they were constructed to undertake cupellation, their actual function can be deduced from their regular association with assemblages of window

Figure 3.5 Lead hearth, Thornton Abbey (scale 1m) (Author).

glass and leads. Surrounding the three hearths at Beverley were dumps of discarded window glass and clusters of window leads, some of which had spilled molten lead on top of them, suggesting they were the primary raw material being melted.[45] This association between small hearths, lead cames, and window glass is replicated at a large number of sites such as Thorney Abbey, Pontefract Priory, Holywell Priory, Durham Cathedral, and Monk Bretton Priory.[46] Whilst it is clear that the hearths would have been too small to handle the melting down of the several tonnes of lead from the roofs of even a modest monastery, they could recycle the smaller quantities used in the construction of windows and for other purposes such as the securing of iron fixtures to masonry. The fact that much of the evidence for this smaller scale activity appears to have been taking place sometime after the initial removal of the roof leads by Cromwell's agents, could suggest this represents a secondary phase of asset stripping, possibly being undertaken by the new owners of the sites rather than for the benefit of the crown.

Other metals

Lead was not the only metal mentioned in post-Dissolution surveys, copper alloys and bells, in particular, were of immediate value to the crown. Bells could be recorded by number, such as the seven listed in the inventory of Monk Bretton Priory, or in scrap weight, such as the 400lb of "belle metalle" recorded at Westwood Priory.[47] Writing in 1540, Sir Richard Rich valued the bell metal from Wenlock at 20s per cwt, nearly ten times the usual value of the equivalent weight of recovered lead, which at Jervaulx was assessed to be 2s 6d per cwt.[48] Bells were just one source of copper alloy, other vessels commonly found in monasteries such as mortars, holy water stoops, and sundry liturgical vessels were all made of alloys of tinned copper.[49]

The immediate fate of these bells is less certain. It is often assumed that they were reserved for the crown and shipped wholesale to London, together with the recovered lead, perhaps to be recast into ordinance to supply Henry's expanding navy and system of coastal forts.[50] Whilst many did follow this route, such as the £832 worth of Lincolnshire bell metal sent to Sir Charles Morris to make guns and other "engines of war," bells also appear in receipts of sale to private individuals during the dispersal of monastic chattels, such as the "thre belles" from Hulton Abbey sold to Stephen Bagott at 18s per cwt in October 1538.[51] Bells sometimes had a value in their own right and found a ready market within local communities. For instance, in July 1538 Cromwell's commissioner Dr. Tregonwell sold four bells from Bodmin Priory to the parish of Lanivet for £36 13s 4d.[52] However, such documented cases of reuse are rare, and the sheer quantity of bell metal being released upon the market might well have impacted upon demand and the price willing to be paid. Following the sale of items from Dale Abbey, which included windows, paving slabs and even feather beds to Sir Francis Pole in 1538, it was noted that six bells weighing 47 cwt "remayneth unsoule."[53] Perhaps to maximize returns, it seems bells, along with other monastic goods, were offered for sale by English merchants on the continent.[54]

Greene has suggested that, due to the higher temperatures required, the melting of bells destined to be scrapped was unlikely to have been undertaken at the site from which they were recovered.[55] Whilst some records do support this, the bells from Neath Abbey sent to Bristol for melting were clearly whole at the time, this was not always the case.[56] For example, on 20 March 1541 the King's plumbers William Wilson and Charles Draye were paid £8 for melting both the lead *and* the bells of Tintern Abbey, and this took place onsite.[57]

Archaeological evidence for the recycling of copper alloys, while less common than that for lead, has been found on several sites in Dissolution and later levels. A typical example is at Battle Abbey where, in an area to the east of the dorter range, scraps of collected copper alloy sheeting were found alongside the evidence for the stripping of lead.[58] Likewise, at Eynsham Abbey, a commingled assemblage of metallurgical debris consisting of leaded copper alloys was found together with slagged hearth material. This led to the suggestion that the recycling of a mix of scrap from a variety of metals was taking place at a single place.[59] Such small-scale, and in the case of Eynsham, inefficient, recycling probably represents opportunistic activities, perhaps by new owners, rather than being the result of the systematic stripping of sites by Cromwell's commissioners.

One site where more professional recycling of copper alloys seems to have taken place is Keynsham Abbey. Cut into the final phase floor of the chapter house, was a well-built and technologically sophisticated reverberatory furnace.[60] It consisted of a sub-circular hearth measuring 1.1 x 1.3m, a smaller square firebox 1.2m deep served by a large underground flue and raking out pit (Figure 3.6). The hearth had the remains of a tapping hole at its base, and the firebox was filled with the wood ash from its last firing and pieces of collapsed superstructure formed from stones set in clay. Shortly after excavation, the furnace was examined by Tylecote who noted its resemblance to one illustrated by Biringuccio in 1540.[61] Metallographic examination of the metal residues found in the furnace showed that they were a bronze formed from 75% copper and 25% tin, a comparable composition to medieval bell metal.[62] At the time the excavators suggested that the furnace represented the activity of an itinerant bell maker sometime between the Dissolution and the 1750s. However, given that there was no evidence that the furnace was built through any post-Dissolution deposits or build up, it seems most likely that it was constructed immediately after the monastery closed. Furthermore, elsewhere in the report, it was noted during the excavation of the chapter house that 130 copper alloy studs, six buckles, and various copper alloy door fitments were recovered.[63] Although not noted by the excavators in the publication, this connexion between the presence of a furnace and the deposit of collected scrap copper alloy, all within the confines of the chapter house, strongly suggests that large-scale recycling of copper alloy was taking place here in the immediate post-Dissolution period. Significantly, shortly after the closure of the abbey, the seven bells of the monastery were recorded as having been sold to Francis Edwards along with various "useless" buildings of the monastery,

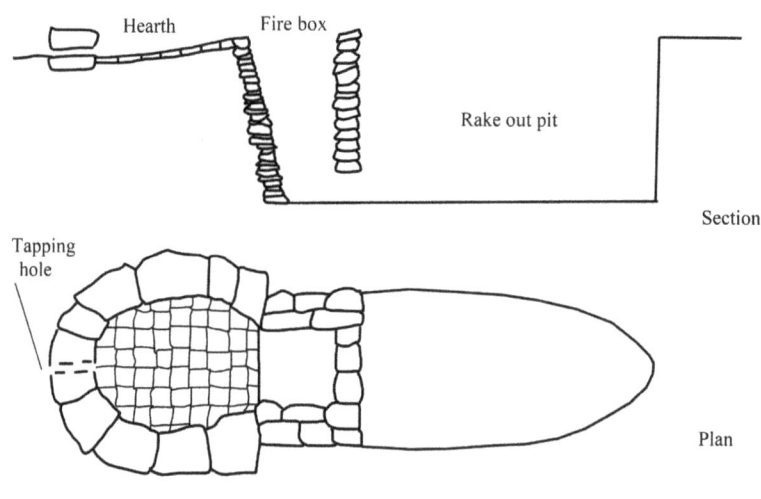

Figure 3.6 Reverberatory furnace, Keynsham Abbey (after Lowe 1987).

which might well have included the chapter house.[64] Given this, it seems that Edwards was the one most likely to be responsible for the recycling taking place at Keynsham.

Dismantling and recycling of building materials

Whilst metals such as lead and copper alloy, as well as being easily accessible, had obvious resale value, so too did other aspects of the monastic architecture, including the stone fabric of the buildings. The motivations behind the destruction of monastic churches and conventual buildings probably varied on a site-by-site basis, dependant on the will of the new owners. Whilst some of the demolitions might have been ideologically driven, it was not a cheap thing to achieve. Writing to Cromwell from Lincolnshire in 1536, John Freeman suggests that rather than incurring significant costs to the crown through the rasing of all the buildings to the ground, merely removing their roofs and letting the walls stand would be sufficient as an interim measure.[65] Even in towns, where pressures of space might make rapid redevelopment more likely, total demolition of urban monasteries and friaries seems not always to have taken place straight away. Dr London's account of the suppression of several friaries across the Midlands during 1539 is perhaps more typical. Whilst certain elements such as the window glass, ornaments, and household goods were routinely sold, he repeatedly included phrases such as "I left the house whole and only defaced the church" and "I pulled down no house thoroughly at none of the Friars, but so deface them that they should not lightly be made friaries again."[66]

Even when total demolition of a building was intended, there might be some considerable delay between the removal of the roof and the demolition of the walls. At Chelmsford Priory analysis of charcoal in demolition contexts suggested that it derived from substantial saplings that appear to have taken root within the roofless structures, before being cleared through burning.[67] Likewise, at Oxford Blackfriars it was observed that a considerable build-up of soil was able to accumulate within the conventual buildings before their eventual demolition in the late 1540s.[68] Finally the excavation at the cathedral and priory church in Coventry revealed that, after the abandonment and initial despoliation of the church, it was left to decay naturally for several decades, while being used as a dump by a local slaughterhouse. Indeed, a natural collapse of a portion of the vaulting of the south aisle crushed a pack of feral dogs who had made the church their home.[69]

Nevertheless, complete and rapid demolition was sometimes required, to either provide revenue through the sale of materials or to enable the sites to be used for new purposes. This process of demolition is well documented both historically and archaeologically and was one that was set to continue from the time of the Dissolution almost until the present day.

Undermining and demolition

Of all sites, the one for which the best evidence survives for the actual process of demolition is Lewes Priory. Following his acquisition of it on 16th February 1538, Cromwell straight away started transforming the site through the wholesale destruction of the monastic buildings, and for this purpose, he hired the services of the engineer Giovanni Portinari. Portinari was a Florentine military engineer who was domiciled in England by 1526, and by the start of the Dissolution was a member of the royal household.[70] Two letters from Portinari to Cromwell survive and are particularly revealing as to how the task of bringing down the vast buildings was achieved. In the first, dated 20th March 1538,[71] he provides a detailed description of the undermining of the walls of the east end of the church;

> First we shall cut away the bottom of the foundation and cut it away to the height of a yard and a quarter so that a man may get under to work and pass to the other side…and put beneath planks of a thickness of 3 inches from one side to the other and put on each side a prop a yard long or thereabouts; and so one goes on, following by degrees, cutting and propping…and when the said chapels and columns have been cut and propped on that side and you wish to bring them to the ground the props on that side only will be burned with fire or with powder.[72]

Archaeological excavations at Lewes Priory have revealed this process in action, in the area of the infirmary chapel.[73] Here at the east end, deep "sap trenches" were dug beneath the line of the north and south walls of the presbytery, but avoiding the foundations of the presbytery arch, presumably because the weight supported at this point would have proved too great to prop. Nonetheless, the undermining was successfully undertaken, as evidenced by the collapse of the side chapel walls into the sap trenches.

Similar undermining techniques were employed elsewhere and to equal effect. In January 1537 the church and conventual buildings of Stanley Abbey were acquired by Sir Edward Baynton for £1,200.[74] Baynton was in the process of building a new house at Bromham, and at least part of the motivation for the purchase of Stanley was to provide materials for this enterprise. Archaeological excavations undertaken early last century revealed that while Baynton did convert the west range of the cloister into a dwelling, he demolished the rest of the church and cloister to foundation level in many places.[75] Evidence for undermining was encountered in the area of the south transept, where the pillars of the east wall were found sunk into pits without their foundations or bases, presumably as a result of having been propped and undermined. The dangers presented by this method of undermining were illustrated by the recovery of the body of one of the workmen responsible, crushed beneath a very heavy fall of masonry from the transept roof,[76] after which the method of undermining was seemingly abandoned as it did not appear elsewhere in the excavated area.

Given the nature of such operations, it is not surprising that similar fatalities occurred elsewhere. During the Earl of Rutland's conversion of Rievaulx into a manufactory, which required widespread demolition of the conventual buildings, two workmen were recorded as having been caught by a fall of masonry while pulling the supports of the chapter house.[77] Such accidents might have been taken by some as divine warnings against the desecration. At Binham Priory it was said that a fall of masonry which killed a workman brought about the abandonment of the attempted conversion of the cloister into a house, whilst in 1781 George Keates told the story of an unfortunate Puritan killed by a fall of stone whilst attempting to deface Netley Abbey during the reign of James I.[78] Given that during this period Netley was a still lived-in mansion, this story is in all likelihood apocryphal. Nonetheless, it may well have drawn inspiration from other tragic incidents preserved in local folk memory. As dangerous as undermining was, it was evidently a successful and widely employed technique. Thus, it was recorded that;

> Payments made and pyd for our Soverign lord the king for work…in undermining and casting down the late abbey church of Barking, for providing of the fairest quoin stones and others to be employed of the King's manor of Dartford.[79]

Whilst excavations at Reading Abbey revealed evidence for severe damage to the outer footings of the north wall at the east end of the church, which was interpreted as a deliberate attempt to undermine the structure.[80]

A second letter survives from Portinari to Cromwell from Lewes Priory, written just four days after the first on 24 March 1537/8 which gives further insight into the scale and organization of the demolition process. He describes the specialist team of 23 workers that he has brought from London, which included "3 carpentars, 2 smythes, 2 plummars and on that kepith the fornance."[81] Still further detail concerning the personnel involved in a large-scale demolition can be found at Chertsey Abbey. While still in the hands of the crown, the materials removed to assist in the construction of the palace at Oatlands were recorded in a surviving ledger book for 1538.[82] Payments were made for goods required in the demolition process including deliveries of straw "servyng to cast downe the stonys for brekynge," "talwood" for scaffolding to be used by the plumbers, and the purchase of demolition tools including hooks, rakes, hammers, chisels, brick axes and mattocks. Further sums were required to pay for a small army of workers which included seven carpenters, 37 bricklayers and 121 labourers, all overseen by a single clerk of works.[83] Monastic stone also proved a valuable resource for other Royal building projects, at the building of coastal forts in particular. Following a visit by Henry VIII to view the defences at Hull in 1541, an order was made for the dismantling of the nearby Meaux Abbey to provide materials to provide rubble footings for the new brick defences, at a total cost of £252;

> 20 masons, some at the Mewesse to see it taken down, and some to hew at Hull, 20 carpenters felling and squaring timber and making store and work houses; 60 bricklayers upon the bulwark next the Humber by the jeotte (jetty), as fast as the foundation can be digged, 10 plumbers to take down and roll the lead at Mewsse, 30 lime-burners, 30 brickmakers, 60 wood-fellers felling wood to make brick and alders for scaffolding, 300 labourers taking down stone and brick at the Mewsse, digging foundations, unloading catches, keels, and coalships, digging chalk, &c.[84]

Archaeological evidence for the activities of these demolition gangs also goes further than just the remains of undermined walls. More recent excavations have produced evidence for scaffolding postholes cutting through earlier late medieval surfaces, such as against the south transept wall at Holy Trinity Priory, Aldgate, and within the church of Guildford Blackfriars.[85] Such ephemeral features are probably common to all sites but have been overlooked by earlier excavations and clearances. Other short-lived structures found in Dissolution phases also seem to relate to periods of demolition. At St Augustine's Abbey, Canterbury, a square building measuring 7 x 7m and built of rough mortared stone was found directly south of, and parallel to, the nave of the church. Being built on top of the monastic cemetery, it dated after the closure of the abbey, but it also respected the line of the church that was all but destroyed by the later 1540s, so presumably was constructed before this. Given this compressed timeframe, the building was probably used as a temporary workshop for the labourers involved in the demolition of the church.[86]

Lime kilns

Whilst elements of the monastic architecture, such as ashlar facings and window or door frames could easily be reused virtually unaltered in new building projects, the vast majority of the masonry walls would have been less useful, consisting of rough rubble cores and shattered

Figure 3.7 Interior of the lime kiln, Thornton Abbey (author).

mouldings. However, in some circumstances, even this debris could be put to profitable use, especially if the stone was chalk or limestone, when these shattered walls provided a ready quarried and handy source of the raw materials for lime production. During the demolition of Dartford Priory an account book kept between June 1541 and April 1542 notes that as well as being charged with breaking down chimneys and walls, bricklayers were responsible for the construction of a new lime kiln.[87]

Limekilns have been found on a number of monastic sites. At Hartlepool Greyfriars, a small example measuring 1.2 x 1m was found built against the south wall in the church. Ash deposits found in association contained large quantities of nails, suggesting that wooden fittings also provided a handy source of fuel.[88] A much larger limekiln measuring 3 x 7m was found inserted into the nuns' chapter house at Watton Priory. It was positioned at the west end of the room so that the original chapter house door could be modified to serve as the entrance to the newly-built furnace.[89] Limekilns have also been found on two sites in York. At Clementhorpe Priory a pair of kilns were built reusing the nunnery's original fabric and to process the same, although no more information concerning their form is given.[90] Better preserved and recorded was a single kiln from St Andrew's Priory.[91] Constructed in the cloister garth was a circular kiln 1.8m wide, built using reused limestone blocks, and with a pair of opposing flues. This kiln is nearly identical to an example recently partially excavated at Thornton Abbey and associated with the demolition and recycling of materials from the abbey hospital (Figure 3.7).

Tomb robbing and the translation of the dead

One of the most emotive images of the Dissolution was the deliberate desecration of tombs and the disinterment of the dead; indeed modern popular culture has sometimes painted a picture of the methodical disinterment of entire religious communities during the Dissolution of the Monasteries.[92] Although there is little archaeological evidence that such systematic assault on the dead was ever made at any site, it is clear that prominent monuments were routinely broken up and ordinary interments disturbed. Accounts refer to the payments made to workmen to destroy tombs; at Dartford bricklayers were explicitly paid for the "breaking uppe of toumes and tome stones."[93] Fragments of broken-up funerary monument are regularly found during excavations of monastic churches, particularly those more decorative elements that could not be usefully recycled. Flat grave markers were also frequently put to new purposes; at Monk Bretton Priory several cross slabs were reused in the post-medieval farmhouse as door lintels and stone tables,[94] a fate that must have been repeated countless times across the country. However, such reuse was far from new and commonly happened in earlier centuries. For example, at Thornton Abbey, a significant number of 12th- and early 13th-century cross slabs were reused both as pillar foundations during the rebuilding of the nave of the monastic church, and as window lintels in the new gatehouse in the 14th century.

Yet it was the treatment of the dead, as much as their final resting places, that has continued to provoke the strongest reactions. The shocked description by a contemporary observer of the callous disregard shown towards the body of St Cuthbert by the commissioners Dr Legh, Dr Henley and Mr Blithman at the shrine in Durham in 1541 is well known but worth repeating.[95] On opening the coffin it was expected that just bones would be encountered, causing Dr Henley to order them to be "cast downe." However, what is important in this account is that once it became apparent that the body was incorrupt, it was carried carefully to the vestry "tyll such tyme as they did further knowe ye kings pleasure." Clearly even to such ardent reformers as Legh and Henley, the undecayed body of a saint still provoked some reverence, and it is interesting that shortly after the monks were able to rebury the remains on the site of the original shrine with many of the original medieval vestments and other grave goods, where they remained unmolested until 1827.[96]

Ultimately the fate of the dead depended upon the new purpose to which their resting places were subsequently put, and with little bearing as to their status in life, even if they were royalty. The tomb of King John at Worcester survives today virtually intact due to the priory's conversion into a secular cathedral. By way of contrast much of the fabric of Faversham Abbey, containing the tomb of King Stephen, was destined to be shipped, along with stone from St Augustine's Abbey at Canterbury, across the channel to help rebuild the fortifications at Calais.[97] When the royal chapel at Faversham was excavated in 1965, it was found to be so thoroughly robbed that only a single sandstone block remained *in situ* within the grave cut, and of the superstructure of Stephen's tomb, only a few pieces of carved stone and plaster were recovered in the backfill of the grave.[98]

This apparent disregard shown to dead by the agents of the crown was not universal. Coppack has highlighted the fascinating example of the tomb of John Ripon (d.1524) at Fountains Abbey (Figure 3.8). At some point immediately after the suppression of the house in

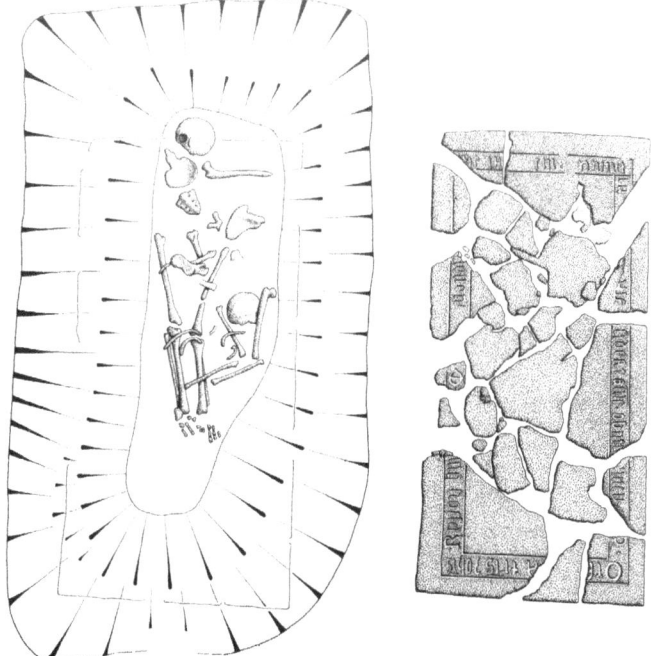

Figure 3.8 Disturbed tomb of John Ripon, Fountains Abbey (G. Coppack).

1539, Ripon's grave slab was lifted and broken and his still semi-articulated body heavily disturbed, possibly to remove the mortuary chalice and pattern.[99] However, following this act the grave slab was carefully replaced and individual missing fragments, which had fallen into the grave, filled in with plaster. This was apparently not an isolated incident at Fountains, excavations in 1851 of the cloister library, which had been crudely walled up, revealed the remains of "a mass of human bones" which seem to have been deliberately concealed there after an episode of looting.[100] Both this, and Coppack's argument that the restoration of Ripon's tomb took place whilst the abbey was still in the care of the suppression commissioners, suggest that acts of unauthorized looting were frowned upon, and if despoliation of tombs was to take place, it should only be after it had been "officially" sanctioned.

Archaeological evidence for the interference of intra-mural burials is commonplace on monastic sites. In most cases it was the materials from which the graves were constructed that were the primary focus of attention, rather than the remains of the occupants, which were either scattered or placed back in the robbed graves. At the hospital chapel at Lewes Priory, several graves had their marble slabs broken with pickaxes so that the lead coffins could be retrieved, the skeletons being emptied out into neat piles in the grave cuts.[101] A similar fate befell those buried in the hospital chapel at Thornton Abbey. Here the grave of the priest Richard de Wispington was opened and the abdomen region his skeleton disturbed by someone rummaging around, possibly looking for a valuable sepulchre chalice, although just the broken remains of a lead one were present. His limestone grave cover only survived as on lifting it appears to have slipped into the grave void, further damaging his mortal remains, and being too troublesome to remove was then left.[102] However, a further phenomenon, that of empty graves, is increasingly being identified on several sites, and these seem to have resulted from the intentional removal of remains elsewhere rather than their deliberate destruction.

The translation of the dead from one location to another was by no means unknown in the Middle Ages, and it is perhaps no surprise the practice continued at the Dissolution. Concern for the fate of ancestors buried within a particular dissolved house appears at numerous times in correspondence between the gentry and Cromwell, usually as a means to bolster the petitioner's request to be granted the site. However, the importance that some members of the gentry attached to their ancestors could result in them exhuming and removing their remains before the churches in which they were buried were demolished or sold to other unrelated owners. Therefore, shortly before the conversion of Carmarthen Greyfriars into a short-lived grammar school in 1543, the tomb and remains of Edmund Tudor, the paternal grandfather of Henry VIII, were moved to St David's Cathedral.[103] However, excavation of the friary church also revealed that at least one other grave was empty save for some 16th-century material in its fill, suggesting that Edmund Tudor was not the only person moved at this time.[104]

Similar empty tombs have been found at other, predominantly urban, sites. At Guildford Blackfriars a grave containing no human remains, or even evidence for Dissolution demolition, was suggested to have once contained a body removed for reburial.[105] Likewise, one completely empty grave from St Mary Graces, Smithfield, and four from Bermondsey Abbey were similarly interpreted.[106] Inevitably, differentiating between graves which were disturbed at the Dissolution with their contents scattered and those which were intentionally removed for reburial, is often impossible. However, it seems likely that the careful translations of burials were probably more common than was previously thought, particularly for the remains of the more recently deceased.

The dispersal of monastic goods

Whilst valuable plate and other metals usually made their way direct to the crown to swell the royal coffers, and the building materials could easily be put to new use by royal agents or the new owners of monastic sites, the fate of other movable fixtures and fittings is less clear. There is often an assumption that what followed was, as Aston has described it, "a scrabble for spoils" and that there must have been:

> a large amount of unrecorded pilfering and fiddling, and it may be assumed that a goodly proportion of monastic property found its way into the households of those who…were watchful for such opportunities.[107]

Such assumptions are usually based upon a few selective accounts, and there is a tension here, as it contrasts very significantly with the far more numerous records of orderly sales of monastic goods, sometimes documented in meticulous detail. Whilst there were clearly incidents of theft and unauthorized spoliation, this was probably not the norm. Archaeologically, where the dispersal of monastic property can be identified, the processes by which it came to be moved is almost impossible to determine.

Of particular relevance here is the study by Howsam into the disposal of medieval books.[108] With the exception of a few documented sales of books, such as much of the library at Monk Bretton, which was purchased by a number of the former brethren,[109] or those collections that were mainly held intact at Durham or Worcester, the accepted historical narrative is that there was wholesale and wanton destruction of monastic books.[110] This is in no small part fuelled by the colourful contemporary description made by John Bale in 1549. He suggested that people used monastic books "to serve theyr jakes (*lavatories*), some to scoure theyr candelstyckes, & some to rubbe their bootes," although he goes on to acknowledge the more probable removal of books "whole shyppes full, to the wonderynge of the foren nacyons."[111] On one level this can be seen archaeologically, as Howsam has shown that particularly high concentrations of book clasps, copper alloy hooks used to hold the leaves of a book tightly closed, have been found in reredorter contexts on monastic sites, although the precise action behind their deposition is still unknowable.[112] However, when considered in a landscape context a different picture emerges.

Book fittings are one of the more common medieval artefact types identified by metal detectorists and reported to the Portable Antiquities Scheme (PAS) in England and Wales, in part due to their very distinctive forms. As of mid-2019, 2,500 clasps, mounts and other book fittings have been registered with the PAS and this probably represents a very small proportion of those found, to say nothing of the numerous examples that have been identified through archaeological excavation.[113] When the PAS data is examined, some interesting patterns emerge. Whilst book fittings are found across England and Wales, there is a significant concentration of finds in eastern and southern England. This should not be a surprise, as these are areas of predominantly arable agriculture, and thus areas more suited to metal detecting. However, even considering these collection biases, a significant pattern still emerges; there is a strong bias towards the deposition of book fittings in Norfolk where a total of 573 examples have thus far been recorded in this single county, well over a fifth of the national total. Furthermore, when their distribution is plotted across the county it is clear that they are evenly spread, found in ordinary fields in virtually every parish, rather than in distinct clusters as might be expected if monastic books were being wantonly destroyed at the monastic houses that originally housed them (Figure 3.9).

It is worth considering what this pattern of disposal represents, particularly as Norfolk was probably one of the most traditional areas of the country when it came to the adherence to the old religion. One possible explanation for this seemingly ubiquitous distribution of books across Norfolk following the Dissolution was that many local people took advantage of the opportunity to acquire religious texts for their personal use. Over the following decades bindings deteriorated and metal fittings came loose and were accidentally lost or intentionally discarded. They

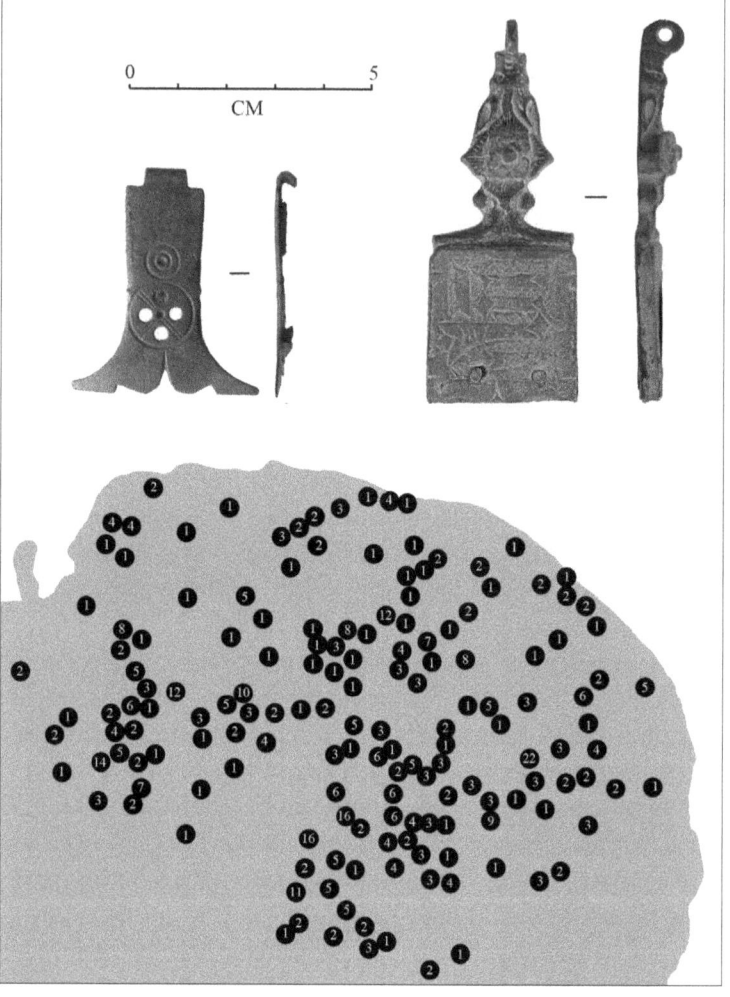

Figure 3.9 Distribution and numbers of book fittings found by metal detecting in Norfolk, data from the Portable Antiquities Scheme (Author).

entered into the normal cycle of household rubbish collection which, outside of the town at least, ultimately ended up being dispersed on the fields as part of the standard manuring process. However, there is an intriguing alternative possibility.

The overwhelming bias in the distribution of book fittings in Norfolk is mirrored almost exactly by another form of late medieval ecclesiastical material culture, the lead ampulla; of the 1,800 recorded on the PAS database, just over 250 come from Norfolk alone. Lead ampullae were simple small containers that from the late 12th century became increasingly popular "souvenirs" collected by pilgrims as they visited shrines or other holy sites.[114] Containing oil or water that had been blessed, they were clearly objects thought to possess some form of spiritual power. Significantly, the ampullae found in such large numbers by metal detectorists are of the simple, often shell-shaped, later form, typically dating to the 15th and early 16th centuries.[115] Mitchiner has made the very interesting suggestion that the reason so many have been found in dispersed rural farmland is that they were used and then discarded as part of ritualized blessing ceremonies, to ensure a successful and productive harvest.[116] Whether these ceremonies were ever officially endorsed, or even undertaken by the church, is uncertain, but even if not there would have been nothing to stop the laity from performing such folk rituals themselves.

If this argument is correct, and it is undoubtedly a persuasive one, what can be seen here is a Christian votive practice that was particularly popular in East Anglia, on the eve of the Dissolution. The Reformation would have put an end to such actions, at least in their original form. With the closure of the monasteries and shrines, lead ampullae would have ceased to be produced, and thus this source of ritual power would have become unavailable to those who still wanted to continue blessing the land. The closure of the monasteries and the destruction of their libraries might have provided an alternative source of apotropaic power for this purpose, medieval texts. Whether Norfolk's farmers sought to improve their harvests through the intentional deposition of portions of medieval books will never be known for sure, but this seems an equally plausible, and somewhat less uncomfortable use, compared with that suggested by Bale in 1549.

Spoliation of the monasteries

Almost every account of the Dissolution of the Monasteries draws attention, and usually reproduces sections from, Michael Sherbrook's *The Falle of Religiouse Howses, Colleges, Chantreys, Hospitalls, &c*. The 48-page manuscript has been published in its entirety, but it is the short passage describing the spoliation of Roche Abbey that has tended to catch the imagination.[117] Taken at face value, Sherbrook is often treated uncritically as if he were an accurate eyewitness account.[118] However, this is far from the case. Born around the year 1535, Sherbrook would have been about three or four years of age at the time of the suppression of Roche, so would have been entirely reliant upon secondary sources to complete his account. Dickens has convincingly argued that *The Falle* was compiled between the years 1567–1591,[119] with the section on Roche probably falling into the late 1560s, so at best Sherbrook might be viewed as a historian looking back at the events of a previous generation thirty years earlier. Yet, even here, his reliability in the most basic factual matters can be questioned. For example, he confidently asserts at the time of the Dissolution there were 10,000 monasteries in England alone, a fantastical overestimation.[120]

However, it is the context of the wider work that it is crucial. Although an Anglican priest, Sherbrook is clearly conservative in many aspects of his religious convictions, and this is the prime motivation behind his writing of *The Falle*. In particular, he reacts against the writings of John Foxe (whose *Actes and Monuments* was published just five years before Sherbrook started his account). He describes Foxe as "an enemy to Monasteries" saying that "when he findeth any writing against the abuse of such Houses, to apply to the Religion itself; descanting thereupon by his own ignorant Censure and Glass, more wickedly, than godly."[121] Given this, it is clear that Sherbrook's intention from the start is to portray the monasteries in the best possible light, and in doing so express his contempt towards those who challenged the religious ideal. Nonetheless, as Dickens has observed, by highlighting the plight of Roche "Sherbrook chose a singularly poor example if he wished to illustrate the hardships of the dispossessed."[122] On the suppression of the monastery the abbot and monks all received substantial payoffs and pensions, and even the servants were dismissed with the reward of half a year's wages.[123]

On first reading Sherbrook's account of the despoliation of Roche, the reader is left with a confusing picture of what took place. On one hand elements of the account clearly suggest an organized sale of the monastic goods, yet on the other the overwhelming impression conveyed is that of a chaotic frenzy of rampant looting by the local population "that they that could this day think it to be the House of God, and the next day the House of the Devil."[124] However, if examined more closely, in amongst the jumbled narrative, a more systematic train of events can be detected, and most of these fall within the familiar pattern of an ordinary suppressed house. First, immediately after the closure, the monks are each given the contents of their cells, a practice noted elsewhere, such as at Coventry Charterhouse.[125] At this point, there might also have been the deliberate concealment of goods by the monks. Sherbrook notes that pewter vessels were found hidden amongst the rocks surrounding the monastery,[126] and whilst he implies this was the work of the looters it would make little sense for them to conceal such items rather than carrying them away with all the other goods.

Second, Sherbrook notes the removal and melting of the roof lead in the nave of the church. Although he does not state it, it is likely that this was undertaken by Cromwell's agents as was usual; if lead were stolen it would most likely have been carried away rather than melted *in situ*. Next is the reference to the defacement of tombs in the church. Whom carried this out is not revealed, but again it is likely to have been Cromwell's men rather than the local populace, perhaps in an attempt to recover lead coffins or valuable materials from the funerary monuments. Once the usual extraction of metals had taken place, Sherbrook notes that the local gentry and yeomanry (including Sherbrook's own father) purchased the timber from the church, and other items were probably sold at this point as well as at a later date. In 1542, nearly four years after the closure of Roche, Ecclesfield church is recorded as having purchased some of the former abbey's vestments,[127] suggesting that many goods had been carefully looked after during the intervening period. Finally, the small fixtures and fittings, such as iron hooks and windows, were stripped from the abbey. Whilst this might have indeed been the result of intermittent pilfering, such items could equally have been legitimately purchased by the local population, although the lack of any contemporary accounts of sale for Roche, as exist for many other monasteries (see below), makes it impossible to say for certain.

Given this, rather than the wild free-for-all implied by Sherbrook, what took place at Roche might have been altogether somewhat different and better organized. Furthermore, the scale at which any despoliation might have taken place, certainly in the short term, is also open to question. Over five years after the surrender of the house, on 20 February 1546 Henry Clifford, Earl of Cumberland, who was leasing the site from the crown, was granted a license to alienate the site to Henry Tyrell.[128] Part of the condition of the grant was that Tyrell was to;

> excepte and reserve all the leade, belles, and belle mettall being in and upon the premises, togither withe all suche superfluous buyldings, tybre, stone iron, glasse, and other thinges as ben excepted out of the former's leasse.[129]

Given that much was still remaining half a decade after the house's suppression, it is clear that the looting of Roche was not as rapid, thorough or as wide scale as perhaps Sherbrook would have us believe.

Despite this re-evaluation of the evidence from Roche, there were still incidents of sporadic looting. On visiting the recently suppressed Reading Greyfriars, Dr London was caused to comment "This is a town of much poor people, and they fell to stealing so fast in every corner of the house that I have be fain to tarry a whole week here."[130] Similarly at Bridlington Priory, following the removal of precious metals by the Duke of Norfolk, the house seems to have been left unattended and, as later reported to Cromwell by Richard Pollard "I never saw so nedy people in my lyve as are in these parties for they have made theare afore my coming great spoyle and robyry."[131] Not all got away with such theft, following the suppression of Pipewell Abbey a tinker was caught stealing lead from the monastery and was hanged for the crime.[132] But these seem to have been relatively isolated incidences of opportunism, and it can be assumed that Cromwell's agents took all precautions to guard against such acts. However, there is one monastery where much more widespread looting was recorded as taking place.

Shagan has highlighted the rather unusual, but particularly well-documented, robbing of Hailes Abbey.[133] Following reports of wide-scale looting, the royal commissioners Bridges, Tracy and Stratford were sent to investigate the situation in January 1542. Their report, which ran to 8,000 words, revealed a pattern of unauthorized yet systematic stripping of the site by the local population. The commissioners compiled as complete a catalogue as possible of what had been stolen and who the perpetrators were. In addition to the more valuable items such as the lead, which had been shipped by the cartload out under the cover of darkness, fixtures such as windows, glazing bars, doors and even the trees and beehives in the precinct had been stolen away. Such was the scale of operations, Shagan argues that the looting "whilst not announced publically…was an open secret."[134]

What is also remarkable are the number of perpetrators involved, and that they came from all strata of society. The 75 individuals indicted included members of the local gentry, yeoman farmers as well as those further down the social scale, and thus rather than the enrichment of just a few, as a whole the people of Hailes integrated the wealth back into their wider community. Indeed, it was not only individuals that profited but also the local church, with stone taken from Hailes at this time being reused and incorporated into the nearby church at Teddington.[135] Shagan has also suggested that what prompted this appropriation of the abbey's wealth was not just pure greed or the work of particular religious zealots. He draws a direct link between the community's willingness to collude in the spoliation and the near-universal enragement of the local population following the very public debunking of the abbey's famous relic of the blood of Christ, which was proved to be just honey coloured with saffron.[136]

The genuine public outrage at the debunking of relics was not limited to Hailes, as a similarly well-documented example can be found at Boxley Abbey in Kent. There the carved statue of Christ on the Rood of Grace was famous for its miraculous blinking eyes, moving lips and even periodic foaming from the mouth. Jeffrey Chamber writing to Cromwell records what happened when he visited the abbey in February 1538;

> On defacing the late monastery of Boxley and plucking down the images, found, in the Roode of Grace, which has been had in great veneration, certain engines and old wire, with old rotten sticks in the back of the same, which caused the eyes to move and stir in the head thereof, like unto a lively thing, and also the nether lip in likewise to move as though it should speak…conveyed it (*the figure*) to Maidstone this present Thursday, being market day, and showed it to the people, who had the matter in wondrous detestation and hatred, so that if the monastery had to be defaced again they would pluck it down or burn it.[137]

The deception caused such a stir, as well as amusement, that after its public display in Maidstone, the figure was taken to London and paraded at court, where it was made to perform before the king and his entourage. It then faced further open ridicule as the Bishop of Rochester preached in public sat opposite the idol, before being finally broken up and burnt before the crowd.[138] In these two cases at least, the revelation of the monks' deceptions might well have fuelled the desire by the local populous to deface and loot the offending monasteries in whom they had previously placed their trust.

Sale and redistribution

Although incidents of theft and looting of chattels, both recorded and unrecorded, inevitably took place following the closure of the monasteries, it was clearly in the interests of the crown that an orderly sale, usually through a public auction, took place so that the maximum financial gain could be realized. Whilst records of sales do not survive for many houses, elsewhere the records are more complete and give a valuable insight into how the monastic goods were sold and redistributed. A particularly well-documented example is from the sale of goods from Burton Abbey on 12 November 1545.[139] The dispersal is a late one, due to the abbey having been temporarily granted a reprieve after being refounded as a short-lived secular college. However, its sale represents the culmination of a well-rehearsed procedure that had been developed through the late 1530s.

The first act of the commissioners Goodrick and Scudamore was to draw up a comprehensive inventory and valuation of all the plate, church ornaments, and household goods. The church plate was measured by weight only and not valued, as presumably it was destined for the king, but the rest of the goods totalled £41 12s 2d, with individual items ranging from a the "sute of Westmts of Whyt Damaske" valued at 36s 8d, a "lectorne of brass" worth 20s, 2 "grett Candlestyckes of latton" 5s, 2d "peyr of Organs" 6s 8d, to an "old ladder" at 2d. With the plate and best vestments, including those of "Whyt Damaske," being reserved for the crown the ensuing sale of the remainder of the goods raised £21 4s 8d. The parish of Burton acquired the lectern and pair of organs, the great candlesticks were bought by William Bassett, while most of the household goods, including the old ladder, were given to Sir William Paget, who had also been granted the site of the dissolved college. From the proceeds of the sale payments of £12 2s 6d were made to the disbanded college household (just as they often were to the religious occupants of the monasteries) and to pay outstanding college debts of £9 13s 8d. Finally, a sum of £25 9s 6d was paid to cover all official expenses incurred by Goodrick and Scudamore, including £10 "geaven in Reward for there pains." Ironically, the final expenses of £47 5s 8d were more than double the cash raised from the sale, and even higher than the original valuation of goods. Given this, with the exception of the plate and best vestments that were sent directly to the king, the financial reward to the crown from the sale of goods of Burton was non-existent.

In some cases, most of the fixtures and fittings of the monastery, once plate and lead were removed, were also sold almost in their entirety to a single individual. Such happened at Dale Abbey. After the de-roofing and part-demolition of the church by the commissioner Sir William Cavendish,[140] presumably to extract the lead and other valuables for the crown, Sir Francis Pole of Radbourne acquired a considerable proportion of the goods for the sum of £77 12s 2d on 28th October 1538.¹⁴¹ Pole had also initially been given tenure then grant of the abbey site, but in 1544 he alienated this to Sir John Porte,¹⁴² suggesting that he was only really interested in the site as a piece of real estate speculation, as well as any short-term value that might be made from the buildings themselves.

Pole's acquisitions¹⁴³ can be broadly broken down into two different categories of goods: specific ecclesiastical fixtures and fittings, and structural building materials. From the presbytery and transepts of the church, he bought items predominantly clerical in nature: altars and altar fittings, seating, wooden panels and partitions, the founder's tomb grate, and organs. Although such items could have been reused in a secular context, their primary value lay in an ecclesiastical context. In contrast, his purchases of roof timber, glass, iron, paving, and gravestones from the nave, cloisters, chapter house, and frater could all be more readily recycled in any building project. It is also interesting to note he also purchased useful items such as kitchen equipment and soft furnishings from the west range, even though these were of little worth. Consequently, Pole clearly saw the value that monastic possessions could have in both continued religious and new secular contexts.

This process can, in part, be seen in the subsequent dispersal of various elements of Dale Abbey that can still be traced today, although that which can still be identified is only a small fraction originally possessed by Pole. Pole used Dale to both embellish his existing properties and to sell for profit. Whilst nothing today remains of Pole's principal seat at Radbourne Hall, where many elements of Dale might have ended up being incorporated, the church survives little altered from the 16th-century when it acted as the family mortuary chapel.¹⁴⁴ Here Pole seems to have transferred much of the woodwork from Dale, including some of the benches, panelling and a particularly elaborate font cover (Figure 3.10). Consequently, it is possible to see Pole taking advantage of his purchase to enrich the family church.

But Pole's purchase of materials from Dale was made for financial gain too, and undoubtedly many now unrecorded sales were made. One that can be reconstructed, in part, are the many elements of the former abbey incorporated into the church at Morley, by Sir Henry Sacheverell. Colvin originally suggested that Sacheverell was directly responsible for removing the materials present at Morley from Dale, as he had been briefly steward of the

Figure 3.10 Pews and panelling, Radbourne church (Author).

abbey following the Dissolution.[145] However, given many of the features present at Morley correspond with portions mentioned explicitly as having been sold to Pole this seems very unlikely.

Although no record of sale exists between Pole and Sacheverell, the two were well acquainted. Sacheverell was a significant figure in Derbyshire, contributing to the *Valor Ecclesiasticus* inquiry of 1535, and taking a key position in the suppression of the Pilgrimage of Grace under the Earl of Shrewsbury.[146] Pole served as a Commissioner of the Peace with Sacheverell in 1541, and Pole and his father German had served together on a Commission of Gaol Delivery in 1540.[147] Given Sacheverell was already well acquainted with Dale Abbey following his stewardship of the site, it is not surprising that he might seek to acquire some of its spoils from Pole.

The most striking elements translated from Dale to Morley are five matching perpendicular square-headed windows, each containing four lights, and interspersed with fine supporting wall buttresses.[148] Four were set in the north wall of the north aisle and one at its east end. Because the windows and their adjoining buttressing had clearly been moved *en masse* the whole north aisle had to be rebuilt to incorporate them. Along with the window frames, the painted glass depicting the story of Robert of Knaresborough, was also brought (Figure 3.11). Although in later centuries the windows did not receive the care they deserved, in 1789 John Byng observed that "There was some stain'd glass in the windows, and some broken pieces laying upon a monument,"[149] and they were restored in the 19th century to give a reasonable impression of how it might originally have looked. Some 19th-century commentators thought that the Morley windows had been brought from the frater of Dale,[150] but as argued by Hope, they almost certainly came from the cloister walk.[151] Not only do they correspond stylistically to the documented rebuilding of the cloister in the late 1470s to early 1480s, they match the width of the excavated foundations found at Dale which indicated the outer cloister walk wall was approximately 20m along on each side, providing enough space for six windows and their supporting buttresses.[152] How Pole disposed of the remaining 19 windows from his purchase of the cloister alley is uncertain, but his purchase of an entire glazing scheme was far from unique. There is also archaeological evidence for the intentional retention of whole windows, although given the fra-

Figure 3.11 Translated window glass from Dale Abbey, St Matthew's Church, Morley (Author).

gility of the material concerned these are rare and hard to identify. Perhaps the best surviving example is a reconstructable late 13th-century grisaille window panel found at Bradwell Abbey, discovered in still leaded state 2m to the north of the church, from which it had been removed with some care. This corresponds to a post-suppression survey of the site that referred to "old glasses… which would be taken down and saved for mending of divers Chancels etc."[153]

Figure 3.12   Tomb slab of Sir Henry Sacheverell, St Matthew's Church, Morley (Author).

Other elements of Morley Church are traditionally believed to have come from Dale, and in almost all cases there is good reason to believe this to be true. Hardest to prove are portions of the porch to the south entrance and a fragment of tomb canopy in the south chapel. The porch, incorporating late 12th to early 13th century early English moulding and shafts is clearly an addition placed against the south wall, yet it covers a late 13th-century decorated door.[154] The late medieval canopy in the south chapel was inserted above a raised altar tomb belonging to Sir Thomas Stathum who died in 1662.[155] Whilst both features are clearly recycled, it is impossible to say for certain whether they originated at Dale or somewhere else closer to hand.

More conclusive are other identified elements more directly connected to Sir Henry Sacheverell, including his own tomb slab, which he shared with his wife, located between the chancel and the north aisle (Figure 3.12). When this slab was moved in the 19th century, it was found that its underside was highly polished and included the matrix for the now missing brass of an ecclesiastical figure with a border and inscription.[156] Colvin has suggested that the original ecclesiastic brass might well have been reused itself to create that for Sacheverell, but without being able to see the underside this is conjectural.[157] Nonetheless, the reuse of what appears to have been the original memorial to an abbot of Dale by Sacheverell seems to have been a very deliberate and almost subversive act.

At Morley a large number of decorative medieval floor tiles also survive, and these are also thought to have come from Dale Abbey. These originally covered much of the floor of the church, but in the 19th century, the better-preserved examples were reset in the north aisle.[158] In 1890 it was noted that tiles found during the then-recent excavations by Hope at Dale Abbey included some of the same design presently at Morley, although unfortunately, these do not survive today.[159] Furthermore, Hope noted in his excavation of the church choir that the tile pavement had been removed and only broken and out of place tiles were found.[160] Very similar tiles, although without precisely replicated patterns, were also found during more excavations of the south range at Dale.¹⁶¹ Given this, and coupled with the fact that it was recorded that the pavements of not only church and cloister but also the south range were sold to Francis Pole in 1538, it seems that in all probability the tiles at Morley originated at Dale Abbey. A tile kiln encountered around the year 1860 outside of the main gate of the abbey seems to have been the original source, although unfortunately this and the tiles recovered from it were broken up and used to mend the local roads.¹⁶²

A final possible relic of Dale Abbey at Morley has never hitherto been noted. Placed against a pillar in the south aisle is the

Figure 3.13   Stone mortar from Dale Abbey, St Matthew's Church, Morley (Author).

majority of a broken stone mortar (Figure 3.13). Clearly not an ecclesiastical object, its presence at Morley is perplexing, although it is certainly large enough to have been reused as a font. Although there is no direct evidence for its origin it is interesting to note that amongst household goods purchased by Pole from the kitchen at Dale Abbey was "a morter with a pestell."¹⁶³

Various other elements of Dale Abbey appear to have been moved to new locations, but this often seems to have happened over the course of several centuries after its closure. The Earl of Stanhope was responsible for the further dispersal of the fabric from Dale during the 18th century. The font was removed to Stanton Hall, before being returned to Dale church at the end of the 19th century,¹⁶⁴ and a considerable quantity of stone was removed to help in the construction of Risley Hall.¹⁶⁵ As late as the 19th-century fragments of glass from Dale Abbey were incorporated into a window at Hathersage church,¹⁶⁶ but it is uncertain whether these came directly from the abbey itself or via Morley. The final pieces of possible fabric from Dale Abbey are two square-headed windows close together at Chaddesden church.¹⁶⁷ Although there is no direct evidence of their sale and they are of different sizes, the windows are of the same style and are clearly inserted into the pre-existing fabric at Chaddesden, so their provenance to Dale is not out of the question.

— 4 —

The Dispersal and Acquisition of Monastic Property

Cromwell's supposed and oft-quoted boast of using the Dissolution of the Monasteries to "make the King the richest prince in Christendom" was in fact coined by an anonymous rebel at the Council of Pontefract during the Pilgrimage of Grace in 1536.[1] If such a boast had been made publicly by Cromwell, it was almost certainly the more modest one to make Henry "the richest king that ever reigned in England" (*il deust promettre de le faire le plus riche que oncques fut en angleterre*), as reported by Emperor Charles V's Ambassador Chapuys in late 1535.[2] Whatever the true scale of Cromwell's ambition on behalf of his monarch, the main asset for its realization would have been the extensive lands, estates, and incomes controlled by the monasteries.

The "golden showre of dissolued abbey lands"?

It is often stated that Cromwell's original intention was for the crown to retain the bulk of the monastic estates intact, favouring the leasing of land rather than its sale.[3] Indeed, the establishment of the Court of Augmentations ensured that there was a mechanism in place for the management of the monastic estates on a permanent basis, so that they could contribute to the royal revenue over a long period.[4] However, as Youings has also pointed out, some sales of land must have been anticipated from the beginning, as the 1536 Act gave the king the right to grant and dispose of the property as he wished.[5] During the first few years of its running, the Court of Augmentations gave only 234 outright grants of monastic lands, before the first formal commission was issued to sell land in December 1539, shortly before Cromwell's fall from grace. In the end, it was political need rather than the Court's expedient management that dictated the rate of sale, and the last five years of Henry's reign saw the sale of over half the monastic estates, a period coinciding with the Anglo-French wars.[6]

Reconstructing this transfer of monastic land is not without its considerable challenges. The initial leases, grants, and alienations are, on the whole, well documented, and allowed antiquarians such as Dugdale, Tanner, Cobbett and even Spelman to note to whom the principal portions of the monastic estate, usually the site of the house and conventual buildings, had passed.[7] However, tracing the fate of the various manors, granges, messuages, and miscellaneous tracts of lands is considerably more complex, although during the 1950s–1970s a number of county based-studies do provide a broader picture of the transfer of land.[8] These overviews, while valuable, still have their limitations; Youings was critical of the fact that most only outline the initial disposal of the land by the crown rather than their subsequent resale and dispersal, which could be an extremely rapid process.[9] Although this is true, it is perhaps a harsh judgement. Even if records of resale are examined, where they survive, it is challenging to be sure whether a plot identified merely as "a tenement" or "land" in a named village in an initial grant is the same as one sold on some years or even decades later.[10]

It is worth noting that, perhaps unsurprisingly, before the extensive estates of the monasteries even passed into the hands of the king, there were attempts by the religious themselves to dispose of their lands once the intentions of the crown became clear. On the eve of the Dissolution, much of the bulk of many monastic estates were already leased to secular individuals, and it is apparent that there was a marked increase in the leasing of land in the 1530s, often at preferential rates, in part to raise the capital required to pay off the crown to prevent early closure. Whilst such transactions were legitimate, if ultimately unsuccessful, in their aims, it is also clear there were numerous examples of monasteries that sought to dispose of land before closure, so that individual members of the community, or those connected with them, could benefit personally after the event.

One notable example, which may well be typical of many others less well recorded, can be seen in the actions of the last prior of Bodmin Priory. Following the death of the previous incumbent Vyvyan, Thomas Mundy who was then a canon at Merton Abbey, was successfully installed in 1534 as the new prior despite the monks of Bodmin having elected one of their own to the office.[11] Such a turn of events was only possible through the support of Nicholas Prideaux, a member of local Devonshire gentry who was responsible for lobbying Cromwell over the matter. The Mundy and Prideaux families were well connected on several levels, not least through the marriage of Mundy's niece Joanna to Prideaux's son William. Whether Mundy and Prideaux were fully aware of the fate that was to befall all the monasteries when they colluded to get Mundy installed as prior is uncertain, but as events unfolded over the ensuing years, they took advantage to advance their particular situations. Following the Pilgrimage of Grace in 1536, Mundy started granting a series of long leases to Prideaux and his family on very favourable terms, helping to solidify a dynastic structure that was of benefit to both families.[12] As was usually the case, these leases were respected by the crown following the Dissolution, as the Act of 1539 only provided for the annulment of leases made less than a year before a monastery's surrender.[13] Consequently, Mundy was able to note in his will of 1548 that Prideaux "oweth me a great sum of money" due to Mundy being "the setter forth of all these foresaid bargains."[14]

Prior Mundy was not alone in his efforts to dispose of leases for his own benefit. Agent John Freeman wrote to Cromwell from Lincolnshire on 3rd October 1538 complaining that:

> for they are in a customed sort all of spoil and bribery, as well the great houses as small, of all the religious houses in England; for they leave neither demesnes unlet nor honest stuff in their houses, but also minisheth the great part of their stock and store. Therefore they would be taken betime.[15]

Corroboration for Freeman's assessment of the situation in Lincolnshire can be found in a range of sources. The prioress of Orford, Joan Thompson, gave a 60-year lease of lands in Golceby and Ranby to her brother Thomas, and the prioress of Nuncotham was reprimanded by the Bishop of Lincoln and ordered not to grant any further leases of property to her brother George Thompson.[16] Where no relatives were to hand to take on leases of land, the religious could resort to more drastic measures to secure their futures. The last prior of Brinkburn, William Hogeson, accused of incontinence with several women by the visitation of Drs Layton and Leigh,[17] attempted to bribe Alexander Hearon of Meldon with £10 saying;

> as I understand th'abbies are like to be suppressed, I have sente unto him the Xli for the which he hathe Revelowe in mortgage, because I am desyrous to have that lande in my owne possession at this tyme of suppression.[18]

but it seems the prior was unsuccessful in his attempts to secure lands for himself.

The demand for land

Over half a century ago, the economic historian John Habakkuk drew attention to what he described as a "schizophrenic" approach by historians, who on the one hand suggested that there was "a scramble for monastic lands" in a market that was extremely competitive, whilst on the other stating purchasers could make significant financial gains through the acquisition of former monastic estates.[19] Likewise, Youings called into question the traditional view that monastic lands were "squandered" by the crown and that bargains were to be had by those in the king's favour, as a way of consolidating changes brought about by the Reformation.[20] Only two decades earlier one historian had felt confident enough to claim, seemingly based on nothing other than his prejudices, that Henry gave away land "as presents, as stakes in a game of dice, in exchange for uncultivated or denuded lands or for practically nothing at all."[21] Whilst clearly such tenuous positions can be dismissed, and indeed have been by a succession of subsequent historical studies, there was a demand for land amongst the secular elite, and the crown was more than willing to meet this through leases and grants.

As has already been noted, it was almost certainly the original intention of Cromwell that the majority of the monastic estates were to be kept by the crown and leased to provide a significantly increased and perpetual income for the king. However, once it became apparent that the disposal of some land needed to take place a mechanism through which sale could take place needed to be established. One of the most colourful near-contemporary descriptions of the acquisition of monastic property is Richard Carew's 1602 account of the duplicitous method by which John Champernowne was supposedly able to gain the site of the priory of St German in Cornwall;

> Now when the golden showre of the dissoluted Abbey lands, rayned welnere into euery gapers mouth, some 2. or 3. gentlemen, the Kings seruants, and master Champernownes acquaintance, waited at a doore where the King was to passe forth, with purpose to beg such a matter at his hands: Our gentleman (*John Chapernowne*) became inquisitiue to know their suit: they made strange to impart it. This while, out comes the King: they kneele down, so doth master Champernowne: they preferre their petition; the King graunts it: they render humble thanks, and so doth M. Champernowne: afterwards, he requireth his share; they deny it; he appeales to the King: the King avoweth his equall meaning in the largesse; whereon, the ouertaken companions were fayne to allot him this Priory for his partage.[22]

However, the reality of how the monastery passed into the Champernowne family was somewhat different.

Despite assertions to the contrary, it is abundantly clear that the crown did not merely give away huge tracts of land for no consideration at all. Savine's review of monastic grants, while now rather dated, nevertheless proves that absolute gifts were a rarity: just 41 (2.5%) of a total of 1,593 grants recorded during Henry VIII's reign.[23] Much, if not most, of the monastic land was already leased under pre-existing arrangements made between the monasteries and private tenants and these usually continued to be honoured after the Dissolution.[24] It has been observed that tenants who had obtained their original leases from the religious were often those who became the first prospective buyers once the monasteries had been closed.[25] Indeed, in the early years after the Dissolution, sites free for immediate possession were usually only available to those who already held the lease, which they could then buy out.[26]

Although in the 1530s there were some more informal and beneficial acquisitions of land, especially to favoured courtiers and individual members of the Court of Augmentations, the first statement outlining terms of sale was issued in December 1539, and the procedure for obtaining a grant was considerably more formalized.[27] Any interested party had to obtain an appropriate valuation of the desired lands based upon its current revenue.[28] Prior to 1543, the "tenth" was then removed, the percentage income reserved for the crown on all property valued over 100 marks,[29] along with the value of any lands that were to be given to the crown in exchange for the new grant, and any other Royal concessions. The fee of the final grant was calculated from this remaining sum at a certain number of years' purchase, which in the 1540s was almost always the standard rate of 20 years.[30]

In examining the sale price of monastic lands, Habakkuk made two important and related, observations. The first was that although most early grants were consistently made at a rate of 20 years' purchase, this rose steadily between the 1540s and 1560s to 30 years' purchase, and later on, there was often considerable variation between sites in the precise figure reached. The second was that despite the very significant amount of land being released onto the market over a comparatively short period, prices were not depressed as might be expected, indeed as already noted grant values actually rose quite considerably.[31]

Taken together, these conditions could be interpreted as having resulted from an insatiable demand for land by would-be purchasers, who were still willing to invest in an ever more competitive and heated market. However, rather than representing an ever-increasing demand for land through the middle of the 16th century, the observed rise in the grant purchase values has been argued to reflect the fact that the original valuations were too low. Thus, in later years a readjustment was required, and it is pertinent to note that the standard rate for private sales of secular land remained at 20 years' purchase.[32] Nonetheless, it is also important to explain why the release of so much property onto the market did not cause a significant devaluation. Habakkuk suggested that before the Dissolution there was already a frustrated demand for land, with too little available for purchase by an increasingly wealthy local gentry and the growing middling sorts.[33] Consequently, when land was released from the 1540s onwards, there was a backlog of would-be purchasers waiting to make acquisitions. However, such an explanation has been argued to be an oversimplification. In Devon, the growth in the land market can be traced to at least the early 1530s, before significant amounts of monastic land had been released, and later sales of crown land merely complemented the existing situation.[34] Where there might have been an effect on the market brought about by the availability of monastic land, this probably was, more importantly, an indirect one, and not just because there were new opportunities to purchase previously unavailable estates. Kew points out that, in the case of Devon, prospective purchasers of the new monastic land frequently had to sell holdings of other property to raise the capital required,[35] and this is likely to have been the case across the country. Thus, many of the sales taking place during the 1540s were of land and property already in secular hands, rather than reflecting a scramble to acquire newly released monastic assets.

One important factor often overlooked in discussions of monastic land purchases is that not all types of land were equal. As previously noted, many manors, granges, and tenements were already under leases which continued to be honoured under the new regime, but the sites of the monasteries themselves would have been mostly vacant and thus available for immediate possession. Furthermore, different monastic assets would not have been equally desirable. As Youings points out, while very early on whole monastic estates were passed intact to individual grantees, more ordinarily estates were broken up, with the site of the conventual buildings and most desirable granges being sold first.[36] But perhaps what made the sites of the houses themselves particularly attractive investments was not only their immediate availability but also the fact that their purchase prices were derived purely from their income and did not take account of the value of the physical fabric present on the site. As has already been noted in Chapter 3, even after the crown had removed valuable elements of the monastic complex, there was still considerable wealth tied up in the remaining buildings, both in terms of what they might realize at sale but also in their ability to be cheaply put to new uses (see Chapters 6 and 7).

Finally, most discussions concerning the transfer of lands tend to focus on agrarian assets. Yet land owned by the monasteries in urban areas was treated differently and perhaps offered alternative opportunities. Houses or tenements without land in London and other towns were officially sanctioned in 1539 to be sold at 15 years' purchase, subsequently lowered to 10 years in 1543.[37] Despite this, such valuations might have been still prohibitively high, and during the 1540s at least they were often sold at rates as low as 8 years' purchase.[38] Given that such urban holdings were not only generally much smaller in size and income compared with the rural manors and granges, but also being sold at far lower rates of years' purchase, it meant that a much wider range of individuals had the potential to buy into the property market, and also put these assets to a wider range of new uses (see Chapter 5).

The beneficiaries

Savine's analysis of monastic land grants gives an, albeit imperfect, overview of the general status of those who benefitted from the Dissolution. His subdivision of grantees into different categories is at best subjective and, as is acknowledged by Fisher, the Duke of Norfolk might be classed as not only a peer but also a courtier, a crown official, and an officer of the Court of Augmentations.[39] Nonetheless, it still provides a superficial insight into the range of people who successfully obtained grants of land. Analysing this data is also problematic. Purely comparing individual numbers of grants given to any group is relatively meaningless when the significant variations in size between each sale or exchange are taken into account. Likewise, merely examining the total monies paid to the crown by each group could be misleading, especially if certain well-connected people benefitted from more generous terms of sale. A more useful measure is the approximate yearly value of the property each group obtained, as this provides a sense of scale to the wealth of land that was redistributed. Another useful comparison that can be made is the number of individual grantees in each category, as this helps indicate how dispersed benefits were, however large or small, between and within different communities.

Excluding grants to corporations, both lay and spiritual, as well as a large number of grantees of uncertain status, several patterns can be observed (Table 4.1, below). In terms of numbers of beneficiaries, the land was equally distributed among peers and crown officials, 130 individuals in each category receiving a grant of land. The remaining third of beneficiaries were from lower down the social scale and included grantees classed as industrialists and entrepreneurs, as well as civic organizations that sought to benefit financially from the acquisition of particular estates. However, such figures are misleading for two reasons. First, while it is clear that equal numbers of peers and well-placed commoners benefitted from grants of land, the amount of land received was not equal; the nobility obtained far larger grants in terms of value. Second, the number of grantees alone is a superficial measure, as it is clear that amongst all categories, specific individuals gained far more numerous grants of land. Although 131 peers and courtiers benefitted, just 16 received the majority of the land granted.[40] Indeed, the beneficiary of the single largest grant of land was the commoner Sir Richard Gresham, mercer and former Lord Mayor of London, who in October 1540 obtained the site and extensive estates of Fountains Abbey, as well as the nunneries of Swine and Nunkeeling, for the sum of £11,137.[41]

Consequently, such raw figures, although impressive, are of limited use in enabling a more comprehensive understanding of those benefitting from the transfer of monastic lands through the middle decades of the 16th century.[42] Not only is the scale of an individual's gains obscured, but also what happened to the land immediately after it passed from crown to subject. It is clear that much land was quickly resold either piecemeal or *en masse*, and this pattern does not emerge from a simple examination of the initial grants made by the Court of Augmentations. Nonetheless, several in-depth county-based studies have provided a more nuanced view of the individuals engaged in the purchase of monastic land. Whilst the narrative varied from county to county, the vast majority of beneficiaries can be more simply grouped into three categories: the nobility and courtiers, the local gentry and possible speculators in monastic property.

The nobility and courtiers

On the face of it, the nobility were the most obvious beneficiaries of monastic land, whether these came in the form of gifts, exchanges or ordinary grants. The staggering amounts of land accumulated by some individuals, such as the Duke of Suffolk (discussed further below), are undeniable. Yet to assume that just the most prominent members of society were to benefit most and that this would be a long-lasting position, would be to overlook a far more complex scenario. In some regions, local conditions meant that there were relatively few monastic lands to change hands, or that there were other competing local interests. For example, in Nottinghamshire numbers of former religious houses were relatively few, and these happened to be not particularly wealthy. Of the thirteen houses present in the county, only Lenton, Thurgaton, Welbeck, and Worksop had incomes stated to be in excess of £200 in the *Valor Ecclesiasticus*, and of the remaining four were considerably below £100. Furthermore, there were relatively few peers with pre-existing and extensive interests in the county, the exceptions being the Earl of Shrewsbury and the Marquis of Dorset, and the major landowners at the Dissolution were the Bishop of Lincoln and the Archbishop of York.[43] As a result, opportunities for the acquisition of land by any individuals in Nottinghamshire was relatively limited, and the only family from the peerage to make any significant gains were the Talbots, Earls of Shrewsbury.

Lancashire was another county that was not particularly well populated by rich monastic properties and prosperous estates. With the exception of wealthy Furness Abbey, and the rather less-endowed Whalley, none of the other nine monasteries had an income of even £100 listed in the *Valor Ecclesiasticus*, and the poorest Kersal was pitifully valued at just £8 6s 8d per annum. Another factor that affected the land market in Lancashire was the Duchy of Lancaster, the long-established government office that had traditionally administered the crown estates in the county.[44] At the Dissolution, around 40% of the monastic property in Lancashire passed to the Duchy, which was unwilling to sell most of its newly acquired lands. The only personage to make a significant gain in Lancashire was Sir William Paget, Chancellor of the Duchy of Lancaster and Privy Councillor, who acquired the sites and lands of Burscough and Conishead, whose combined value in the *Valor* was £177 7s 6d.

Elsewhere, those of the elite were able to make more significant gains. In the West Country, Edward Seymour, 1st Duke of Somerset was initially granted the site and estates of Maiden Bradley Priory in Wiltshire,[45] which became the family's principal seat, and he later acquired the sites and lands of Muchelney in Somerset and Amesbury in Wiltshire, along with a numerous other West Country properties.[46] In neighbouring Devon, John Russell, 1st Earl of Bedford, was able to secure substantial grants of monastic land during the reign of Henry VIII, unusually including generous gifts from the king that amounted to £650. Later during the reign of Edward VI, Thomas Wriothesley, 1st Earl of Southampton, was also granted extensive Devonshire lands, as well as grants in other counties.[47]

Even though the nobility and other courtiers might have been the significant beneficiaries of land grants in some areas such as the West Country, this might not have always been the case. In the case of Somerset, while it has been argued that the nobility did indeed gain significant grants of land at preferential rates, this was primarily confined to the period when the system for sales was laxest, in the 1530s.[48] Furthermore, although those well-placed at court might have initially benefitted most, this was not the case in the longer term. Not only did many of the key figures in the 1530s and 1540s, such as Edward Seymour or even Thomas Cromwell himself, subsequently later fall out of political favour and have their lands seized by the crown, but many others also sold their newly acquired lands to an eager provincial audience. Thus, it has been observed in many locations that despite the gentry's initial gains via royal grants, it was through the subsequent resale on the private market that much of the land ended up in the hands of the local gentry.[49]

Local gentry

That it was the provincial gentry that gained the most from the redistribution of monastic lands in the long term is probably of little surprise. They would have had extensive dealings with the monasteries, and in many cases were leasing manors, granges, and tenements from them before to the Dissolution. More often than not, the local gentry had been patrons of their local abbey or priory, and many of their dead would have been buried within their precincts, so it was perhaps understandable that they also wanted to acquire the sites of the houses too. This has long been recognized and where suitable data survives the numbers of entirely new families that became established through the acquisition of monastic land can be seen to be very small, with most ultimately going to traditional dynasties who sought to consolidate and expand their estates.[50]

The extent to which former monastic land transferred into the hands of provincial elites during the 16th century is often hard to assess accurately, and inevitably varied considerably depending on the local situation. As has already been discussed, in Lancashire the presence of the Duchy of Lancaster affected to some degree the opportunities for wealthy buyers to secure significant grants. Nonetheless, of the monastic land that was available on the Lancashire market, a total of 23 grants were made, with fourteen of these going to local families, and these particular grants were the highest in value.[51] Although speculative, it is possible that this was in part a result of the Duchy seeking to disperse its assets to a local supporting gentry. In Glamorgan, where no such restrictions were present, still very little land was acquired by the nobility, and the majority passed into the hands of around five local families, of which the most successful were the Mansels. Sir Rice Mansel took advantage of his position as a commissioner who had received the surrender of several of the local houses, and over the course of seventeen years, between 1540–1557, acquired property amounting to the value of £2,482 13s 1d, an enormous sum for a man of his status.[52] Yet Mansel's success was unusual, and the majority of land passed in the form of far smaller parcels amongst the other established local families, and thus it is clear that a new class of gentry was not created in the county.

Perhaps more typical is what happened in Nottinghamshire, where there was a division of land between peers and local gentry. George Talbot, 4th Earl of Shrewsbury, was granted first the site and lands of Rufford Abbey, on rather generous terms in exchange for far less valuable Irish estates. Following his death, his son Francis received a grant for Worksop and most of its lands in 1541, while in 1584 his grandson George, the 6th Earl, was able to purchase Welbeck Abbey.[53] Consequently, in Nottinghamshire at least, the Talbot family was not only able to hold onto the grants made in the immediate aftermath of the Dissolution, but also to increase their holding of monastic lands during the 16th century. However, despite the Talbot gains in Nottinghamshire, the majority of monastic land still ended up in the hands of the local gentry, primarily in the form of leases in the first instance. The Walleys gained control of Welbeck Abbey and held it for 45 years, the Stanhopes secured a 60-year lease on Shelford Priory, and the Byrons bought Newstead outright.[54] Consequently, although both members of the peerage and the gentry managed to increase their holdings of land in Nottinghamshire, the Dissolution had little impact on the social structure of the county, merely having the effect of enabling them to consolidate their holdings.

New men of the moment

Although it has long been the general consensus amongst most historians that the redistribution of monastic property usually benefited pre-existing families, whether they be from the peerage or from the gentry,[55] there were indeed some exceptions to this position that have been overlooked. In particular, there were those who sought service under Thomas Cromwell and succeeded in rising from very humble origins, as did their master. Two such individuals were William Blithman and John Tregonwell, and their lives and careers followed very similar paths that were typical for many of the new men who prospered under the Tudor regime.

William Blithman was born in the early years of the 16th century at New Laithes in the West Riding of Yorkshire, to family of yeoman stock.[56] He was first recorded as having been admitted as Bachelor of Civil Law at Cambridge University in 1519/1520 and was later incepted Doctor of Civil Law.[57] By 1535 his legal career had taken off, and he was appointed a commissioner for first fruits and tenths within the Diocese of Durham, and the archdeaconries of Richmond, Northumberland and Westmorland.[58] By March of that year he was involved in the compilation of the *Valor Ecclesiasticus* in Yorkshire, acting as one of Cromwell's most trusted agents in the north, and in 1536 was active in the monitoring and reporting of the Pilgrimage of Grace. In 1538 he was appointed a receiver to the Court of Augmentations spending much of the next 18 months accepting the surrenders of houses in Cumberland, Staffordshire, Nottinghamshire, and Yorkshire, and he was present at the opening of the tomb of St Cuthbert in 1541.[59] On 24 April 1540, he paid the not inconsiderable sum of £892 3s 4d for the site and lands of Monk Bretton Priory, just a couple of miles from where he had been born.[60] This was clearly a move by Blithman to establish himself as a gentleman in his county of birth, but within two years he was dead, and the property passed out of his family fairly rapidly after.

John Tregonwell followed a very similar, if ultimately longer and more successful career, to Blithman. Indeed, his path serves to illustrate what might have happened to Blithman had his life not been brought to a premature end. Born around 1498, just a few years earlier than Blithman, Tregonwell came from obscure Cornish origins, but he was almost certainly of yeoman stock.[61] Like Blithman he is first recorded when he gained first a bachelor's and then a doctorate in civil law in 1522 at Oxford.[62] He rose quickly in legal circles, perhaps first gaining official recognition for his involvement in Henry's divorce from Katherine of Aragon, for which he was rewarded with an annuity for life of £40.[63] Cromwell first employed him on monastic business in 1533, and by 1535 he was engaged in visitations of monasteries in Oxfordshire.[64] The following year he too took an active role on behalf of the crown in the Pilgrimage of Grace, and in 1537 was one of the chief interrogators of those implicated in the rebellion.[65] However, perhaps his most important role from 1536 onwards was as the chief commissioner receiving the surrenders of monasteries across the West Country.[66] Tregonwell was evidently unsuccessful in his early attempts to gain grants of monastic lands, as on 11 August 1539 he complained to Cromwell that despite the king's assurances he would be provided for, nothing had fallen to his lot.[67] He was finally rewarded for his good service a few months later when he was granted in February 1540 the site and lands belonging to Milton Abbey, along with the right to hold a fair for the fee of £1,000.[68] Unlike Blithman, Tregonwell lived to continue to advance his career and capitalize on his investment. He saw service in government under Mary, was knighted in 1553 and became MP for Scarborough.[69] He retired to Dorset shortly before the accession of Elizabeth, and thereafter he continued to consolidate his estates, dying a prosperous country gentleman on 13 January 1565.[70] His transformation from yeoman to gentry landowner is epitomized by his choice of the traditional altar tomb that survives in the Milton Abbas parish church today. The memorial brass depicts him wearing a medieval tabard typical of knight's attire of at least a century earlier, and the latest dated example of this form of dress surviving on a memorial in England (Figure 4.1).[71] It is perhaps ironic then that a man who more than almost any other sought to end the old way of life chose to depict himself so anachronistically in death, a symbol of the old traditional order.

On one level, both Blithman and Tregonwell were very similar individuals; both were yeomen who after gaining an education in law used their talents to serve the crown in the visitation and suppression of the monasteries. Both

Figure 4.1   Memorial brass to Sir John Tregonwell, Milton Abbey church (Author).

were sufficiently rewarded financially that they could acquire landed estates and achieve a newfound social status. However, to depict them as having led parallel lives would be simplistic, and there were significant differences in their character, and religious convictions in particular. Blithman was an evangelical reformer writing of the visitations made to the monasteries "I dare well say there is no religious man that will avowche any grief for that matter."[72] Tregonwell, by comparison, was conservative in religious matters. Throughout his visitations of the Oxfordshire monasteries, he was equally full of praise for houses that were ordered and well ran, as he was quick to condemn those he felt were breaking the rule.[73] Yet despite these differences in faith, both men demonstrated the desire and ability seen in of some of those of relatively lowly birth to take advantage of the changing situation for familial advancement. It is quite likely that others of a similar humble status did too, albeit usually on a more modest scale. This could have been either directly through the lease or purchase of small parcels of monastic land from the crown, as evidenced by the small but significant number of grants made to professionals, clerks, and yeomen (Table 4.1), or through the acquisition of portions of former monastic property that continued to circulate through private hands.

Table 4.1   Summary of Grantees and Land (Data extracted from Fisher 1913, 499).

Grantees	No Grantees	Yearly Value of Lands
Peers and courtiers	131 (32%)	£23,000 (51%)
Crown officials and servants	137 (34%)	£14,000 (31%)
Industrialists	86 (21%)	£6,000 (13%)
Professionals, clerks, yeomen	51 (13%)	£2,500 (5%)

Speculators?

One of the traditional narratives arising out of the Dissolution was that the sudden availability of so much monastic land gave rise to a wave of property speculators who entered the market to take advantage of the situation and to make short-term but significant profits from the immediate resale of the land.[74] This assumption arose from the often-huge recorded grants made to individuals or groups of London and other provincial city merchants, which were rapidly followed by resale or grants of alienation from the crown. Such a supposed orgy of speculative greed fitted well with the narrative of Henry's squandering of the land, and likewise has long been critiqued and usually dismissed by more recent historians. Habakkuk has made the most comprehensive debunking of the notion that there was widespread speculation in land at this time.[75] He stated that the fact that land was sold at a standard and consistent rate argued against the extensive competition for land which would have pushed up prices. There were no auctions of land or evidence for "bidding wars" between speculators, where land was contested between two different claimants they generally would have both been expected to pay the same standard price and other considerations decided the success of their claims. Habakkuk further suggested that the fact that prices remained stable suggested that the motivation for the purchase of land was not on the whole due to the speculative profits that could be made in the short term. He explained the often rapid resale of granted land as resulting from an over expenditure of resources by the purchaser, who had initially intended their procurements to be long-term investments.

Subsequent studies have drawn the broadly similar conclusion that the dispersal of monastic land did not create a golden opportunity for the speculator at either a national or local level,[76] although there is still the need to explain the acquisition and usually rapid dispersal of land by individuals who had no intention to settle on and manage these new estates. Habakkuk noted that time and again specific individuals, such as Lawrence Shryfe and Thomas Reeve, appear as grantees, and yet are not readily identifiable elsewhere historically, indicating they were of relatively humble origins.[77] Consequently, instead of viewing these individuals as wealthy speculators they should more appropriately be seen as agents acting on behalf of those either not wishing to be identified or who wished to draw upon their expertise in navigating the complex procedures required by the Court of Augmentations, a view that has continued to prevail more recently.[78]

However, this revisionist position has also had its challenges, with Woodward being caused to comment "the present tendency to transform all those who formerly were regarded as speculators into honest brokers must not be allowed to go too far."[79] In justification of this position, Woodward cites the single example of the case of Selby Abbey, first granted in 1540 to Sir Ralph Sadler, a secretary at court, which was alienated four months later to Leonard Beckwith, the augmentations receiver in Yorkshire, and presumably a man with a knowledge of any good bargains to be had.[80] On the face of it, this was a simple transaction, with Sadler using his position at court to acquire land on behalf of Beckwith and it would have received no further attention, but for the fact that Beckwith was later accused of fraudulent dealings, and called to account by the Court of Augmentations. As part of these investigations the testimony of Henry Whitereson, a middleman and business associate of Sadler comes to light. Sadler purchased Selby from the crown for the sum of £736, after which Whitereson offered £846 for an immediate sale on deferred terms, meaning payment was due sometime after the sale. Whitereson had little ready cash and originally intended to sell the land off piecemeal to meet the price of the purchase from Sadler, but ultimately was prevented from doing so by illness. As a result, he was forced to sell the whole estate to a new buyer, Beckwith, so that he might meet his obligations to Sadler and at a price less than he might have been expected to receive had things gone originally as planned.[81] Nonetheless, Beckwith still paid the sum of £1,040, so not only had Sadler made a quick profit on his initial investment of £110, Whitereson had made £194 without having to pay a penny of his own money, and in just four months, the property had risen in value by 23%.

Such wheeler-dealing was probably taking place across the country and yet went mostly unrecorded in the formal record of the Patent Rolls unless licences to alienate were granted. Haigh identifies the example of Richard Crimbleholme, who was engaged in similar acquisitions of property which were subsequently broken up for resale in Lancashire.[82] In May 1543 he was granted the lands formally of Whalley Abbey for £168 16s 7½d which in May of 1544 he was then given permission to alienate to local individuals.[83] Therefore, it is clear that there were opportunities for quick profits to be made, and especially in towns. As previously discussed, Habakkuk has noted the more volatile urban market which saw property being sold at the more variable rates of 8–15 years' value.[84] Not only did this mean that land was available at more manageable costs, but also it seems this "less desirable" property provided would-be investors with better opportunities. Urban property was particularly popular amongst the city merchants first identified as speculators (see below) and was often resold shortly after at significantly higher prices.[85] The fact that so many of these potentially speculative purchases were not made by single individuals but by two or more, and sometimes even small consortia, strongly suggests that these people were not merely acting as agents purchasing land on behalf of others and with capital that was not theirs. Instead, such cooperation would seem to represent the pooling of assets to enable purchases that could be financially beneficial to all parties involved.

Of course, to draw such distinctions between greedy speculators and honest agents is ultimately simplistic and naive. Even if acting for third parties, property brokers would have done so for a fee, and thus could have profited handsomely from the sale of monastic land during the decades following the Dissolution. Likewise, speculators were probably successful because they knew how the system operated and had established contacts in the Court of Augmentations. Consequently, the lines between the two groups are inevitably blurred and differentiating between the two impossible. However, there can be no doubt that fortunes could be made through dealing with monastic property. In his will written on 31 May 1575, John Braddyll reflected on his good providence many years before. He had been born to a reasonably lowly station, but after a career as a servant to the Sheriff of Lancaster and then as a rising official within the Dutchy of Lancaster, he had amassed significant wealth in dealing in monastic land.[86] Braddyll was very clear concerning the debt he owed the monarch who had died 28 years earlier, putting this most eloquently when he asked that prayers be said;

> Moste specially for Kinge Henry the Eight whose soules God padon by whom my firste risinge and gaine was gotten by byenge and sellinge of lande and other dive bargaines.[87]

Regardless of how modern debates concerning the nature of land speculation and acquisition might pass back and forth, to Braddyll, there was no doubt as to the source of his good fortune or where his gratitude lay.

The topography of acquisition

Most county-based studies of the dispersal of monastic land amongst the peerage, local gentry and other speculators have tended to focus on the economic value of the land, whether it be from the perspective of the sums paid for these acquisitions, or whether they represented the best value for the crown. However, such discussions are often in the abstract and fail to recognize that land was often, as is still the case today, the most emotive of assets and that the patterns of acquisition during the 1530s and 1540s might have been driven by factors beyond simple short-term financial gain. Instead of viewing such grants and purchases as simple economic decisions, a much more nuanced picture of the motivations behind purchases can be achieved. In particular, one way to bring fresh insight to the debate is to look at the topography of acquisition and examine the geographical choices made by purchasers, as well as the types of asset acquired. In this way, such transactions can be contextualized, and the personal motivations of the purchasers of the newly available monastic lands explored.

A case where the use of this approach has been demonstrated is in Swales' study of the redistribution of monastic lands in Norfolk.[88] Superficially, this provides few surprises nor insights into the motivations of the purchasers. Thomas Howard, 3rd Duke of Norfolk, as the predominant peer in the county received the most substantial grants of land, totalling £720 between April and December 1537 alone, whilst other county gentry such as Sir John Spelman, Sir Edmund Beddingfield, Sir Richard Southwell, and Sir Osbert Eckingham all expanded their holdings through grants of monastic land. Men of lower birth with good associations at court also benefited, such as William Butts, the king's physician and Thomas Cromwell himself.[89] As such, the narrative conforms to the familiar pattern seen across much of the country.

That Norfolk used the Dissolution as a means to increase his holdings, there can be little doubt. Until the death of the 2nd Duke, in 1524, Thomas Howard had relatively little wealth of his own. On inheriting the bulk of his father's estate, which was valued at £2,241, his net landed income was £1,900 in 1526, yet by 1538 this had increased 50% to £2,638, directly as the result of the acquisition of monastic land.[90] Greed must have been a motivating factor here, but it has also been suggested that perhaps Norfolk had, in part at least, some higher motives for his acquisitions: to prevent monastic land from falling into less sympathetic and more reforming hands. At the start of the Dissolution in 1536, Norfolk had actively tried to shelter Thetford Priory from closure, as the site had long been patronized by his family and was the burial place of his recently deceased father. Furthermore, even when his attempts had failed, he took some responsibilities seriously: in 1538 he claimed to be spending £72 a year in support of the former monks, and there is no reason to doubt this figure.[91]

However, Swales provides a further explanation of the motivations behind Norfolk's desire for monastic land, especially when the topography of these acquisitions is understood (Figure 4.2).[92] In 1536, the majority of Thomas Howard's inherited Norfolk lands had been in the southeast of the county on the Suffolk border, as well as along the north coast. In addition to bolstering his holdings in and around Norwich through the acquisition of St Leonard's Priory and Norwich Greyfriars, Norfolk actively sought to establish his hold on the central and western portions of the county, where formerly the Howards had held little land.[93] To achieve this, he specifically chose to purchase monasteries and their holdings in these areas: Croxford, Castle

Acre and Normanburgh in 1537, followed by Thetford in 1540.[94]

As well as seeking to enlarge his income through the appropriation of significant portions of monastic lands, the Duke of Norfolk was trying to consolidate his holdings across the county, quite probably with the goal of creating a permanent estate to pass onto future generations of the Howard family.[95] However, the duke seems not to have been acting entirely on his own, nor was he the only person to have a vested interest in how the former monastic land was redistributed. It is notable that, except for a few relatively modest grants to the 1st Earl of Lincoln and the Dukes of Somerset and Suffolk, none other of the nobility made any other gains in Norfolk.[96] Furthermore, despite Thomas Howard's significant acquisitions, it is still notable that in the county of Norfolk as a whole, the gentry and lower social groups still acquired three times the value of the land that the nobility did, over £3,000 worth in total.[97] The lack of substantial grants to any peer apart from Norfolk cannot have been coincidental, and indeed it served the crown. Not only was consolidating Thomas Howard in Norfolk suited to his dynastic ambitions of securing a legacy for his sons, the effective exclusion of other peers and the Duke of Suffolk in particular, from the county defused a growing potential conflict at the top of English society.

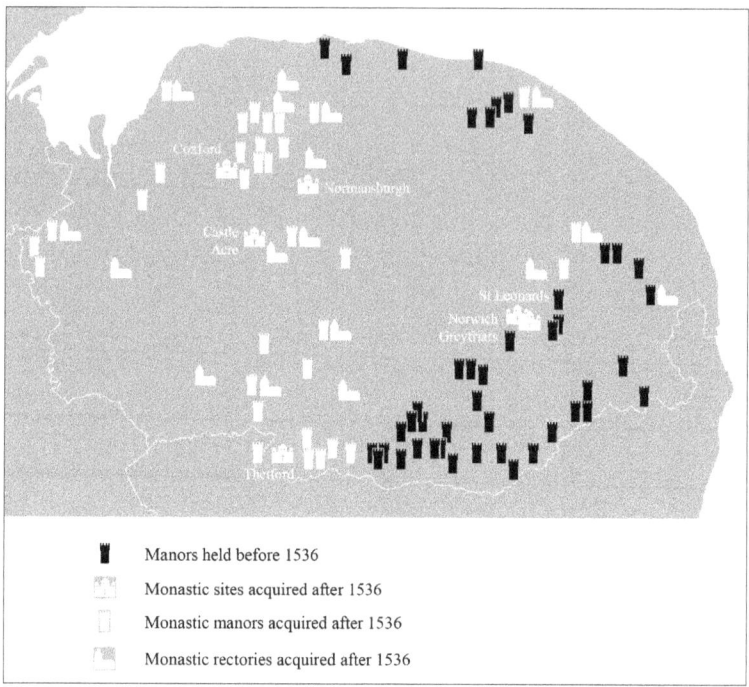

Figure 4.2   Lands held in Norfolk by Thomas Howard, Duke of Norfolk before and after the Dissolution (Author).

Land acquisition in Lincolnshire

Charles Brandon, 1st Duke of Suffolk

The Lincolnshire Rising, which took place in October 1536, saw the first serious and violent opposition to Henry VIII's religious reforms and has received extensive historical attention.[98] While less than two weeks in duration and quickly dispersed by Charles Brandon, 1st Duke of Suffolk, the rebellion resulted in an acceleration in the process of dissolution in the county and rapid changes in land ownership (see Chapter 2). Just as the Dissolution saw the establishment of Thomas Howard as the preeminent peer in Norfolk, Charles Brandon saw his position consolidated in Lincolnshire in the late 1530s. Everson and Stocker have noted that Brandon was granted the monasteries of Barlings and Kirkstead in a single grant on 20th March 1539,[99] and attach great significance to this due to the two monasteries' act of having sided with the rebels in the rising just over two years earlier (see Chapter 7).[100] They argue that this was a highly symbolic move, whereby Suffolk, through converting the former monasteries into country residences, was demonstrating his new power over the county with a very visible lesson of what fate befell those who opposed the king.[101] Whilst there is a convincing argument that there was an element of symbolism at play here, to focus solely on the Duke of Suffolk's Lincolnshire implantation is only to see part of the contemporary situation. Indeed, if such actions were primarily motivated by a desire to express Brandon's vice-regal authority, it seems strange that Bardney Abbey, the third monastic house that took an active role in the rising and for which six monks were subsequently executed, was not similarly granted to Suffolk.[102] Indeed, Bardney was instead acquired by Sir Robert Tyrwhitt, a member of the local gentry, who during the rising had been under some suspicion, albeit unfounded, of being compliant with the rebels.[103] Given this, it would seem strange that if this dispersal of monastic land was driven by symbolic motivations alone, that such a politically important site was granted to one of the Lincolnshire gentlemen the crown had suspected "did wink at this rebellion or might have stopped it at the first had they been willing."[104]

Understanding the topography of land acquisition in Lincolnshire, and the role of Charles Brandon within this picture, requires a broader overview. It is true that before the 1536 rebellion, the Duke of Suffolk's interests in Lincolnshire had been minimal, indeed it is probable he had never visited the county.[105] Since 1516 he had leased three manors from the de la Poles and from 1535 the former Percy estates,[106] and although his wife Lady Willoughby did have significant interests in the east of the county, she kept careful control of these, and continued to retain them long after Brandon's death in 1545.[107] Instead, the majority of his estates had been based in East Anglia, and there had been growing conflict during the early 1530s between the tenants and followers of both the Dukes of Suffolk and Norfolk. On the eve of the Lincolnshire Rising in 1536 and into the following spring, Brandon was still seeking to secure his position in East Anglia, petitioning to obtain grants of land from the recently dissolved Suffolk monasteries of Leiston and Eye.[108]

It appears that it was the deliberate intervention of the crown in 1537 that resulted in the move by Brandon to Lincolnshire. The reasons for the crown in wishing to see the move were probably in part to help re-establish control over the rebellious former county, but it was also a conscious attempt to quell once and for all the growing conflict between the two preeminent peers of the realm.[109] Whichever the case may be, the transformation was rapid, and in late 1538 and early 1539, Brandon exchanged most of his pre-existing estates for massive grants of former monastic land across Lincolnshire.[110] Such grants included not only the aforementioned sites of Barlings and Kirkstead, but also the houses of Boston Blackfriars, Bullington, Elsham, Greenfield, St Katherine's Lincoln, Louth Park, Markby, Newsham, Nocton, Thornholme, and Vaudey, along with numerous manors and granges (Figure 4.3). With these new estates, and those held by his wife, Brandon became the predominant landowner in Lincolnshire, with one of the largest property portfolios in the kingdom. From his extensive will drafted in 1544, it is clear that the original monastic estates belonging to twelve different houses were all still largely intact and in his possession.[111] Despite the suggested redevelopment of some of his new former monastic sites, it is clear that Brandon made Tattershall Castle, which the king gifted him in 1537, his new principal seat.[112] As has been pointed out, this was a fitting family seat with historical connections to the county that befitted his new status in the region,[113] and unlike any of his former monastic possessions, there is ample evidence that he resided at Tattershall and made extensive renovations to the fabric. However, whatever long-term plans Brandon had for his newly acquired Lincolnshire estates were cut short by his death in 1545 and that of his two sons in 1551, after which the holdings were dispersed amongst the heirs of his daughters.[114]

The Lincolnshire gentry

Whilst the Lincolnshire Rising and its aftermath resulted in the greatest, if brief, transferal of land in the county to the Duke of Suffolk, it was the local gentry who were the ultimate long-term beneficiaries, with seven families receiving substantial grants.[115] Whether any of these gentry families had had serious sympathies with the protagonists of the Lincolnshire Rising is unclear, but it is probably unlikely. Indeed, many members of the Heneage and Tyrwhitt families who subsequently benefitted most from the dispersal of monastic land had acted as commissioners valuing benefices in Lincolnshire in 1535.[116]

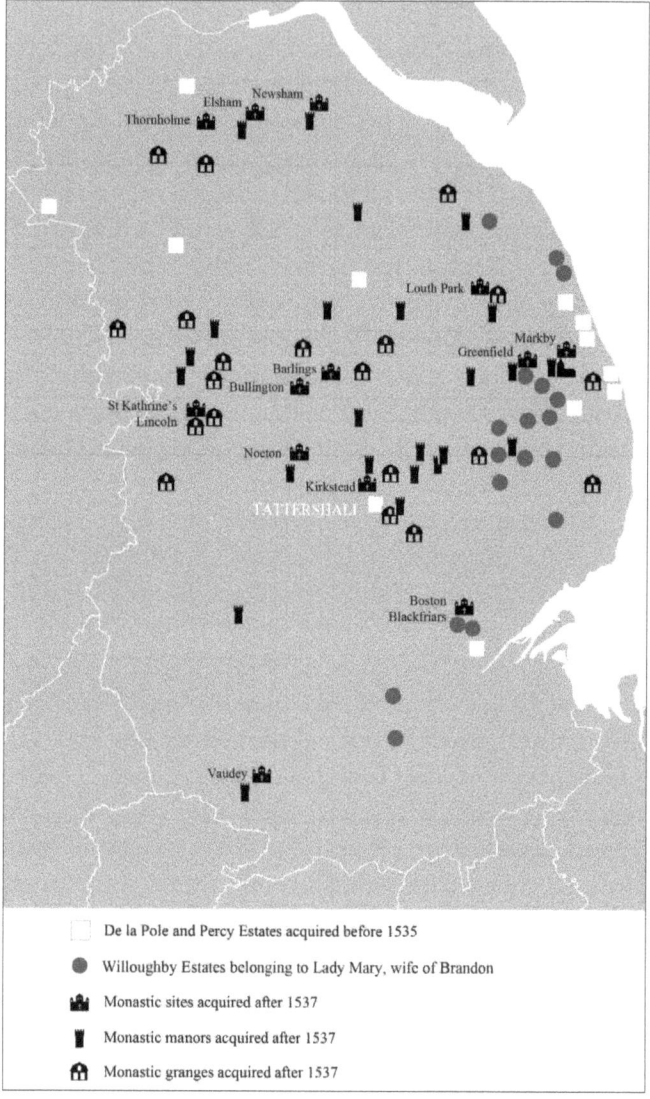

Figure 4.3   Monastic land acquired by Charles Brandon, Duke of Suffolk in Lincolnshire (Author).

Not only were they complicit in the Dissolution itself, but they also had inside knowledge of what potential prizes there were to be had. So keen were the Lincolnshire gentry to acquire land that it caused minor local disputes. As early as August 1536 a Mr Edgare was writing in complaint to Cromwell about the way the local gentry were trying to gain hold of the parsonage and farm of the recently suppressed Abbey of Marksey, which he had recently been granted. A member of the Heneage family had already been successful in securing the farm and Edgare now feared that he would lose the parsonage to a member of the Skipwith family;

> By means of Master Hennege I am disappointed of the farm of the parsonage, worth to me yearly 20 marks; and now I would to God the said Master Skipwith his belly and guts were stuffed with all the tithe corn this year gathered in sheaves as it is on the said parsonage, and then I trust he

would once rest of craving; for he hath the whole abbey, and yet he would have my said corn besides.[117]

The Heneage family cited in Edgare's complaint were one of the bigger beneficiaries of monastic lands in Lincolnshire. They had only recently come to prominence in the county at the turn of the 16th century when John Heneage (d. 1530), a prominent lawyer, acquired the Manor of Hainton as the family seat.[118] John had four sons, who were all to play significant roles in local politics and the church, and all but one, George, Archdeacon of Lincoln from 1542–1549, acquired monastic lands.[119]

Of the remaining sons the youngest, John, was elected twice Member of Parliament for Grimsby.[120] His Lincolnshire acquisitions were relatively modest, mainly small parcels of land scattered across the north of the county, although he was also granted the site of Hull White Friars across the Humber.[121] Perhaps John, as the youngest saw the short-term opportunities for making modest acquisitions of land in Lincolnshire; indeed, he may have lacked the resources to not only buy but more crucially con-

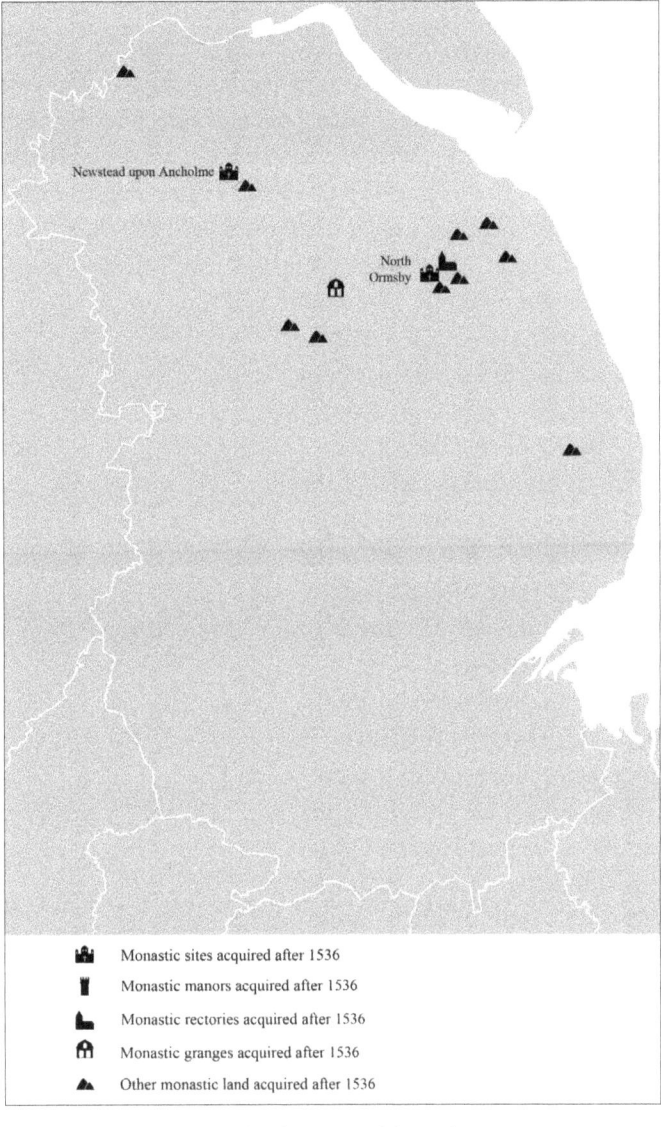

Figure 4.4 Monastic land acquired by Robert Heneage in Lincolnshire (Author).

vert the site itself of a monastic house to domestic or profitable use. However, more substantial gains were made by his elder brothers Thomas and Robert, which suggest they were more concerned with establishing themselves more securely in the county. Robert, the second son, was an auditor of the Duchy of Lancaster,[122] and his purchases appear to have been more deliberate (Figure 4.4). The majority of Robert's acquisitions centred on the former monastery of North Ormsby, where he secured the site of the house and a number of its former possessions.[123] He also acquired the site of Newstead upon Ancholme, but it seems he was more focused on establishing himself in North East Lincolnshire.

The eldest Heneage, Thomas, was the best connected at court and the greatest beneficiary of former monastic land. He had started his career in Wolsey's household but after his fall from grace took up a key position in the new administration of Cromwell. By the 1530s he was frequently acting as a go-between for the king and the Vicar General, rising to be a senior gentleman of the Privy Chamber.[124] Given his connexions, Thomas Heneage was well placed to take advantage of the disposal of monastic land and seems to have made a series of very strategic purchases (Figure 4.5). Having inherited his father's estate at Hainton in 1530, he consolidated his holdings through the acquisition of Sixhill Priory and much of its lands, located in the neighbouring parish.[125] He was also granted further monastic sites and lands elsewhere in the county, mainly focused on Heynings Abbey in the west, Wellow Priory in Grimsby and Tupholme to the south.[126]

Whether the original intention for the acquisition of monastic land focused in various locations in the country was to provide for the future of several intended children is uncertain, and in the end he only had a single daughter Elizabeth,[127] but there is the possibility this pattern of acquisition was, in part, the result of dynastic planning.

Whether this was the intention of Thomas Heneage is uncertain, however, in the purchases made by the Tyrwhitt family it is more certain that in using the newly acquired monastic land, explicit provision was deliberately being made to secure futures for their offspring. By the time of the Dissolution, the head of the Tyrwhitt family was Sir Robert Sr. He was the second son of Sir William Tyrwhitt, an established county figure, and although he had an elder brother Philip, he appears to have played no role in county life and died without issue.[128] Robert inherited his father's lands and seat at Kettleby in 1522, which became his principal residence until he died in 1548.[129]

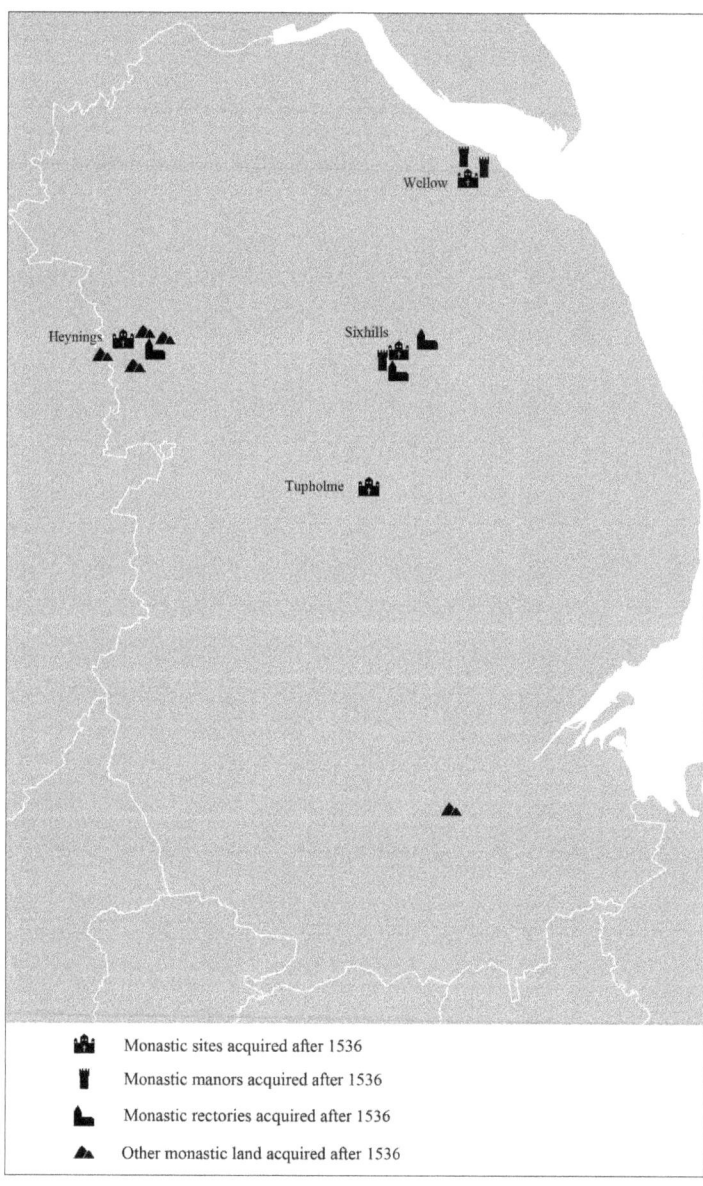

Figure 4.5   Monastic land acquired by Thomas Heneage in Lincolnshire (Author).

Robert Tyrwhitt was well connected at court, being an esquire of the body, and along with his son William, had acted as one of the king's commissioners valuing monastic land in 1535, the next year being captured at Caistor by rebels during the Lincolnshire Rising.[130] Despite contemporary suspicions by the crown that many of the gentry had been complicit, albeit passively, in the rebellion this is unlikely, certainly in the case of Tyrwhitt. As Gunn has pointed out, the rebellion helped unite the gentry who had previously been at odds, with Robert Tyrwhitt agreeing to end a long-running feud with William Ayscough in light of a new united fear of the "commons."[131] Whatever Tyrwhitt's sympathies might have been, it did not prevent him from seeking to prosper from the Dissolution, nor did it deter the crown from making him significant grants of monastic land. From 1538 until at least 1545 Tyrwhitt was involved in a large number of transactions involving monastic land. Some of these were in partnership with other buyers, such as those made in conjunction with Thomas Manners, 1st Earl of Rutland (Figure 4.6), and were probably opportunistic purchases, intended to be sold on again rapidly for a short-term profit. However, many of his solo acquisitions of monastic land were intended to be kept within the family, as a means for securing the futures of his children and even his grandchildren.

Amongst the purchases Robert Tyrwhitt made on his own, three stand out as significant, both in their location and how they subsequently passed through the family (Figure 4.6). The first was concluded on 22 February 1538 and included the site of Stainfield Priory with adjacent lands and property.[132] The second was granted on 9 December 1539 and included the site of Orford Priory, whilst a third on 8 October 1545 included Cammeringham Priory, its manor, and rectory.[133] What is interesting is that unlike Thomas Heneage's acquisition of monastic land that bordered his pre-existing estates

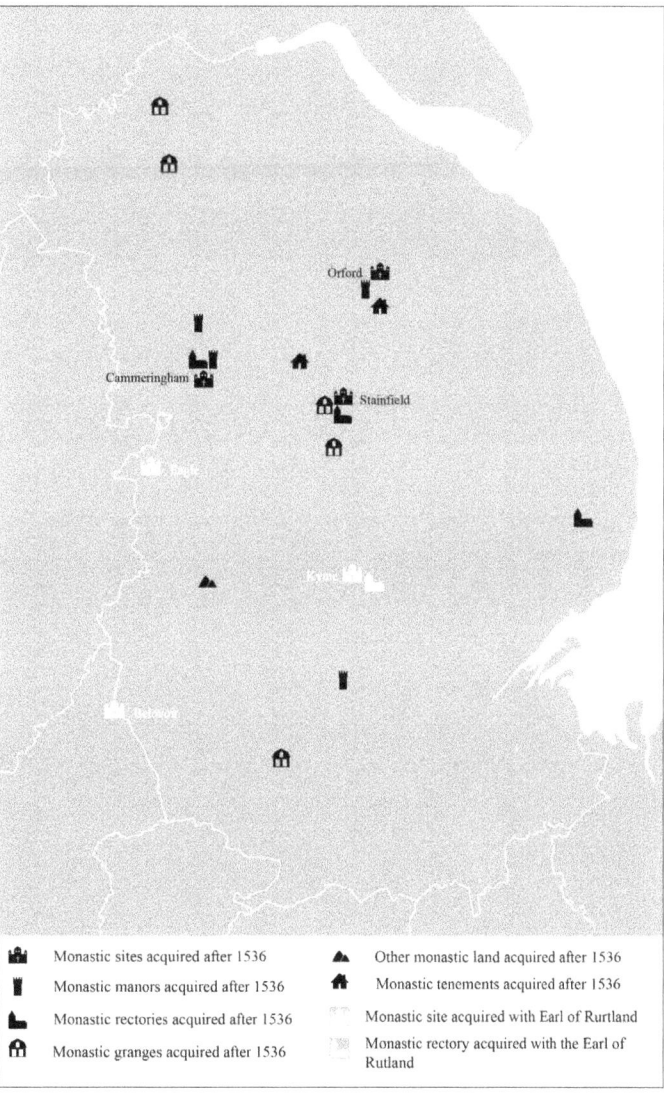

Figure 4.6 Monastic land acquired by Robert Tyrwhitt in Lincolnshire (Author).

at Hainton, none of the land granted to Tyrwhitt in these grants was particularly close to his holdings at Kettleby. This is not to say he did not acquire property closer to home, as in 1544 he bought the site of Nuncotham Priory from Edward Skipwith who had been originally granted the site in 1540. However, the reason for his purchases directly from the crown in distinct locations seems to have another purpose.

When Robert Tyrwhitt died in 1548, he passed on much of his monastic gains to his children and grandchildren, and although his will does not survive it is possible to reconstruct the passage of many of his monastic holdings through subsequent documentation (Figure 4.7). His eldest son William had predeceased him, but two other sons were still living.[134] His second son, Robert Jr., had held political office initially in Lincolnshire, and then in Huntingdonshire, later establishing himself through the purchase of the manor of Leighton Bromswold.[135] Robert Tyrwhitt's youngest son Phillip appears to play few public roles, but was briefly a member of parliament in 1554.[136] With his eldest son dead, Robert Tyrwhitt Sr. passed the Kettleby estates directly to his grandson Robert II (b. 1526). An *Inquisiton Post Mortem* undertaken upon Robert II's death in 1581 revealed that many of the monastic manors and other lands he inherited from his grandfather and the original grantee were still intact and continued to be passed down this line of the family for several more generations.[137]

To his second son Robert Jr. no monastic lands are recorded as having been passed, but it is entirely possible that those associated with Orford Priory were, as they are not mentioned in conjunction with any other relative. Robert Jr. died in 1572 with no male heirs and afterwards any monastic holdings he may have held had presumably passed out of the direct family line. Robert Tyrwhitt's youngest son Philip inherited the Stainfield estates, which in turn passed to his second son Edward upon his death in 1558, with his eldest son Thomas being described as "residuary legatee of his mother."[138] Robert Sr. appears to have willed the Cammeringham

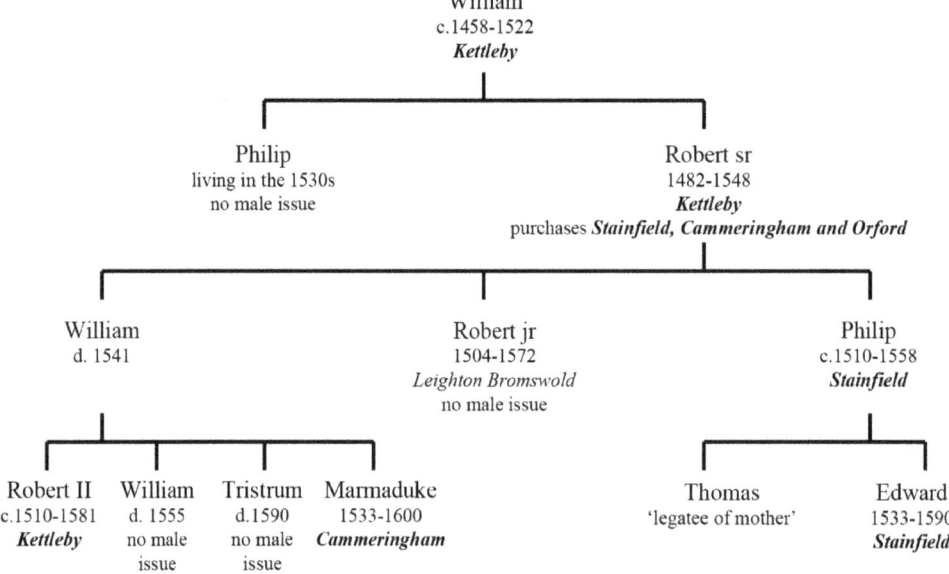

Figure 4.7 Tyrwhitt family tree (Author).

estates to another child of his eldest son William, Marmaduke in 1558.[139] Cammeringham passed from Marmaduke to his son Robert in 1601 and remained in that branch of the Tyrwhitt family until the middle of the 18th century.[140]

Although the surviving documentary sources can only provide partial insight into the complex provisions made over several generations, it is clear that at least some of the initial purchases of monastic land made by Robert Tyrwhitt Sr. in the 1530s and 1540s were for long-term strategic reasons. In particular, the purchase of the sites of the former monastic houses of Stainfield, Orford and Cammeringham, is particularly telling as these would not necessarily be profitable investments in themselves in the short term; indeed, in converting them into country residences (see Chapter 6) they would incur further expense. Instead, it shows the very deliberate establishment of several branches of the family, strategically placed across the northern half of the county.

Agents of the land

Just as the gentry appear to have been making particular choices as to what land to acquire so too were other groups, amongst them the so-called property speculators. As Hodgett has noted, during the summer of 1544 it was not uncommon for consortia of London merchants to apply for grants of monastic lands that consisted of diverse holdings scatter right across the country.[141] However, in Lincolnshire two individuals were particularly prolific, John Bellow and John Broxholme, and although they were involved in land grants in other counties, by far the majority of their acquisitions were in Lincolnshire, a county they knew well.

John Bellow's origins are somewhat obscure, but he appears to have come from Lincolnshire yeomanry family. He first comes to attention in the early 1530s when he was in the employ of Cromwell, and by 1536 was acting as crown surveyor and taking part in the first wave of the Dissolution of Monasteries.[142] He appears to have been particularly ruthless in his work and made himself unpopular, and although it was incorrectly reported to Cromwell that during the Lincolnshire Rising the rebels had "baited Bellowe to death with dogs, with a bull skin upon his back,"[143] it reflected popular sentiment. Bellow prospered personally from his dealings in monastic land, although until 1539 he is described as being from Legbourne, shortly after which he was establishing himself in Grimsby where he became mayor and member of parliament several times before his death in 1559.[144] Bellow's association with the Court of Augmentations, his role in the Dissolution in Lincolnshire and his local connexions in the county, put him in an ideal position to capitalize upon the opportunities provided by the sale of monastic land.

Less is known about John Broxholme. Although he was referred to as "of London" in various grants, he too was of Lincolnshire stock.[145] He appears to have come from a yeoman family from Utterby, although there is also a suggestion he might have mercantile links in Lincoln.[146] He stood unsuccessfully as a candidate for Member of Parliament for Lincolnshire in 1547 and bought estates at Corringham outside of Gainsborough, where his family continued to reside until the late 17th century.[147] After the Dissolution of the Monasteries, Broxholme continued to be involved in the Lincolnshire property market and during the closure of the chantries in 1547 he acted as an agent for the Mayor of Lincoln in an attempt to acquire their rents.[148]

Between them, Bellow and Broxholme made substantial acquisitions of monastic land. Before July 1545, this was either personally or in conjunction with other individuals

(Table 4.2). Bellow is first mentioned as being the recipient of a grant of monastic land with Robert Brocklesby in October 1543, for a fee of £946 16s 8d, the majority of which lay in Lincolnshire. In August the following year, Bellow was in receipt of a grant with Robert Gowche and Robert Lawrence for £560 10s 6d, and in March 1545 he and Edward Bales were awarded a grant in fee for £1,386 13d, again both of these were for holdings almost entirely based in Lincolnshire. John Broxholme received his first grant in August 1544 for £1,220 15s 6d, again

Table 4.2 John Bellow and John Broxholme's Lincolnshire Acquisitions

	Tenements/ messuages/ cottages	Land	Manors	Rectories/ vicarages	Granges	Other
Bellow & Brocklesby 21/10/1543 L. & P. XVIII (ii) 327 (17)	3	41	4	3		Greyfriars, Grimsby
Broxholme 22/08/1544 L. & P. XIX (ii), 166 (40)	21	8		12		White Friars, Linc.: 1 wind mill, 1 water mill
Bellow, Gowche & Lawrence 23/08/1544 L. & P. XX (i) 465 (61)	2	7		1		
Bellow & Bales 06/03/1545 L. & P. XX (i) 465 (22)	11	16	1	6		Shops in Sleaford
Bellow & Broxholme 04/07/1545 L. & P. XX (i) 1335 (11) & (12)	341	21	1	5		5 windmills, 10 water mills, 4 fulling mills, 1 corn mill, 1 fishery
Bellow & Broxholme 10/12/1545 L. & P. XX (ii), 1068 (19)	111	55	4	5	3	Blackfriars, Linc.; Austin Friars, Linc.; Shops in Linc.; 2 windmills, 1 water mill, 1 wood
Bellow & Bigott 22/11/1546 L. & P. XXI (ii), 476 (85)	7	8				
Bellow & Broxholme 24/11/1546 L. & P. XXI (ii), 476 (96)	2	11	1	1		
Total	498	167	11	33	3	4 friary sites, 25 mills, 1 wood, Shops in Linc. & Sleaford

primarily for Lincolnshire lands. The one-off collaborations between Bellow and other individual grantees seem to be a marriage of convenience. It is unclear whether these individual grantees wanted to again hold these new properties for their personal use, or were themselves smaller time speculators. Either way, they evidently benefitted from Bellow's experience in the monastic land market and his personal connections with the Court of Augmentations.

However, it was between July 1545 and November 1546 when Bellow and Broxholme appear to have gone into business together and received four separate grants for a total of £7,800 16s 10d. Unlike the nobility and gentry, Bellows and Broxholme could not have possessed the immediate wealth to undertake these transactions, indeed as Hodgett has pointed out, had they held these gains and not sold them, they would have become amongst the leading landed families in the county, which was never the case. Instead, they probably borrowed the sums of money required from London lawyers and other city sources on the promise that grants to alienate the land would enable its rapid resale for profit.[149]

There was a further difference between the purchases of these speculators or agents and those magnates such as the Duke of Suffolk or local gentry such as the Tyrwhitts that have largely been overlooked; the types of acquisitions being made. The peerage and gentry who petitioned for monastic land tended to opt for investments that would provide long-term yields. These consisted of either the sites of the monastic houses themselves that could be converted into residences for personal use or to be leased, or elements of the former monastic estates that could provide a steady income: granges, manors, and rectories. This contrasts with the acquisitions made by Bellow and Broxholme (Table 4.2). Whilst their huge investments did include around eleven manors, thirty rectories and the advowson of vicarages, the majority of their grants were formed from numerous small tenements, messuages, crofts, cottages or simple pieces of land. Unlike the much more costly elements of their portfolio, these would have been much easier to sell on rapidly, in many cases quite possibly, to the tenants who were already occupying them. It is particularly noticeable that Bellows and Broxholme did not seek to purchase a single site of a rural monastic house, their only purchase of this kind consisted of the urban-based friaries, which could be more easily broken up and for which there was a ready market. For example, following their purchase of the Austin Friars in Lincoln, Bellows and Broxholme were able to immediately lease the site and two tenements to Robert Dighton for 29s.[150] Likewise, following Bellows and Brocklesby's purchase of Grimsby Greyfriars, they were able to straight away let the house to Thomas Hatcliff, who had been initially leased the site following its closure in 1538, and whose family continued to live there for some years.[151]

— 5 —

Avenues for Common Opportunity

It is perhaps inevitable that following the closure of the monasteries, the immediate discussion has always focused on their asset stripping and plunder. Whilst aspects of their infrastructure were indeed systematically removed and repurposed, primarily for the financial benefit of the king, those houses that were left in a relatively unmolested state did provide opportunities to parishes, civic corporations, and entrepreneurial individuals. Particularly in towns, but also sometimes in rural communities, the former monastic houses provided communities the chance to repurpose them, so they continued to serve the common good and provide valuable local services and products.

The continuation of public worship

The Dissolution did not necessarily end religious life in all the monasteries of England and Wales, and in many cases, it continued, albeit in significantly altered form. Indeed a few monastic houses remained almost unaltered, these being the eight cathedral churches, Canterbury, Carlisle, Durham, Ely, Norwich, Rochester, Winchester, and Worcester, which were served by communities of monks. These churches, along with the counterparts served by communities of secular canons such as York and Exeter, were the centres of their bishoprics and continued to hold important roles within the reformed church of Henry VIII. In addition to the maintenance of these traditional medieval dioceses, the new church authorities added six former abbeys to become the cathedrals for newly created sees focusing on Bristol, Chester, Gloucester, Oxford, Peterborough, and Westminster.[1]

Although there appears to have been a clear vision for the conversion of the existing cathedral monasteries and establishment of the new bishoprics, how that was affected on the ground appears to have been less well thought through, and certainly did not take place in a single movement. The great cathedral monasteries were all suppressed as usual with their communities signing the same deeds of surrender, thus effectively ending religious life temporarily. However, former monastic priors were usually swiftly appointed as the new deans, and many of the former monks became the prebendaries. However, as Knowles has noted, not all of the former religious occupants were automatically transferred, some perhaps taking advantage of the opportunity to leave religious orders, and the new establishments were generally half the size of their predecessors in terms of personnel.[2]

The adoption of the new cathedrals was similarly haphazardly structured, and the transition to secular status could take many months. However, ultimately for these fourteen former monastic institutions and many of their inmates, life continued much as before, and perhaps most significantly their churches, conventual buildings, and other structures were spared the destruction seen elsewhere. A further two abbeys were, temporarily at least, retained for ecclesiastical use as colleges to train secular priests. Burton Abbey, Staffordshire (briefly mentioned in Chapter 3) was suppressed in 1539 and refounded in 1541, headed by a dean who was the former abbot, while Thornton Abbey, Lincolnshire was also suppressed in 1539 and likewise converted.[3] Both of their new lives were brief: Burton always small in size in its new guise appears to have failed to fulfil its initial intentions and so was closed in 1545, whilst the arguably more successful Thornton College failed to survive the death of Henry VIII by more than a few weeks with the accession of a more fervently Protestant king.

Had the religious climate not changed so quickly under the reign of Edward VI, the creation of new colleges of canons might well have helped preserve at least a few more of the former abbeys. On the direction of the King, Fountains Abbey was initially "mothballed" following its suppression in 1539, with the intention it could be converted into a college, although this was short lived.[4] Likewise after the Benedictine priory in Coventry was closed in 1539, Bishop Lee expressed the hope that it could be reopened as a college for preachers, as well as a place for the former pensioned religious to live out their days. While the monastery was initially saved from destruction, this was only a temporary reprieve, and in 1545 its sale and demolition began.[5] Whether this might have been the intention at other sites is uncertain, but what is clear is that by the later 1540s only those abbeys that had been elevated to cathedral status would remain intact.

However, it has long been appreciated that the boundaries between institutions that were purely monastic and those that were secular in the Middle Ages could be considerably blurred, especially when it came to the places of worship used by both groups. In the 19th century, Hodgson emphasized the important role some monastic churches played in parochial life, and in particular he identified 37 Augustinian and 119 Benedictine houses where local communities held parochial rights to worship within the main monastic church, amounting to around a quarter of the national total.[6] Such figures have been subject to more recent revaluation and criticism. Heale has pointed out that working out which communities may have held parochial rights is extremely difficult due to the lack of surviving documentation and the fact that medieval practice was very fluid, meaning rights could and did change through time. However, he concludes that Hodgson's estimations might actually be a significant underestimation and that as many as 284 monastic churches of differing orders might have also been parochial at some point in their history, although not necessarily all at the time of the Dissolution.[7]

Despite the fact that the absolute numbers of monastic churches in partial parochial use cannot be calculated with any certainty, what is significant is which orders were most likely to have been affected. Out of Heale's list of 284, almost exactly half were Benedictine, while Augustinians made up the significant proportion of the remainder; in contrast, not a single Cistercian church was also shared by the parish.

The relationship between the monastic church and its lay community before the Dissolution had a significant bearing on what happened to the monastic church, at least, after the suppression of the monastery. This dependence grew from the legal responsibility faced by the monastery to provide lay altar and worship space, which usually arose from their acquisition of the established parish church as part of their original foundation, a factor particularly likely when foundations were made in densely populated areas.[8] In more isolated areas, monastic institutions may have also felt the need to provide parochial provision, even if there had not been a parish church before their foundation; provisioning both the physical and spiritual needs of growing communities that they relied upon was clearly within their interests. Often monasteries might choose to build and endow a separate parish church, but for smaller Benedictine houses or the canonical orders such as the Augustinians whose own inmates could serve the parish altar without the need to employ a secular priest, there might have been less incentive to do so. Either way, established parochial community rights to worship within the monastic church did not cease with the suppression of the house that supplied them.

Whilst the legal rights to worship may have remained after the Dissolution, the physical means to do so were not so straight forward. Such monastic churches remained a valuable asset for the crown, which parishes were still expected to purchase, along with all others who sought to acquire monastic property. As a result, examples of communities acquiring whole monastic churches are rare, although not unknown (see below), partly due to the overall cost of acquisition and the fact the entire monastic church would have been far too large for the average parish's needs, so would be an unacceptable drain in resources to maintain.[9] However, more significantly the parochial rights only applied to the part of the monastic church where the parish altar was kept, and not the entire building. For this reason, it is usually suggested that local communities were only able to lay claim to, and continue to preserve, those portions of buildings originally under parochial control.[10]

It is impossible to be sure how many monastic churches remained, in part at least, places of worship in the years following the Dissolution. Hodgson asserted that every such church where they existed would have continued in parochial use, but the surviving evidence does not corroborate this claim.[11] To date, the only comprehensive overview of parish churches that contain elements of surviving monastic fabric was a brief survey undertaken by Clifton-Taylor in 1974, which names a total of 89 examples.[12] Inevitably this list cannot be seen as exhaustive, medieval fabric can be hard to identify, medieval churches have been destroyed and rebuilt in the centuries following the Dissolution, and of course contemporary records are patchy at best. Nor should this list be viewed as entirely accurate, since some of the churches named were actually formed out of monasteries dissolved long before the 1530s (see below), while others can now be categorically stated not to have been formed from former monastic buildings but were built from the start as parish churches.[13] Whatever the actual numbers involved were, it seems that ecclesiastic life lived on at a significant proportion of monastic sites for decades if not centuries to come. This is an aspect of the Dissolution that has been underplayed by many of the more traditional narratives that have sought to emphasize the more destructive side of the events of the 16th century. Nonetheless, the process of conversion to parochial use is undoubtedly worthy of further examination as it shows how local communities sought to benefit from the suppression, or at least continue to maintain their existing rights, as well as how they overcame the physical challenges of adapting these buildings of prayer to more limited use.

As has already been eluded to, as with many aspects of the Dissolution, there were earlier precedents for the conversion of monastic churches into purely parochial places of prayer. The suppression and closure of many of the alien priories in the 15th century, and in the year 1414 in particular, presented such a chance. While many alien cells were transferred to the control of English orders, those that came

Figure 5.1   St Andrew's church, Stogursey, former Benedictine priory (Author).

under the possession of secular colleges no longer needed to service a community of the religious, and were often transferred to total parochial control. This is precisely what happened at Stogursey Priory. Granted to the new college of St Mary at Eton in 1440, the church remained completely intact, indeed, this even extended to the former prior who remained as "custos" of the new parish church (Figure 5.1).[14]

A similar pattern can be observed at Great Bricett Priory after it came into the possession of the College of SS Mary and Nicholas, Cambridge (now Kings). Again the whole church was retained for the parish, the only alterations being the removal of the short transepts and the small side chapels, which were presumably now redundant (Figure 5.2).[15] The same transformation took place at Lapley Priory where, on becoming the possession of Tong College the whole cruciform church was retained for the parish, and again the only major alteration being the removal of the transepts and nave aisles.[16] Although occasional examples of more drastic alterations from these earlier conversions are known, at Monk Sherborne Priory, Hampshire, only the crossing and presbytery remained in use once it was granted

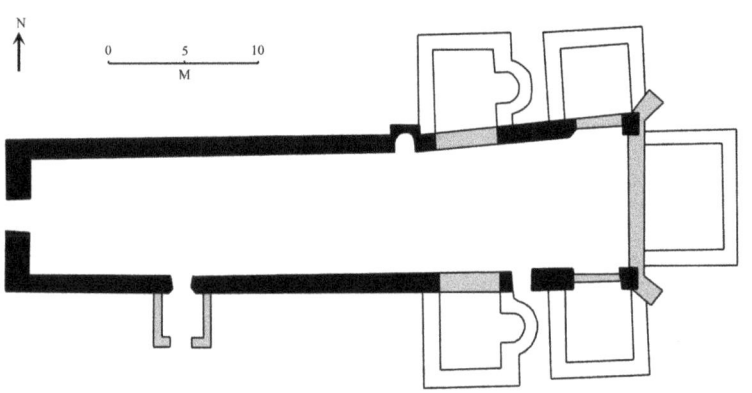

Figure 5.2   Reduced church, Great Bricett Priory (after Fairweather 1926).

to God's House, Southampton, in 1414,[17] it seems that before the Henrician Dissolution, there was no great desire on the part of the crown to split up churches. Downsizings, where they occurred, were probably an effective response to make the building more manageable for the parishes who were now responsible for their upkeep.

This pattern is in stark contrast to that seen after the suppressions of the 1530s, where only around one fifth of those monastic churches identified by Clifton-Taylor as having continued in parochial use that this time remained substantially intact.[18] Although parochial rights only extended to certain portions of the monastic church, there are still examples of where communities successfully acquired the whole building. One such was the priory church at Great Malvern. Newly built the century before, it provided the opportunity for the parish to gain a more extensive and far superior building to replace their present parish church that was inadequate for their needs, although for this they had to pay the sum of £20.[19] In the case of Great Malvern, this move by the parish has ensured the preservation of one of our finest surviving monastic churches, with an almost unparalleled collection of original window glass, tile, and woodwork; a building far superior to one they could ordinarily expect to possess. However, such larger expensive purchases could potentially be tricky undertakings. Spelman tells what might be a somewhat apocryphal story about the purchase of the church and former shrine at Walsingham. Thomas Sydney was tasked by the local population to acquire it for the town for the sum of £90, but subsequently kept the property for himself, and much of the site was then sold on to Sir Thomas Gresham, further increasing Sydney's gain.[20]

Where the whole church was not available to or was not wanted by the parish, then it is generally assumed that only the nave, where the parish altar was located and separated from the monastic choir by a physical barrier such as a screen, was retained for parochial use. Perhaps the "typesite" for this form of conversion can be seen at Binham, Norfolk. The conventual buildings were purchased by the Paston family, who intended to convert the cloister into a domestic dwelling.[21] However, the nave at Binham had always had parochial rights and was thus reserved for the parish.[22] The response was the separation of the nave from the choir at the point of the rood screen and the walling off of the nave aisles, which were allowed to decay (Figure 5.3). This was not, perhaps the most practical response, given the architecture of the building. The most robust way to separate the nave would have been at the western piers of the crossing. However, this would have given the parish the additional small area of the choir to which they were not entitled

Figure 5.3 Binham Priory church (Author).

and which the Pastons may not have been willing to grant. The family was certainly keen to capitalize on their investment as much as possible, as receipts in 1553 for the sale of rubble and stone, most likely deriving from the demolished east end of the church, attest to.[23] Apparently, it was only after an accident during demolition that killed a workman that Edward Paston decided to cease the destruction of the remaining parts of the cloister (see Chapter 3), leaving the parishioners with a parish church surviving among the remaining ruins.

Similar conversions can be seen at other former Benedictine houses, and perhaps the one most often cited is at Crowland, Lincolnshire. However, this example also serves as a useful reminder that subsequent events also affected the parochial use of churches. Today, the parish church occupies the north aisle of the nave and the northern tower, yet it is clear that following the Dissolution the original extent of the parishes' control extended over the whole of the nave and the south aisle too, with only the original presbytery and crossing being demolished. This situation only changed during the Civil War, when in 1642–1643 it was fortified by the Royalists, then besieged by Oliver Cromwell, during which the nave and south aisles were irreparably damaged and subsequently abandoned.[24] As a result, the actions of the Parliamentary forces were far more instrumental in shaping the longer-term fate of the church at Crowland than the Dissolution itself.

Such nave conversions were not restricted to Benedictine houses, several Augustinian houses were treated in a very similar fashion. This can perhaps be most clearly seen at Bridlington Priory. Suppressed in early 1537, the house might have expected to have been treated harshly, as its last prior, William Wood, was executed for his involvement in the Pilgrimage of Grace.[25] However, the parish held parochial rights over the nave, which ensured its preservation,[26] although the remainder of the priory was destroyed and used to maintain the town's quay (see later in this chapter), even if this seems to have occurred sometime later in the 16th century as the crossing tower was still clearly depicted in Lord Burleigh's atlas of the 1560s or 1570s.[27] The conversion of Bridlington was similar to those already discussed, with the nave separated from the remainder of the building at the western piers of the crossing, but in this case the aisles were retained, perhaps due to the urban parish's larger population and needs. Subjected to a thorough "restoration" by Edmunde Sharpe and later Sir Gilbert Scott, surviving engravings from before these improvements show a building in very similar condition and appearance to Binham, illustrating what many of these conversions would have looked like before being repaired, tidied and gentrified in the 19th century (Figure 5.4).

Figure 5.4 Bridlington Priory church prior to restoration in the later 19th century (J. Hornsey 1812).

A further site treated very similarly was Bolton Priory, another Augustinian house where parochial rights were well established.[28] Here, the nave was walled off from the crossing and the single northern aisle retained for parish, no southern aisle ever existed. Interestingly, such was the connection between the parish and the monastic house that after the Dissolution the last prior, Richard Mone, who died shortly after in 1541, left all his vestments to the parish to "serve them that comes to hear service at Bolton."[29] However, these vestments were not the only legacy Mone left his parishioners, but they also had to cope with the stub of an unfinished monumental tower that had only been completed to the level of the top of the nave wall. The original design would have called for this to be three or four times higher than it was and once completed the western nave wall would have been removed to extend the whole building beneath it.[30] However, this ambitious building project was left uncompleted, and the tower base remained an unroofed extension to the building until it was covered over in the later 20th century. Why the parish never chose to remove the inconvenient folly to the former prior is not known, but perhaps its solid construction presented them with too great an expense to do so.

In London, former monastic churches were potentially in even higher demand than elsewhere, due to the rapidly increasing population of the 16th century city, even when there was stiff competition to acquire monastic properties. When St Bartholomew's Priory, Smithfield was suppressed in 1539 it came to the attention of one of the most prominent courtiers, Sir Richard Rich, who intended to convert it into a significant townhouse.[31] However, the parish held rights over the church which prevented Rich from completely redeveloping the whole site.[32] It seems that Rich's solution to maximize his gains was to present the parish with the presbytery and crossing of the church, even though this was not the portion of the building where they would have traditionally worshiped. However, in doing so, it enabled Rich to demolish the much larger nave and transepts, providing him with more space for redevelopment.

When influential courtiers were not set on acquiring London's religious houses, monastic churches were put to much wider public benefit and use, and the Benedictine nunnery of St Helen's, Bishopsgate, is a good example of this (Figure 5.5). Prior to the Dissolution, the parish had occupied the main nave of the church, while the nuns had a choir to the north.[33] Following the house's suppression the nave was retained by the parish, but the northern choir was purchased by the Leathersellers' Company, who seem to have transferred it to the parish shortly after. As well as securing the survival of the whole church, the Leathersellers, who were also located in Bishopsgate, ensured that increased provision was made to the parish which served a large number of their members.

In towns, the potential availability of monastic churches, and those of the friaries in particular, enabled new religious communities to establish themselves where they had not formerly existed, and this was particularly the case for Protestant immigrants and refugees arriving from continental Europe. Sir William Paulet acquired the Austin Friary in London after the Dissolution, and like Rich, intended to make it the focus of a new townhouse. Acquiring first the northern, and then in 1546, the main cloister he built his mansion house (see Chapter 6). In 1550 he added the church itself to his possessions, demolishing the presbytery which he turned into a stable, leaving just the walled-off nave.[34] Interestingly, it was a condition of his purchase of the church that he repair the nave so that it could be given over to serve as a church for Dutch protestant refugees who were arriving at this time in increasing numbers.[35]

Whether Paulet was really that desperate to acquire the presbytery that he was willing to take on the expense of repairing the nave is uncertain, however, during the reign of Edward VI, Paulet was known for his reputation as an evangelical Protestant so it might also have been he had slightly more altruistic motivations for doing so.[36] With the accession of Mary to the throne in 1553, the Protestant community left, and the church reverted to Paulet's ownership, but this was short lived as by 1560 a Dutch congregation had returned to worship there.[37]

Even if redundant monastic churches were not turned to this purpose immediately, their fabric could still be put to good religious use many years later. At Norwich Blackfriars, the site was initially purchased by the city corporation, with the nave to be used as a hall for the mayor and the east end

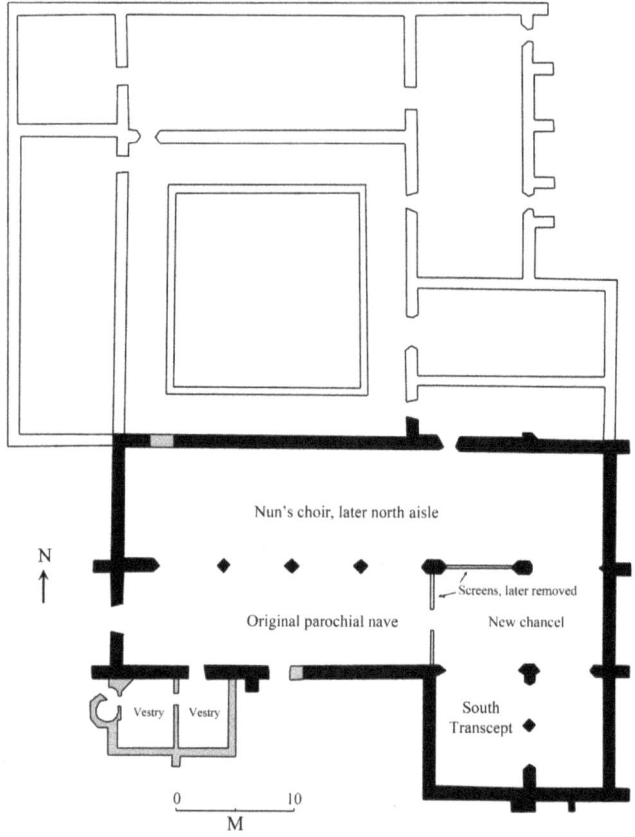

Figure 5.5 St Helen's church, Bishopsgate (after Reddan and Clapham 1924).

retained as a chapel. However, later in the 16th century, the building was returned to its original use when the former monastic church was given over to Dutch protestant immigrants who formed an increasingly important part of the early modern population.[38]

At several sites, the presence of pre-existing burials seems to have affected what parts of the former monastic churches were preserved, irrespective of pre-existing parochial rights. The Duke of Norfolk famously petitioned for the preservation of Thetford Priory's church as it was a family burial place, his own father having been interred there only a few years previously (see Chapter 4).[39] Whilst Norfolk was ultimately unsuccessful, others were not. At Boxgrove Priory, upon its suppression, Lord de la Warr petitioned Cromwell that the church be left unspoiled as the parish church, even though the parish held no legal rights to it. He was partially successful, and the presbytery was indeed saved for this purpose. However, the motivations for de la Warr's pleas were not entirely altruistic, nor was the preservation of the presbytery as opposed to the nave, which might have benefitted the parish more, coincidental. As de la Warr explained to Cromwell, his interest lay in the church (and thus the presbytery) as many of his ancestors were buried there and he had already built "a poor chapel to be buried in."[40] Even if local gentry did not have ancestors already interred in prominent tombs in the presbyteries of monastic churches, the Dissolution provided the opportunity to create lavish personal mausolea.

Breedon Priory was a relatively modest Augustinian house, where the parish held rights to worship in the nave.[41] Following the Dissolution, the priory was acquired by the Shirleys, a notorious recusant family. Instead of the parish retaining the nave as might ordinarily be expected, this was demolished, and the presbytery and central tower formed the focus of the new parish church. Whilst this might have been less convenient for the ordinary parishioners, it provided a grander setting for the Shirleys' new dynastic ambitions, as evidenced by the succession of exceptionally large funerary monuments they went on to build there during the second half of the 16th and early 17th centuries.[42] No doubt placing their dead at the heart of the former monastic church appealed to their Roman Catholic leanings.

Thus far, discussion of the retention of monastic churches for parochial use has focused entirely on buildings formally occupied by the Benedictines or Augustinians, and this is primarily because these orders were much more likely to have had shared the right of worship within their churches. Some houses from other smaller orders did have parishes using their naves; Heale has identified nine Cluniac, four Gilbertine and two Premonstratensian houses where parochial rights existed.[43] However, as already noted, not a single Cistercian house seems to have also fallen into this category, and very few appear to have been purchased after the Dissolution for this purpose. Only at the former male houses at Dore and Hulme Cultram, and the female houses at Heynings and Swine is there any evidence for the reuse of former Cistercian monastic churches in an ecclesiastical way.[44]

However, a small number of parish churches were formed from Cistercian buildings, most notably extramural chapels situated outside the main precinct gate. In Essex, the *capella extra portas* at both Coggeshall and Tilty abbeys was appropriated by the parish.[45] There are probably various reasons why local communities might have been able to exercise a claim over extramural chapels. At Merevale, Warwickshire, another *capella extra portas* passed into the control of the local lord.[46] Although not a true parish church until 1889, the chapel remained a place for lay worship, and its former medieval function as a chapel endowed explicitly for the use of pilgrims might have facilitated its transfer after the house's suppression.

Just occasionally other elements of the claustral ranges that had never functioned as a church or chapel could be retained for secular purposes. Following the dissolution of Birkenhead Priory, a small Benedictine cell, the site was acquired by Ralph Wolsey in 1545.[47] The church was destroyed, and most of the cloister left to decay. However, the chapter house, being on a suitable west-east alignment was retained by Wolsey, initially as a private chapel. Shortly after Wolsey's acquisition, there is evidence that it was used as a place of worship for the extra-parochial district of Birkenhead until a new and much more suitable parish church was built in the 19th century.[48]

Perhaps the most unusual ecclesiastical conversion took place at Cistercian Beaulieu Abbey in Hampshire. The whole site was purchased by Thomas Wriothesley, one of the most prolific converters of monasteries into domestic dwellings (see Chapter 6). In the case of Beaulieu, he unusually chose to focus his redevelopment on the inner gatehouse, which formed the core of the new mansion.[49] This did not save all of the claustral ranges from destruction, as the church and east range appear to have been largely demolished at this time, but the western range was retained for domestic purposes. Most interestingly the former refectory survived and was converted into a new parish church. On the face of it, the refectory would not seem to be the most suitable building for this new purpose, principally because it was orientated north-south. However, measuring around 10x40m, it was a large building and, reordered, closely resembled a single-celled church, once the orientation was overlooked.⁵⁰ Perhaps most

Figure 5.6 Interior of Beaulieu Abbey church, the former monastic refectory (Author).

significantly, the refectory possessed a fine pulpit set into its western wall, originally built so that the monks might hear the scriptures during dining (Figure 5.6). However, this striking feature may well have appealed to the Protestant converters of Beaulieu, as it provided a singular focus for the new church, and facilitated the developing practice of preaching in English that was being introduced into the new liturgy of the Protestant church.

Finally, it is important to remember that the ecclesiastical reuse of monastic churches could occur many decades or even centuries after they were originally closed and their religious communities expelled; where the fabric survived sufficiently well preserved a parish church could be created relatively easily. Following its suppression in 1537, Beauchief Abbey, Yorkshire, was largely demolished for building stone, so that most of the claustral buildings were reduced to near foundation level, the exception being the robust western church tower. In 1662, 125 years after its closure, the then owner Edward Pegge restored the tower to act as the main body of a church, building a new small chancel in the ruins of the former monastic nave.⁵¹ An almost identical fate befell Humberston Abbey, Lincolnshire. The original house was dissolved in 1536, with most buildings falling into ruin shortly after. However, following a bequest from Matthew Humberston in 1710, the western tower was restored and a new nave and chancel added to it to form a parish church for the local community.⁵² Perhaps the site that waited longest to be converted back to ecclesiastical use was Buckfast Abbey, Devon. Although the medieval buildings had long since been demolished, following the reacquisition of the site by a group of French Benedictines in 1882, the new monks exposed the former Abbey's foundations and constructed the new church and cloister directly upon their footprint, thus recreating the original abbey in plan if not precise architectural design.⁵³

For the civic good

In discussions of the Reformation, it is often stated that the Dissolution had the benefit of releasing large amounts of property for civic redevelopment within England and Wales' already pressurized urban spaces.[54] In particular, it seems that it was the friary buildings and precincts of the mendicant orders that received the most significant reuse by civic authorities, although on the whole they were located on the margins of towns rather than within their centres. This was, in part, due to their prevalence in the urban landscape, for even a very modest town might be expected to have had a small Franciscan or Dominican house. However, as Butler has suggested, civic authorities might have seen friaries as being slightly different to those properties belonging to the other major orders, feeling they had some pre-existing rights of ownership over them, not in a legal sense but because the town and burgesses had financially supported them through the centuries.[55] Even if the precincts of the friaries were not of immediate interest to local authorities, other aspects of their infrastructure could be. At Grantham, the water supply to the Franciscan friary, and its great conduit, was taken over by the Corporation, and similar moves were made in Lincoln to secure former monastic water supplies.[56]

Whilst, as shall shortly be outlined, this was certainly the case in some instances, in many towns, the precincts of the former monastic houses remained derelict and undeveloped for decades and sometimes centuries after their closure. For instance, although the site of the Carmelite friary in Newcastle experienced considerable robbing following the Dissolution, much of its precinct remained as open waste ground throughout the 16th and 17th centuries, only being redeveloped from the 1720s onwards.[57] Nonetheless, if the buildings and land upon which the former monastic houses lay provided little interest to individuals, urban authorities often saw that immediate benefit could be derived from the surplus of building materials from the now redundant houses; the dissolved monasteries provided an abundant source of cheap materials that could contribute to civic building and repair projects.

Such a reaction was seen at Boston, Lincolnshire, when Thomas Paynell petitioned Cromwell on behalf of the town to be granted materials from the former Austin and Carmelite friaries to maintain the town's sea defences;

> The Visitor has been at Boston and suppressed all our Friars' houses. My duty is, being the King's officer, to certify what is necessary to keep up his Grace's tenements, staythes (*landing stages*), and sea-banks in the said town. Considering how barren our country is of stone, timber, and tile, the said houses were meet for this behalf.[58]

Such requests, particularly in the north of England, were not unusual. At Bridlington as late as 1566 the town corporation sent a request that "all old stones of the monastery not yet sold" be turned over for the repair of town's pier, which had formerly been the responsibility of the now-closed Augustinian priory and required continuous repair throughout the 16th century.[59] The pier and waterfront at Scarborough were similarly in need of repair, and in October 1541 a petition for timber was made for this purpose, as well as stone from the town's three former friaries.[60] The urban monasteries did not just provide useful quarries for waterfront development, for in Carlisle stone from the Franciscan friary found its way into improvements to both the castle and the city defences, while at Coventry stone from the former Greyfriars was used to repair the town walls and roads.[61] These, of course, are just instances where official requests were made for monastic materials to be used in civic building projects, in reality, there were probably few towns that did not benefit to some degree from more "informal" acquisitions.

Civic authorities did not just benefit from the potential materials coming from former monastic sites, and their upstanding buildings could easily be adapted for use by the town.

Although, and in a similar fashion to their rural counterparts, urban houses would have been subject to the removal of roof lead and other disruptions, it is clear that in most cases such stripping was limited and buildings could be put back to good use. It was perhaps with a potential civic afterlife in mind that, after closing the Franciscan friary at Aylesbury, Dr London reported "I left the house whole and only defaced the church, which is well covered with lead and has a good new roof."[62]

That such properties should attract the interest of civic bodies should be of no surprise, as both the burgeoning guilds and the developing town corporations needed increasing amounts of property during the 16th century. Occupational guilds had been present in many towns from the 14th century onwards, initially operating through a system of controlled membership to regulate the various trades, but by the end of the Middle Ages they had developed into complex social originations, often focused on a guildhall.[63] Schofield has charted this rise of guilds and their property in London; around 1400 only four to five craft companies possessed halls, rising to 27 by 1475, and 60 on the eve of the Dissolution.[64] Given this, and the relative lack of available property in the expanding 16th century town, there was a long established and growing demand for suitable property for guild use, with the former monastic property often seen as being ideally suited for this purpose.

Such demand did not just come from the craft companies; the town corporation increasingly sought to express its emerging power and identity through the building of town halls. Tittler has documented the sharp rise in the numbers of town halls from the 1530s–1540s onwards and suggested that such institutions were given additional purpose following the Dissolution, stepping in to fill some of the voids created in social and civic life.[65] Although many of these emerging town halls were new builds, from the 1550s onwards many were also formed from the adaptation of former monastic buildings. Such conversions might have been undertaken due to financial expediency, but as has already been suggested, town corporations might well have felt some sense of pre-existing ownership over their urban religious houses. As Giles has suggested in the case of York, the medieval guildhalls were some of the few prominent secular buildings to survive the 16th century and provided "a sense of continuity with the medieval past."[66]

Perhaps this was what was in the minds of the mayor and citizens in Chichester when the town purchased the whole of the former Franciscan friary complex in 1541.[67] It is unclear what the authorities' initial intention for the former claustral ranges was, but the east end

Figure 5.7 Chichester friary church, retained as a town hall (F. Grose 1790).

of the monastic church was converted with little effort into a new city guildhall, and subsequently acted as the assize court. The choice of this portion of the church to be the new guildhall was a sensible one, as not only was the broad and lofty choir amply suited for this purpose once the stalls and other fittings were removed, but it had only recently undergone a thorough restoration, so was one of the newest elements of the friary complex (Figure 5.7).

In other instances, it was the claustral ranges that were chosen by civic corporations to be preserved. It is possible that the reason for this was due to the sensitivities involved in reusing the former church, or possibly the fact that the royal agents had already damaged this element of the complex most heavily. However, the domestic nature of cloister might have been the key factor in its preservation. In Newcastle, on the surrender of the Augustinian friary in 1539, the Council of the North successfully requested the reservation of the friary for their use, due to the lack of suitable alternatives, stating "there is no house there to meet to receive them but the friars Augustines."[68] Although the church was probably demolished relatively soon after, throughout the 16th century there are well-documented instances of repairs and periodic refurbishing to all the claustral ranges to preserve them for the councils' very occasional use.[69] Perhaps in adapting and reusing former monastic property, the town corporation was also making a conscious reconnection with its medieval past, which was being rapidly swept away by events beyond the control of the civic authorities.

Alternative civic uses for the friary cloister can be seen at Bristol, and the house of the Dominicans in particular, which at the time of the suppression was a relatively large complex, possessing two separate cloisters as well as a wide range of other buildings (Figure 5.8). Following the house's suppression, it was initially leased to William Chester, a Bristol merchant who bought the site in 1540, although even before the Dissolution elements of the claustral complex were already in secular use.[70] As was not unknown for some friaries late in their history, the Dominicans at Bristol had since at least 1499 been leasing the upper floor of their infirmary building in the lesser cloister to the Bakers' Company.[71] Following the house's suppression, this existing lease continued to be honoured and at some point soon after the company bought the hall outright, where it continued to be based until the second half of the 18th century.

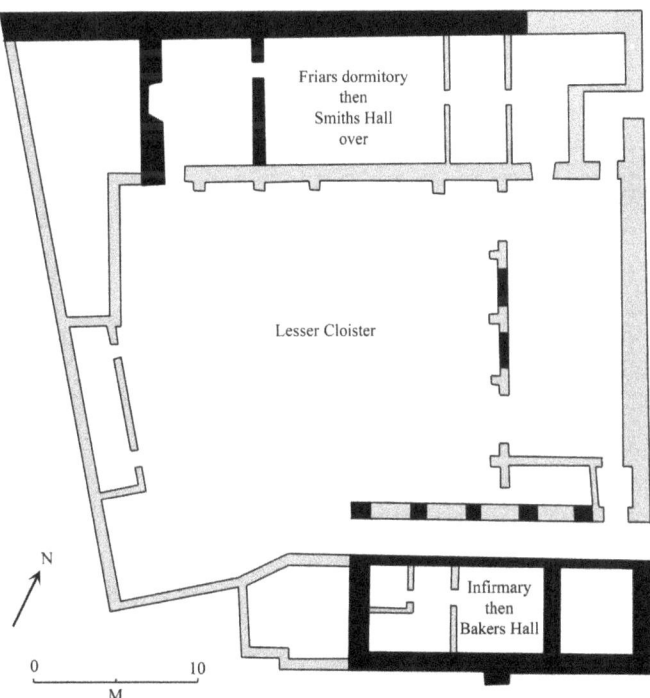

Figure 5.8 Post-Dissolution division of the cloister, Bristol Blackfriars (after Leighton 1933).

This was not the only element of the friary complex to come under company ownership. In the great cloister, the east range is recorded in a deed of 1610 as being the location of the Tanners Hall, although it probably first occupied this site at some point during the second half of the 16th century, and it continued to operate here until shortly before 1802.[72] Likewise at some point during Elizabeth's reign, the south range of the main cloister became the property of the Cutlers' Company, who again used the first floor as their hall until 1654, when the corporation turned it over to become a workhouse for children.

The picture at Bristol is of a rather *ad hoc* acquisition of elements of the former friary by individual companies at different points in time following the suppression. However, in Newcastle, there was a much more coordinated response by the city authorities to provide new guild accommodation. Here, following its closure in January 1539, the whole site of the Dominican friary was sold for £53 7s 6d to the mayor and burgesses for the town. As elsewhere, the church was probably demolished shortly after this, but by 1552 both the claustral ranges and the wider precinct were leased to nine craft companies (Figure 5.9).[73] The claustral ranges were subdivided and the precinct fenced into individual closes to be used by members of the Bakers and Brewers, Butchers, Skinners and Glovers, Cordwainers, Saddlers, Smiths, Taylors, Tanners, and Fullers and Dyers companies. To achieve this conversion of the cloister, a considerable amount of adaptation was required. There is clear evidence for the removal of more ritualistic elements of the complex, such as the former chapter house, and this necessitated the repair and rebuilding of individual sections of the main fabric, as well as inserting partition walls to create the new spaces for the nine companies (Figure 5.10). In this case, from the start there was a clear and concerted effort by the town authorities to create well-needed space as well as, of course, the additional revenue it brought through leasing it to the companies eager to occupy the new premises. This does contrast, however, with the fate of other monastic institutions elsewhere in Newcastle; when the Trinitarian priory was also finally acquired by the town in 1582, it saw little purposeful redevelopment by the corporation.[74]

Company halls were not the only public benefit to which former monas-

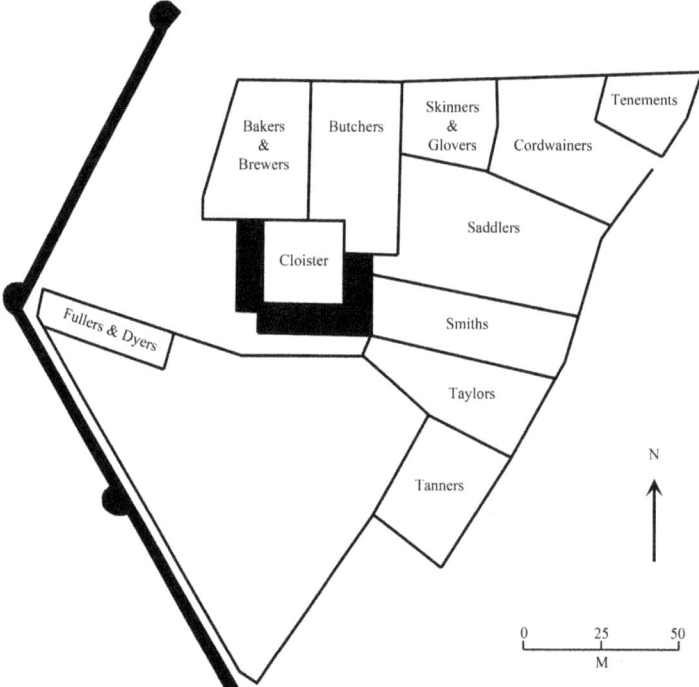

Figure 5.9 Post-Dissolution division of the precinct, Newcastle Blackfriars (after Harbottle and Fraser 1987).

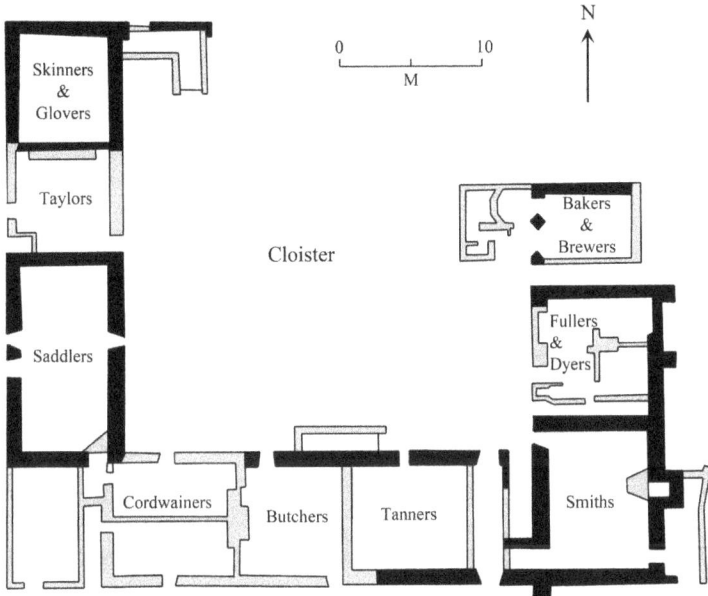

Figure 5.10 Post-Dissolution division of the cloister, Newcastle Blackfriars (after Harbottle and Fraser 1987).

tic buildings could be put, a further less charitable, but arguably equally important function, that former urban houses could be turned to was as prisons and houses of correction. At the Franciscan friary at Dunwich, according to the 18th-century antiquarian Thomas Gardner, parts of the standing remains of the cloister were acquired by corporation to serve as a hall and a gaol, and although no further details are known, it is possible this was located in the refectory range, elements of which are still upstanding.[75] A similar conversion seems to have occurred at the Dominican friary in Boston. The town corporation acquired the principal part of this site to be used both as a prison and a granary, but again details concerning how the friary might have been converted are sadly lacking.[76] A more educated guess might be made about the use of the Dominican friary at Carlisle as a prison. Initially reserved for the use for the Royal Council, around 1608 it was converted into the county prison. Palmer tells us that this took the form of "buildings around a considerable yard," suggesting that the cloister was converted to this purpose.[77]

How the domestic ranges of the cloister could easily be converted into a prison are not certain, but presumably would have required a considerable amount of adaptation, including the blocking of windows, partitioning of rooms and securing of doors. At Bodmin Greyfriars, a more straightforward conversion was made. Bought by the town corporation in 1566, the choir of the church was converted to an assize court and its nave a corn market. However, the main gatehouse to the precinct was retained as a prison.[78] Medieval gatehouses were ideally suited for such a purpose, naturally "defensive" in nature if not intent, they had very restricted access points and first-floor halls where it was relatively easy to confine individuals. Indeed, from the late Middle Ages onwards, it was not unusual for town gates to function as gaols as well, as was the case at Durham and Gloucester, which were used for such a purpose between the 16th and 18th centuries.[79] A final example where a portion of a friary was known to have been used as a gaol was at Ipswich Blackfriars. This site saw a complex conversion, which is discussed in more detail below, but the undercroft of the east range immediately to the south of the chapter house appears to have been subdivided into individual cells of a bridewell or house of correction.[80]

A secular education

One of the perhaps unintended consequences of the Dissolution of the Monasteries was the closure of those schools run by the religious institutions that had recently been suppressed. The foundation of schools by religious institutions had its origins in the 12th century with the establishment of cathedral free schools, and by the 15th century, a range of religious educational establishments was also financially supported by members of the mercantile classes.[81] It has been estimated that on the eve of the Dissolution there were around 175 monastic houses engaged in some form of educational activity, yet following the Acts of Suppression all but one of the former nunnery schools were closed, along with the vast majority of those run by male houses.[82]

It is not that the authorities were unaware of the problem created closure of the monastic schools. To partially mitigate against this, eleven new grammar schools were founded in association with the establishment of the new secular cathedrals in the 1540s, although these could only cater for a fraction of those who had previously been educated by the monks.[83] A second blow came with the Dissolution of the Chantries Act of 1547, which immediately threatened a further 300 or so schools supported by these local institutions. Although the act contained a clause that where appropriately supported schools should be saved, and provision was made for two commissioners to judge when this was appropriate to do so, between half and 80% of the chantry schools nonetheless closed.[84]

Given this potentially severe blow to public education, even the government was caused to take action, albeit slightly belatedly. Following the Dissolution, and during the last eight years of his reign, Henry VIII contributed to the establishment of nearly two dozen schools, whilst under Edward VI from 1550 onwards the Court of Augmentations was tasked with overseeing the re-establishment of schools where necessary, probably resulting in around 50 institutions, a trend that continued under Mary.[85]

Despite these centralized efforts to preserve educational provision, it is hardly surprising that several civic bodies and private individuals also sought to establish new schools, primarily in the urban centres, and utilising the buildings of the recently closed monasteries. Some-

Figure 5.11   18th-century view of Ipswich Blackfriars (J. Kirby 1748).

times such arrangements could be rather informal. Following the closure of Wellow Abbey in Grimsby in 1536, the former prior Robert Whitgift continued to teach the sons of the local gentry in the claustral ranges, including his nephew John who was later to become the Archbishop of Canterbury, apparently with the full blessing of the site's new owner Sir Thomas Heneage.[86] That the buildings of the former urban religious houses might serve to host these new schools made sense, as not only were they often lying vacant, but in many cases they had served this very function before the Dissolution. This must have been at the forefront of the famous polemicist Henry Brinklow's mind when he preached in 1545 that grammar schools and almshouses should be built in every town in the kingdom and that former monastic property used to achieve this aim.[87]

Despite this clear interest in the establishment of new secular schools, and the obvious suitability of the former religious property to house these, the actual evidence for the conversion of monasteries into schools is slight. This is in part because many do not appear to have lasted for very long in their new educational roles, or are not documented in significant detail in the secondary sources. For example, the Dominican friary in Bangor was recorded as having been acquired by Dr Glynne in the 1550s to create a new free grammar school, and while it was still evidently in use in 1611, when it appears on Speed's map of the town, little more is known about it.[88] A similar situation exists at the site of the Dominican friary at Chelmsford where a free school was established on the site shortly after 1542. Shown on a plan dated 1591 no other evidence for this school survives, despite the area having been subject to some archaeological excavation.[89]

In some instances, mainly where the school survived beyond the 16th and 17th centuries, a better idea of how the former monastery might have been occupied can be gained. The site of Ipswich Blackfriars has been briefly alluded to earlier in this chapter. Here, shortly after the Dissolution, the town corporation acquired the entire site of the Dominican friary with the intention of putting it to a variety of civic uses, including a prison, hospital and a grammar school.[90] A plan and view of the former monastic complex was drawn up by Joshua Kirby in 1748 (Figure 5.11), shortly before much of the site was subsequently demolished, and although drafted two centuries after the original division of the site it probably represents the original 16th century plan, elements of which have been confirmed by excavation.[91] As a result, a detailed picture of the site shortly after its suppression can be gained (Figure 5.12). As with many urban redevelopments, the monastic church appears

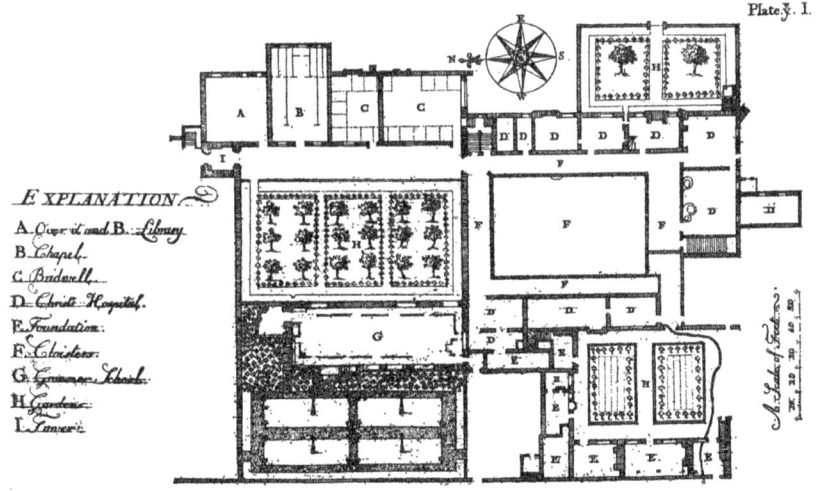

Figure 5.12 18th-century plan of Ipswich Blackfriars (J. Kirby 1748).

Figure 5.13 18th-century view of London Greyfriars (W. Tom c.1740).

to have been demolished soon after coming into secular hands, but the rest of the complex was reused. The outer cloister became the focus of the newly established Christ's Hospital for the poor, while the east range of the great cloister was, at least in part, used as the bridewell, with the former chapter house becoming a small chapel. The new grammar school was located in the west range, including the former refectory, a building with its seating already ranged running around its inner walls and possessing a prominent pulpit that was ideally suited for its new educational purpose.

A similar conversion can be seen at the expansive complex of the Franciscan friary in London that was granted to the citizens of the town in 1547.[92] The choir of the monastic church was turned over to parochial use as the new Christ Church, but the rest of the complex adapted to form the new orphanage and poor school, Christ's Hospital, which opened in 1555. The great cloister of the friary was the focus of the orphanage, the west range functioning as the dining hall, the north range the library, and the dormitory in the east.[93] Although partly destroyed by the Great Fire of 1666, William Tom's engraving of c. 1740 clearly shows that medieval cloister arcade and upper library windows preserved within the north range of the hospital (Figure 5.13).

Schools were established within the cloistral ranges of other urban friaries. At Carmarthen Blackfriars, the precentor of St David's Cathedral, Thomas Lloyd, established "The King's Scole of Carmarthen," which flourished until Lloyd died in 1547.[94] Archaeological excavation of the site has revealed tentative evidence for the refurbishment and occupation of elements of the south and west cloistral ranges that date to the immediate post-suppression period, and therefore likely indicate that these portions of the complex were the focus for Lloyd's school.[95] Other buildings within the precinct also seem to have been suitable for conversion into schools. The site of Lincoln Greyfriars passed through several owners after the Dissolution until Thomas Monson obtained it in 1568, and founded a free school there. This he conveyed in 1574 along with the water conduit to the city, where it continued until 1612.[96] The building used still survives, albeit in much-altered state, and there has been some debate as to which element of the former friary was used as the school. Martin thought this building, due to its east-west orientation, was part of the friary church, a suggestion confirmed more recently by Colin Hayfield, to be the case.[97] What all these examples go to show is that when it came to creating a suitable space for a school, virtually any open hall or building could easily be adapted to this purpose.

Where the cloistral ranges were not available, or suitable, for conversion into a school, the monastic church was also ideally suited to being transformed to this purpose. This was certainly the case at Atherstone, where Sir William Devereux founded a grammar school in the presbytery of the former Dominican church in 1547. As the school expanded, the nave of the church was later donated by Amyas Hill to the school, which continued to occupy the site until 1863.[98] A similar conversion took place at Thetford Blackfriars which was acquired by Richard Fulmerson in 1541. In this instance Fulmerson initially turned the cloister into a house, although afterwards in his will dated 23 January 1566, he donated the nave of the church to be the location for the newly established school, the remains of which were still much in evidence in the 19th century.[99]

However, the one site for which the best historical and archaeological evidence for the establishment of a school is in the conversion of the Carmelite friary in Coventry, despite the fact it was only in operation for just over a decade. Acquired by John Halls in 1545, a royal licence was granted for the foundation of a school which lasted until 1557 when it was relocated to St John's hospital church.[100] Excavations in the 1960s–1970s revealed an impressive amount of detail about the layout and operation of the school, in part due to its unusual preservation but also the precise nature of the archaeological work undertaken. Hall's school was located in the east end of the Carmelite church, primarily focused in the area of the former choir, although some activity was also observed in the area of the sanctuary to the east. What is clear is that the original choir stalls were rearranged and repurposed as school desks, and remarkably some of these survive today still in St John's hospital church after they were also moved when the school relocated.[101] As a result, an unparalleled reconstruction of the layout of the school is possible (Figure 5.14).

Further intriguing details concerning everyday life at the school come from the unique assemblage of artefacts recovered. These survived due to the presence of "resonance passages" that ran beneath where the desks were placed.

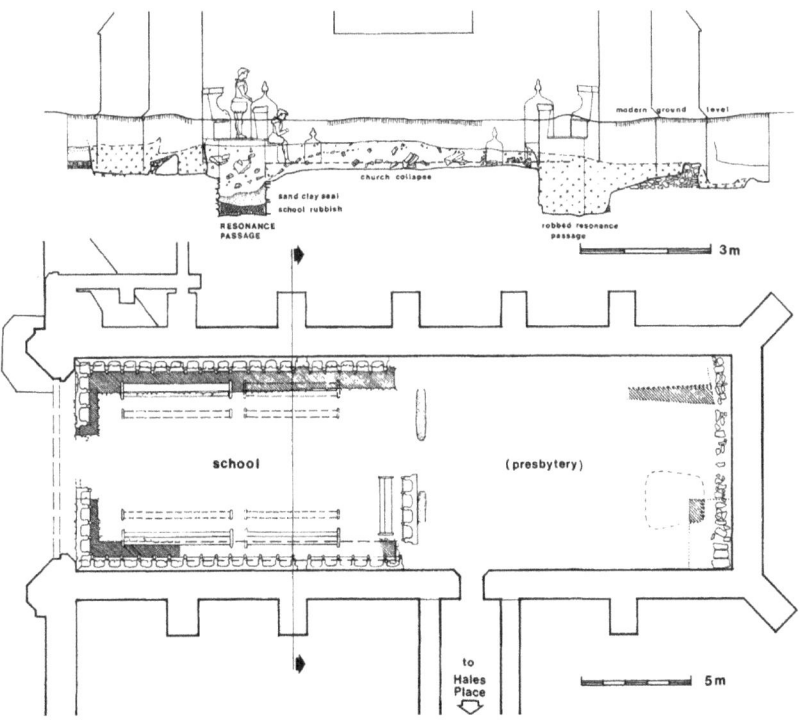

Figure 5.14 The Free Grammar School, Coventry Whitefriars (© Society for Post-Medieval Archaeology).

Formerly functioning to carry sound in the monastic church, in the school setting they became redundant, instead filling with rubbish that either accidentally dropped, or was intentionally swept, into them. These included objects associated with the day-to-day activities of the school, and the most distinctive of these were the remains of twelve inkwells. These were all made from small pieces of church building fabric, usually the finer carved mouldings, which were repurposed by having recesses for the ink carved into them (Figure 5.15). One example even had the owner's initials HW scratched onto it, leading the excavator to suggest that this was because scholars were expected to provide their ink themselves.[102] In addition to the inkwells, 31 pointed lead styli were recovered. Resembling traditional mason's pencils for marking up stonework, such a large number from post-Dissolution contexts suggests that they were more probably used by the pupils, perhaps on writing slates.[103]

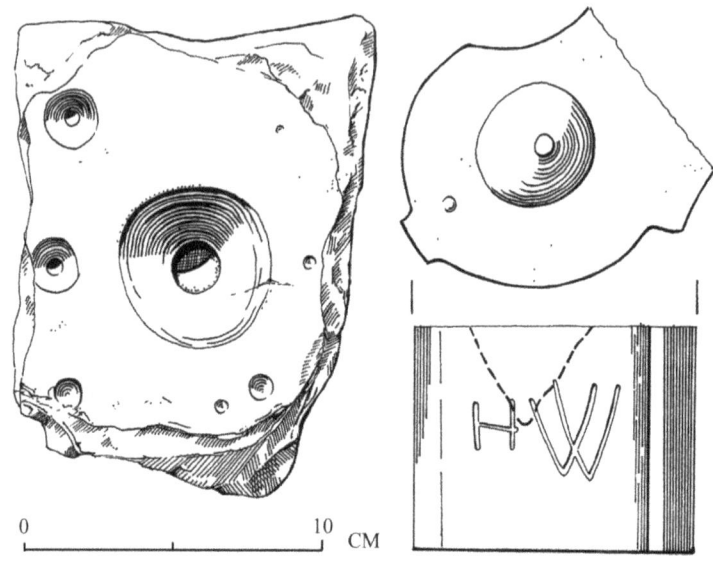

Figure 5.15 Inkwells found at the Free Grammar School, Coventry Whitefriars (© Society for Post-Medieval Archaeology).

Other aspects of school life also came to light during the excavations. Most interestingly, the nature of the school meals consumed could be reconstructed from the faunal assemblage present. Unsurprisingly, mutton and beef formed the majority of animal bone recovered, but in small quantities venison, swan and even peacock were present. This led to the suggestion that not only were pupils bringing "packed lunches" from home, as it is doubtful the school provided any food, these often included the leftovers from festive family feasts.[104] Finally, hints of the breadth of education a Tudor boy might be expected to receive were encountered. The excavations revealed seventeen arrowheads, ten of which were blunted for target practice, in addition to six musket balls, demonstrating that more than just academic skills were on the curriculum.[105]

What constituted a "school" might vary considerably, particularly with those focusing on the emerging field of the dramatic arts in later Tudor England, and monastic buildings could also be used to house these nascent institutions. Following its closure, the Carmelite friary at Hitchin appears to have fallen rapidly into ruin, with the church, in particular, being robbed of many of its portable assets.[106] However, in 1553 the complex was acquired by Ralph Radcliffe who established a school on the site. Little is known of its early history, but presumably it was located with the claustral ranges. Nonetheless, it also included a room specifically reserved for the pupils to develop good speaking, and for the presentation of plays.[107] Such fostering of the dramatic arts can more famously be seen within the confines of the Dominican friary in London. In 1576, Richard Farrant, deputy master of the Children of Windsor, a children's company of performers, established one of London's first playhouses at the Blackfriars. Without the capital to build a new playhouse, he leased a "long apartment" within the Blackfriars precinct, which Smith has suggested was the former friars' refectory.[108] Within this building, a purpose-built stage, equipped with curtains and even a trap door was constructed. Coincidently, in the same year that Farrant was establishing his playhouse, James Burbage leased the former service court of the Augustinian Holywell priory in Shoreditch. Shortly after he built "The Theatre" in the centre of the courtyard, not making use of any monastic buildings, but choosing instead to construct a circular timber structure, now recognizable as being the precursor to the typical late Elizabethan theatre. Although dismantled in 1598, the timbers from Burbage's theatre were transported south of the river and reused in the construction of the Globe in 1599.[109] Thus, both the former Dominican and Augustinian houses can arguably be claimed to have been seminal to the birth of modern English theatre.

Almshouses for the poor

It was not just upon the established monastic provision of education that the Dissolution significantly impacted; it had a more disastrous consequence upon the poor and sick who had traditionally relied upon the religious for some modicum of charitable relief. The suppression first of the houses that provided dole at their gates, and then the closure of the monastic-run hospitals in 1547 under the Chantry Act, at a stroke removed much of the poor relief available. Whilst some of the newly established schools, such as Christ's Hospital in London, were established ostensibly to provide support and education for children of the poor, they were not intended or equipped to provide relief to the destitute in need of food, clothing, and shelter. The growing problem of what to do with the poor was recognized by the government, which passed the 1547 Slavery Act, making it a requirement for civic authorities to provide accommodation for "idle, impotent, maimed and aged" persons. However, it seems such legislation was largely ignored, and it was only when later acts passed in 1597 and 1601 specified that such housing should be built and paid for by parishes on waste ground, that more organized civic provision became the norm.[110]

Despite the passing on the Chantries Act, not all existing monastic hospitals were closed, some survived by finding new secular supporters to replace their former religious patrons. Such was the case for the hospital of St Nicholas at Lewes. Established by at least the mid 13th century and initially functioning as a *domus leprosum*, the hospital was under the direct control of Lewes Priory. At the priory's suppression, the royal commissioners Cromwell, Pollard, and Mylsent made the promise that the hospital could retain its original function, although made no financial provision for this.[111] However, the hospital continued to be supported by the Earl of Dorset who eventually took ownership of the former priory site, and several local individuals made further bequests to the new secular almshouse. One, William, a former inmate who had benefitted from its care made a donation in 1559 of 6s 8d for repairs to the buildings and requested that he be buried "within the hospital where I now dwell."[112]

Other monastic hospitals survived the Dissolution due to the multiple roles they fulfilled at the end of the Middle Ages, one such site being the hospital of St Mary Magdalen, Colchester initially founded in the early 12th century as a leprosarium. As with many hospitals, its function changed through the course of its life, first to cater for the more general sick and poor, and at some point in the early 13th century the hospital chapel also became the parochial church for the burgeoning community of Colchester. Despite being the least well-endowed of Colchester's four hospitals, Mary Magdalene was the only to survive the Dissolution, mainly due to its parochial status.[113] This did not stop the speculators in monastic land, Nicase Yetsweirt and William Tunstall, gaining grants of the hospital's meagre lands that supported it in 1565, although some of these were subsequently returned to the now secular institution in the 1580s. Despite these financial difficulties, the former monastic hospital continued to operate for the good of the local community throughout the 16th century as a poorhouse and hospital, until James I formally refounded it as a church and almshouse in 1610.

Quite how these hospitals might have been physically affected by their transition from religious to secular run institutions is often unclear; most of these sites were either short-lived or were rebuilt into more suitable premises for the provision of charity during the 17th and 18th centuries. However, some indications survive archaeologically at the site of the hospital of St John at Cirencester. Founded in the early 12th century, the hospital was supported by the canons of Cirencester Abbey throughout the Middle Ages.[114] Following the passing of the 1547 Chantries Act, the newly appointed first commission into the state of hospitals and chantries related that "The hospitall of Seynt John Evangeliste was ffoundyd to fynde a master or keper for ever" and that it "ys a parish curch for the said pore folke."[115] It seems that again the parochial status that this hospital held saved it from immediate closure, and it continued to operate at least as an almshouse with the occupants documented as being housed in six tenements, although it appears soon after the Dissolution it had ceased to be a place of public worship.[116] Excavation of the former hospital chapel showed clear evidence for the subdivision of the presbytery and nave into separate units, presumably corresponding to the creation of the six tenements (Figure 5.16). Although precisely when these alterations were made is uncertain, it was probably soon after the Dissolution; indeed, by the late 18th century these tenements were described as being old and sufficiently dilapidated that new cottages had to be built on adjacent land to house the inmates. What is clear is that with the secularization of this particular hospital, the medieval chapel lost its original function, and thus was converted to more profane use, even if this was still that of the founder's intentions.

Existing hospitals were not the only former monastic institutions that could be used to care for the sick and destitute in the post-Dissolution

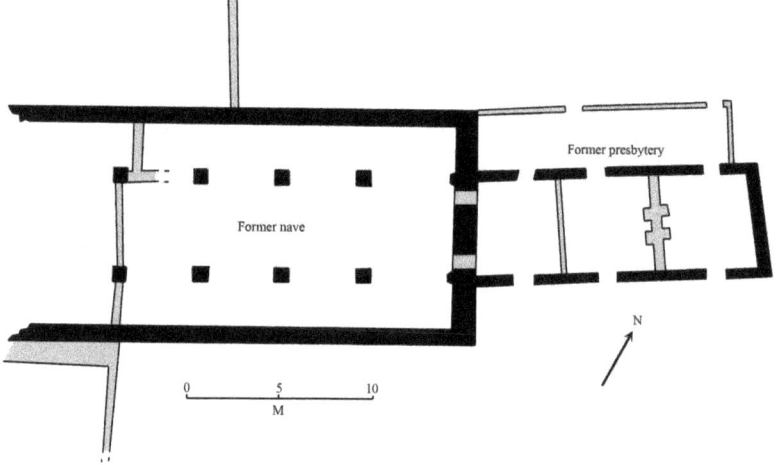

Figure 5.16   Hospital of St John, Cirencester (after Leech and McWhirr 1982).

period, and charitable repurposing of other urban monastic houses and former friars could also be undertaken on the instigation of civic-minded individuals. In Ludlow, the Carmelite friary appears to have passed relatively unaltered through various hands until part of the site was acquired by Charles Foxe for the explicit purpose of serving as an almshouse.[117] The choir of the monastic church seems to have been retained as the almshouse chapel, and Foxe even replaced the bells removed from its steeple immediately after its suppression. Where the residential element of the almshouse was located is not known for certain, but it might be reasonable to assume it was located in some, if not all, of the cloister.

Such conversions could be undertaken many decades after the original closure of the monastic house. In London, the Carthusian Charterhouse was converted after its suppression into a grand secular residence first for Edward North and then the Duke of Norfolk (see Chapter 6). This conversion resulted in the demolition of much of the former cloister of individual cells, which was turned into a garden. However, the potential of the site to be used for more charitable purposes was still apparent many years later, as in 1611 the site was purchased by Thomas Sutton to found a hospital for 80 "brothers."[118] The original cloister plan was rebuilt in brick and provided an ideal arrangement for the new almshouse that Sutton established for the good of the city's poor.

Entrepreneurial business opportunities

The appearance of large tracts of monastic land and buildings within, or close to, urban contexts also provided new opportunities for businesses and manufactories to establish themselves in locations previously unavailable. The reasons for such industries to set up within the former religious buildings were probably varied, but several factors made them an attractive location. For a start, the former urban precincts of the friaries, in particular, were located in the heart of their local communities, meaning that there was an immediate customer base for any products. Furthermore, the stone-built buildings of the former friaries provided some level of natural protection, within a town that would have been primarily constructed out of timber, for any high-temperature industries that might have operated ovens, kilns or furnaces. As a result, in the decades following the Dissolution, a variety of entrepreneurial businesses were to establish themselves within the former monastic properties and started to supply an ever-expanding market eager for their goods and services.

In his examination of the post-Dissolution evidence from London, John Schofield has observed that whilst in the period immediately following the closure of the monasteries most redevelopment that took place was large scale, high status and domestic in nature (see Chapter 6), from the 1560s onwards there was more of an emphasis on the fragmentation of monastic property and the establishment of new industries.[119] As an example, he points to the case of Holy Trinity Priory. Following the site's initial occupation as a high-profile residence following its closure, towards the last quarter of the 16th century the monastic precinct was broken up and became the location of several new businesses. As early as 1544, part of the precinct had been leased to William Grene, a member of the Merchant Taylors Company, and although it is uncertain whether he was commercially active on site, he also purchased over fifty tenements belonging to the former monastery, so it is entirely possible he was purely acting as a property speculator.[120] Nonetheless, by the 1580s part of the site was used by William Kerwin,

The Dissolution of the Monasteries in England and Wales

Figure 5.17 Pottery wasters from Holy Trinity, Aldgate (© Museum of London Archaeology).

a master of the Masons' Company, who was undoubtedly using part of the priory as a builders yard.[121] Kerwin was also engaged with the remodelling of the former prior's garden, which was by the start of the 17th century known as Sugar Baker's Yard, which has led to the suggestion this was the location of an early sugar refinery, although this has yet to be corroborated archaeologically.[122] Furthermore, during the 1580s–1590s, a baker named Brian Naylor was in residence in the precinct and occupying the former great kitchen, which he seems to have been using for his business.

Perhaps most significant, however, is the record of thirteen immigrant potters being resident on the site, including Jacob Jansen from Antwerp who was one of the wealthiest foreigners in the parish.[123] Jansen and a colleague, Jasper Andries, are known to have operated a workshop near Aldgate, and archaeological excavations on the west side of the cloister of Holy Trinity Priory revealed a pit containing an assemblage of tin-glazed earthenware wasters (Figure 5.17). These consisted mainly of jars and dishes, and it is significant that Jansen and Andries' original petition for permission to manufacture ceramics specifically mentioned the production of drug jars.[124] Precisely where the manufacturing was taking place is uncertain, as no archaeological evidence for a kiln or other industrial structures have thus far been found. However, it was likely to have taken place somewhere within the former priory precinct as it is unlikely such pottery wasters would have been moved far before disposal.

Similar parallels between this industrial endeavour and those of glassmakers can be seen at the former house of the Crutched Friars, near Tower Hill. After the Dissolution, the friary came into the possession of Sir Thomas Wyatt who constructed a house in the southeast corner of the precinct and leased the remainder of the property out to a variety of tenants. The property passed to the Lumley family in 1571 who lived in the mansion and continued the pre-existing leases.[125] One of those renting property from first Wyatt then Lumley was the Antwerp merchant Jean Carré, who, following his success in gaining a monopoly to produce window glass in 1567, built a glass furnace in the former friary, which he staffed with Venetian glassmakers. One of these, Giacomo Verzelini took charge of the works in 1572 and two years later received a further monopoly to produce high-quality crystal drinking glasses.[126] Little is known about the precise location of the glass manufactory, although John Stow recalled a disastrous fire in 1575 which destroyed it;

The Fryers hall was made a glasse house...which house in the yeare 1575. on the 4. of September brast out into a terrible fire...was all consumed to the stone wals, which neuerthelesse greatly hindered the fire from spreading any further.[127]

Stow's use of the term "Fryers hall" suggests the manufactory was not in the church, but perhaps in the refectory. Either way, the fact that the fire did not spread any further than its immediate building does suggest it must have been contained within the secure stone walls of a significant monastic building. Verzelini rebuilt his furnace, and by 1579 a new lease between him and Lumley has led Holder to suggest it was again located somewhere in the complex to the north, or northwest, of the mansion house.[128] As with Jansen's ceramic production, glass waste found nearby at Aldgate almost certainly derived from Verzelini's works in the former friary (Figure 5.18).[129]

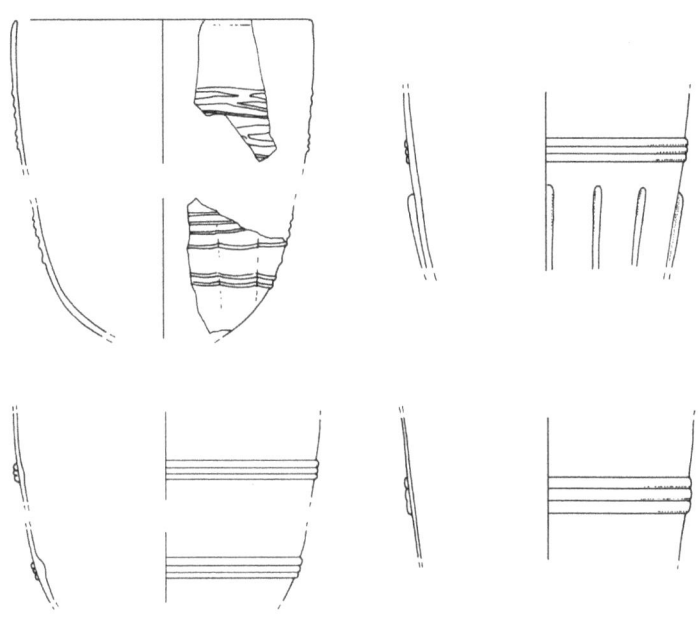

Figure 5.18   Wine glass fragments from Verzelini's furnace at Holy Trinity, Aldgate (Author).

In addition to housing industries newly introduced from the continent, monastic precincts also provided opportunities for merchants to expand more traditional operations within the confines of the town. One such craft was that of weaving. In Canterbury, the "priory, church and buildings there on" of the former Dominican friary were leased in 1539 to John Bathurst, a major Kentish clothier, to establish a weaving factory.[130] Bathurst had been keen to secure other properties for his industry, although the particular suitability of the Blackfriars was noted by Sir Christopher Hales who wrote to Cromwell stating;

> If Batherst or another of the best clothiers in Kent were disposed to set up cloth making in Canterbury the house of the Blackfriars would be sufficient for the purpose.[131]

Bathurst finally settled on the use of the Blackfriars for the next twenty years or so, holding several leases on the property until it was eventually sold to John Harrington and George Burden in 1560.[132] Which portion of the friary complex was used as the weaving factory is not immediately clear from the documents. A 1595 map by Thomas Langdon showed the church and all conventual buildings still roofed and intact, although by the 17th century the north and the west ranges were recorded as dwellings and the former guesthouse named as "Weavers Hall" (Figure 5.19). That this was the location of the business has now been confirmed archaeologically.

Figure 5.19   Infirmary Hall, Canterbury Blackfriars (Author).

In 1929 Martin confidently asserted, but without sourcing his information, that massive irregular brick and rubble foundations had recently been unearthed in the undercroft of this building, which he interpreted as being the bases for looms.[133]

It was not just at Canterbury, where those involved in the cloth trade took an interest in the potential that former monastic property could offer. In Gloucester, Thomas Bell, the prominent draper and clothmaker, acquired the entire site of the Dominican friary in 1539.[134] Bell adapted the friary church into a house, demolishing the presbytery end and focusing the dwelling within the body of the nave, and his new weaving factory was then located within the former cloistral ranges.[135] Although the manufactory did not seem to survive past Bell's death, when William Stukeley visited in the early 18th century, his published engraving still shows this arrangement,

Figure 5.20   18th-century view of Gloucester Blackfriars (W. Stukeley 1721).

although the very schematic depiction of the west and north cloistral ranges suggests they might have been substantially altered or even demolished by this time (Figure 5.20).

Perhaps the most profane industrial use to which an urban monastery was put after the Dissolution also occurred in Gloucester, at the Franciscan friary. John Jennings acquired the lease of this site in 1544 who converted the nave and north aisle of the friary church into a brewery.[136] This was a major operation intended to quench much of the city's thirst, as it had its own dedicated water supply piped in from Robinswood Hill, and the brewery continued in operation up until the middle of the 18th century. Interestingly, excavations in the 1970s revealed evidence for brewing in the church (Figure 5.21). The nave was subdivided into separate cells or units for the different activities, a brick cellar was constructed and several clay-lined pits dug which probably acted as vats.[137] Perhaps most significant of all was the identification of a circular tread from a horse mill, used to crush the malt, again emphasizing the industrial scale of the brewing taking place in this former House of God.

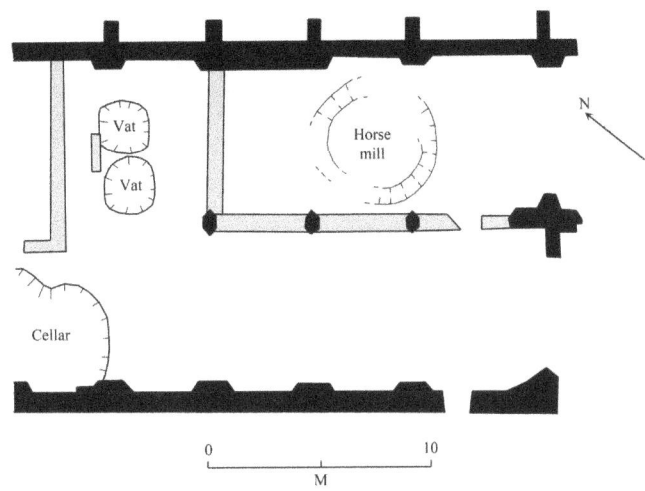

Figure 5.21 Plan of the post-dissolution brewery, Gloucester Greyfriars (after Ferris 2001).

— 6 —

The Conversion to Domestic Use

Although almost all former monastic houses suffered some degree of damage immediately following their surrender to the crown, such as the removal of lead roofing and other elements of their fabric that had immediate resale value, at least to begin with most remained relatively unmolested. Whilst the fabric of the church and conventual buildings themselves represented an opportunity to make a short-term gain through the sale of window glass, furnishing and even the building stone itself (see Chapter 3), perhaps their greater value lay in their ability to be transformed into new domestic dwellings, and at a fraction of the cost of building from new.

That many of the 800 or so religious houses closed at the Dissolution went on to have a transformed afterlife often as private domestic residences is not disputed. However, perhaps the scale to which this happened has not been fully appreciated; there is good archaeological or historical evidence for at least 250 having been converted to domestic use in the period 1536–1600, and this is likely a vast underestimate of the actual total. Indeed, it would probably be safe to say that only a minority of houses did not experience some form of secular occupation during the 16th century, even if only temporarily. This, of course, is not surprising, as even the poorer houses contained an array of stone-built buildings that could be cheaply re-roofed, if necessary, and put to immediate use.

Despite the assumption that because all monasteries were built to a fairly standard plan, and this would have placed similar restrictions and challenges upon their new owners in how they might be converted,[1] the reality was that there was a very diverse range of new uses to which monastic buildings could be put to use. Nonetheless, the majority that were converted became private residences, ranging in grandeur from royal palaces and great houses for the nobility through to humble farmsteads and agricultural enclosures. Differentiating between these different types of conversion in any systematic way is challenging, especially in the absence of historical documentation detailing the new owners. Furthermore, even over a relatively short period, the status of a site could shift, so that over the course of the 16th century a religious house could have been put to multiple different uses. A further complicating factor was that many monastic sites were divided between several new owners. At Thornton Abbey the majority of the claustral ranges were granted to Henry Holbeach Bishop of Lincoln in September

1547, yet the church to the north and the adjoining monastic cemetery and infirmary yard to the east came into the ownership of Robert Wood in 1549, significantly affecting how Holbeach could approach and develop his new residence (see Chapter 7).[2]

Another consideration that should be borne in mind is that even before the Dissolution there were sometimes members of the laity in permanent residence at some monastic sites. The presence of corrodians, men and women who effectively paid the monastic house for the opportunity to live there in comfortable retirement is an often-overlooked occurrence.[3] It is usually assumed that corrodians would have resided in the infirmary or another precinct building partially given over for this purpose. However, by the early 16th century, more permanent and substantial secular structures may have been present at some sites. In 1518 Sir John Sharpe was recorded as residing at Coggeshall Abbey in Essex. This house was later granted to Clement Harleston in 1528 when the property was described as being next to the infirmary and consisting of "one little garden...and the mansion on the east."[4] In this case, at least, a substantial secular mansion was present coexisting alongside the religious house for several decades before the Dissolution.

Concealed conversions

A further complication in understanding the process of domestic conversion is the relative lack of surviving archaeological evidence. While very large numbers of dwellings were made out of monastic complexes, few have survived significant subsequent alteration, and the fabric of those that have is usually obscured by render, panelling or plaster. Part of the problem is that even as they were being converted, many of these new domestic dwellings were already what has been described as "throwbacks to the past."[5] With architectural fashions rapidly changing during the second half of the 16th century, most monastic conversions fell out of fashion, and where owners could afford to do so, they were totally rebuilt or substantially modified beyond all recognition. A typical example would be the Benedictine abbey at Walden, which was granted to Sir Thomas Audley in 1538, who converted the monastic buildings into a substantial house.[6] On Audley's death, the estate passed to Thomas Howard, Earl of Suffolk, who set about rebuilding the house in grand Jacobean style and setting in motion a programme of building evolution that was to last for the next 140 years.[7] So thorough was Thomas Howard's rebuilding that no trace of the original 16th-century conversion

Figure 6.1 Inserted Tudor windows, Netley Abbey (Author).

remained visible, so much so that it was suggested that the abbey site might lie some distance from the upstanding house. It was only from the 1950s onwards that excavations revealed that portions of both Audley's conversion and the original abbey were preserved within the later fabric and that Audley's conversion incorporated the monastic church, the west and southern ranges, and very possibly the eastern range too, although this was subsequently completely demolished.[8]

Even on sites where there was relatively little later development, especially those abandoned and left to ruin, it can be frustratingly difficult to understand the full extent of any domestic conversion. This is primarily due to three causes: natural decay, robbing, and "improvement." These factors can be found to a greater or lesser extent at most former monastic houses but can be amply illustrated at two, Netley Abbey and Monk Bretton Priory.

The very nature of monastic conversion generally meant that the newest adaptations and additions were those likely to suffer greatest from subsequent abandonment and decay. One of the attractions of using the medieval monastic building in a conversion was that it provided a solid core onto which more delicate and contemporary features such as brick chimneys and inserted windows might be affixed, and partition walls attached, with the transition between the two styles hidden beneath carefully applied render, plaster, and stucco. The moment the building was exposed to the elements, it was these later elements that were prone to the fastest degradation, decay, and ultimately disappearance. Such natural removal of the Tudor alteration of the building's adaptations is amply illustrated at Netley Abbey. Although evidence for William Paulet's conversion of the site is still visible through the use of brick, mainly inserted windows and doorways (Figure 6.1), most of the substantial alterations made, particularly in dividing the monastic church with partitions and internal floors to make the principal apartments have virtually disappeared. This happened relatively rapidly; the Buck brothers' north view of the abbey church engraved in 1733 showed that less than half a century after the house ceased to be occupied no divisions were surviving in the church, even though it formed the core of the mansion.[9] Likewise, more detailed engravings dating to the early 19th century, before the first excavations and clearances of the buildings, such as those published in Mudie's 1839 *Hampshire Past and Present* show that despite the ruins still standing to a significant height, few Tudor dividing walls or other insertions survived beyond ground level (Figure 6.2).

Figure 6.2   Early 19th-century view of Netley Abbey church (Mudie 1839).

It was not just natural decay that could hasten the removal of the Tudor additions to the monastic fabric, since many of the additional elements added during the conversion were attractive to subsequent robbers. Inserted door lintels, quoining, and other stone elements would not only have been less weathered than the corresponding medieval masonry, but having been inserted into the monastic fabric they would have been easier to remove compared with their earlier counterparts which were integral elements of the original structure. Likewise, Tudor brickwork could have been easily dismantled and the bricks recycled much more readily than the rough rubble cores of the monastic wall. At Monk Bretton Priory, this clear preference in the scavenging of the Tudor fabric can be seen. Whilst the site went through two phases of rebuilding, first by William Blithman in the 1530s and then subsequently by the Earl of Shrewsbury in the 1580s, relatively little diagnostic stonework from these conversions remains.[10] However, only 100m from the site, the original monastic water mill was rebuilt during the later 17th century, and this renovation included the use of a significant number of Tudor door lintels, chimney breasts, and string coursing, which must have been scavenged from the priory.

The final factor affecting the modern reconstruction of many monastic conversions was the conscious "improvement" of the sites after they had begun to attract the attention of antiquarians, and ultimately when they came into state care. Most significantly, the influence of first the Office, then the Ministry, of Works has been noted.[11] During the first half of the 20th century, many of the more prominent monastic sites were taken into state care, and as part of this process, most were cleared to make them more presentable and accessible to the public. However, this tidying did not merely stop at providing practical or even aesthetical access, but often took on a more fundamental purpose, to present an idealized version of the medieval, rather than Tudor, past. Where there was a conflict between the two archaeologies, the latter was frequently removed, even if at times it was to the broader detriment of the monument. At Monk Bretton Priory in 1937, the medieval gatehouse had not only the early modern additions to it removed, but strict instructions were also given by the then Inspector of Ancient Monuments P.K. Baillie Reynolds, following the policy devised by Sir Charles Peers, for the stripping of its roof timbers.[12] Whether the gatehouse roof was the original medieval one or a later replacement is unknown, but this act turned the building into a ruin for the first time in its history, much to its subsequent structural degradation (see Figure 1.3).

Although the scale of clearance, tiding and deliberate ruination undertaken by the Ministry of Works during the 20th century was enormous, it was not a new phenomenon; during the 19th-century landowners often undertook substantial and at times damaging, work on their sites. At Thornton Abbey, the 1st Earl of Yarborough cleared the monastic church and part of the cloister shortly after acquiring the site in 1816, perhaps unintentionally removing vital evidence for the Tudor conversion of the site. The family would later reroof the gatehouse and build a custodian's cottage out of medieval and early modern standing remains close by to encourage visitors. Antiquarians could also be destructive in their pursuit of tracing monastic plans. Although, as has already been discussed, much of Paulet's adaptations to the monastic church at Netley Abbey had fallen victim to natural decay or casual robbing, excavations undertaken by the in the early 1860s were also clearly destructive. For example, it was stated that the workmen removed the "large brick or stone partitions erected by successive lay occupants for their own especial convenience."[13] Fortunately, in the case of Netley, the Reverend

Kell made frequent note of the Tudor adaptations his workmen removed, helping in part to aid a partial reconstruction of Paulet's conversion (see below).

These complications aside, it is possible to identify four broad categories of domestic developments: total cloister conversions, lesser gentry adaptations, farmsteads and agricultural occupation, and urban housing.

From cloister to courtyard, the elite house

Unlike the full range of county-based historical studies that have been undertaken examining the transfer of land following the Dissolution (outlined in Chapter 4), there has been a surprising lack of attention paid to the process of conversion itself. There are, of course, a number of individual site-specific studies that have been undertaken, at sites such as at Norton Priory, Haughmond Abbey, and Monk Bretton Priory to name but a recent few.[14] Despite these, there have been few more regional overviews. Exceptions are Coppack's review of Lincolnshire and Doggett's study of Hertfordshire, but unfortunately the former, while very astute in its historical observations, is hampered by a relative lack of upstanding architecture or more modern excavations, whilst the latter is limited in scope with a small poorly surviving sample set.[15]

To date, the most comprehensive overview has been undertaken by the architectural historian Maurice Howard, who has completed a more detailed survey of the process of conversion, primarily focusing on still-upstanding remains.[16] Howard's work has been seminal in many ways, most notably through stressing the positive aspects of the Dissolution and the opportunities it provided for architectural development.[17] Rather than stemming from a particular interest in the Dissolution, Howard instead seeks to frame his study within a broader exploration of the development of early Tudor polite architecture, in which the monasteries played just a supporting role. Consequently, he is understandably only interested in the architecture and conversions of the elite, stating it is the "earliest conversions that are of greatest interest...the best illustrations of a different kind of conversion come from buildings belonging to the most powerful men."[18] In particular, Howard is interested in the relationship between the monastic cloister and the secular courtyard house, so understandably only focuses on the grandest conversions that saw the majority of the former religious buildings converted into a new secular house.

Howard is at pains to stress that initially only the courtiers, taking advantage of their positions at court, and following the lead of the crown, were involved in purchasing and adapting monasteries and that only around 30 "recastings" of sites took place in the first years following the Dissolution. He further contends that it is only later in the 16th century during the reign of Elizabeth that the gentry "picked up the leftovers, the poorer pickings."[19] This is clearly an oversimplification, as Chapter 4 has shown, whilst the nobility were indeed initial recipients of very large numbers of sites these were often very rapidly sold on, and even then there were still plenty of former monastic houses to go around the gentry and others eager to acquire and develop such sites.

Perhaps because of his more general interest in the development of polite architecture, when looking at individual sites Howard's focus is only on those that conform to the classic "courtyard" model. Here he rightly stresses that it was the church that suffered most harshly, with either the presbytery end that projected beyond the east range or the majority of the structure being demolished very rapidly.[20] However, much of the discussion is in rather general terms, and in some cases, such as at Titchfield and Netley, additional historical and archaeological data has not been included within the analysis (see below). This is not to say that Howard's work or general conclusions are incorrect, indeed they are ground breaking, but they do provide a somewhat simplistic picture that lacks sufficient nuance. In many ways, the issue lies in the fact that the architecture is mostly dealt with in isolation, both from other sources of evidence but also divorced from the people who built and inhabited it. Consequently, it is worth revisiting a number of these "classic" courtyard conversions.

Titchfield Abbey

Probably the most quoted example of a courtyard conversion, and certainly one of the earliest to receive academic attention, is Titchfield Abbey, Hampshire. The site was granted to the prominent courtier Thomas Wriothesley (later 1st Earl of Southampton) in 1537. Straight away, he set about converting it into a residence, and there survives an interesting set of letters from his agents on the ground discussing their plans and reporting the progress of the works.[21] From these letters, a significant amount of detail concerning the conversion of Titchfield is preserved, in particular emphasising how fluid the plans for its transformation were and determined by practical considerations on the ground. For example, the conversion was estimated to cost 300 marks (£200), and initially it was planned to convert the refectory into the principal lodgings with the kitchen and hall in the southern range. However, the plan changed, and the refectory later became the great hall due to the savings that could be made by reusing the original monastic kitchen.[22] Unfortunately, the majority of the Tudor house was demolished in 1781, leaving only the western and central portions of the south range, but Hope supplemented dates from the surviving fabric and documentary sources with the excavation of the eastern range, demolished presbytery and south transept of the church. The combination of both the documentary and archaeological sources has allowed for a basic reconstruction of the conversion by Howard.[23] This saw the demolition of the south transept and presbytery of the church with the remaining portion of that building being converted into the gatehouse and access route into the site. The frater was converted into the hall, as the main focus of the house, with the principal apartments occupying the east range and north transept of the church, although it is clear that neither Hope nor Howard were aware of additional sources that shed light on the wider composition of the house.

The first was an inventory made on 12th May 1699,[24] which provides a detailed description of the layout of the house at the end of the 17th century.[25] There were 39 principal rooms, including galleries, dining rooms, and several halls. Interestingly the first floor of the gatehouse range appears to have been the most important quarters, divided into King's and Queen's rooms, and there is no reason to suppose that these were not principal apartments in the 16th century as well. The second source is a series of very detailed measured plans of both the ground and first floor of the house drawn by John Achard in 1737,[26] giving not only a much more comprehensive overview of the original house plan but also a location for many of the main rooms.[27] Taken together, these later sources provide an invaluable overview of the house before its destruction. Inevitably, developments would have taken place between the conversion in the 1530s and these later surveys, indeed it appears that at a later date a new service wing was built to the northeast, however, the broad arrangements of some of the key rooms would have remained the same.

Wriothesley created his house in a most expedient and cost-effective manner, and virtually the whole of the original monastic fabric was used in its construction (Figure 6.3). The eastern portion of the north transept, the entire south transept, and the cloister walk were demolished, and the western range narrowed possibly for aesthetic reasons as it originally protruded further west than the north or south ranges. However, it is now clear that the whole of the east range and the reredorter were also adapted for secular use so that new ground plan of the house was very similar indeed to its medieval precursor. From the 1727 survey, several additional details can be added. The hall was located on the first floor of the north range and accessed by a new external flight of steps. The internal arrangement followed the traditional pattern of a screens passage with the buttery and pantry on one side and the great hall on the other. The monastic chapter house was adapted into a chapel open at the east end to the height of the first floor but covered over by a long gallery that ran from the choir of the church along half the eastern range. At the northern end of this range was located the great chamber and beyond even the reredorter was reused, although for what purpose is unclear. As indicated in both the 1699 inventory and the 1727 survey the principal apartments lay at first floor level in the southern range (with offices below), and not in the eastern range as suggested by Howard,[28] and it is likely that other lodgings were located in the west range.

On one level Wriothesley's conversion does seem quite brutal, perhaps symbolically so, especially in his treatment of the church and the creation of a gatehouse in the nave. However, this does not necessarily represent the intentionally "harsh" treatment suggested by Howard,[29] as in fact the presbytery was preserved to its full length and not destroyed. Instead, Wriothesley's workmen chose to fossilize the majority of the original monastic plan in the new house, making practical choices to create the desired result rather than any bold political or symbolic statements. Indeed, it has been noted that while the south face of the house was radically altered and modernized, the rest of the conversion made little attempt to hide its medieval origins.[30] In this way, the house was a reflection of its owner. Wriothesley,

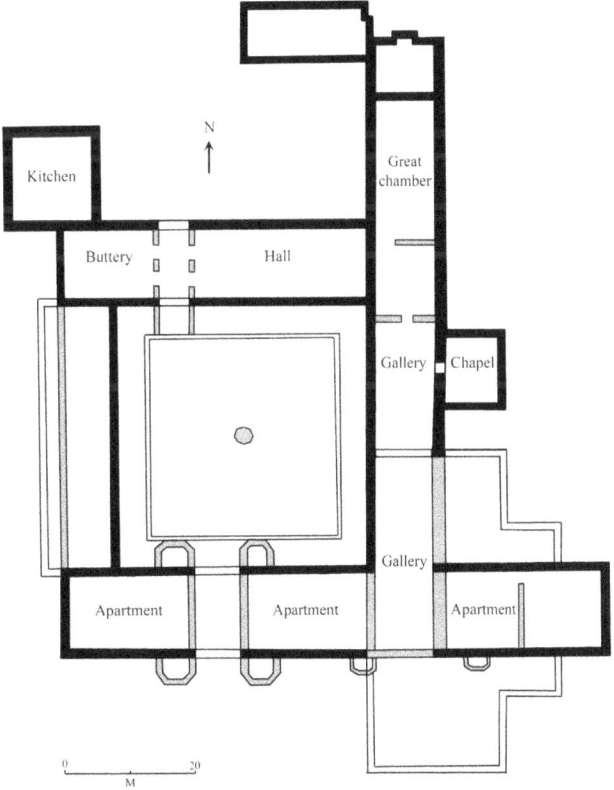

Figure 6.3 Plan of Titchfield Abbey (after Hope 1906b; Tamkin 1989).

an ambitious and astute political operator, was also a pragmatist and religious conservative, more noted for his persecution of Protestant evangelicals rather than the condemnation of Catholics.[31] The conversion at Titchfield merely represents the most straightforward and cheapest way to create a grand courtyard house, while all the time below the new façade much of the fabric of the old religion remained the same.

Leez Priory

Sir Richard Rich, then Chancellor of the Court of Augmentations, took an alternative approach to creating a courtyard house at Leez Priory, Essex. He immediately set about creating an extremely grand house focusing around two courtyards, in the manner of Hampton Court and Nonsuch Palace. The former monastic remains were converted into the inner court, while a new and even larger outer court was constructed to the west, and to the east a sizeable walled privy garden laid out (Figure 6.4). The inner court was totally demolished in 1753, and today only the south range of the outer court remains. Early in the 20th century, excavations were undertaken by Clapham in the area of the inner court and have revealed the plan of the original monastic buildings and their later conversion. The original report suggests that Rich completely levelled the medieval buildings, but admits confusion as to why the rebuilding should still follow the earlier lines.[32] However, Howard has rightly noted that this was not, in fact, the case; instead, the medieval fabric was encased in later brick, so that there was a uniformity of design between the converted inner court and newly built outer.[33]

The conversion undertaken at Leez seems to closely resemble that originally intended at Titchfield with the eastern nave becoming the location of the hall, just as requested by Wriothesley. The church north of the crossing was completely demolished, as was its north aisle and the cloister walk, the northern arcade being adapted as the new outer face for the southern range. The kitchen was not located in the church, instead being sited in a new service block immediately to the south, and a new entrance leading from the former cloister into a screens passage was created, opening out to the hall on one side and the buttery on the other. Clapham's excavations

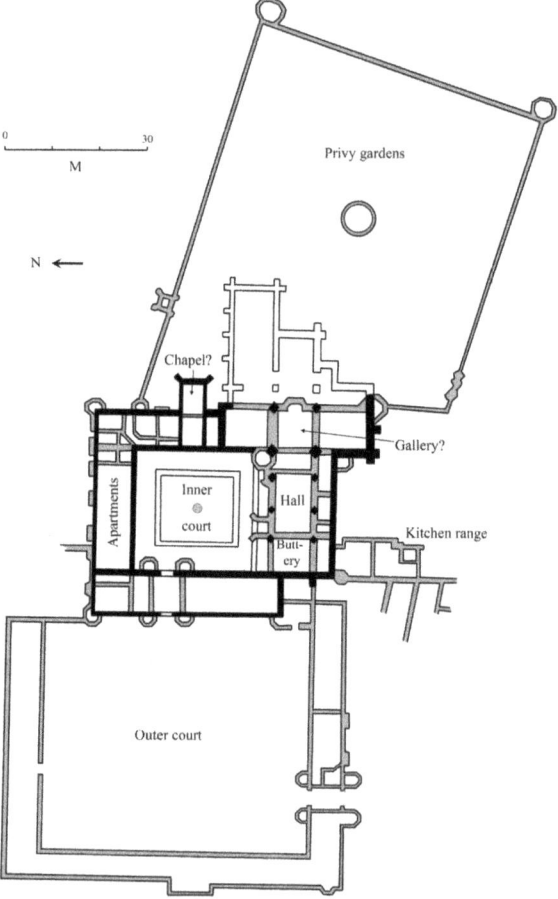

Figure 6.4 Plan of Leez Priory (after Clapham 1915).

revealed at times a bewildering array of later walls, and it is not entirely clear from his plan what they might all represent. The one element of the inner court that still survives relatively intact is the connecting gateway that had been built through the west range of the monastery. The new functions for the east and north ranges are less certain. Clapham suggested the chapter house may have been converted into a chapel, and although he found no direct evidence for this it is a distinct possibility.[34] The transepts of the church and possibly the eastern range too seem to have functioned as a first-floor gallery, while the addition of a large number of chimneys to the outer wall of the north range suggests this was developed into apartments.

Rich's approach to the conversion of Leez was markedly different from Wriothesley's at Titchfield. Clearly, resources were not an issue, although no records survive, as Rich must have expended many times more than the 300 marks Wriothesley was quoted at for Titchfield. However, more importantly, there was no element of compromise in Rich's conversion of Leez. First, the entire east end of the church, which would have caused a deviation of the quadrangle plan of the courtyard house was demolished, likewise the reredorter and the medieval kitchen projecting to the north. Then, a second outer court was constructed free from any earlier confines, but most crucially turning what would already have been an impressive house into a building of almost palatial status. Finally, and perhaps most tellingly, Rich tried to obliterate all evidence of the former religious nature of the site. Old fabric was clad in brick to create the impression of a coherent build between the old inner and new outer courts, complimented by an elaborately walled privy garden over the east end of the church, built over the former cemetery and which must have required the removal of the infirmary and other now redundant buildings. There was to be no visible reminder of the ecclesiastical past in Rich's house, or indeed the very active role he had personally played the suppression of the monasteries.

Netley Abbey

A further site that benefits from a re-evaluation is Netley Abbey, Hampshire. Although not small in size, the monastery was poorly endowed and was closed during the suppression of the lesser monasteries, being granted shortly after to Sir William Paulet.[35] Like many who prospered in the early 16th century, Paulet was from relatively humble stock, but became an accomplished courtier, rising to be treasurer of the household by the time he acquired Netley.[36] As mentioned earlier, the conversion undertaken by Paulet is at times hard to trace in the surviving ruins. However, the original excavation account, along with a more recent geophysical survey and interpretation,[37] allow for a detailed reconstruction of how Paulet chose to transform Netley, as well as hinting at some of the motivations behind the decisions made.

Superficially, the conversion of Netley quite closely resembles that of Rich's at Leez, in that the monastic church became the location of the hall and core of the house (Figure 6.5), although, a much more detailed picture of Paulet's conversion of the church at Netley can be gained. Except for the north transept, which was demolished, the entire church remained largely intact. The west door was walled up, the south transept was closed off, and the north and south aisles largely blocked off from the nave and presbytery with dividing walls.[38] The kitchen with inserted fireplaces occupied the western half of the nave, and the pantry and hall the eastern nave and choir, while a new service block containing "a very large oven, capable of baking bread made from two bushels" was found to the north of the former nave.[39]

However, an essential difference between the conversion at Leez and Netley is that at Netley the east end not only remained entirely intact, it still retained an ecclesiastical function as it became the chapel for the house. Other elements of the former monastic fabric were demolished, but primarily for practical reasons. To be able to create a new entrance into the cloister directly opposite the door to the new hall, the refectory, which was orientated perpendicular to the south range in the standard Cistercian fashion, had to be demolished. In its place, a relatively modest entrance was placed in the south range, which from the presence of inserted fireplaces appears to have been converted into apartments at first-floor level. Geophysical survey has confirmed that the infirmary lay in the standard location between the east range and the abbot's lodge and was also demolished at this time but only so a formal garden could be created here.[40] Likewise, the cloister walk was demolished to open the space to create a new fountain court. Otherwise, the monastic plan remained relatively unmolested.

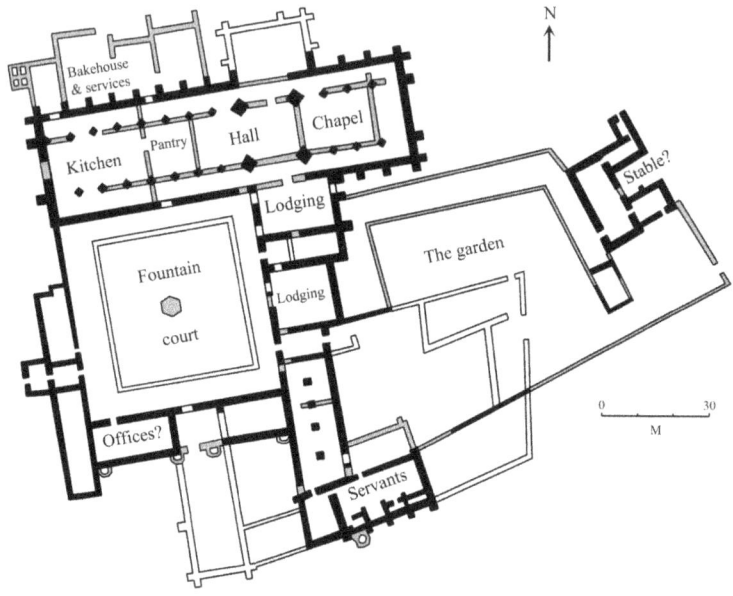

Figure 6.5   Plan of Netley Abbey (after Hare 1993; Barker et al. 2005).

There is ample evidence for the division of rooms in the eastern range at both ground floor and first-floor level to create private lodgings or apartments, and as at Leez, a gallery would likely have formed part of this arrangement. The reredorter was also retained and improved with newly inserted windows, and it has been plausibly suggested that this might have been adapted as a servants hall. Finally, even the former abbot's lodge was preserved mostly intact, with only minor modifications; Kell stated that in the 19th century it had been turned into a stable.[41] Whilst it is possible that this might have been the case in the 16th century too, the fact that the abbot's lodge was incorporated as an integral element within the new formal garden suggests it would have had a higher status role, perhaps as a banqueting house.

Paulet's conversion of Netley is on first sight as similarly pragmatic as Wriothesley's at Titchfield. Where possible monastic fabric was retained, and comparatively few changes were made to the overall ground plan; it might be considered a relatively cost-effective conversion. Indeed the 19th-century excavations also showed that Paulet did not renovate many elements of the building and the former medieval fittings were still much in evidence. Whilst it is not surprising that decorated medieval floor tiles survived the conversion of the presbytery into the private chapel of the new house, they were also found *in situ* and still in use during the later 16th century in the chapter house and south transept, which had been converted into domestic lodgings.⁴² Likewise, decorated medieval window glass survived in large enough pieces in the eastern range that individual scenes could be recognized, indicating that they must have come from panels that remained in position even after the house was converted. Indeed, one of the reasons the conversion is hard to see in the fabric of the building is that so little that could be changed was altered. Even though it could have been replaced comparatively cheaply, all the original monastic window tracery was retained throughout the church (Figure 6.6); despite the internal divisions that were inserted, the core of the house would still have appeared externally to strongly resemble a monastery.

Figure 6.6   Medieval window tracery surviving in the church, Netley Abbey (Author).

Such a conservative approach to the conversion of Netley could not have been due to lack of funds, since Paulet developed his principal residence at Basing House into what was the largest private house of its day, with over 300 rooms.⁴³ Furthermore, it is essential to consider why Paulet chose to not only retain almost all of the external fabric of the monastic church but also chose to maintain a continuity of ecclesiastical use. Whilst at both Titchfield and Leez the conveniently located and orientated chapter house was chosen as the site of the new domestic chapel, at Netley the presbytery was chosen for this role, the most sacred space of the former religious community. Such an obvious continuation of use cannot have been coincidental.

Some insights into the motivations behind this decision have been recently proposed by Smith, who suggested that Paulet had a very personal interest in preserving the church at Netley, through his friendship with Richard Foxe, Bishop of Winchester.⁴⁴ Despite being Foxe's junior by many years, the two men had been close friends and shared conservative, but more importantly pragmatic, views of religion.⁴⁵ Foxe had been a generous patron of several religious establishments, but particularly Netley Abbey due to its relative impoverishment and proximity to Winchester. Furthermore, Foxe's patronage was reflected in the fabric of the building; roof bosses originating from the east end of Netley Abbey's church depicting identical devices to those found on Foxe's chantry chapel in Winchester suggest his support for the abbey was immortalized in stone before or shortly after his death in 1528.⁴⁶ It is no coincidence then that Paulet chose to maintain this portion of the former church as a sacred space in memory of its former patron and his friend.

The argument put forward for Paulet's intentional retention of certain aspects of the fabric at Netley is a convincing one, however, it is probably just part of the motivation behind his very "light touch" conversion. Had he wished to retain a portion of the former church as a private chapel, he could easily have done so while still radically altering and modernising the remainder of the buildings relatively cheaply through the insertion of new windows or other more contemporary features. Yet he chose not to. Perhaps the reason lay in his political acumen and foresight to be "made of the pliable willow, not of the stubborn oak" as he supposedly claimed.[47] Unlike Rich at Leez, through preserving so much of the visible monastic fabric in its original state, at least externally, Paulet was making an ambiguous statement that could suit all political times.

Courtyard conversions in context

Although some courtiers were choosing to create new courtyard houses incorporating all three claustral ranges and the church, these are in fact comparatively rare. More often than not, high-status conversions that might be usually be thought of as "typical" courtyard conversions, were in reality only focused upon the claustral ranges and saw the church destroyed or left as an unoccupied ruin. Whilst it might be argued the choice not to incorporate the church into the subsequent house might have been due to the fact this would have been the most challenging and costly building to convert, and thus been beyond the budget of some, this cannot have always been so. A good case in point is Lacock Abbey, often cited as being the archetypal courtyard conversion.[48] Following its suppression, Lacock was sold to Sir William Sharington, at that time a page of the privy chamber and member of the royal household. Sharington was subsequently appointed the head of the newly established mint in Bristol and was able to amass an enormous wealth through embezzlement and fraud; when he was found guilty of his offences in 1549 and his lands confiscated, he was found to be in possession of bullion and coin worth £14,000.[49] Later that year, after being pardoned, he was able to gain restoration of his estates by paying a fee of £12,867 and demonstrating the enormous wealth he had at his disposal.

Despite these tremendous resources, Sharington, in his conversion of Lacock, still chose not to include the church within the scheme of renovation (Figure 6.7). When the site

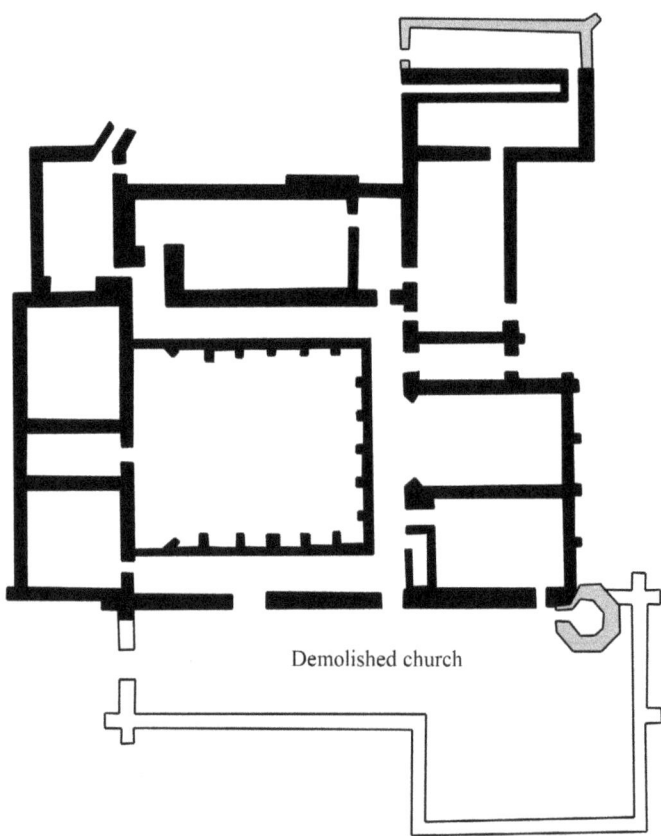

Figure 6.7 Plan of Lacock Abbey (after Brakspear 1900).

was excavated in 1898, this element of the complex had been so thoroughly demolished that in parts even the lowest foundations had been removed.[50] The failure to reuse the church was not the result of a lack of funds to renovate it; indeed Sharington further improved the property by constructing a new large stable court to the north of the monastic cloister, over doubling the size of the house. The reasons for Sharington's reluctance to include the church in his conversion are thus unclear, especially as it resulted in the new inner court of the house only comprising three ranges rather than the customary four of grander Tudor houses. Perhaps he saw the demolition of the church as a way of ensuring the site could never be put back to religious use. However, unlike Rich's conversion at Leez, where medieval masonry was covered over with fashionable Tudor brick, at Lacock Sharington felt no need to hide the medieval fabric, but left it plainly on show.

Even if the fabric of the church was often not incorporated into the new house, it could still be left conspicuously visible. Perhaps the site where this is best illustrated is Newstead Abbey, Nottinghamshire. On one hand, the conversion is straightforward, the three claustral ranges, the abbot's lodging and possibly the kitchen were all incorporated into a house on three sides. The only element of the church incorporated into the house was its south transept, and part of the south wall of the nave, both to complete the square symmetry of the post-Dissolution mansion. However, while at Newstead, the majority of the rest of the church was demolished apparently at the time of initial conversion, its west front was retained to its full height (Figure 6.8). This was a conscious decision made by its new owner, as the west front could quickly and for relatively little extra cost have been pulled down at the same time as the rest of the monastic church.

Newstead was dissolved in 1539 and granted the following year to Sir John Byron.[51] As well as being a prominent courtier, Byron was also nominated Sheriff of Nottinghamshire and served as a local MP. Like many men in his position, he had been actively engaged in the Dissolution, acting as a commissioner in the north and being present at the surrender of Furness Abbey. However, despite Byron's active role in the Dissolution and his willingness to acquire monastic property, it is clear that he still adhered, at least in private, to the old religion. In his will, made just three months before the death of Catholic Queen Mary in 1558, although unaltered before his death in 1567, he left money to pay for the saying of masses and expressed the hope that others might return back to the "right faith."[52] The possibility that Byron's intentional retention of the west façade of the nave at

Figure 6.8   View of Newstead Abbey (J.P. Neale c.1810).

Newstead was a tacit acknowledgment of his Catholic faith is an interesting one, although it would still not explain why he was still content to destroy the rest of the church, and the most sacred east end in particular. Nonetheless, the remains of the church were deliberately incorporated into the design of the new house as a very visible reminder of its monastic origins, and a testament to where the source of Byron's fortune, as well as his obligations, lay.

Figure 6.9   19th-century view of Egglestone Abbey (T. Higham after J.M.W. Turner 1822).

Not all such partial courtyard conversions were as grand, and at times the retention of church fabric might have been for less symbolic reasons. A good example is Egglestone Abbey, County Durham, a site acquired by Robert Strelley in 1547. Strelley was from a minor Nottinghamshire gentry family, and while he prospered in the household of Princess Mary, he was hardly of the same status or had the same level wealth as Sharington or Byron.[53] Egglestone had been a poor foundation, with an income of only £36 3s 3d at the Dissolution, and its buildings were modest in size. Strelley's conversion of the site was equally modest, the north and east ranges of the cloister became the residential focus, while the west range was converted into a kitchen. There is no evidence that the church was in any way utilized, but it seems that the majority of its structure was left unroofed, until parts of the structure collapsed in the 19th century (Figure 6.9). The abandonment but preservation of the church at Egglestone might well have been due to financial constraints, since the initial development of Strelley's house did not require its demolition, and he died shortly after in 1554 without any children.[54] Unsurprisingly, the site ceased to be developed further and rapidly fell into a poor state of repair, occupied by several different tenants.

However, there may have been other reasons why Strelley was reluctant to damage the church any further than it had been following its initial despoliation by Cromwell's commissioners after its initial surrender. The church contained what Leland had described as "to very fair tumbes of gray marble."[55] The first belonged to Sir Thomas Rokeby (d. 1357) Sheriff of Yorkshire, but more significantly a noted soldier who in 1346 had fought with great ferocity and helped defeat the Scots at the Battle of Neville's Cross, just 25 miles away.[56] The second, more prominent, tomb belonged to Sir Ralph Bowes (d. 1512) (Figure 6.10), who had been High Sheriff of Durham between 1482–1502.[57] As many of the Bowes family had been over the centuries, his son Robert had also been prominent in the Anglo-Scottish hostilities in the 1540s, just at the time Strelley acquired Egglestone.[58] Consequently, although Egglestone was a relatively impoverished and unimportant monastery, it contained the tombs of two of the key families involved in the border wars with Scotland, and were highly regarded in the region.

Figure 6.10   Tomb of Sir Ralph Bowes (d. 1512), Egglestone Abbey (Author).

These would not be monuments to despoil lightly, and instead, Strelley appears to have left their tombs untouched and the church in which they lay unmolested, even if it meant compromising upon the look of his newly converted house.

Other considerations often affected the types of claustral conversion undertaken, and necessitated a more economical transformation. Whilst many of the peerage or nobility were able to purchase sites outright and were thus in a position to invest in them for the long term, those who were only able to acquire sites under a long-term lease had less incentive to do so. Such was the case at Cleeve Abbey, Somerset. Dissolved in 1537 it was almost immediately obtained on a 21-year lease by Anthony Busterd for the rent of £42 2s 8d, which was reserved for him despite the ownership of the site passing from the crown to Robert, Earl of Sussex, shortly afterwards.[59] Little is known of Busterd's background or circumstances. In 1536 he was described as "gentleman" and in possession of lands in Oxfordshire,[60] and seems to have held some connection to the Court of Augmentations; in April 1537 he was cited as reporting to Lord Audley a conversation between Cromwell and Lord Darcy, one of the chief rebels during the Pilgrimage of Grace.[61] However, he seems not to have played any more prominent role at a national or even local level, and despite his aspirations to own monastic property, did not have the resources to purchase it outright.

Consequently, Busterd's conversion of Cleeve, while effective in providing him with a country residence, was undertaken as economically as possible (Figure 6.11). The church, except for the south nave wall which enclosed the newly created domestic court, appears to have been quite rapidly demolished, although whether this was for the immediate benefit of the tenant or new owner of the site, the Earl of Sussex, is unclear. At the same time the west range, apart from its east wall, and three sides of the claustral walk were removed, as was the reredorter, while the chapter house was shortened to bring its east end in line with the rest of the range. The rest of the conversion mainly utilized the remaining medieval buildings, with very little new building work. The refectory, which had been lavishly rebuilt by the monks in the later 15th century, became the new hall with no adaptations required, and the monastic kitchen was retained for its original purpose. The eastern range appears to have become the focus of the principal lodgings, and no substantial evidence for the conversion remains, suggesting any changes were superficial and lightweight in construction. A new fashionable gallery was created through the retention of the west range wall and the modification of the west cloister walk, but this required little expensive building beyond the insertion of a new chimney and the blocking off of specific passages.

Such economical conversions made by the tenants rather than the owners of such sites were probably more common than is currently appreciated. Given their conservative reuse of pre-existing structures and their potentially shorter period of occupation, evidence for this type of conversion is the least likely to survive. Whilst many new lessees might have hoped ultimately to purchase their properties and then redevelop them more ambitiously, many such as Busterd failed to do so. Cleeve's occupation as a mansion was relatively short-lived, passing first from Busterd to the Boteler family by the 17th century,[62] before shrinking to become a farmhouse.

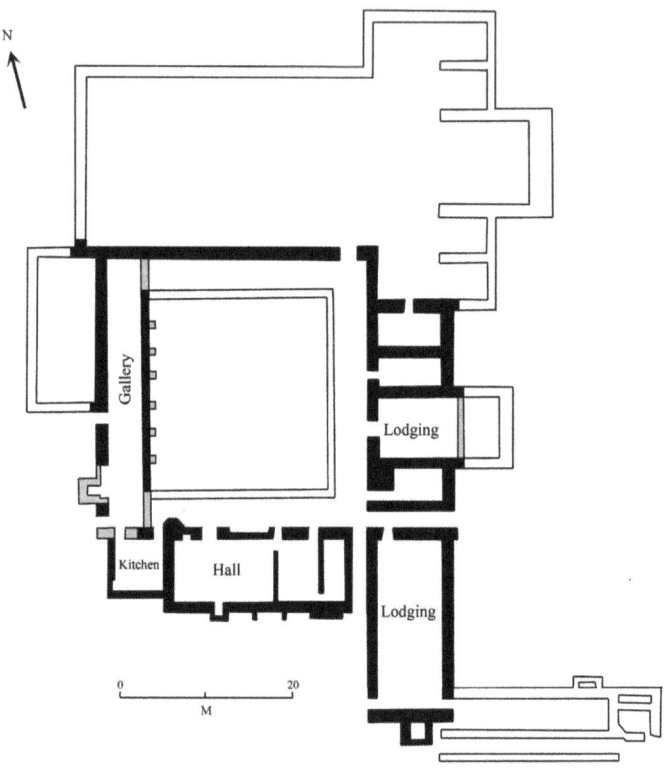

Figure 6.11 Plan of Cleeve Mansion (after Parker *et al.* 2007, 74; Gilyard-Beer 1960; Robinson 1998, 86).

Range conversions

Inevitably, it is larger scale, often more ambitious, conversions of former monastic sites that has attracted the most academic attention. Likewise, the concentration of scholars such as Howard upon the close architectural parallels between monastic cloister and Tudor courtyard house has tended to shift focus away from the many more sites that were developed in other less complete ways. Whilst Howard's suggestion that in the years following the Dissolution only around 30 monastic sites were transformed into courtyard-style houses,[63] with either three or four fully developed ranges, is probably an underestimation, many more saw the development of just one or two ranges. This did not create a classic courtyard house at all, but rather a residence focused on a single rectangular or L-shaped block.

Factors that drove the decisions of the new owners of how to develop which range or ranges varied from site to site, and of course some properties were divided between multiple owners preventing a total cloister conversion. Other factors including the level of finances available and the suitability of the surviving medieval fabric probably all affected the choices made.

However, the one element of the claustral complex that was very rarely incorporated into the subsequent residence, as a residential building at least, was the church itself. Despite Howard's assertion that renovation of the church alone as a residence was a phenomenon of the later 16th century,[64] seemingly based solely on the example of Buckland Abbey (discussed below), conversion of just the church on its own at any point during the 16th century was extremely rare indeed. There were undoubtedly some practical reasons for this, as the church was probably the building already suffering the most decay following its initial despoliation by the Cromwell's commissioners, unroofed and stripped of most of its fittings. However, the church also presented far greater logistical problems compared with the rest of the cloister for those seeking a cost-effective conversion. Not only was it an often a vast open space that required careful and clever division, it contained none of the pre-existing domestic elements such as fireplaces, stairs, or facilities such as kitchens for a swift conversion. Consequently, the church only presented a viable option for those with a breadth of vision and resources to convert it, such as Paulet at Netley Abbey, or those for whom it represented the only viable element of the site still surviving.

It is possible that some might have felt uncomfortable focusing their residences on the former church, and instead preferred to remove the reminder of an ecclesiastical past. Certainly, the use of the church as a house was sufficient in some cases to merit comment by a contemporary audience. Calwick Priory, Staffordshire, was granted to the Fleetwood family in 1543,[65] who immediately converted it into a residence. In the late 16th century, the antiquarian Sampson Erdeswicke (d. 1603) observed in slightly astonished tones "I have heard (*John Fleetwood*) hath made a parlour of the chancel, a hall of the church, and a kitchen of the steeple."[66] Whether such a conversion had actually been undertaken as described, the placing of the kitchen in the steeple seems particularly unlikely, it was seen as sufficiently unusual to merit mention.

Archaeological corroboration for the sole conversion of the monastic church into a residence is hard to find. One possible site where this might have occurred around the middle of the 16th century is at Canons Ashby, Northamptonshire. The priory was granted to Sir John Cope who built a house that was completed shortly before his death in 1558.[67] The precise location of Cope's house is not known. The western portion of the nave was converted to use as the parish church, and excavations in 1970 in the claustral ranges to the south produced no evidence for their reuse until the 17th century, although they were the focus of the dumping of waste during the middle of the 16th century.[68] Given this, it seems possible that Cope's house lay in the area of the east end of the church, now occupied by the parish churchyard, although the evidence for this is far from conclusive.

Indeed, one of the few definite examples for where the church was the sole focus for domestic reuse is Buckland Abbey, Devon, which was granted in 1541 to Sir Richard Grenville, of the substantial West Country gentry family.[69] However, the premature death of Sir Richard's son Roger on board the Mary Rose followed soon afterwards in 1545, and seems to have stalled any redevelopment of Buckland.[70] It appears that it was only after Richard's grandson, also called Richard (b. 1542), regained his estates in 1563, after they had been confiscated following a murderous student brawl, that conversion started in earnest.[71] Certainly, they seem to have been completed by 1576, when the dated plasterwork was added to the hall. The reason why this conversion focused on the church rather than the cloisters, as would usually be expected, is far from clear. Perhaps the delay of over two decades before the rebuilding started had resulted in significant deterioration of the claustral ranges, while the intervening years since the Dissolution had probably eroded any sense of ill-ease in repurposing the former sacred space. The conversion was a relatively simple one,[72] and given the original monastic church was modest in size, probably not particularly taxing or expensive (Figure 6.12). The nave of the church was retained, although its arcades were removed, as was the crossing and the choir. The north transept was completely removed, and crossing blocked, with a new entrance porch being added. The south transept was also removed with the exception of its southern wall

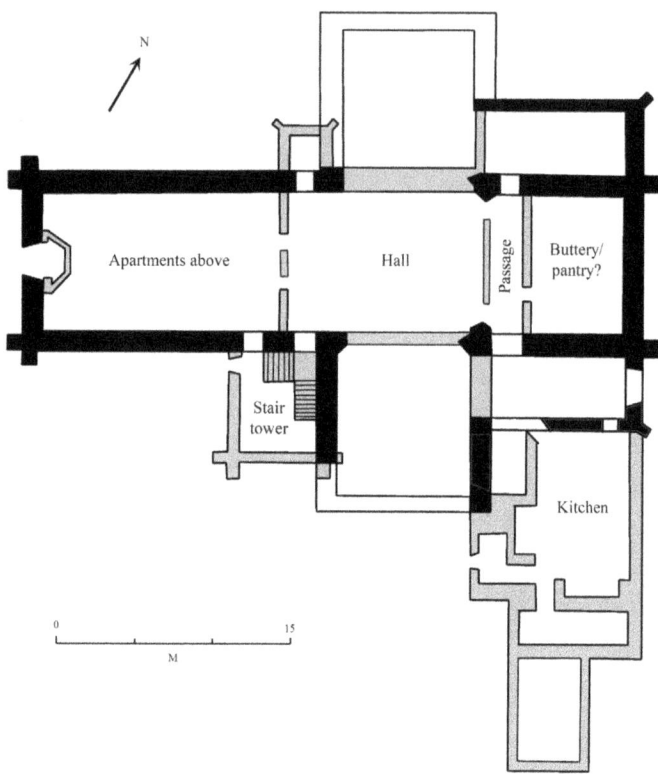

Figure 6.12   Plan of Buckland Abbey (after Cherry and Pevsner 1989, 288).

which was in part retained to form part of a new external stair tower. The side chapels flanking the choir were also removed, perhaps because they were not substantial enough, since the northern one was rebuilt on its original footings to create a separate room, whilst the southern was built over by a new kitchen and service range that extended to the south. The east wall of the original choir was partially rebuilt, probably to remove a large eastern window that did not fit within the revised scheme. As the conversion was occupied until the 20th century, with so many small internal alterations being made, most of the functions of the modified Tudor spaces are not known. The exception is the former crossing, which, with its grand fireplace and plasterwork, was repurposed as the hall. Gaskell Brown suggests that, to the east, beyond a newly created screens passage, the former choir was retained as a chapel, the function it performs in the house today.[73] However, sited as this is between the kitchen range and the hall, this seems unlikely, and Copeland states that this use as a chapel only started in the early 20th century, and before this it functioned as a servants hall.[74]

Although the church could be adapted as the principal residence, by far the most common element of the site to form the focus of a Tudor conversion was the west range, as this section of the cloister was the easiest to convert.[75] Although variations existed between the different monastic orders, and even between houses within the same order, the west range often combined several common features that made them particularly conducive to conversion. On most sites, the west range comprised an open vaulted undercroft, which may have been simply divided but was free from the specialized spaces such as the chapter house found in the east range. At first floor level, they were also economical to convert; in many houses of different orders, the west range was the location of the prior or abbot's residence, providing a space already created for domestic use.

As a result, a wide range of sites demonstrate some evidence for the post-Dissolution reuse of the west range, although the full extent of this adaption is often unclear due to subsequent development or decay. The conversions focusing on the west ranges of former Cistercian houses are sometimes the most obvious, as the insertion of chimneys and stairs into what had been the lay brethren's quarters is particularly conspicuous. The form that these conversions took could vary quite considerably. At Rufford Abbey, for instance, the domestic transformation seems fairly modest in scale despite the high status of its new owner; the site was granted to George Talbot, 4th Earl of Shrewsbury, in 1538, but almost immediately afterward he died.[76] Little seems to have happened to the site for over two decades until it came into the possession of the 6th Earl, who converted the west range into a residence, with an imposing new entrance in the outer wall of the western range leading to a first floor hall, but otherwise little else of the monastic complex appears to have been used and was demolished at this time.

Modest conversions undertaken by local gentry can be seen at several other Cistercian sites. Typical is Croxden, which was granted to Godfrey Foljambe in 1545.[77] Here the house which survived largely intact until the early 18th century seems to have been centred on the southern portion of the west range,[78] and although the rest of the monastic complex was not actively used, the church was left as a prominent ruin. In other conversions of sites, additional elements of the Cistercian complex were incorporated. At Sawley Abbey, acquired by Sir Arthur Darcy, the west range had already undergone significant remodelling in the late 14th and 15th centuries and the medieval kitchen was incorporated into a west range conversion, continuing to fulfil its original purpose.[79] Likewise, at Boxley Abbey, Kent, a conversion dating to the 1540s by Sir Thomas Wyatt reused the west range and the medieval kitchen, whilst the church was levelled to create a terraced water garden over the nave (see Chapter 7).[80]

Conversions that focused on the west range could also make good use of other portions of the cloister, and the refectory range in particular. An example of this is the Vale Royal Abbey, another Cistercian house located in Cheshire. Vale Royal was granted to Sir Thomas Holcroft, the youngest son from a minor gentry family in neighbouring Lancashire. Holcroft was another of the men who used his position at court to significantly advance his status, first in service to Cromwell and then the king himself becoming a capable and trusted diplomat and solider.[81] He benefitted considerably from the purchase of monastic land, making Vale Royal his seat. Unlike some of his contemporaries, whose fortunes were also made at this time, Holcroft did not create a traditional courtyard style house, rather choosing a design centred on a principal range with wings projecting to the west and east.

The main focus of the house was the west range, which also incorporated the former west cloister walk, and became the location for the hall (Figure 6.13). Entry was through a newly constructed stair and entrance porch in its west face, leading into a screens passage, and the southern portion of the range was converted to a pantry or buttery and kitchen. The principal lodgings of the new house were located in the half-timbered south range, which was refurbished with new windows inserted into the pre-existing frame.[82] Holcroft embellished his new house with panels of armorial stained glass, some of which survive in the Burrell Collection, a visual expression of his new social status.[83] In addition to the conversion of the monastic fabric, further additions were made. The most significant of these were two wings projecting from the west range, forming additional sets of private apartments. Much altered in subsequent centuries, the dating of these is slightly uncertain; they appear in a sketch view from 1616 and McNeil and Turner argue they formed part of the original redevelopment of the house by Holcroft, a likely suggestion that would have provided a residence of sufficient size and status for his new rank.[84]

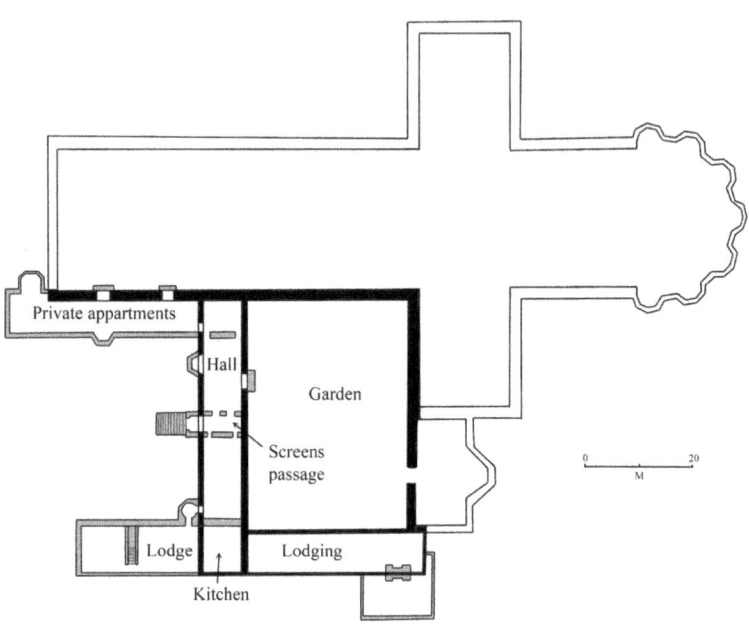

Figure 6.13   Plan of Vale Royal Abbey (after McNeil and Turner 1990).

It is not just at former Cistercian houses that substantial developments focusing on the west range can be seen, with the same often being the case in other orders. Perhaps the example examined most thoroughly in recent years is at Augustinian Norton Priory, also in Cheshire. Whilst little of the medieval or Tudor masonry remains upstanding due to the later construction of a Georgian mansion, the demolition and clearance of much of the site in the 20th century allowed for a thorough investigation of the monastery and its subsequent redevelopment.[85] Dissolved in 1536, the house was granted to Sir Richard Brooke soon after. Brooke was of relatively low birth but had risen to prominence as a successful soldier, being created a Knight of Malta in 1531 and following the Dissolution he was appointed Vice-Admiral of England.[86] Although he found favour at court, his positions would not have been as financially lucrative as those who prospered in the Court of Augmentations, for example, and it is clear that the family did not possess the wealth that Holcroft had accrued in the same county.

Brooke's conversion at Norton, while superficially not dissimilar to that done twelve miles away at Vale Royal, appears to have been undertaken under considerable financial constraints.[87] The church was apparently demolished rapidly after the Dissolution and the west range made the focus of the Tudor house. As at Vale Royal, this faced westwards and was given a new courtyard incorporating the medieval gatehouse, enclosed by a wall on all sides apart from the south, which was formed from a wing projecting from the west range. Overall the excavators concluded that the conversion was undertaken with little "substantive structural modification,"[88] and this is amply demonstrated in an engraving by the Buck Brothers from 1727 (Figure 6.14).

This view gives a clear impression of the degree to which the existing medieval fabric was adapted and incorporated in the conversion. To the north is the prominent 15th-century abbot's tower, seemingly retaining its former residential focus. Next to this in the southern portion of the west range lay the Tudor hall at first-floor level, now accessed by a new entrance stair, one of the few pieces of evidence for new building work. To the south of this, and separated by the medieval passage at ground level, was the monastic kitchen, which again was probably retained for its original purpose. The upper floor of the south-west range and the kitchen are of half-timbered construction in the print, and it is uncertain whether this is original medieval work or later rebuilding. Even if the latter, this is still fairly modest in scale and expense, and confirms the picture of an expedient conversion.

Two further, slightly puzzling, adaptations took place at Norton during the 16th century. First, excavation of the cloister revealed that, rather than becoming a rear garden for the house, as might be expected and is suggested for Vale Royal, it became an open midden, with kitchen and other household waste accumulating continuously throughout the 16th century.[89] The dumping of potentially unpleasant waste in such close proximity to the house is unexpected, even though the prevailing winds would ordinarily have carried any noxious smells away from the house. Second, it is clear from the Buck engraving and other documentary sources, that the Brooke family chose to save a 3.37m high statue of St Christopher, dating to the last quarter of the 14th century, which originally had been located in the monastic church.[90] This statue was prominently set against the west front of the new house. The reason for such public retention and display of an icon of the old religion by Brooke is not known, but perhaps the patron saint was held in some affection by a gentleman who had made his career in large part travelling across Europe.

Whilst Brooke had the means to convert the substantial Augustinian house at Norton Priory, albeit conservatively, many others who could not afford such grand renovations had to settle for a more modest undertaking. One way this might be achieved is through the acquisition and conversion of smaller and much poorer monastic houses, and nunneries in particular.

Figure 6.14   View of Norton Priory (S. and N. Buck 1727).

Not only were these available for purchase, or lease, at much-reduced rates due to their low incomes at the Dissolution, but being smaller properties, they could be converted much more manageably by those of modest means. Indeed, although it is hard to quantify accurately, it appears that small poor monastic houses were much more likely than their larger counterparts to be converted to domestic use immediately after the Dissolution.

Figure 6.15 Late 17th-century sketch of Kington Priory by John Aubrey (© Wiltshire Archaeological and Natural History Society).

Two examples of nunnery conversions that exemplify how smaller yet still comfortable dwellings could be made from portions of their ranges can be seen at Kington Priory, Wiltshire, and Burnham Priory, Buckinghamshire. Kington was a poor Benedictine nunnery, recorded as having an income of just £35 15s in the *Valor Ecclesiasticus*,[91] and following its suppression, it was granted in 1537 to Sir Richard Long, from a minor gentry family based at Wraxall.[92] As was usually the case with a larger male house, the church was soon demolished; certainly writing in the 17th century Aubrey describes its site as being a garden.[93] Aubrey also made a sketch of the west range of the nunnery, the focus of the conversion, where he reconstructs the missing church, but also shows that very little change had been made to the medieval fabric, at least externally (Figure 6.15). The conversion itself was also cost-effective and straightforward and survives mostly unaltered today (Figure 6.16). As well as the demolition of the church, the east range was removed, probably along with the cloister walk, if this indeed had existed in any other form but timber. The west range was retained as a small hall and buttery, accessed from a pre-existing entrance, when it had originally functioned as a possible priest's lodging, and the

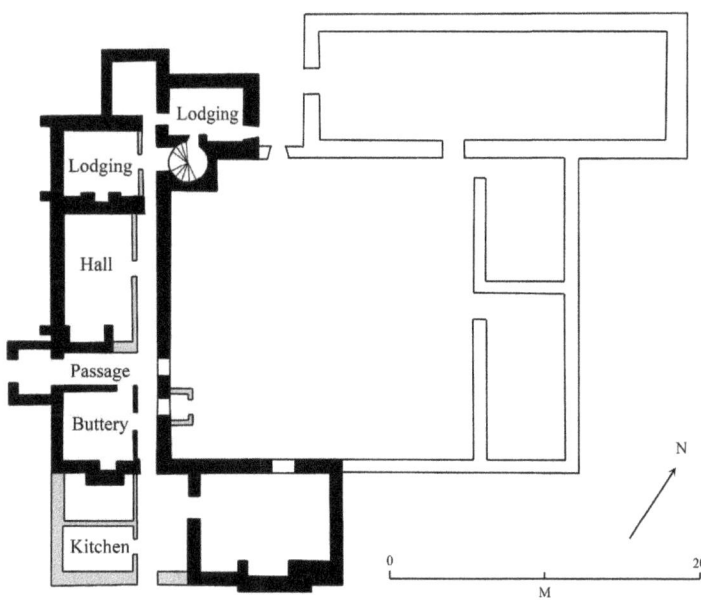

Figure 6.16 Plan of Kington Priory (after Brakspear 1923).

former prioress' apartments in the north of the range were reused for residential use. The former nuns' refectory was also retained, although for what purpose it was put to in the 16th century is uncertain. As a result, little modification or building work was required, except for some internal divisions in the west range and the construction of a kitchen to the south, which possibly replaced a pre-existing medieval one, built in timber.

Burnham Priory in Buckinghamshire, a house of Augustinian nuns, underwent a similar if slightly more complex conversion. It was a little larger and more developed house than Kington, and in 1535 had an income of £50 2s 4d.[94] It was leased for 21 years (between 1539–1561) to William Tyldesley, a gentleman about which little is known.[95] During his tenure, he undertook a thorough conversion of the site, but one that required little substantial rebuilding on his part (Figure 6.17). As might be expected, the church was demolished, as was the western range. The principal foci of the conversion in this instance were the north refectory range, which was embellished with a new entrance, and the eastern range which became the lodgings of the house. Interestingly the conversion also included the former reredorter and infirmary, although to what new purposes these were put is unknown. Unlike Kington, which remained a residence until the present day, Burnham fell in status during the 17th century, being converted to barns and agricultural purpose, so that many of the details of its initial conversion are now lost. Nonetheless, it still demonstrates how a smaller nunnery provided a good opportunity for an individual like Tyldesley to create a comfortable dwelling on a site he could only afford to lease.

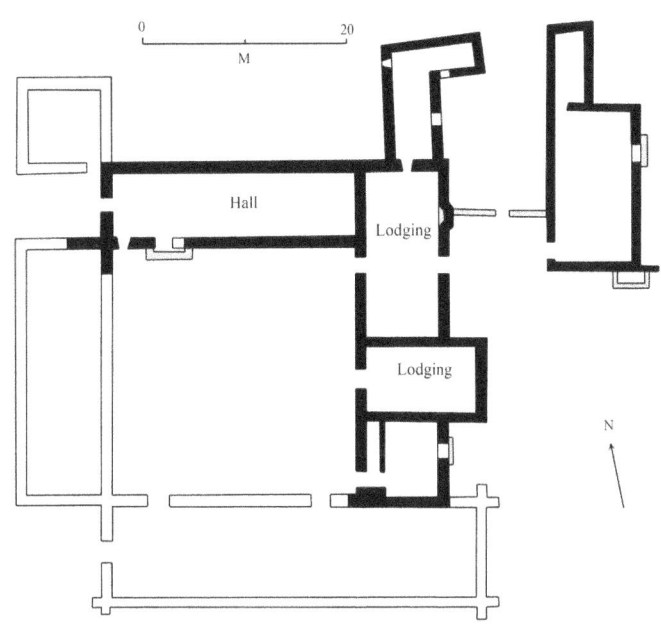

Figure 6.17 Plan of Burnham Priory (after Brakspear 1903).

Agricultural conversions

Former monastic cloisters provided new owners with a variety of possible opportunities, from full courtyard conversion to just the adaptation of a single range as a dwelling. However, other repurposings were not only domestic in nature, and several sites were transformed not into grand private residences but farms. This was particularly the case when the grant of the monastic buildings also came with elements of the original estates, thus providing a ready-made economic unit. Whilst farms also contained residential components, and thus there is a degree of crossover with what might be classed purely as a house conversion, a feature of an agricultural conversion was that principal elements of the claustral complex were also turned into barns and other agricultural buildings. Such neat distinctions between purely domestic and agricultural conversion are not always easily made, especially as the upstanding architectural evidence is now lacking. Indeed, a single site might have been adapted to both purposes at different stages of its life. Nonetheless, owners and lessees of monastic property were faced with a slightly different set of alternatives and challenges if they sought to convert their new holdings into profitable agricultural use.

Farm conversions were usually much more diverse, and it is hard to see any consistent pattern as to how they were undertaken. Perhaps the most important factors were the buildings available and what had already taken place on the site, and an example such as Cleeve Abbey illustrates the point well. As previously outlined, Cleeve was first developed into a gentry house, which resulted in the demolition of the church and conversion of the three remaining claustral ranges, but by the start of the 17th century it had passed to the Stewkeley family who converted it into a farm.[96] Because of its size, the former frater in the south range, which had initially been converted into the hall of the mansion, reverted to being a barn. The same was the case for the narrow west range, while the former east range which had also formed part of the Tudor house, but was inconveniently subdivided, was now surplus to requirements and left to become roofless (Figure 6.18). With the rest of the complex being unsuited to, or unavailable for domestic occupation, a new simple farmhouse was constructed attached to the south-west corner of the former cloister.

The conversion of Cleeve into a farm took place over half a century after the Dissolution, and while this is perhaps a particularly late example, relatively few agricultural conversions appear to have been undertaken immediately following the Dissolution. Instead, several decades had usually elapsed after the closure of the monastery, during which time perhaps the buildings had decayed too much to make them an attractive prospect for more high-status conversion

Such was the case at Sandwell Priory, Staffordshire, a poor Benedictine house which was closed in 1525 under Cardinal Wolsey's "Little Dissolution."[97] Following its suppression, the site remained undeveloped until it was acquired by Robert Whorwood in 1569.[98] At this point what remained of the decayed church was demolished, and a farmhouse and associated buildings were created out of the ruins of the east range, which was

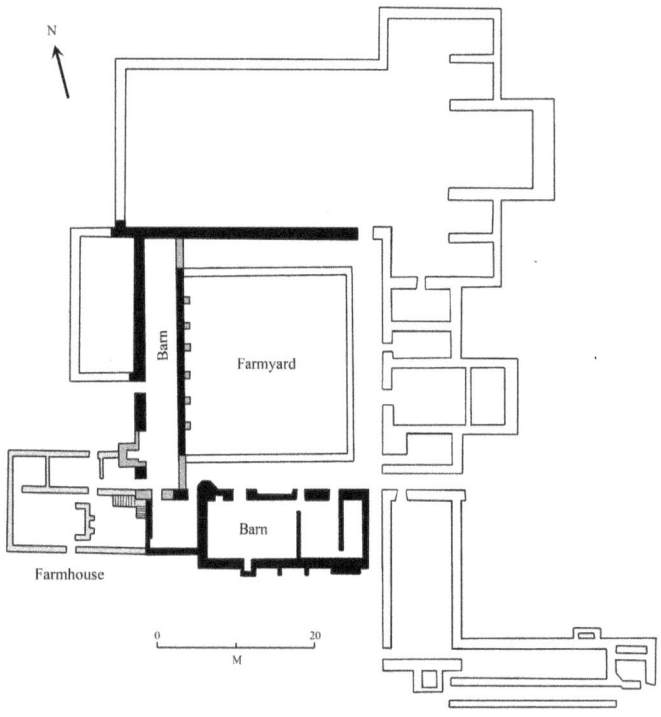

Figure 6.18   Plan of Cleeve Farm (after Parker et al. 2007).

divided into compartments for the purpose. A similar sequence of events can be seen at Bradwell Abbey, Buckinghamshire, where a period of perhaps four decades elapsed before the site was converted, with a farmhouse being fashioned out of the ruins of the former prior's hall and with other elements of the cloister buildings being put to agricultural use.[99]

Perhaps one of the most extensive and complex agricultural conversions is found at Denny Abbey, Cambridgeshire, and this was in part a result of the site's unusual development as a monastic house. Initially founded as a Benedictine priory in 1159, after just a decade it was transferred to the Knights Templar who constructed a cruciform church with a small northern cloister. Following their expulsion from England the site was then granted to the Countess of Pembroke (d. 1377). She converted the western portion of the church into her private lodgings, and it seems that the original cloister was probably part of this domestic dwelling. The countess built a new church to the east, and a new claustral complex to the north, to be inhabited by the Poor Clares, a small female order. At the Dissolution the site was retained by the crown but leased, resulting in a complex farm conversion incorporating elements of the Templar and later buildings (Figure 6.19). The later nunnery church was demolished, but the former Templar church that had formed the basis of the Countess of Pembroke's lodgings was retained. This became the site of the farmhouse, with a new kitchen in the former south transept and a dairy in the northern one. Much of the original cloister was demolished and turned into a yard, but the original east range was kept as a barn and a new timber passage constructed leading up to the residence.[100] The later northern cloister became the main focus of agricultural activity, with the east and west ranges being demolished, but the frater to the north was converted into an imposing barn.[101]

Whilst many of those responsible for domestic conversions appeared reluctant to incorporate the monastic church into their designs, individuals creating farms appear to have been less unwilling to do so, perhaps because such agricultural conversions were generally later in date. Therefore, at Thetford Priory, while the choir of the church was demolished and left as a heap of rubble, the remaining nave was converted into a barn measuring 23m long and servicing

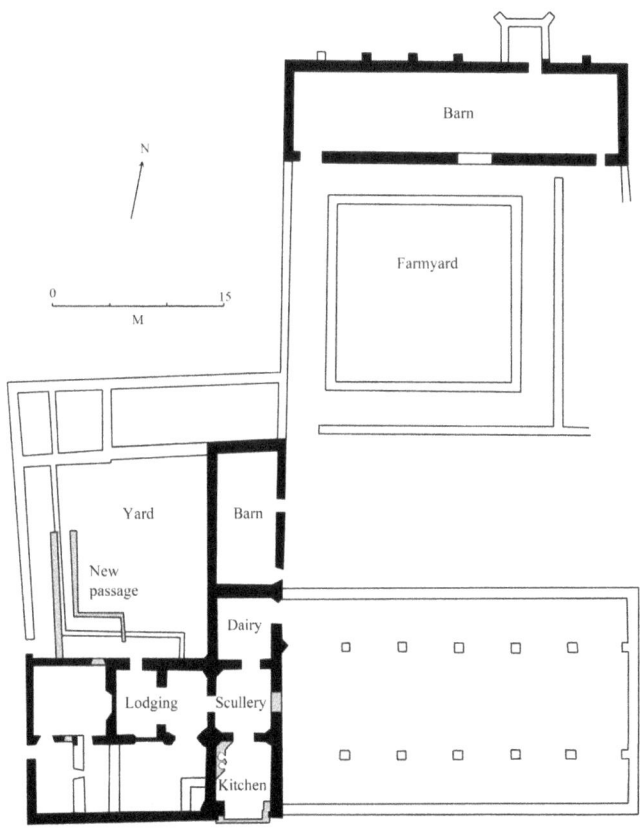

Figure 6.19 Plan of Denny Abbey (after Christie and Coad 1980; Poster and Sherlock 1987).

a newly built farmhouse that was situated in part of the former cloister.¹⁰² A more modest, but similar, conversion can be seen at the Cistercian nunnery at Pinley, Warwickshire, where the nave formed the focus of a barn conversion, and the former prioress' lodgings were converted into a farmhouse with few changes save the addition of several chimneys. However, at Pinley the motivations behind the conversion might not have been purely practical. A poor house at the Dissolution, it was granted to Sir William Wigston along with other monastic property in 1544.¹⁰³ Wigston was a wealthy man, the son of Roger Wigston (d. 1542), a wool merchant and lawyer from Coventry, and heir to his uncle who was also a prosperous merchant.¹⁰⁴ Clearly, Wigston did not need such a modest house as a dwelling, and his purchase of the site and its conversion to a farm might be seen purely as an economic decision. However, Wigston had existing connections with the nunnery, as he had been a steward of the house in the 1530s,¹⁰⁵ and a close relative, Margaret Wigston, was the house's last prioress. Although there is no surviving evidence for who dwelt at the site after its conversion, an intriguing possibility is that it might have been the former inmates. After the Dissolution, Margaret Wigston was granted a very small pension of £4 and the other three sisters nothing at all,¹⁰⁶ and the conversion of the nunnery into a farm, with the retention and improvement of the former prioress' lodgings, immediately after its closure might have been an attempt by Wigston to provide a more lasting income for the ex-religious who had formally been in his care, and may well have continued to live on the site.

Further forms of domestic conversion

Whilst the central cloister provided the obvious focus for a domestic conversion, with its well-developed ranges of buildings, almost always built in stone, other portions of the inner precinct could become the focus of later alteration for residential use. This was particularly the case for other buildings that were already designed explicitly for domestic purposes, especially if the whole of the site was not available to the new owner or lessee to convert. In particular, free-standing abbots' or prior's lodges could be cost-effectively transformed, as they were already in effect private houses. Perhaps the clearest example of this can be seen at Watton Priory, Yorkshire (Figure 6.20). This Gilbertine house was one of the last in the country to be dissolved, surrendering in December 1539. Immediately afterwards, its last prior and master of the order, Rob-

Figure 6.20   The medieval prior's lodge with Tudor additions, Watton Priory (Author).

The Conversion to Domestic Use

ert Holgate, began petitioning the Court of Augmentations for a grant of the site for life.[107] However, despite his insistence, the principal church and buildings of the nun's cloister were reserved for the King, and only part of the site, the canon's chapel, precinct, and the attached prior's lodge was grated to Holgate.[108] Even if Holgate might have been disappointed with the arrangement, it did result in him gaining what had been his former lodging as a permanent residence and as apparently little or no adaptations were made at this time, very little additional expenditure would have been incurred beyond the cost of the lease.

The abbot's lodge at Muchelney Abbey, Somerset, also provided an economical residence. Following the granting of the property to Edward Seymour, Earl of Hertford, it was leased to tenants rather than becoming the focus of a large residence.[109] At Muchelney the abbot's lodge and the south range to which it had been attached had already been rebuilt in lavish style during the 15th century, and thus would have provided a still comfortable and relatively fashionable residence with no further expense required on the part of the tenants. The same was also the case at Haughmond Abbey (discussed in detail in Chapter 7), and at Castle Acre Priory, Norfolk, where the prior's lodge had been largely rebuilt in the 14th century and then further renovated in the late 15th or early 16th century[110], continuing to provide a fully developed and comfortable house for its new owner, the Duke of Norfolk.[111]

The Duke of Norfolk was also to make use of another former prior's lodge, but this time at Thetford Priory (Figure 6.21). Granted to the Duke in 1540, unlike Castle Acre, Norfolk's motivation for the purchase appears not to have been the creation of a private residence.[112] The long narrow prior's lodge, already an old and plain building, was hardly altered at all at this time, the exception being the addition of a few internal partitions, and only towards the end of the 16th century were specific windows replaced in brick.[113] Instead, Norfolk's motivation for the purchase seems to be the fact that his father had been buried here shortly before the Dissolution, and after these remains had been translated to Framlingham he had little further interest in the site.[114] However, the retention of the prior's lodge as a modest residence, coupled with the fact that the monastic church went relatively unmolested at this time, suggests that Norfolk might have maintained an emotional connection with the site, which was

Figure 6.21   Converted prior's lodge at Thetford Priory (Author).

expressed through the keeping of a residence there, even if it was rarely, if ever, intended to be occupied by the Duke.

Although not as well appointed domestically, gatehouses could also be converted into free-standing residences, when they were not to be kept for their original purposes.[115] A typical example is Butley Priory, Suffolk. Although initially granted to the Duke of Norfolk, it soon passed to William Forthe of Hadleigh in 1544.[116] Prior to this, Forthe's estates appear to have been modest, but upon his death in 1559 they were worth £143 per annum.[117] The gatehouse at Butley, whilst by no means the largest in the country, was probably one of the most decorative. Dating to around 1320–1325, the frontage was dominated by a frieze of 70 heraldic panels, comprising the devices of European states, members of the English peerage and local gentry families.[118] To a man of Forthe's new pedigree, such associations to a chivalrous past may well have provided a strong attraction for the retention of this building over others in the claustral complex. Later decay and alterations prevent accurate reconstruction of the Tudor conversion. However, the medieval gatehouse seems to have seen little dramatic modification, though the 1738 view by the Buck brothers clearly shows a Tudor wing, perhaps containing the kitchens and other service elements, was added onto the eastern side.

Although largely demolished, excavation has shown a similar conversion took place at Leicester Abbey.[119] After the site was dissolved in 1538 there was extensive robbing and dismantling of buildings so that by the time it was acquired by Henry Hastings, 3rd Earl of Huntingdon, it was in a ruinous state. There the earl "built a fair house…out of the old materials,"[120] which was focused on the gatehouse as the most complete portion of the monastic complex. Although obscured by a later 17th-century mansion built by the Cavendish family, which in turn was destroyed during the Civil War, some elements of the first conversion can be reconstructed. The original gatehouse appears to have been a relatively simple structure, at ground floor level consisting of a central passageway flanked by single cells. Excavation revealed that following the Dissolution, a new wing was built to the northeast, with a large cellar below, and this was probably mirrored by a second wing on the north-western side. Between the two a new northern porch was added, providing a more contemporary entrance. The gatehouse by itself would have been far too small to have provided all the rooms required for the new mansion and was probably extended in various ways that have not survived. The exception was to the west, where a surviving portion of medieval precinct wall was incorporated in a new service building, which from the presence of two large fireplaces placed side-by-side can be identified as a kitchen.

A gatehouse might have been too small to act as the focus of a later house, but it could still be modified to perform some subsidiary domestic roles. The imposing 14th century gatehouse at Thornton Abbey never formed the core of a principal residence, and was retained and reused by a succession of secular owners as an entranceway. Yet peg holes on the interior walls show that during the 16th century the first-floor hall and other rooms were subdivided into smaller rooms and wood panelling installed, suggesting that at least occasional occupation was also intended by those who expected some level of fashionable comfort.

Even if too small to form the core of large mansions, gatehouses of smaller size made could still serve as modest dwellings; those at Montacute Priory, Somerset, and Pentney Priory, Norfolk, appear to have been turned into farmhouses. An alternative gatehouse conversion can be seen at Wetheral Priory, Cumbria. Dissolved in 1538, the monastery was granted to the Dean and Chapter of neighbouring Carlisle. The majority of the site was plundered for materials and left to decay, except for the gatehouse which was maintained as a new vicarage.[121] The original building was small in scale, consisting of a passage and side chamber at ground level and single rooms on both the first and second floors, requiring little adaptation other than the replacement of the roof, which dendrochronology has revealed took place at this time.[122] This made a convenient vicarage conversion for the Dean and Chapter of Carlisle, and one much cheaper to undertake than the renovation of any element of the claustral ranges. However, there might have been an added incentive to reuse the gatehouse, as architecturally it was not dissimilar in form to a fortified tower house. Thick walled and securely built, the first and second floors were only accessible by a single spiral stair and punctuated by small windows. Located just 12 miles from Scotland, Wetheral was in a position vulnerable to border raiding during the 16th century, and the relative defensiveness of the gatehouse might well have been seen as a considerable advantage when it was converted into the new vicarage.

New builds on old foundations

Many sites, whilst providing the land on which to build, contained buildings that were not deemed fit for conversion. Nevertheless, the former monastic buildings could still be of some use, not only as a source of building materials but also providing a firm footing on which new residences could be constructed. Such was the approach taken by Edward Fiennes, 1st Earl of Lincoln, at Sempringham Priory, which he acquired in 1539 and proceeded to convert into his principal residence in Lincolnshire. Early excavations in the 1930s revealed evidence for what was thought to be two separate post-Dissolution houses on the site.[123] However, a recent re-evaluation by Cope-Faulkner has suggested they were contemporaneous and formed part of a very substantial mansion consisting of three connected courtyards.[124] Although such a house could make little use of the rather ramshackle arrangement of the Gilbertine double house, there was a practical reason to reuse the location of the former monastic buildings. The ground upon which Sempringham was built was low lying, and the Marse Dyke which ran past the site was prone to flooding; in 1349 this had been so bad that the monastic church had been drowned under six feet of water,[125] and although subsequent drainage works had probably improved the situation a little, it was not the most promising land to build upon. Nonetheless, by placing the inner court of the new mansion over the former church and its west range over the canon's east range, the new house sought to benefit from the added stability and solid platform the medieval foundations provided. This was further enhanced by the deposition of a layer of sand over the areas where the house was to be built just prior to its construction, adding further height to the house platform and improving drainage.[126]

Such intentional reuse of earlier monastic footings to provide foundations for the Tudor mansions that replaced them was probably commonplace. However, because the new buildings tended to obliterate the medieval structures that they replaced, above ground at least, such deliberate reuse usually goes unnoticed. An exception is at Launde Abbey, Leicestershire.[127] The site of the Augustinian priory was granted to Thomas Cromwell who started the conversion of the site, which was completed by his son Gregory. In the case of Launde, it is known that the house was deliberately sited on the former eastern range of the monastery only because it incorporated a side chapel of the old monastic church as a private chapel in the new house, even though the remainder of the construction was built anew. Without this small inclusion of a portion of an earlier building the house would have appeared as if it was an entirely new build, and the significance of its placement on the foundations of the earlier monastery unrealized.

The one site where the reuse of monastic foundations in the footings of the later Tudor house has been best illustrated is at Sopwell Priory, Hertfordshire, purchased by Sir Richard Lee in 1539. Lee was a skilled building surveyor and soon rose in status through working on the home of Thomas Cromwell at Austin Friars, London before being appointed Surveyor of Works at Calais.[128] Given his profession, it seems likely Lee took a direct interest in the construction of his new house. Whilst this retained many of the elements of the pre-existing monastic plan in its arrangements, the former claustral buildings were demolished and just their footings used. The house built on top incorporated a considerable amount of reused monastic stone, yet it was ostensibly a brand-new building. Indeed, it appears the superstructure may have been timber-built.[129] This new mansion took the form of a typical courtyard house, with the new hall built over the location of the former church, and wings over the western and eastern ranges, so although invisible, the old monastery directly influenced its ground plan (Figure 6.22 top).

Following his work improving the fortifications at Berwick-upon-Tweed in 1564–1565, and being in his 60s, Lee appears to have reduced his work commitments and resided permanently at Sopwell.[130] However, his retirement was not a quiet one, as he immediately set about constructing a second brand new house. This necessitated the demolition of the former residence, but the new construction still reused many of its foundations, as well as the earlier medieval ones. The second house was built on a much more massive scale, a new hall constructed over the old and new wings

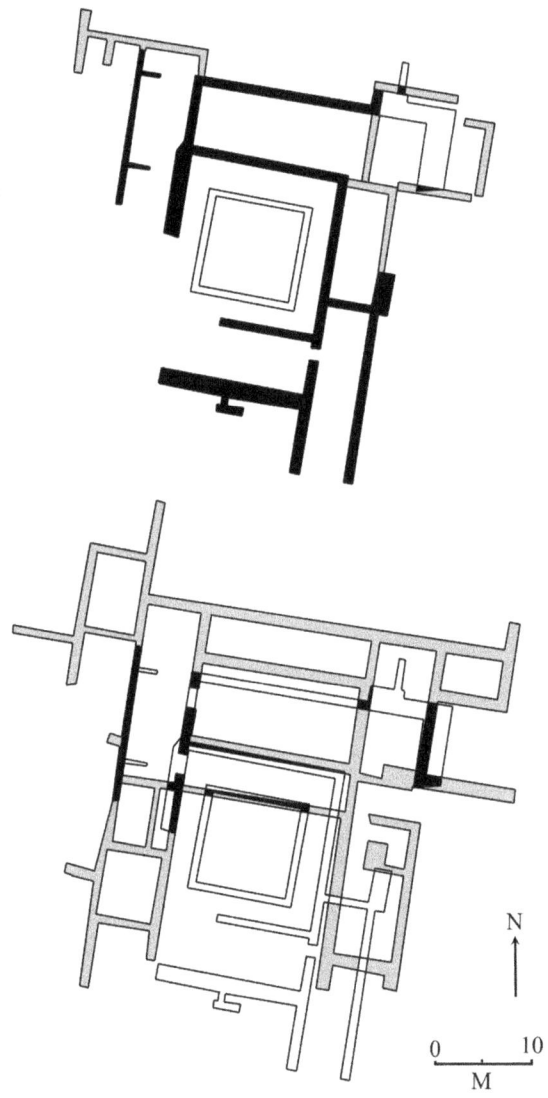

Figure 6.22 Post-suppression house plans at Sopwell Priory. Top: Lee House 1 over priory; Bottom: Lee house 2 over priory (after Johnson 2006).

projected both southward as before but also northwards, creating a more compact H-shaped building (Figure 6.22 bottom). It is tempting to see Lee as the ultimate "fiddler," a professional surveyor and architect unable to leave even his own house without radical alteration. However, Lee's constructions were symptomatic of their time; his first mansion fitted the fashions of the earlier Tudor courtyard house, which by the 1560s had become out-dated as architectural styles evolved towards more compact, taller buildings that would ultimately result in the so-called "Midland high house" of the late Elizabethan reign.[131] Under his ownership, Sopwell transformed as a house beyond recognition, not once but twice. However, to a man of Lee's professional experience, the importance of the earlier underlying foundations were always clearly of importance. Although carefully concealed, the old played a critical role in supporting the new.

Urban palaces

Thus far, the discussion presented here has almost entirely focused on rural monastic conversions, and yet, of course, 16th-century towns possessed a vast number of religious houses within them, or at least on their boundaries. Despite this, it seems that relatively few urban houses were converted into private domestic use in the decades following the Dissolution. The reasons for this are probably varied and certainly differed from town to town, and as has already been noted, urban monasteries could often be put to other civic uses as new parish churches, schools, almshouses or gaols. Furthermore, it is entirely possible that urban populations in the provinces had neither the appetite nor, more crucially, the resources for large-scale conversions; indeed in many regional towns former monastic property was left derelict for decades or even centuries after the religious had been ejected. There was, however, one exception to this: London.

In his study of the afterlife of London's monastic houses, Schofield has identified what he coins the "era of urban palaces," which ran from the Dissolution to approximately the 1570s.[132] This phase, he argues, saw the creation of large palatial houses by the elite, although these were often short-lived in their grandeur and subsequently fragmented into smaller properties. Why this phenomenon occurred in London is perhaps obvious. It was the only city in England of any real considerable size or wealth, and with London and its hinterland being the seat of government and court, many nobles and wealthy courtiers desired to maintain a fashionable townhouse here, to be close to the political heart of the country. The sudden availability of monastic land in the heart of the city provided an opportunity for some to create a new residence in the heart of the capital.

As in the countryside, conversions of urban monastic houses could be equally varied, and there was no template in how to create an urban "palace." The same factors such the availability of what the new owner could lease or purchase, along with their wealth, affected the domestic conversions seen in the capital. One problem that inevitably exists for the archaeologist is that most of these conversions, along with their earlier medieval fabric, have long since been swept away by fire and the remorseless redevelopment of centuries, so there is an even greater reliance on surviving documentary sources and opportunistic archaeological excavation to provide their reconstruction. Nonetheless, at several sites a good impression of what took place immediately after the Dissolution can be gained.

Some of these new urban palaces could be both grand in scope, and ambitious in design, although in the case of the conversion of Holy Trinity, Aldgate, this was still constrained by the original medieval fabric. The site was initially acquired by Thomas Audley, but following his death in 1544, it passed to Thomas Howard, later 4th Duke of Norfolk. Recent archaeological excavation, combined with plans drafted by John Symonds around 1592, has allowed for the reconstruction of the conversion undertaken by the Duke of Norfolk after he acquired the site.[133] In this case, it was the monastic church that formed the core of the conversion. The nave was unroofed and became an open area, but perhaps unusually so was the main body of the presbytery. However, the crossing and side aisles were converted into a new domestic block, referred to as the "Ivy Chamber," and the sanctuary and side chapels were also retained in domestic use. The result was to create a rather curious courtyard structure, with an open area over what had been part of the choir but still surrounded by the new residence. Other elements of the cloister and precinct appear to have been retained for domestic use, but probably these were more for service functions, whilst still other elements of the original precinct were developed into small tenements to be leased out.

Given the demand for former monastic land in the capital, elements of the former monastic precincts could be granted to several different individuals and identifying who precisely obtained what is often difficult to disentangle. One excellent case study where this has been done is by Holder at the site of the Austin Friars.[134] As was the case with a number of mendicant houses who needed the additional funds, this precinct had in fact been the focus of secular domestic occupation for at least two decades before the Dissolution. For some time, Thomas Cromwell had leased land there fronting onto Throgmorton Street, which he ultimately purchased in 1534, and where he started to construct a grand urban palace that would, by the time of his death in 1540, consist of three connected courtyards. Cromwell's house was a new build, not incorporating any monastic fabric, and passed to the Drapers' company shortly after his fall from grace.

However, other secular owners did not necessarily have the wealth or the opportunity to create such a grand mansion from scratch. Following the suppression of the Austin Friars, elements of the precinct were sold to a variety of owners including

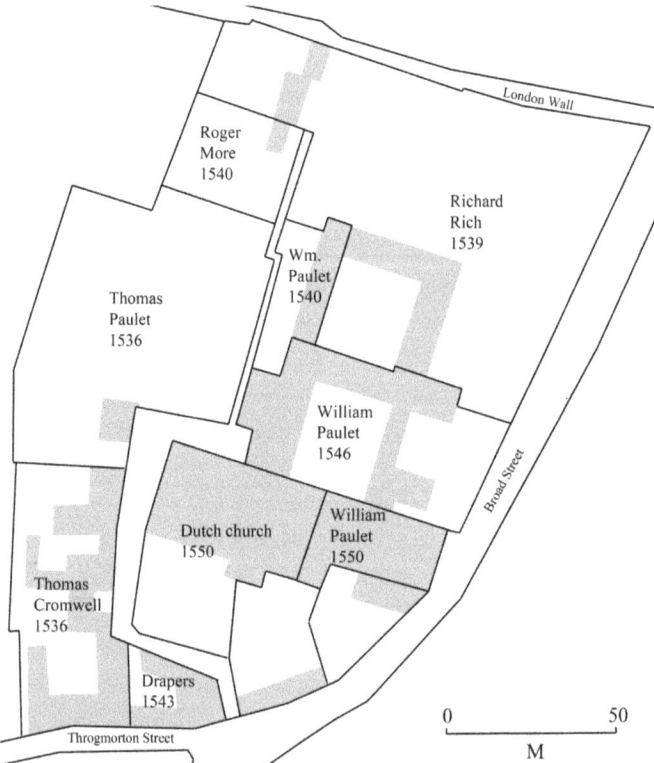

Figure 6.23   The division of the former precinct of the Austin Friars, London (after Holder 2011).

the courtier Richard Rich and other lesser figures such as Roger More. However, Holder has shown it was the Paulet family who secured the majority of the site, albeit over time and in a piecemeal fashion (Figure 6.23). The first was Thomas Paulet, perhaps acting on behalf of his elder brother William who acquired a parcel of mostly open land in 1536, followed by William who gained the northern cloister. Agents acting for William Paulet then acquired the southern cloister in 1546, with Paulet himself purchasing the presbytery of the former monastic church in 1550, but as we have already seen this was conditional on him establishing the Dutch church in the nave (see Chapter 5).

Figure 6.24　View of Winchester House, London (J. Smith 1800).

Holder has reconstructed the broad layout of Paulet's conversion, known as Winchester House, which seemed to focus on the north range of the southern cloister, with two rebuilt wings on the east and west ranges of the northern cloister forming a new courtyard fronting onto what is now Great Winchester Street.[135] A view by John Smith in 1800 from this road, apparently looking south to the north face of the converted medieval range, shows this to be an imposing structure (Figure 6.24), although there is little visible evidence for medieval fabric, and the whole house was entirely demolished *circa* 1839.

Those seeking to develop new urban palaces were not always so constrained in either the portions of the former precincts they could acquire or the need to reuse existing medieval fabric. The London Charterhouse was sold en masse in 1545 to Edward North, Chancellor of the Court of Augmentations, before passing on to Thomas Howard, 4th Duke of Norfolk, in 1565, who presumably wanted a less constrained property than his earlier converted house at Holy Trinity, Aldgate. Both families appear to have contributed to the conversion of the monastic house into an urban mansion, and while this was almost entirely a new build, just as with Sir Richard Lee's conversions at Sopwell Priory, the layout and foundation of the monastic house still affected the final design of the secular one.[136] A further factor influencing the Tudor layout was the fact the Carthusian cloister consisted of a radically different design to the usual monastic norm, being far larger and surrounded with individual cells for the monks, and the remaining buildings such as the church clustering to the south in a diminished form (Figure 6.25). This resulted in a cloister that was ill-suited to standard conversion, the individual cells were demolished and a garden formed using the 14th-century cloister wall as its boundary, with the new mansion built upon the medieval foundations of the frater and one of the adjoining cells. The only substantial medieval buildings that were retained in use were the church tower and the

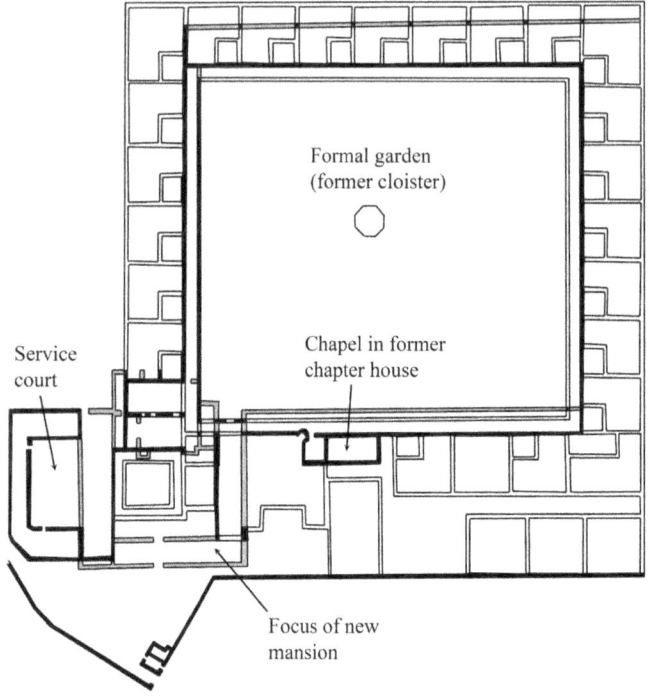

Figure 6.25   Plan of the London Charterhouse (after Barber and Thomas 2002).

chapter house which seem to have continued in use as a chapel, although the church proper was demolished, and the wash-house or service court which was retained for its original purpose. As a result, although the North/Howard palace would have appeared an entirely new and lavish construction to its contemporary audience, it was still fundamentally shaped by the charterhouse that had preceded it.

Despite Schofield's observation that many of these early London conversions were palatial in scale and ambition, not all urban houses in the capital were subject to such lavish domestic redevelopment. What might have been more typical were new owners having to recoup the cost of their purchases through maximising the return that their new property could make; in several instances, in addition to the owner's own house, it was necessary to create several dwellings that could be leased out. It has already been observed that the Duke of Norfolk's conversion of Holy Trinity, Aldgate, seemed to contain several additional tenements around the edges of the precinct, but at St Mary Spital this subdivision was more explicit following its acquisition by the courtier Stephen Vaughn.[137] Vaughn himself seems to have occupied rather modest apartments on the eastern, and possibly the northern, claustral range (Figure 6.26). However, a more substantial house focused on an open courtyard, the west range of the cloister containing the former prior's lodge, the north aisle of the church and a western range founded on the footings of the north wing of the infirmary building, was let by Vaughn to Edmund Issak. A further substantial property was built to the south of the presbytery and this was leased to Sir Edmund Huddlestone, while various other elements of the precinct were divided up into smaller tenements. In so doing, Vaughn was able to finance his rather ambitious acquisition, resulting in good long-term investment, but still a relatively simple personal dwelling.

Other London houses saw more modest conversions. At St Mary Graces, East Smithfield, the new owner, Sir Arthur Darcy, focused on converting the abbot's lodge in the western range of the cloister, and the church and remaining claustral ranges were almost totally destroyed at this time.[138] In 1544, the leather seller Thomas Kendall was able to acquire just the east range of the cloister at St Helens, Bishopgate, and from this his family and heirs created a relatively small but well-appointed house over many decades, presumably as and when they had the funds. In 1567 the upper part of the chapter house was rebuilt as a parlour, and as late as 1610 the first-floor dormitory was still being transformed into a hall.

Such limited urban conversions were probably much more common in the so-called "era of urban palaces" than is usually appreciated, but being small in scale they are less likely to have been well documented and are archaeologically much harder to identify. However, Schofield's observation that from the 1560s onwards there was a breaking of these large urban properties is certainly correct,[139] but in truth, they probably were always rather more fragmented than is currently appreciated. Whatever the case may be, by the time the 3rd Baron Rich came into the possession of St Bartholomew's Priory in 1581 he was content to redevelop much of the site into three new streets of small tenements described as "at least respectable."[140] By the end of the 16th century, the incentive for conversion had developed from the desire to create grand courtier dwellings to the maximization of the profit that the former precincts could provide, through the supply of tenements and cheap housing for rent.

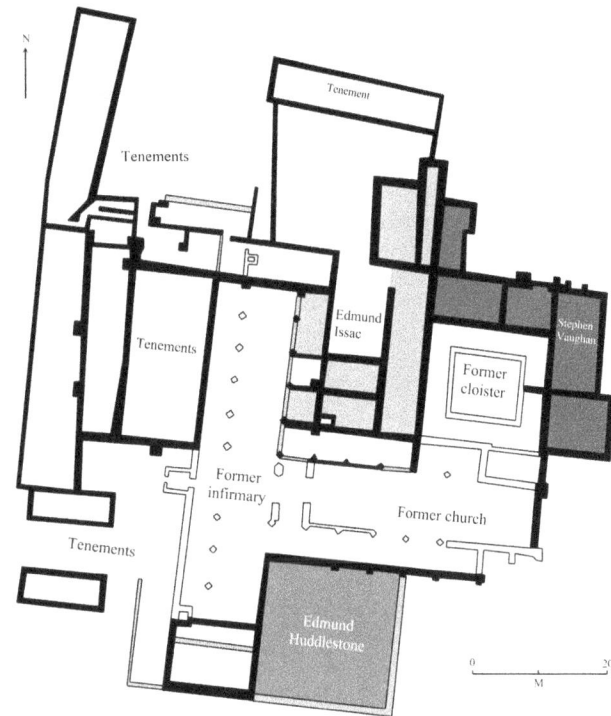

Figure 6.26   The division of St Mary Spital, London (after Sloane and Philpotts 1987).

― 7 ―

NEW LANDSCAPES OF LEISURE

To date, most studies of the physical effects that the Dissolution had upon the monasteries have focused upon the destruction and transformation of the church and claustral ranges. After all, these formed the core of the institution and changes and alterations to these elements have been the easiest to observe, date, and phase. Furthermore, this bias towards the focus on the post-Dissolution conversion of buildings is understandable, given that is has been architectural and, to a lesser extent, art historical, studies that have been in the vanguard of academic attention in this area. However, the monastery was a much more extensive complex, and the former religious precincts were full of open spaces, enclosures, subsidiary buildings, and watercourses, all of which could be repurposed to secular ends. Over the last two decades, it has become increasingly apparent that the post-suppression developments that took place on many sites not only included the establishment of secular houses and mansions, but also the creation of landscaped parks and gardens to surrounded them.

Medieval gardens

It is important to remember that, even before the Dissolution that swept away many of the pre-existing monastic features, medieval precincts were not only occupied by religious buildings and structures that were required to support the community, they were also verdant and at times lush landscapes. It has long been appreciated that, unlike the current sterile clipped-lawn image perpetuated by English Heritage or CADW, medieval monasteries abounded with groves and gardens. The very core of the monastery, the cloister, was a green open space and may well have been cultivated, while other open areas within the precinct would have been planted in various ways. Many of these may well have been functional, kitchen and physic gardens provided much-needed sources of food and medicine alike, while within larger monastic precincts orchards and even vineyards would have been a common sight.[1] Such gardens might not necessarily have always been purely functional; Coppack cites the example of Brother Thomas Suthewell who was admonished by the abbey's sacrist for planting a garden in the cloister garth at Bardney Abbey in 1444.[2] Not all church authorities necessarily disapproved of the provision of leisured spaces, especially if they were in more appropriate locations than the cloister. The post-suppression survey of Rievaulx Abbey identifies an open space adjacent to the abbot's house called the "Abbottes garden,"[3] this presumably being a pleasure garden provided for the enjoyment of the head of the monastic house and any guests that might lodge with him.

Indeed, for certain orders, such as the Carthusians, gardens were central to monastic life, and careful excavation of several cells at Mount Grace Priory revealed evidence for borders, planting pits, and pathways.[4] Gardens were not just a feature in rural houses; those located in towns could also have planted areas. Perhaps one of the best examples is at the Augustinian friary in Hull, where excavations revealed a rectangular garden laid out in formal fashion with four bays, each defined by clearly visible, manured, planting trenches that had been dug into the clay below (Figure 7.1).

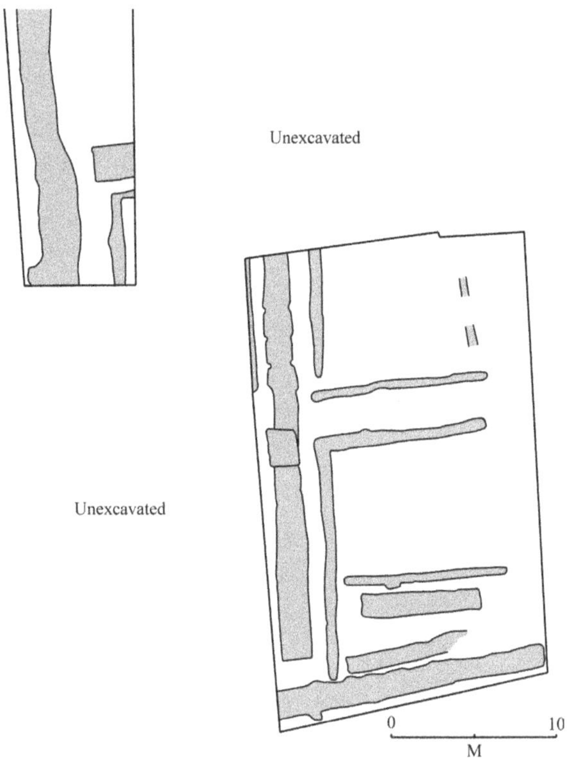

Figure 7.1 Monastic garden at the Austin Friars, Hull (after Coppack 1990).

Landscapes of conversion

Given that most monastic precincts would have contained such functional and ornamental gardens, it should be of no surprise that later occupiers of these spaces would also continue to cultivate the land for domestic and leisure purposes. Indeed, just as the fabric of monastic buildings were ideally suited for conversion to secular use, so too was the wider landscape of the precinct in which these structures lay. Furthermore, it has become increasingly apparent over the last few decades that, where they have survived modern development or ploughing, the majority of earthwork features within many monastic precincts in fact related to the post-Dissolution occupation of the site rather than its monastic phase of use.[5]

Despite this, there is a comparative lack of studies focusing on the wider monastic precinct in the post-suppression era when compared with those examining the conversion to, and creation of, secular houses. This is in part due to the attention traditionally paid by archaeologists to the cloistral ranges or other areas of identifiable buildings. Furthermore, where fabric is still standing on sites, this enables a relatively straight forward and quick architectural analysis. Conversely, by their very nature landscape and garden features are much more ephemeral and usually consist of rather unassuming "humps and bumps," difficult to read and even more impossible to interpret meaningfully. As a result, it is only through much more time consuming and meticulous survey, and importantly one that is backed up with some form of "ground truthing" through excavation, that an understanding of the scope and extent of the creation of new landscapes of leisure in the post-Dissolution period can be appreciated.

One of the challenges to be faced by those trying to understand the post-Dissolution development of the precinct is the prevailing narratives that are already well-established at many sites. Often this is the desire to understand and recreate the monastic phases of a given site, but even when archaeologists and historians have looked at the later developments that took place, this is sometimes skewed to particular events or periods in time. A case in point is Lewes Priory. The site is well known for having been acquired by Thomas Cromwell in 1537 to provide a suitable house for his son Gregory, and for the rather dramatic details that survive for the destruction of the monastic buildings by undermining and gunpowder by the Italian engineer Giovanni Portinari (see Chapter 3). This account features in nearly every traditional discussion of the Dissolution, primarily as it fits so well the desired theme of these accounts, which seek to emphasize the destructiveness of the events of the 1530s-40s.[6] However, until recently somewhat less emphasis has been given to what happened to the site after the walls had come tumbling down. Certainly, as early as 1538 a house described as "commodious" was said to be there, and this soon passed into the Sackville family, the Earls of Dorset, when it was known as Lords Place, surviving until its demolition in the late 17th century.[7]

However, the real significance of the landscape setting of the post-Dissolution house only became apparent following a recent appraisal by Paul Everson.[8] He demonstrated that the house was, in fact, a conversion of the former prior's lodge, and not a new build as had been supposed, and pointed out that this sat right at the centre of a series of landscaped gardens that surrounded it (Figure 7.2). These consisted of formal arrangement to the north of the house, "The Court," and a pond or water garden to the south. However, more significant was Everson's reassessment of two features known locally as "The Mount" and the "Dripping Pan," in the north-western corner of the precinct. The Mount, being a large mound 50m in diameter at the base and 6m at the top, and 14m tall had previously been identified as a Norman motte, and the Dripping Pan, a rectangular earthwork-defined terrace, was suggested to be a possible medieval pit or quarry.[9] However, Everson convincingly argued that both must be closely interrelated due to their juxtaposition and, given the fact they respected the turn of the monastic precinct boundary, both must post-date the foundation of the priory.[10] In the absence of any archaeological excavation the precise dating of these features is not possible, but given it seems impossible that the mount was an earlier Norman feature, a post-suppression date for this and its associated terrace is now entirely likely. If so, they were clearly garden

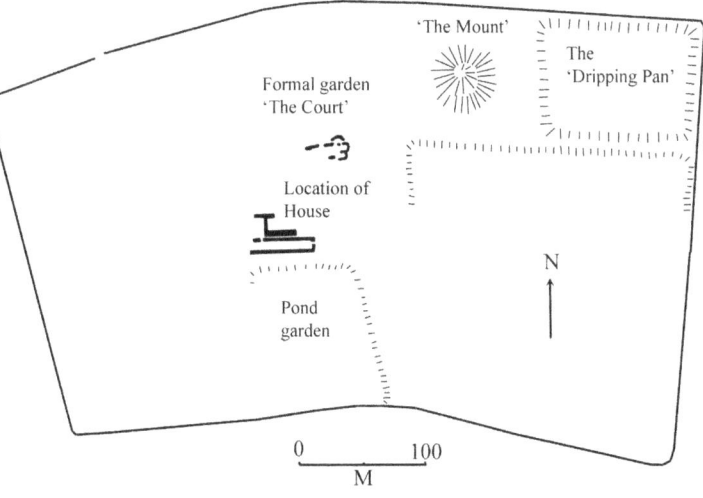

Figure 7.2 Post-Dissolution gardens at Lewes Priory (after Everson 2005).

features. The mount, which has a spiral walkway, would have made for an impressive viewing platform, or belvedere, and the rectangular terrace upon which it was focused was almost certainly a formal garden. However, what is most significant is the sheer amount of effort that was expended to create these two features. Crudely estimated as a truncated cone, the Mount alone consists of around 40,000m³ of soil that had to be moved; for the new owners of Lewes, the effort and expense expended upon the construction of the new gardens were as significant, if not more so, as that which went into the house itself.

The possibility of reconstructing the post-Dissolution gardens at Lewes was aided, in part, by the fact that once the house was demolished in the 1680s there was relatively little subsequent occupation on the site. However, as often as not, the subsequent evolution of the surrounding landscapes with the changing fashions of the day has masked or eradicated the original Tudor gardens. One site that typifies the difficulties posed by later development is Rufford Abbey. The former monastery was acquired by George Talbot, 6th Earl of Shrewsbury, and converted into a residence first occupied by himself and then following his death, by his eldest son Gilbert, the 7th Earl. Given the house belonged to one of the preeminent peers of the realm, and in the early 17th century it was certainly grand enough to play host to the retinue of James I three times, it can be assumed it possessed an equally lavish set of gardens laid out throughout the former monastic precinct. However, a landscape analysis by Smith has failed to identify any of the original Tudor design.[11] This is hardly surprising, since the initial gardens were replaced in around 1680 by a formal Baroque layout, and then again in the 18th century by a fashionable English landscape style, inspired by Lancelot Brown. Consequently, in the absence of a sustained programme of geophysical survey and targeted archaeological excavation, it seems unlikely any hint of the leisure landscape that entertained James I will be gained.

The archaeology of garden features

The difficulties in reconstructing the garden layouts that accompanied new post-Dissolution residences go beyond the fact they may have been obliterated by subsequent redevelopment. Even where features survive, in the absence of proper archaeological excavation it can be hard to ascribe a definitive date to an observable garden feature, and this applies not only to those that survive only as earthworks, but also those that might be detected through geophysical survey. For example, at the Charterhouse of Sheen, a geophysical resistance survey revealed the clear impression of a formal rectangular garden with paths and planting beds, which lay to the south of, and was orientated upon, the great cloister.[12] Following its closure in 1539, Sheen was granted first to the Duke of Somerset, then the Duke of Suffolk, before briefly reverting to monastic use under Mary.[13] Whilst in secular ownership during the 16th century it might be assumed that the former cloister was the focus of occupation, as was typical for an early conversion. It was only in 1640, when Lord Lisle was in possession of the site, that a new mansion was built to the north of the former cloister and earlier Tudor house, and the whole site was re-landscaped again.

The dating of the garden identified through geophysical survey is problematic. It clearly was post-monastic, as it overlaid the assumed location of the church. In style, it was thought by Gater to be later 17th century in date and in keeping with Lisle's remodelling,[14] yet its juxtaposition with the cloister would equally make it likely that it belonged to the earlier house. In essence, neither possibility can be ruled out, and only if the garden were dated through excavation, not necessarily an easy task in itself, could its origin be resolved. Furthermore, this was just a single element of what would have been a complex leisure landscape that was constantly evolving over several centuries.

Similar difficulties in dating geophysical features have been encountered at another Carthusian charterhouse, this time at Witham. After the Dissolution, Witham was granted to the Hopton family, who resided in a house located in the former claustral ranges. Following the site's passage to the Wyndham family in the 17th century, a new mansion was built around the year 1717.[15] This historical sequence was corroborated by a resistivity survey, which located the claustral ranges of the charterhouse, as well as the later early 18th-century mansion to the north.[16] However, this survey also showed clear evidence for a formal garden being laid out within the cloister garth, taking the form of radial paths and bedding areas. Whether this garden related to the initial Tudor mansion or the later 18th-century house, when it is suggested the whole of the former claustral ranges might have become a garden, is again unclear in the absence of excavation, although it seems on balance of probability that it was related to the first house. However, what it demonstrates was the apparent suitability of the former cloister garth in forming the centrepiece of any more extensive garden and landscape design. In essence, what had been created as a naturalistic space for religious contemplation also served the new secular owners equally well.

The cloister was not the only element of the former monastic precinct that could be converted into a garden; almost any element of the inner court could be adapted. One of the more ambitious examples of this can be seen at Boxley Abbey. Here, a post-Dissolution house was focused on the former southern west range and the attached abbot's lodge. The remaining claustral ranges and the monastic church were demolished at this point, and the cloister became a privy garden for the house. A later plan of 1801 shows that after the church's demolition the original south aisle became a terrace and an artificial ornamental pond had been dug into the area of the nave. Excavations undertaken in 1971-2 demonstrated that the terrace had been constructed immediately after the Dissolution, so in all likelihood the water feature also originally formed part of this Tudor garden design.[17] The use of the church to form an artificial pond is, at first sight, a puzzling one; however, on a practical level the general topography of the site, along with the ready amount of rubble from the church to construct the required banks made this not an impractical task. However, there might have been a more symbolic reason for the church's treatment. The new owner of Boxley was Sir Thomas Wyatt, the courtier, famous poet, protégé of Thomas Cromwell and alleged lover of Anne Boleyn. A fervent Protestant, it was while serving as ambassador to the court of Charles V he got into trouble with the Inquisition for distributing illegal literature and was even involved in the conspiracy to assassinate the exiled English Catholic Cardinal Reginald Pole.[18] Perhaps to a man so committed to the new religion, literally submerging the former monastic church so flamboyantly under water might have provided some poetic irony.

Other elements of the former claustral ranges could sometimes be adapted as garden features. At Haughmond Abbey an expedient conversion was made, where the principal residence focused on the former abbot's lodge, while the former canon's kitchen was retained for its original purpose to serve the new house. The majority of the remainder of the conventual buildings and the church were demolished, but the rather elaborate chapter house survived intact and was retained in use as a garden pavilion or possibly a banqueting house.[19] The fact that it remained in its unaltered medieval form suggests that it was intended to act as a folly or romantic feature, in contrast to the modernized house. Yet, this was just one element in a much more comprehensive scheme of works undertaken by the new owner of the site, Sir Rowland Hill (Figure 7.3). Hill, a local Shropshire man, had made his fortune as a merchant adventurer, later served as master of the Mercers' Company and in 1549 became Lord Mayor of London.[20] He acquired considerable property in the Marches and set about transforming Haughmond into a country seat worthy of a man of his now elevated status. This involved not just the alteration of the former monastic buildings, but the laying out of an ambitious garden scheme. Surrounding the new house were a series of walled gardens, one to the north focused on the former cloister that utilized some of its original walling. Others were created from scratch defining new areas to the south and east.[21] However, it was not just the area in the immediate proximity of the house that was re-landscaped at this time, but rather the whole of the wider precinct was included. Elements of the former enclosure moats and internal medieval watercourses were transformed into ponds and other water features, while further pre-existing enclosures became terraced gardens and other domestic spaces.[22] What is preserved at Haughmond is not just a series of garden features, but a whole leisured landscape that was integral to the creation of the private residence.

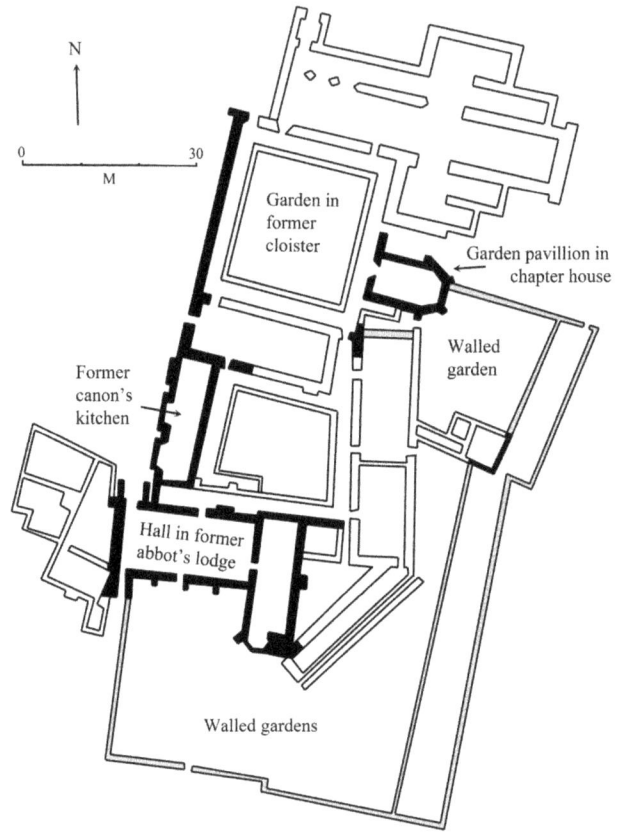

Figure 7.3 Gardens at Haughmond Abbey (after West and Palmer 2014).

The conspicuous preservation of the Haughmond chapter house as a garden feature by Hill was by no means an unusual occurrence. As Coppack, amongst others, has observed ruinous medieval fabric was intentionally preserved, or at least tolerated, by the new owners of these estates.[23] Sometimes, this was very close to hand, as has already been discussed in Chapter 6, such as at Newstead Abbey where the former west front of the monastic church was retained as a dramatic feature immediately adjoining the new house (Figure 6.9). At other times, the former monastic remains were meant to be viewed from afar; the Tyrwhitt family, whose principal residence was over two miles away at Stainfield Hall, appear to have actively maintained the ruinous tower of Barlings Abbey through the late 17th and early 18th centuries so that it could act as a distant landscape feature (Figure 7.4).

Figure 7.4 Detail showing the ruins of Barlings Abbey, with Stainfield Hall in the distance (S. and N. Buck 1726).

However, such ruins were not necessarily intended to act as passive reminders of the past, and the new owners of these sites often actively encouraged visitors to engage with these monuments through their setting within wider garden landscapes. Such an example can be seen at Egglestone Abbey, a relatively modest conversion made by the Strelley family in the 1540s (see Chapter 6). Here the house was located in the claustral ranges, while the church was left as a fully standing, if roofless, ruin. Survey work undertaken by English Heritage has identified three adjacent garden enclosures, which overlie earlier medieval features, immediately to the south of the church ruins and set squarely on to them as if to make them an integral feature of the overall garden design (Figure 7.5).[24] Furthermore, to the east lies a smaller possible garden enclosure with a 5m wide flat-topped mound immediately to the south. This has been variously interpreted as a possible stock stand or demolished dovecote, but it would equally well have functioned as a belvedere, affording as it does commanding views across the ruins in a similar fashion to the Mount at Lewes, albeit on a somewhat more modest scale.

A very similar use of ruins can be observed at Tilty Abbey, Essex. An early suppression dissolved in February 1536, it was granted to Thomas Audley, the Lord Chancellor of England. A map of 1594 shows that the house built here was focused on the east and south ranges of the abbey and that even sixty years after its suppression the abbey church still remained as a substantial ruin. Detailed earthwork surveys undertaken by Oxford Archaeology have revealed that significant remodelling of the landscape east of the claustral ranges took

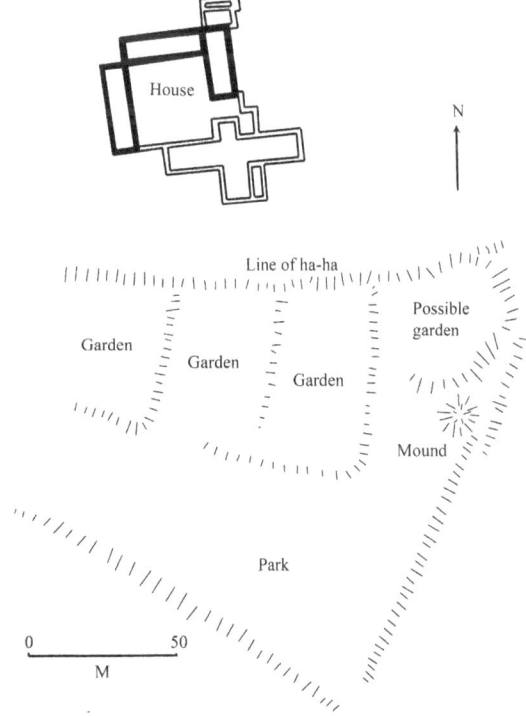

Figure 7.5 Gardens at Egglestone Abbey (after Dunn and Lax 2001).

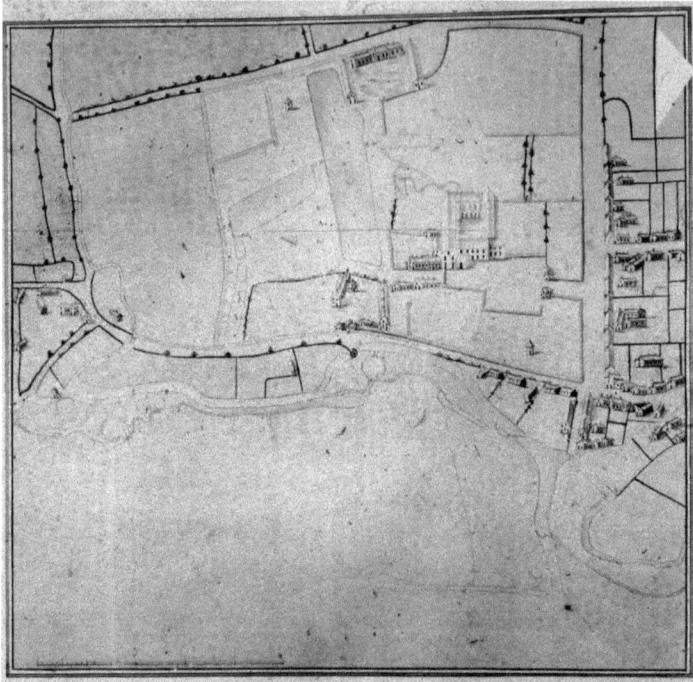

Figure 7.6 18th-century copy of a 16th-century plan of Audley End (© Historic England).

place after the Dissolution, with the establishment of a series of platforms and paths.²⁵ These, it is argued, were carefully placed to provide scenic walks and well-placed vistas of the ruins, maximising the visual effect of the former church. That Audley was keen to do this might be of no surprise; as Lord Chancellor he was active in the suppression of the Pilgrimage of Grace, and he was the one responsible for condemning a number of its ringleaders to death. As has been suggested for Charles Brandon, another key individual involved in the crushing of the revolt (see Chapter 4), perhaps Thomas Audley wished to deliberately showcase the fate of a dissolved abbey through his creation a ruined landscape.

Tilty was one of several monastic properties acquired by Audley in Essex, with his principal residence being built between 1538–1544 in the former Benedictine house of Walden Abbey.²⁶ Audley's mansion, modestly named Audley End, was established in the cloister, and although destroyed in the later rebuilding of 1603, a lost contemporary plan that was copied in the 18th century shows that in this case Audley chose to totally remove the church rather than use it as a romantic ruin (Figure 7.6). Nonetheless, what this plan also clearly demonstrates is the extent to which the original monastic watercourses were preserved and reused in the wider landscape design of the house. In part, this was probably a practical consideration, since both the monastery and mansion required water to be sourced and drained, and the outer moats would have provided a convenient boundary to the new house. However, it is clear that from the start the use of water was integral to and drove the garden design. Ponds, moats, and streams were not just small elements of the design; in the case of Audley End water was one of the most essential features.

The presence of the pre-existing monastic watercourses can be seen as central to the design of most post-suppression gardens, and not just during the 16th century. At Norton Priory, the original Tudor house and gardens built by the first owners, the Brooke family, were swept away in the 18th-century remodelling of the site (see Chapter 6). Despite this, a 1757 estate plan for the Georgian mansion clearly shows the medieval hydrological system in place and intact.²⁷ The later gardens continued to be enclosed by water-filled moats, while modified medieval ponds and other water features continued to define this landscape over two hundred years after the monastery was closed. Given the long-lasting importance of water to post-suppression garden planning, it is of little surprise that the reuse of earlier hydrological systems can be seen in almost all of the best-documented Tudor conversion gardens.

For the pleasure of princes

The extent to which some garden layouts could be truly palatial in scale and ambition has only recently become apparent following the systematic archaeological survey of some of England's largest monastic precincts. Perhaps one of the most important, yet least well known, was undertaken at Jervaulx Abbey, North Yorkshire by the RCHME (Figure 7.7).[28] What made

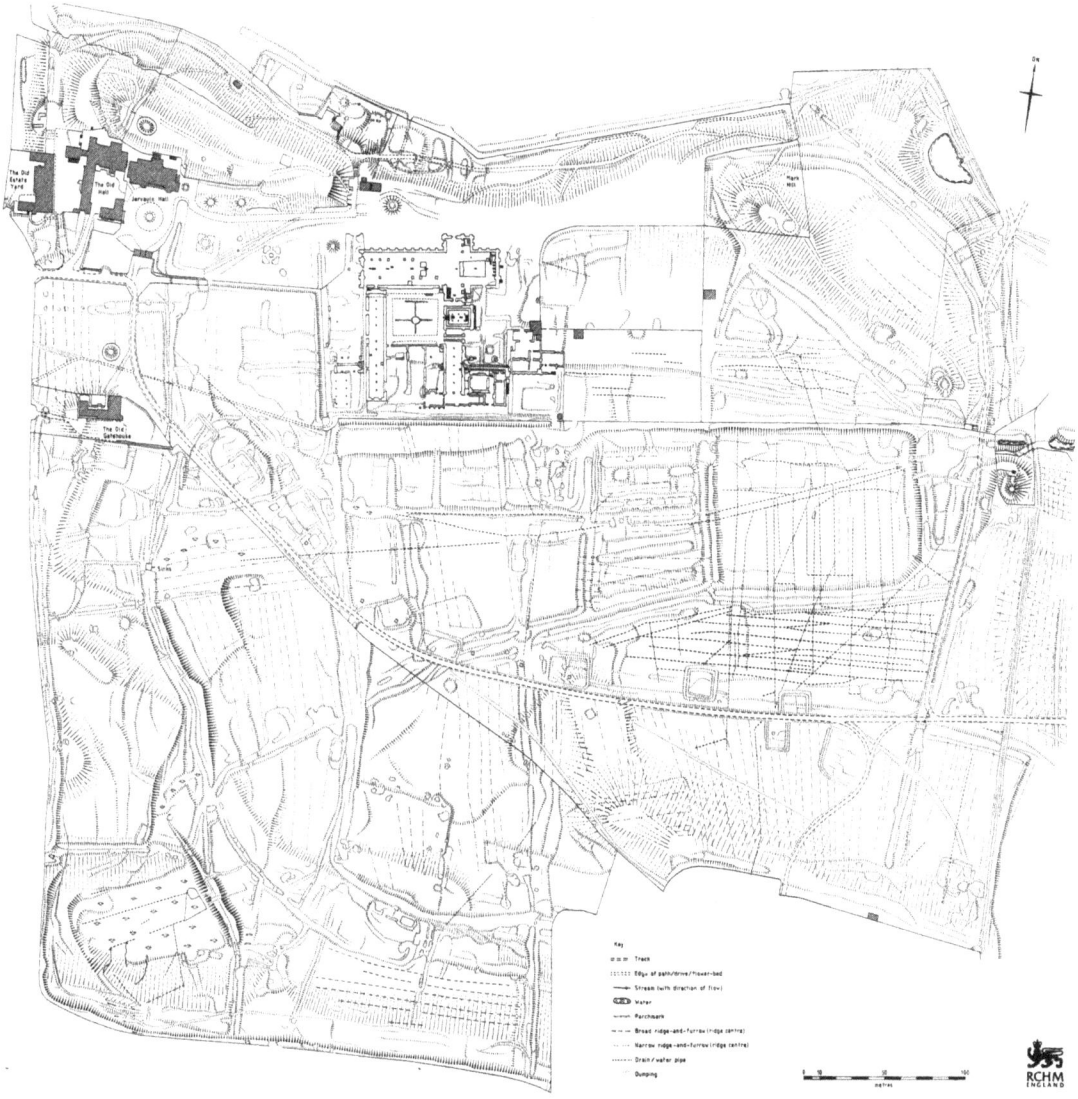

Figure 7.7 RCHME survey of Jervaulx Abbey (© Historic England).

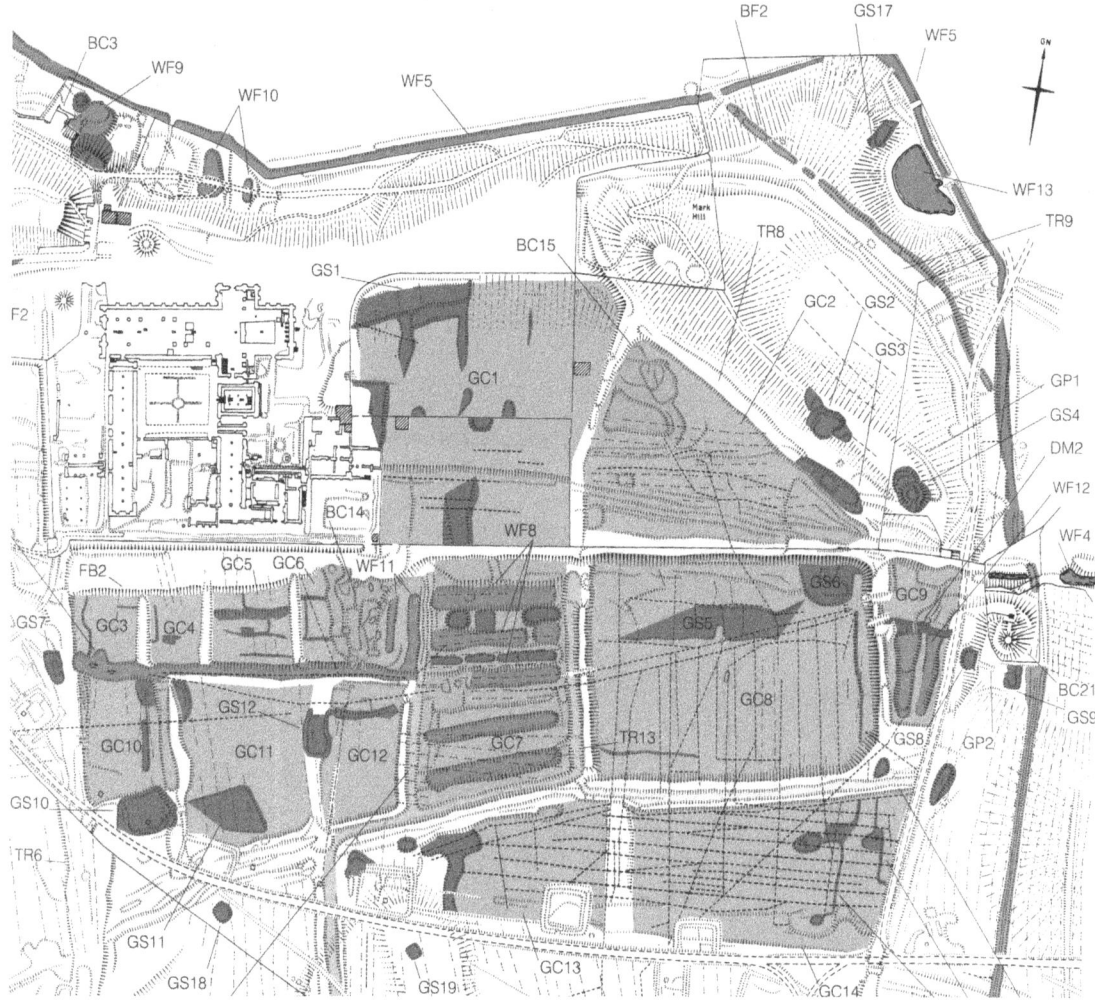

Figure 7.8   Reconstructed gardens of Jervaulx Abbey (© Historic England).

this survey even more surprising is that before it was undertaken, there was no real historical indication of the importance of its immediate post-Dissolution occupation.

The estate of Jervaulx was granted to Matthew Stewart, the 4th Earl of Lennox, the grandfather of the future James I of England, and remained in the family until it was bestowed by the newly enthroned king on Sir Edward Bruce in 1603. Jervaulx had been thought to be a minor holding, since in an estate plan of 1627 it is shown as subdivided into several small closes for rental and apparently of limited importance. However, the systematic survey of the precinct undertaken in the 1990s revealed a hitherto unknown major phase of activity relating to the Stewart period of occupation (Figure 7.8).

To the south-east of the claustral complex, the robbed-out foundations of a sizeable post-suppression house (BC14), measuring approximately 25x30m, were identifiable. This proved to be at the centre of an extremely complex and extensive system of formal garden compartments, as well as water features, walkways, and viewing platforms. Fourteen separate garden areas were identified by the Royal Commission (GC1-14), of which at least three contained water features (GC6, 7 & 9).[29] These were all self-contained areas defined by prominent banks and overlay, and paying little respect to, the earlier monastic phase features. The former claustral complex to the north of the new house, with its upstanding walls, many of which are still prominent today, almost certainly formed a further garden showcasing the abbey ruins, and being located to the rear of the house would have had an impressive presence.

The Royal Commission survey was not just able to identify general garden areas, more specific features were recognized across the precinct. Whilst some caution is required in their identification, as in the absence of excavation their precise date and function cannot be ascertained for certain, it seems likely that most of these were part of the larger Tudor landscaped design. They included probable pavilion buildings, one GS7 measuring 15x8m with a central doorway and a second GS9, although without an obvious entrance, was also of a similar size. In addition to pavilions, the landscape also included several viewing platforms, GS2 and GS4, the latter seeming to have a flight of steps leading to the top, while at least one, GS17, appeared to be specifically related to water features and positioned to provide the best vistas over it.

The transformation that took place at Jervaulx is impressive, but perhaps should not be that surprising. This was, after all, an estate belonging to a royal family, so its palatial scale might be expected. That it was only occupied at this social level for a short period has of course allowed for its complex of earthworks to be relatively easily unpicked and interpreted; it is a leisure landscape fossilized and lacking in substantial later development. Although there is clearly much still to learn about this conversion, and probably few sites merit some form of excavation more than Jervaulx, it provides a clear example of how a monastic precinct could be transformed, and clearly demonstrates the value of intensive archaeological survey.

Other prominent members of the aristocracy, and not just those from royalty, could also create landscapes of palatial power; Paul Everson and David Stocker have argued just this for the treatment of two Lincolnshire houses, Barlings and Kirkstead Abbeys, following their suppression.[30] As outlined in Chapter 4, both abbeys were active in their support of the Lincolnshire Rising of 1536, and both were dissolved because of their involvement and formed part of a massive transfer of monastic land to Charles Brandon, Duke of Suffolk, the man principally responsible for the revolt's brutal suppression. Everson and Stocker have argued that the way Brandon treated both rebellious monasteries reflected both his new felt presence in the county, but also acted as a visible reminder of what happened to those who challenged the king's authority.

Although Brandon's principal residence in the county was Tattersall Castle, he seems to have invested considerable effort in converting both abbeys into private residences. At Barlings, which has probably received the most intensive documentary and archaeological survey of any post-Dissolution site, Brandon set about creating a grand house and garden landscape.[31] Part of the monastic church may have been retained for parochial use, at least initially, but the remainder was unroofed and left ruinous, while a new L-shaped house built of brick was constructed to the southwest (Figure 7.9). Associated with the house to the north are what Everson and Stocker have suggested were stables, further lodgings, and a possible meeting house. The mansion complex itself was set in a range of now familiar Tudor gardens; to the rear was a privy garden with a water pool and cascade, and set around the rest of the precinct a series of other garden compartments. Perhaps the most striking of these is what Everson and Stocker have termed a "ruin garden" where the dilapidated church and claustral buildings were set out on deliberate show, as a visible reminder of the former abbey's treacherous past. An engraving of a drawing by W. Millecent from around 1730 depicts the now abandoned and collapsing remains of Brandon's mansion, paradoxically still dominated by the ruin of the impressive abbey tower (Figure 7.10). Nonetheless, it was clear that the remains of the abbey were intended to be clearly seen by all around.

Some potential issues in Everson and Stocker's thesis have already been discussed in Chapter 4, including Brandon's death soon after his acquisition of Barlings in 1545, and the site's continued occupation by various families throughout the later 16th and early 17th centuries.[32] Despite this, the convincing argument remains that Brandon intended to demonstrate his dominance over both the abbey and Lincolnshire more generally through his redesigned landscape at Barlings, even if this was never fully completed within his actual lifetime.

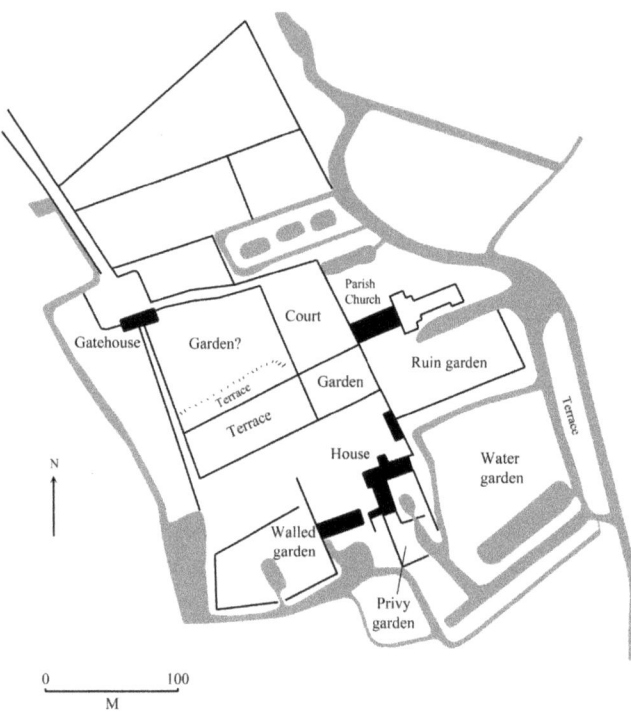

Figure 7.9 Brandon's gardens at Barlings Abbey (after Everson and Stocker 2011).

The other rebellious site acquired by Brandon, Kirkstead Abbey, also underwent a thorough transformation after its suppression. Here, the conversion into a house was more modest, with the cloister appearing to have been remodelled for this purpose rather than a complete new build. The smaller scale of the conversion has prompted Everson and Stocker to suggest that rather than a great house, Brandon was creating an equestrian centre at Kirkstead, drawing parallels to similar lodges created for Henry VIII.[33] However, they argue that

Figure 7.10 View of Barlings Abbey (right) and Brandon's house (left) (W. Millecent 1730, © Lincolnshire Archives).

more effort seems to have been placed on the redesigning of the wider landscape around the house or lodge, and note that this is depicted in remarkable accuracy in the 1724 survey undertaken of the abbey by William Stukeley (Figure 7.11).

Although Stukeley was attempting to map the medieval cloister and church as it would have appeared in its final monastic phases, the features depicted in the inner precinct around the cloister in fact almost entirely reflect changes made to the site by Brandon. As the more recent survey of the site by Coppack and Harrison has noted, the moat drawn by Stukeley and still visible today was entirely a creation of Brandon, who chose not to reuse the original monastic watercourse.[34] Whilst Everson and Stocker suggested Brandon might have left the former church unmolested, as it would have served well as an equestrian stable, Coppack and Harrison have pointed out the moulded voussoirs from the nave arcades of the church were visibly built into Brandon's boundary bank on the near side of the post-Dissolution moat. This suggests that a large portion, if not all, of the monastic church must have been swiftly demolished.[35] So in many ways, Brandon's transformation of Kirkstead was rather different to that at Barlings. At his mansion at Barlings, where he might have been expected to receive a range of political and professional persons when he was in residence, he chose to emphasize the site's monastic past as a visible lesson. In contrast, at the

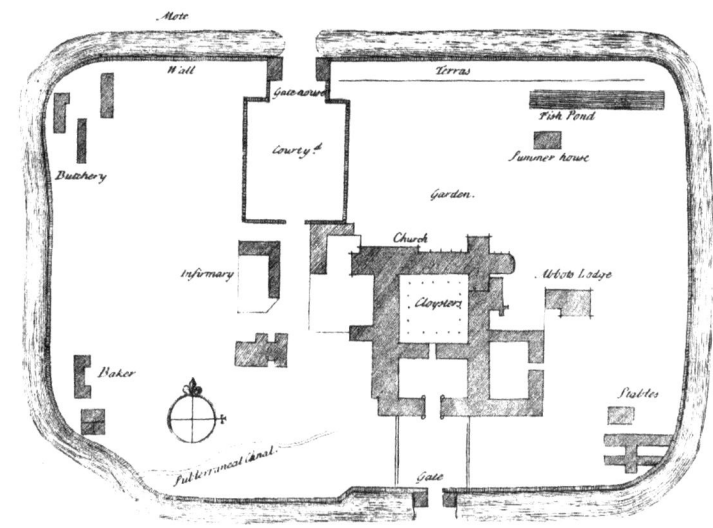

Figure 7.11 Stukeley's 18th-century survey of Kirkstead Abbey (W. Stukeley 1724).

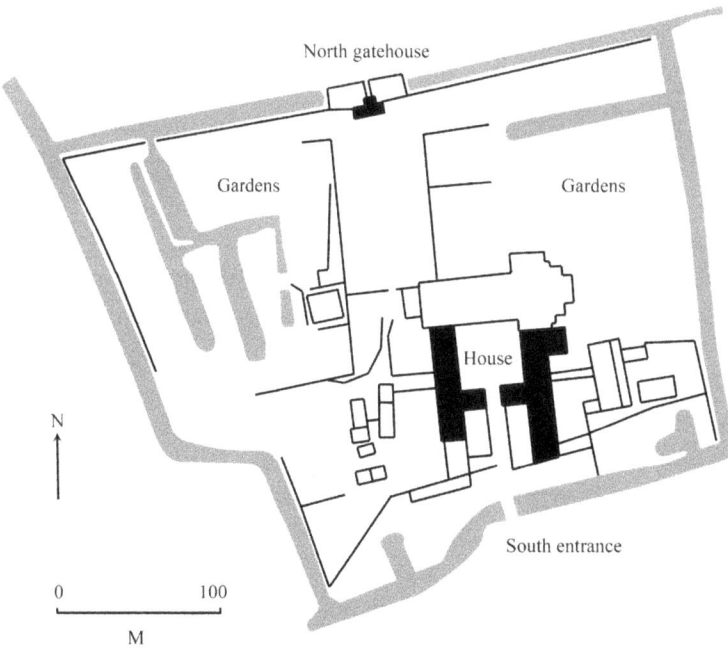

Figure 7.12 Brandon's gardens at Kirkstead (after Everson and Stocker 2009; Coppack and Harrison 2014).

more private lodge at Kirkstead, which was dedicated to leisure rather than the dealings of court, evidence for its former life was effectively eradicated and built over anew.

Although there are some differences of opinion between the analysis of Everson and Stoker and that of Coppack and Harrison, a reasonably detailed and consistent picture of the new landscape created by Brandon at Kirkstead can be discussed (Figure 7.12). The house or lodge occupied elements of the claustral ranges, being broadly H-shaped and focused on two courtyards, while other monastic buildings such as the church and infirmary ranges were demolished. The house seems to have been approached from the south, but there was also a second new entrance across the northern moat. This entered into a large new walled courtyard, so clearly depicted by Stukeley, and possibly the main equestrian yard if Everson and Stocker's interpretation is correct, and new gardens were laid out on either side of this new courtyard. That to the west contained a series of water features. To the east Stukeley's plan records a northern terrace or platform overlooking an ornamental pond and to the south of this a "summer house," which must be a feature of the Brandon landscaping.

Unpicking the palimpsest—Thornton Abbey

Whilst earthwork, geophysical and aerial survey have transformed our understanding of the extent to which new secular owners often transformed monastic precincts, there are still problems in the interpretation of such data. As has already been suggested, while such survey techniques present a range of hypothetical reconstructions, ultimately their absolute dating and interpretation is only possible through archaeological excavation. Furthermore, landscape features could fulfil successive roles dependant on period, both through passive reuse or active remodelling. For example, a medieval drainage moat might become a landscaped pond with no alteration save the addition of some waterfowl, who were probably in residence there already, while a demolished and robbed medieval building might be easily transformed into a terrace or platform with little effort. As a result, *any* interpretation based purely upon survey alone is likely to be at best simplistic, compressing discussion into just two crude and contrasting "pre-Dissolution" and "post-Dissolution" phases, thus creating a very flat narrative. Even worse, interpretations based on survey work alone might simply be wrong.

This is not to say the case studies discussed already should be disregarded, and each certainly has its merits. For instance, the work by the RCHME at Jervaulx had fortuitously identified a phase of garden works that must date between its suppression in 1537 and 1627, when the surviving estate plan was drawn up. However, as the surveyors themselves admit, it cannot be said for certain that every one of these possible garden features dates to this period. Perhaps more crucially, within this 90-year window, it is impossible to achieve a more fine-grained chronology for the landscape's development and to say which member of the Stewart family might have been responsible. Whilst the majority of the gardens probably were laid out at the time of the construction of the house, this cannot be proved for sure, and possibly the gardens developed over decades. There are similar issues when considering the fate of sites acquired by Charles Brandon in Lincolnshire. At Barlings the interpretation of the laying out of the gardens fits well the very plausible thesis developed by Everson and Stocker, but they are not definitively able to prove that the Wray family did not create some or all of these features in the 17th century. Even at Kirkstead, whose occupation appears to have been even shorter-lived than

Barlings, from survey alone the garden remodelling cannot be absolutely dated to the 1540s, and it equally could be the work of a subsequent, albeit undocumented, owner.

That having been said, archaeological excavation is by no means the panacea to this problem. Unlike a building that can be carefully excavated in its entirety, only a tiny percentage of even a modest monastic precinct can be examined, and even extensive targeting of features through numerous small trenches may prove problematic, as they are often not big enough to produce the crucial dating evidence or provide an adequate interpretation. A good illustration of this point can be seen at Thornton Abbey. The majority of the precinct was subject to intensive earthwork survey and interpretation by English Heritage between 2007–2009 (Figure 7.13), building on earlier earthwork survey undertaken by Caroline Atkins.[36] Between 2011–2016 the author undertook geophysical survey across almost the entire inner precinct (Figure 7.14), which was followed by targeted excavation of what were thought to be post-Dissolution features. Given this, Thornton's precinct is one of the most intensively examined in England, yet, as shall be seen, it is still only partially and very imperfectly understood.

Thornton has a complex, but well-documented post-Dissolution history. Furthermore, in the inner precinct at least, its archaeology has been relatively undisturbed except for the church and claustral ranges that were cleared in the 19th and 20th centuries. Thornton was one of the wealthiest monastic houses by the Dissolution, since in 1534 its clear income was £591 0s 2¾d, and this wealth was reflected by the size of its precinct, around 75 acres, and the magnificence of its buildings.[37] Following its initial closure it remained in ecclesiastical use as one of Henry VIII's new colleges for secular canons, but after six years it was closed under Edward VI in 1547. However, during this time the former abbot's lodge in the west range and an unspecified area surrounding it had been "divided off by walls and ditches" and remained in possession of the King, whom Coppack has suggested intended to establish it as his primary residence just south of the Humber.[38]

Thornton's passage into secular ownership was more complicated than its Lincolnshire neighbours of Barlings and Kirkstead. Following the closure of the college, a grant was given to Henry Holbeach, Bishop of Lincoln, on 2nd September 1549. This consisted of the west range, formerly in the king's hands and the southern refectory range, and these presumably formed the nucleus for the new mansion.[39] Also included in the grant was the great western gatehouse (Figure 7.15), the court between this and the west range, the conduit and laundry house as well as the park enclosed with pales and walls of 80 acres, and rights to the game contained within it. English Heritage has noted that this park roughly equates to the same size as the whole of the monastic precinct,[40] but given substantial portions of this were not included in the grant to Holbeach (see below) it is uncertain what this land consisted of. Interestingly in the grant, it is stated that this park was already in the tenure of the property speculator John Bellow, possibly since shortly after the initial suppression of 1539, so it implies that the park was not thought essential to the running of the short-lived college.

Two years after this initial grant, a second considerably larger one was made to Robert Wood on the 21st July 1549. This included the former monastic church, east range, the cemetery, infirmary yard as well as a range of subsidiary buildings including the watermill, great barn, cow house, dovecote, and kiln house.[41] The grant also consisted of "a great garden," suggested by Coppack to be the cloister,[42] the precinct called "Uttercourt" and 240 acres of land in the

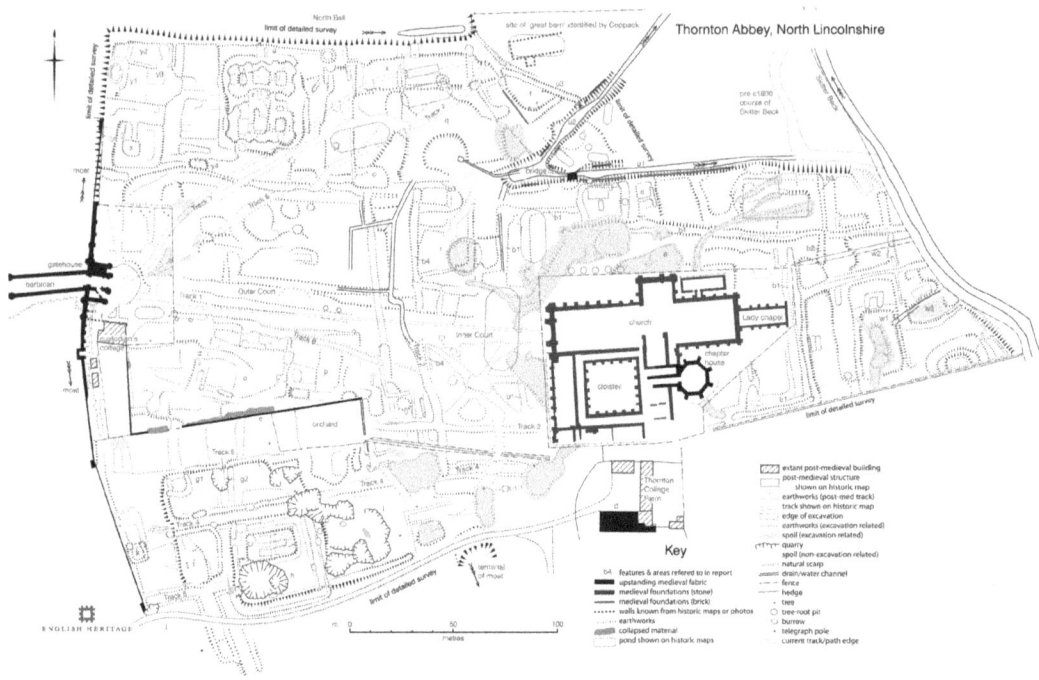

Figure 7.13   Earthwork survey of the inner precinct at Thornton Abbey (© Historic England).

Figure 7.14   Resistivity survey of the inner precinct at Thornton Abbey (Author).

Figure 7.15   The gatehouse at Thornton Abbey (Author).

north and south fields of Thornton. These 240 acres must represent the demesne land in the parish, formerly held by the monastery as lords of the manor. However, the "outer court precinct" is hard to identify for certain, but given its close association with other elements of the grant, including the mill, barn, and dovecote, it might well have been the north bail of the monastery, identified as the location of the home farm, and an area of land measuring approximately 22 acres.[43]

Despite the uncertainties of where much of this land lay, it is possible to see the division of Thornton into two central units (Figure 7.16), although the fate of the southern portion of the site is less clear. However, beyond this, and the relative size of the grants, there is a clear difference in what each of the new owners intended to use their portions for. In Holbeach's case, the grant of the domestic ranges, the imposing but rather impractical gatehouse, and the park with its hunting rights is entirely domestic in nature, fitting the requirements of a gentleman of newly elevated status. Wood's grant, in contrast, with its emphasis on the industrial and agricultural elements of the former precinct, along with the former demesne lands, is suggestive of the establishment of an economic enterprise. Whether Wood managed this directly, or more likely through a lease is unknown, but his acquisition was more motivated by the generation of income than to create a country seat.

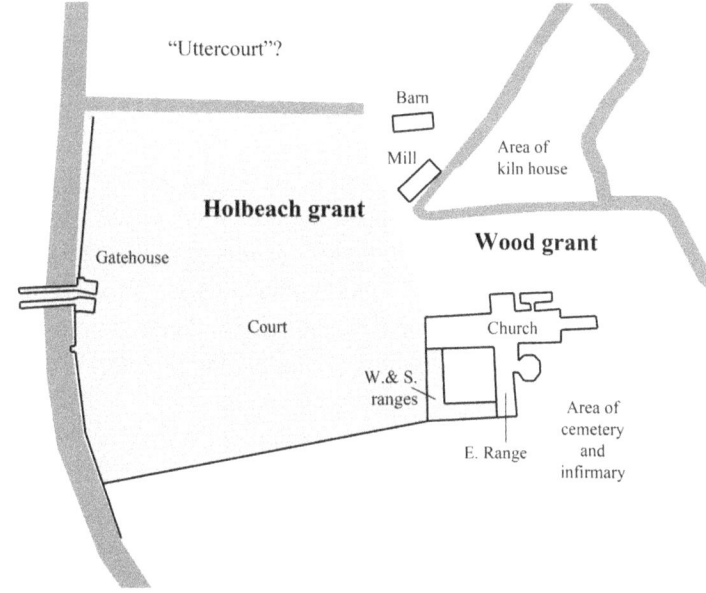

Figure 7.16   Division of the precinct at Thornton (Author).

The former monastic precinct remained divided between these two families until 1575 when Sir Robert Tyrwhitt purchased the estate held by Holbeach from his son. This passed to his grandson, also Robert, who by 1591 had also acquired the remaining lands from the monastery originally granted to Wood.[44] Little else is known of the Tyrwhitt occupation of the site, although they were still occupying the house centred on the former cloister. Clearance of the south claustral range in 1952 revealed a small hoard of 23 silver coins, two silver thimbles and four Nuremburg jettons hidden under a tile in the floor of the undercroft.[45] Whilst the earliest coin was a Mary I groat, the majority dated to the 1570s, with the latest being a crescent shilling of 1587–1590, clearly demonstrating that the range was still in occupation at this time.

The final phase of intensive occupation started in 1603, when Vincent Skinner acquired the whole abbey, on 28 February 1603, from Robert Tyrwhitt for the sum of £3,000.[46] Skinner was from a wealthy local mercantile family, prospered under the patronage of Lord Burghley, and became MP for Boston.[47] He was an early supporter of James I, being knighted by him before his actual coronation on 25 July 1603. As a result, Skinner's purchase of Thornton, in late February 1603, less than a month before Elizabeth died, and when she was known to be ailing, was made in anticipation of his soon to be elevated status through his financial backing of James' claim to the throne. Thornton represented the kind of estate an emerging member of the gentry might aspire to, yet Skinner's dynastic hopes were short-lived. It seems that he overextended himself financially in his ambitions, and throughout his occupation of Thornton appears to have sunk increasingly into debt, before dying in a debtor's prison in 1616. Members of the Skinner family continued to live intermittently and in reduced circumstances at Thornton until it was bought by Sir Robert Sutton in 1720.[48]

At Thornton, it is, therefore, possible to see three clear historical phases of secular domestic occupation, that of the Holbeach (1547–1575), Tyrwhitt (1575–1603) and Skinner (1603–1616) families, all who had the potential to make a significant imprint upon the landscape. The descendants of Skinner were almost certainly in no financial position to make significant alterations to Thornton, beyond the repair and maintenance of a few of the buildings, indeed it is clear that by the time the site passed out of their ownership in the 18th century many, such as the great gatehouse, were roofless and in significant decay.

Thornton's wider precinct can be divided into three broad areas: the inner precinct, the north bail, and the southern enclosure. For the purposes of this discussion, only the main inner precinct is discussed. This is in part due to historical and archaeological bias, as this has been the area of most intensive study. However, it is also likely to have been the main focus of the most intensive secular occupation and landscaping; here too were to be found the principal buildings of the monastery, inevitably the first focus of any later development, and what activities that took place in the southern enclosure are uncertain, both for the medieval and post-suppression phases. However, there are few earthworks or building platforms suggestive of intensive occupation, so it is likely this area was also used for agricultural purposes throughout its occupation.

Earthwork and geophysical survey have allowed for the combined reconstruction of the garden landscape at Thornton Abbey, and this has been partially phased and dated through targeted excavation (Figure 7.17). Combined with the historical context of ownership, a tentative reconstruction of the sequence of development as it took place over a century can be made. The focus of the first extensive secular occupation of the site by Holbeach was the west and south

New Landscapes of Leisure

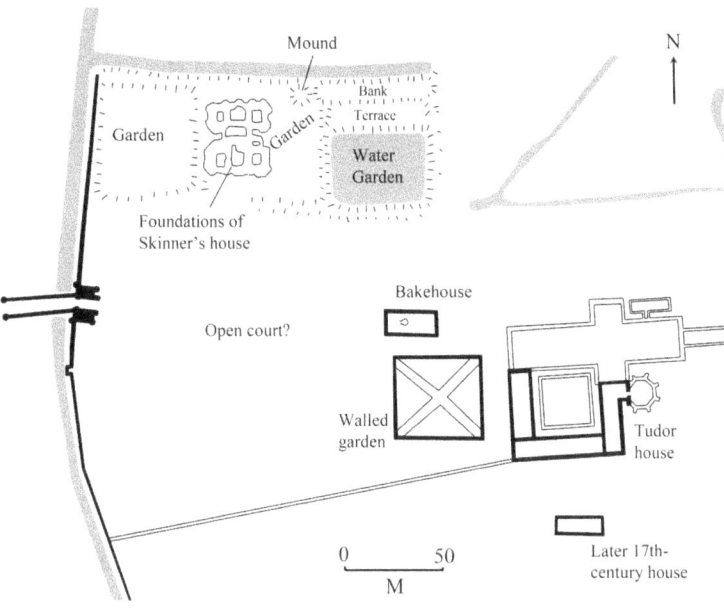

Figure 7.17 Garden plan of Thornton Abbey (Author).

claustral ranges, although technically before this the King had already claimed elements of this for himself, even if only on paper. Given that the west range faced towards the imposing gatehouse and entrance, it seems likely that its western face formed its principal front. Furthermore, the somewhat awkward arrangement, whereby Robert Wood was in possession of the eastern range, and maybe even the cloister garth, meant that Holbeach would have had to orient his house westwards. This probably explains the positioning of one of the earliest of the garden features, a sub-rectangular formal garden aligned square to the west range. The garden had been disturbed on its western side by a later track way, distorting its appearance, but originally this was a regular area measuring around 50x60m. The geophysical survey clearly showed that running from corner to corner were two high resistance features, crossing at the centre, where there also appeared to be a solid structure. Small-scale excavation revealed the precise form of this garden (Figure 7.18). Its outer edge was defined by the robbed-out trench of what had been a brick wall surrounding the garden on all four sides. The transverse features proved to be cobbled paths, and although the trench was too small to reveal details of the planting plan between these, it was clear that there were several

Figure 7.18 Cobble path of the formal garden, with gravel in fills (Author).

153

phases of the garden which utilized patches of light coloured gravel, presumably to enhance the horticultural planting. Ceramics of a wide range of dates were found in the garden soils, but those within the matrix of the paths, appearing to have been trodden in, were of broadly mid to late 16th-century date.

Immediately to the north of this garden was the footprint of a W–E oriented building. Given its apparent association with the northern edge of the garden, although separated by the garden wall, it was assumed that this might in some form of pavilion. Excavation of half this structure revealed this to be a rather rough-built building, with low un-mortared sleeper walls, probably to carry a timber-built superstructure, floored internally with robbed and reused flags, including one that was part of a grave slab with an incised cross, identical to one still *in situ* in the floor of the monastic church. The function of the building was that of a bake house and kitchen as it contained the base of a bread oven, a subsidiary hearth and fireplace and a portion of broken stone dough trough (Figure 7.19). This was a relatively short-lived building, early post-suppression in date, as material culture found within its demolition layers, including a surprising number of diagnostic dress accessories, suggested this probably took place in the third quarter of the 16th century, so dated to the Holbeach phase of occupation. The positioning of such a utilitarian building in such a prominent location is at first sight surprising. Nonetheless, the divided nature of the initial grants probably explains its construction here. Being one of the key service buildings required by Holbeach it had to be close, but possibly separate to the main residence for safety reasons. Furthermore, a new bake house might have been necessary, as although its medieval predecessor was not specifically mentioned in the original grant made to Wood, this had included the former canon's kitchen, and thus Holbeach was required to build a new bake house and kitchen for his mansion. As the land to the rear of his new mansion was not available to him, he had to place the new service range to the west and north of his house and newly constructed garden. It was probably only in the Tyrwhitt occupation of the site, when the whole precinct came into their ownership, that this kitchen became redundant and was demolished.

Few other features can be said for certain to date from this earliest phase of remodelling, the only other landscaped element might be what is clearly the remains of a large courtyard that can be seen in the geophysics which encompasses much of the area between the gatehouse and Holbeach's formal garden and kitchen. Whether he constructed this is not known, as this has

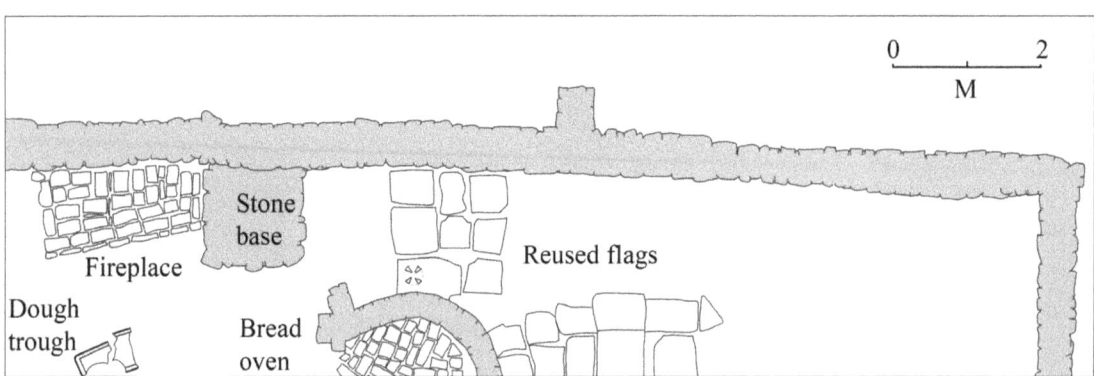

Figure 7.19   The bakehouse at Thornton Abbey (Author).

yet to be excavated, and it is possible it was a pre-existing medieval feature that continued in use.

The next phase of landscaping seems to have occurred later under the occupancy of the Tyrwhitts. Running along the northern boundary of the inner precinct were a series of three clearly connected and evenly sized garden compartments formed by low banks, and measuring approximately 50x50m square. The westernmost is the most disturbed of these gardens. Excavation here revealed that it had been subject to modern quarrying and the dumping of substantial amounts of concrete, masonry and other rubbish relating to the 20th-century refurbishment of the gatehouse by the Ministry of Works. The middle garden was also largely obscured by later activity relating the Skinner family (see below), but the easternmost remained fundamentally intact, save for some modern agricultural disturbance. This area has already been identified by English Heritage as a possible garden compartment, although this and all other associated features were rather erroneously suggested to be related to the Skinner period of occupation.[49] The northern edge of the garden was formed by a low flat-topped bank 4m wide running parallel to the moat, the other three sides defined by low, degraded earthworks. To the south of the northern bank was a flat garden terrace approximately 15m in width, with the remaining southern two-thirds of the garden being an irregular depression. A natural spring, that still flows today, was located in the south-eastern corner of this area, and would have resulted in filling this depression with water and creating an ornamental pond.

These three garden compartments were laid out simultaneously and can be dated to the Tyrwhitt phase of occupation for a variety of reasons. First, the south-facing vista from the terrace of the water garden would have been severely interrupted had the utilitarian kitchen building immediately to the south still been in existence. As a result, it seems likely the garden was established at the same time this was demolished, so that not only could the viewer look over the water garden, they could also see past this to the formal garden directly beyond. Second, the flat-topped bank that provided the viewing platform was found on excavation to consist almost entirely of broken up medieval roof tiles. Such a large quantity of roofing material must have come from several substantial buildings that had at that stage started to be demolished, and the church and cloistral ranges in particular. Following his grant of 1547, Holbeach had not been granted these elements of the monastery, apart from the portion retained intact as his house, they only came available once the Tyrwhitts had gained control of the whole precinct. Finally, Thornton is not the only site occupied during the sixteenth century where a comparable embanked garden with a raised terrace can be seen. Similar earthwork features, albeit of a slightly different arrangement and scale, can be seen at Stainfield Priory, the Tyrwhitt's principal seat, as well as at Nuncotham Priory and Bardney Abbey, both of which were also owned by the family after the Dissolution.[50] The final feature within this phase of landscape design is a small circular platform, or belvedere, located in the north east corner of the middle garden compartment. Although somewhat eroded and obscured by scrub and trees to the north today, it was placed in a central position along the length of the northern moat and afforded an uninterrupted view across not only the inner precinct with its monastic ruins, gatehouse and secular mansion to the south, but also the enclosed park to the north. Interestingly at least one similar mound is again present at the Tyrwhitt site of Bardney, also in direct association with the embanked garden.

The final period of occupation, the thirteen years Sir Vincent Skinner resided at Thornton, is much misunderstood and appears to have made the least impact on the precinct. However, it is this phase that has received the most attention and attempted reconstruction by English Heritage, perhaps unsurprisingly given the sensationalist events said to have taken place there at this time. These are recorded in the rather contradictory accounts of the late 17th century antiquarian, Abraham de la Pryme. De la Pryme mentions Skinner's presence at Thornton twice; first he tells the apocryphal tale of his downfall. In Skinner's apparent transformation of the site he;

> "built a most staitly hall...on the west side of the abby plot within the moat, which hall, when finished fell quite down to the bare ground without any visible cause, and broke in pieces all the rich furniture that was therein...After that...Skinner built another hall out of part of the stones that the other was built of. Which hall now stand on the east side of the court of the abby, and is all built on arches of some old building."[51]

De la Pryme's tale of the construction of a new build hall in the western side of the precinct is apparently corroborated by the presence of some very prominent earthworks resembling the outline of a house (Figure 7.20). Furthermore, David Roberts identified two slightly different versions of a plan for a house drawn by the renowned architect John Thorpe and annotated as being for Sir Vincent Skinner at Thornton in the archives of the Soane Museum. These almost identically matched the earthwork on the ground, as well as a 19th-century measured drawing of the feature made for the Earl of Yarborough, the then owner of the estate.[52]

Therefore, the presence of Skinner's ill-fated house has been taken for granted to be represented by this earthwork, so much so that English Heritage has installed reconstructed views of it in interpretive panels on the site. However, there is a problem with this connection apparent from the

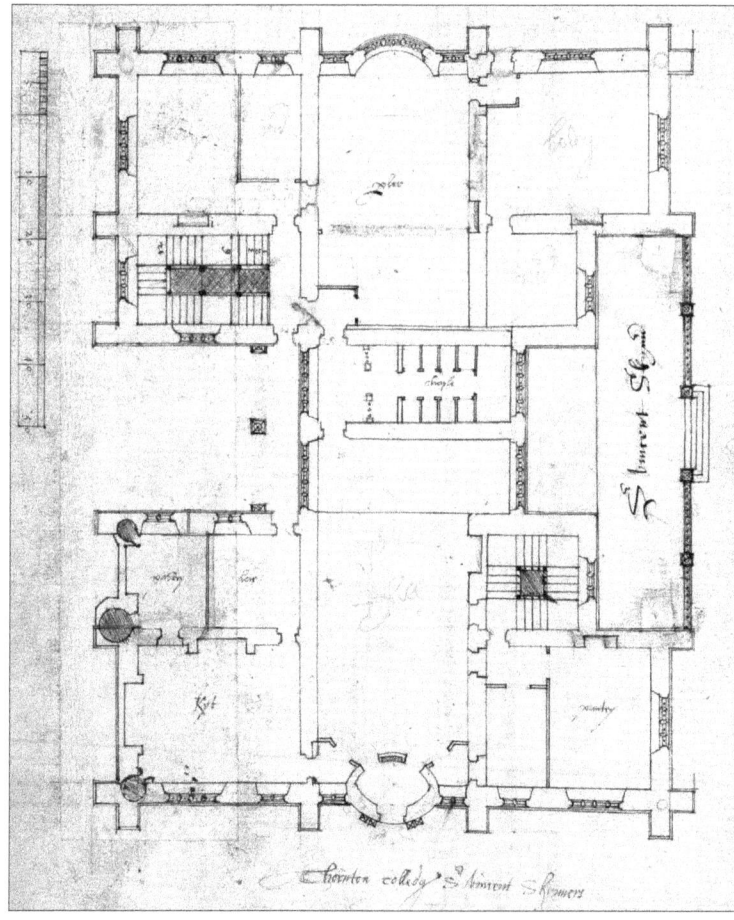

Figure 7.20 Plan by John Thorpe for a house for Sir Vincent Skinner at Thornton College (© Sir John Soane's Museum).

earthworks alone. The chief of these is that as the monument stands today, where the walls should be are steep-sided trenches surrounding mounds in the place of the rooms. This is an extremely unusual if unique archaeological monument, since ordinarily, even if the walls had subsequently been robbed, as de la Pryme suggests, the remaining earthwork would remain as a low uneven mound.

Figure 7.21   Excavation of the foundation trench of Skinner's "house" (Author).

Excavation of a section of the northern part of the earthwork which related to rooms that were marked as the "parlour" and a flanking "lodge" on the Thorpe plan, provided a clear explanation for this unusual feature. Although there was evidence for an earlier medieval building of uncertain form or function here, this had been cut through by steep-sided foundation ditches along the line of the putative house's walls; yet that was the furthest its construction had ever progressed. There was not a single building stone or sizable piece of rubble within these trenches, and no evidence for internal floor layers was encountered (Figure 7.21). Even if the house had been so thoroughly robbed as to remove every brick, stone, floor tile or beam, there still was no broken-up plaster, window glass or other detritus that would have been left behind from the collapse or removal of a large building; its construction had never progressed beyond the cutting of the foundations.

This leads to the only possible conclusion, that Skinner's new house was never built here, or anywhere else in the precinct for that matter, as there are no other earthwork or geophysical features to match it. Nonetheless, he must have been residing somewhere in the precinct during this time, and the only logical conclusion is that it was within the original claustral conversion. In his follow up to the description of the catastrophic collapse, de la Pryme then stated that Skinner built a new hall on old foundations, and this is commonly believed to be the so-called "Abbot's Lodge," the only upstanding and roofed building remaining (Figure 7.22).[53] However, this building is, even by today's standards fairly modest in scale, and it currently serves as the tenanted farmhouse for the estate. It also contrasts with a further account that de la Pryme gave when first visiting the abbey, when he recalled being shown the residence of Skinner's descendant who by then lived in London. He stated; "out of part of the old building is built a _large_ and somewhat _low_ hall, not farr of of the aforesayd chappel" (author's emphases).[54]

This description does not fit well with the rather small Abbot's Lodge, which is a compact and upright building. However, this account would provide a better fit for the mansion originally created by Holbeach from the former cloister; this would have been broad but comparatively short in height, as it reused the original medieval ranges. Perhaps what can be seen in the de la Pryme's account is a conflation of events, with a bit of moralising added for dramatic effect. It now seems probable that Skinner was in residence in the cloistral conversion, but planned a far grander new build residence to reflect his new status. Plans for a Jacobean mansion were commissioned, and his workmen cut the foundation trenches, but when it came to the added expense of materials and specialist labour Skinner was undone. The collapse may have been financial and social rather than physical, but the result was the same, he was ruined and his fine furniture removed by creditors rather than crushed.

Figure 7.22 The "Abbot's Lodge" (originally the guesthouse) at Thornton Abbey (Author).

Whatever the precise turn of events was, the fact it seems that no grand mansion was ever properly started, let alone completed, makes it extremely unlikely that Skinner would have undertaken any wider landscaping of the site to create gardens and associated features. This is also borne out by the archaeological evidence. Skinner's new house is placed asymmetrically within the central garden compartment and it is clear that its foundation trenches cut through the pre-existing enclosure, and its western bank in particular. With the exception of these foundation trenches there are no other features that can definitively be said to date to this period of occupation, and the only evidence for it physically the alterations and adaptations made to the former monastic guesthouse.

Consequently, the research undertaken to date at Thornton Abbey, although still far from comprehensive and with scope for much further work, has demonstrated the importance of an approach that utilizes not only historical research and field survey, but also intrusive excavation. Either approach on their own, while revealing to a certain degree can only present a partial reconstruction of how the landscape of the precinct was transformed, and for a more nuanced and integrated narrative a much more holistic approach is required.

— 8 —

CONCLUDING REMARKS

At the start of this book, I stated that I wanted to look again at the Dissolution and try to go beyond the often-polarized discussions concerning the motivations of those who enacted it, and instead to look at the physical effects that it had upon the hundreds of monastic houses across England and Wales. I also wanted to put the people of Tudor England and Wales back into the narrative, insofar as that was possible. The king, Cromwell and some peers of course feature in every account of the Dissolution, but archaeologists, in particular, have been prone to see the whole process being imposed from the top down. Whilst, of course, the Dissolution was initiated by the king, in reality, it was countless individuals in the shires, whether they be individual private purchasers, civic authorities or even the former religious themselves, who shaped what happened at each monastic house after it was closed. It was their motivations, ambitions, successes or failures that moulded the afterlife of England and Wales' monasteries as much as the king himself. Each chapter in this book has presented different aspects of the Dissolution that can be observed in both the historical sources and archaeological record to varying degrees, and it not my intention here to reiterate all these discussions and arguments. However, there are several broader themes it is worth highlighting here, if just briefly.

The first is the complexity of the Dissolution, and the fact that it was not just a simple political act. Whether Henry VIII and Thomas Cromwell did, or did not, start with the original intention to reform rather than repress the monasteries will probably be debated for years still to come.[1] However, to dismiss these individuals as solely being motivated by greed and personal ambition is to ignore the fact that both were men of deeply held religious conviction. This is also reflected, to some degree, in the fate that some of the former monastic houses experienced after their closure; far from being swept into oblivion, many continued in ecclesiastical use in some form. The full extent to which this happened is still unknown and it is an area that has largely been overlooked by scholars, possibly because it sits ill at ease with the dominant narrative of greed and destruction. Eight former monastic communities continued largely unchanged in their diocesan roles, and six more were preserved to serve the creation of new secular sees. In addition to these, were the numerous monastic churches that continued in parochial use, due to the pre-existing rights the local communities held to worship there. Assessing the numbers of churches that continued to be the focus for prayer after the Dissolution is challenging, but estimates between a quarter and one-third of the 800 or more monasteries closed at the Dissolution seem to be reasonable.[2] The conversion to parochial use is an area that deserves more academic attention, since to date there has been an absence of more detailed site-specific case studies examining how parishes adapted the former monastic churches to serve their needs. It is also striking how rigorously these parish rights were maintained, even when they might have been at odds with some of the most influential men in the realm. One cannot imagine that a man as powerful as William Paulet, Marquis of Winchester, was best pleased that he was only granted the site of Austin Friars in London with the condition that its church should continue in parochial use.[3] Even Sir Richard Rich, chancellor of the Court of Augmentations, could not ignore such legal rights and was forced to allow the parish to continue to worship in the church of St Bartholomew Priory, which he had acquired for himself.[4]

Another traditional image of the Dissolution, the so-called "scramble for spoils," is now hard to sustain.[5] From an organizational point of view, whatever one's personal feelings about the Dissolution, the way it was so efficiently enacted cannot fail to impress. Whether it was the arranging of the visitations, the compiling of the *Valor Ecclesiasticus*, or the organized sales of land at official regulated prices, the way that the Court of Augmentations was run so efficiently nearly 500 years ago almost beggars belief. From an archaeological perspective, it is the at times meticulous post-suppression surveys detailing the possessions and buildings of the monasteries that are of particular importance, and they still remain today a largely overlooked source for understanding the state of the monasteries on the eve of their closure. Nonetheless, it would be hard for even the most revisionist interpretation to deny that greed played its part, especially amongst those who sought to benefit personally from the Dissolution. The financial benefits to the crown, down to those who bought and sold on the smallest fixtures and fittings belonging to the former religious houses, are clear enough to see.

However, what the evidence shows is that far from this being a "free for all," the process was highly controlled and regulated. In particular, the problem created by an uncritical reading of the well-known account of Michael Sherbrook has been highlighted. Taken as an "eye witness" account by many authors,[6] it was nothing of the sort, and its tale of the frenzied stripping of Roche Abbey by the local populous is at best misleading. Despite this, the supposed message is one that is still attractive to some contemporary audiences, and a nostalgia they seek to curate. For example, English Heritage, who currently manage Roche, are happy to describe Sherbrook's account as "How a vivid eyewitness account reveals the shocking speed and scale of destruction of Roche Abbey after the Suppression of the Monasteries—and the fragility of human goodness."[7] Instead, I have argued that, if one reads between the lines of the Sherbrook account, it is possible to see the organized removal of metals for the king, the granting of possessions to the monks, and the controlled auction of the remaining goods. Whilst it makes for a less dramatic story, and clear-cut moral narrative, what is seen at Roche, and undoubtedly repeatedly at countless other houses, was a highly structured processes where everyone was engaged and complicit to a certain degree, and this including the religious.

Where archaeology, in particular, has been able to contribute significantly has been in shedding light on how first the crown, and then the new owners of sites, actually went about profiting from their new estates. Accounts of the stripping of the roof lead, as well as the techniques employed by Portinari in undermining and blowing up monastic buildings with gunpowder, are well known. However, the archaeological evidence from sites such as Northampton Greyfriars shows how the lead was melted and the fodders cast, while excavations at Lewes Priory have revealed how Portinari was able to bring the walls crashing down.[8] What is less well appreciated is the extent to which the new owners of sites looked to maximize their gains through the burning of building materials to produced slaked lime, and perhaps the most ubiquitous of all, the small-scale recycling of window cames and other lesser leadwork in small bowl hearths.

However, it is important to emphasize that the new owners of monastic sites did not just seek to profit from destruction, goods, and even the architecture that was of value was retained and sold on. Whilst it is unlikely that preservation would have been at the forefront of Pole's mind when he bought the glazed windows from the cloister walk of Dale Abbey, nonetheless, those translated to Morley church are very unlikely to have survived at all had Dale continued to operate for several more centuries. Chance survivals such as these were clearly accidental, but they still provide a valuable resource to modern scholarship. It is worth bearing in mind that the reason so much elegant medieval monastic architecture survives in England and Wales today, albeit in ruinous form, is that the monasteries here were spared the horrors of the Baroque that blighted so many of their continental counterparts.

Despite the scale of destruction, we should not underestimate the extent to which aspects of the monastic world were saved and curated, at least in the short term. In this study, I have highlighted the example of the fate of the monastic libraries. To a modern scholar, there is no more emotive topic than the wanton destruction of books, especially those of such beauty and value, which were contained within the monastic libraries. Thus, it is easy to latch onto the melodramatic suggestion made by Bale that such holy works were put to base uses in the lavatories of Tudor England, however impractical vellum might be for this purpose. I am not suggesting for a moment there were not great losses, but much of what was destroyed would have been the standard and well-copied, if exquisitely illustrated, biblical texts, to say nothing of more mundane account books and other day-to-day writings. There is, however, the pervasive romantic, and largely erroneous, notion exploited by modern fiction writers such as Umberto Eco or Dan Brown, that untold "ancient" or "secret" works might have been lost. Books were undoubtedly destroyed, the presence of their metal fittings in Dissolution contexts on monastic sites attest to this. But perhaps rather more survived than is often appreciated.[9] John Leland's exhaustive search of the monastic libraries, undertaken as the Dissolution was unfolding, resulted in many important and rare works being saved for the royal collection.[10] Furthermore, it seems more than likely that those who bought up the former assets of the monasteries would have sought where possible to profit from their gains by selling books, as they did with every other good, rather than just destroying them. I have made the suggestion that local populations may have acquired some texts and repurposed them for apotropaic use in ritual blessings of the land, and it is highly likely that other elements of monastic material culture were curated for the benefit of individuals and broader communities. Indeed, just as in the case of Morley church, many parishes profited from the donation of monastic vestments, liturgical items and other ecclesiastical furnishings following the Dissolution.

One of the major themes I wanted to pursue in this book was longer term and probably entirely unexpected outcomes of the Dissolution. There is little doubt that for the king and Cromwell, their concerns were with the here and now, and they would never have envisaged, or probably cared about, some of the developments that resulted from the Dissolution. Some were attempts to mediate against the negative social impact felt by the closure of the monasteries. It is interesting to see a spate of grammar and free school foundations utilising the former religious buildings but, of course, these could hardly replace the level of education formerly provided by the monks and nuns. What is more significant are the new and unexpected opportunities that the Dissolution offered to urban groups in particular, whether that be the provision of raw materials for civic building projects or complete buildings that could be repurposed to house the emerging trade guilds.

Likewise, the release of vast amounts of monastic land onto the property market also had profound and enduring outcomes. I am not claiming this to be "social revolution" affecting all classes, certainly not; if you were a peasant or yeoman farmer life continued as usual. Yet the release of so much land inevitably had a transformative effect. Last century, there were a significant number of county-based historical studies that examined the redistribution of monastic lands in detail. Whilst these are useful up to a point, the problem with many of them is they merely equated land as a unit equivalent to its stated financial value. However, as anyone who has formed an attachment to a place, area, or notion of the landscape will attest, not all land is equal, and it is certainly not passive in the emotions it evokes. Given this, it is imperative to try and understand what, and most crucially, why people made the transactions they did; the acquisition of land was not merely about accumulating wealth for wealth's sake. The validity of this approach was first demonstrated by Swales' plotting of the Duke of Norfolk's acquisitions in Norfolk, showing how monastic property enabled the peer to extend influence over areas of the county where he had previously held few possessions, rather than just being a simple exercise in increasing his holdings and revenue.[11] I have taken a similar approach here in Lincolnshire, but as well as looking at peers such as the Duke of Suffolk, I have also focused on the choices and motivations of local gentry families, such as the Heneages and Tyrwhitts.

That the Dissolution provided new creative opportunities is, of course demonstrated by the possibilities it provided for the development of new secular housing. Most archaeological works that discuss the Dissolution touch on this as an outcome, albeit in superficial depth, but the full extent to which there was secular occupation of the former religious sites is usually underappreciated. Although it would be impossible to say precisely how many in total, it now seems likely that the vast majority of monastic sites experienced some form of secular occupation utilising the former medieval buildings in the years following their closure. Certainly, where historical or archaeological evidence survives in sufficient quantity, it is extremely hard to identify sites that were erased off the map or ceased to exist after they were dissolved. This, of course, is what should be expected, as not only was the total destruction of a monastery a formidable and expensive task, it was an illogical one for any new owner who might wish to create a residence for themselves, or simply profit from leasing the asset out to others.

This book has explored in some depth the mechanics of conversion, as many previous discussions have been rather simplistic. The exception has been several studies by Howard, who has established a model for the creation of gentry courtyard houses focused on the monastic cloister in the years immediately following the Dissolution, followed by a later wave of conversions often utilising the church.[12] Whilst both variations are known, they are the exception. Few conversions utilized the full claustral arrangement, instead focusing on one or two of its ranges, and conversions focused on the church are quite rare. What is now clear is that there were a diverse range of options available to the new owners of these properties that could suit their circumstances, resources and most crucially what parts of the former monastic complex were available to them. Furthermore, the reuse of monastic buildings was a phenomenon that extended further down the social scale than perhaps has been traditionally appreciated. For each Laycock, Netley or Titchfield Abbey that feature in every work that discusses such conversions, there were a greater number on a much more modest scale, such as those of the nunneries at Kington and Burnham priories. Furthermore, monastic buildings could be repurposed for more mundane ends, being adapted to agricultural use in the countryside, or locations for industrial processes in towns. Consequently, the conversion of buildings was a much more complex process than the evolutionary model of "cloister to country house" would suggest.

If there is an area in recent years where archaeology has made a particularly significant contribution to our understanding of the development of the monasteries following the Dissolution, it is through the examination of the changes that took place within the wider monastic precinct. Over the last two decades, a range of detailed topographical, and to a lesser extent geophysical, surveys have been undertaken focusing upon several precincts, which have emphasized that secular owners, more often than not, transformed entire landscapes, creating parks, gardens, and leisure spaces. Indeed, where detailed surveys have taken place, it is often apparent that the majority of earthworks that survive today, in fact, relate to the post-Suppression, rather than earlier, activity. Although for convenience in this book I have separated the discussion of house and garden conversions, they should, in reality, be viewed together as part of the same transformative process; house, garden, and ruins were all experienced as one. One of the interesting elements to emerge from these studies is that for some secular individuals, garden landscapes were as important, if not more so, to their owner than the houses they occupied. This is evidenced by the "theatrical" landscaping of Barlings Abbey by Charles Brandon, as argued for by Everson and Stocker, or the sheer scale of effort undertaken in the construction of the many gardens around Jervaulx Abbey, or the monumental Mount at Lewes Priory.[13]

Despite the recent advances in this area of archaeological investigation, some caution is still required. Meticulous archaeological survey inevitably provides a very "flat" chronology, at best just divided into pre- and post-Dissolution phases, and one that is usually entirely speculative. Where it is possible to undertake excavation to provide more fine-grained data, this inevitably is limited and cannot possibly cover the whole landscape. As a result, while I feel this is probably the most productive avenue for future research, it is also the one that requires the most cautious and judicious approach; it is far too easy to create narratives that are purely a corroboration of the researchers own perceptions or biases.

The Dissolution of the Monasteries was, without doubt, one of the most complex, divisive, and tumultuous moments of the 16th century. Indeed, it is often viewed as a defining moment of transition, where the old medieval world was brought to an end, and the Renaissance could finally flourish free of the shackles of the old religion. Whether from the standpoint of defining the start of a historical period, or in drawing to a close the narrative of monastic life, the Dissolution is frequently defined as an "act," and while in a political sense this is true, its wider social ramifications lasted for the rest of the century. Just as the former religious did not disappear overnight, neither too did the monasteries. Their original function may have ceased, but the vast majority went on to evolve in new ways under secular ownership. Whether as assets of capital to be exploited, sources of land to be redistributed, buildings to be converted, or landscapes to be developed, the monasteries provided a wealth of opportunities that ensured that they had an afterlife that lasted far longer than those responsible for their closure. It is the archaeological wealth of this legacy that this book has sought to highlight.

NOTES

Chapter 1

1. Both Prescott 1952 and Mantel 2009 provide meticulously researched, albeit contrasting, views of The Dissolution, most notably in their portrayal of the Pilgrimage of Grace and the character of Thomas Cromwell. Nonetheless, they still largely play to the traditional narrative themes of greed and opportunism.
2. Beckett 2008.
3. Colvin 1999, 52.
4. Baskerville 1937, 273–275.
5. Marsh 1998, 13–15.
6. Trigge 1589, 7.
7. Handley 2004.
8. Spelman 1853, 247.
9. Spelman 1853; this work was not published until the end of the 17th century and while mildly entertaining, should be treated as a curiosity rather than historical fact.
10. Handley 2004.
11. Gasquet 1888.
12. Bellenger 2006.
13. Gasquet 1888, xi.
14. Brooke 2004.
15. Knowles 1940, 1948, 1955, 1959).
16. Knowles 1959, 292.
17. Youings 1971; Woodward 1966.
18. Shagan 2003, 163–164.
19. Shagan 2003, 163.
20. Lowe 2010, 3–4.
21. Shagan 2003, 163. He points out that Duffy 1992 completely ignores the monasteries, whilst Haigh 1993 contains less than ten pages specifically dedicated to the Dissolution.
22. Bernard 2011.
23. Coppack 1990, 146.
24. Platt 1984, 222 and 240.
25. Coppack 1990, 129–146; Greene 1992, 178–198.

26. Clarke 1984; Steane 1985.
27. Crossley 1990, 100.
28. Johnson 1996.
29. Coppack 2000, 123-132; Coppack and Aston 2002, 129-150.
30. Brown and Howard-Davies 2008.
31. Everson and Stocker 2003, 2011. Whilst I happen to disagree with some of their conclusions, I would argue this is an excellent attempt to contextualize the site.
32. Willmott and Bryson 2013.

Chapter 2

1. Knowles and Hadcock 1953, 364-365,
2. Huggon 2018.
3. Greene 1992, 1.
4. Knowles 1940, 4-15; Ryan 1931.
5. For recent discussions summarising the debates on the identification of possible early medieval monasteries see Willmott and Daubney 2020; Willmott and Wright in press.
6. Knowles and Hadcock 1953, 364.
7. The difference between what constituted a priory (ruled by a prior) and an abbey (ruled by an abbot) is at times a little confusing and dependent on the order involved. For the Benedictines (but also other orders such as the Augustinians), a priory was a house of lesser wealth and status, but for the Cistercians all houses however large or small were classed as abbeys. For our purposes, the distinction is largely academic, as archaeologically no meaningful distinction can be made.
8. Knowles and Hadcock 1953, 360; Coppack 1998, 15-17.
9. Knowles 1940 146-7; Knowles and Hadcock 1953, 360.
10. Coppack and Aston 2002, 11-13; Molvarec and Yocum in press.
11. Graham 1901.
12. O'Sullivan 2013, 2-3.
13. Gilchrist 1995, 62-65.
14. Knowles and Hadcock 1953, 364.
15. Knowles and Hadcock 1953, 364.
16. Page 1974, 178-179.
17. Gilchrist 1995, 108.
18. Knowles and Hadcock 1953, 231.
19. Knowles and Hadcock 1953, 171-172, 178.
20. Taunton 1897, 74.
21. An accessible overview of the differences between the churches of various monastic orders, and their development through time can be found in Coppack 1990, 32-60.
22. See Coppack 1993, 49.
23. Greene 1992, 158-159.
24. Wrathmell 2018.
25. Hope 1901.
26. Townend 2017.
27. Breeden 2018.
28. Hadcock 1955, 162-163.
29. Doubleday and Page 1903, 226-229; Slazman 1948, 219.
30. O'Sullivan 2013.
31. Knowles 1959, 167-170.

32. Woodward 1966, 5-9-60.
33. Hodgett 1975, 23.
34. Hughes 1950, 283.
35. Knowles 1959, 270.
36. Bernard 2011, 397–398.
37. Logan 1991.
38. TNA SP 1/102, mm. 91-114, summarized in L. and P. Henry VIII, X 364, p.137–144.
39. Woodward 1966, 59–60.
40. Bernard 2011, 399–400.
41. Woodward 1966, 69.
42. Woodward 1966, 79–85.
43. See Gunn 1989 and Hoyle 2001 for comprehensive discussions of the Lincolnshire Rising and the Pilgrimage of Grace respectively.
44. Woodward 1966, 107–108.
45. Youings 1971, 63.
46. Woodward 1966, 114.
47. Dickinson 1968; Holder 2011, 34.
48. Bernard 2011, 405.
49. Page 1906, 363–369.
50. Elton 1982, 380–385.
51. Cunich 1998; Huggon 2018, 44.
52. Dickens 1964, 205–210.

Chapter 3

1. Savine 1909, 98.
2. Wright 1843, 224.
3. Wright 1843, 144.
4. Wright 1843, 257.
5. Cook 1965, 198.
6. Beckett 2001, 71–72.
7. Walker 1926, 52.
8. Summarized in Gasquet 1889 II, 535.
9. e.g. Greene 1992,185.
10. Walbran 1863, 294.
11. Cook 1965, 137; L. and P. Henry VIII, XII (ii), 432, p.174.
12. Willmott and Bryson 2013, 142.
13. Woodward 1966, 126.
14. L. and P. Henry VIII, VII, 237, p. 97.
15. L. and P. Henry VIII, XII (ii), 432, p.174.
16. Dunning 1952.
17. Peers 1927, 277.
18. Cook 1965, 136–137.
19. Sunley and Stevens 1995, 54.
20. Thomson 1964, 10.
21. Barker 1907, 214–215.

22. Rees 1987, 21.
23. Walbran 1876, 146.
24. Elliston Erwood 1923, 196.
25. Baker 1873, 125.
26. Barker 1907, 214–215.
27. Williams 1978, 106–107.
28. Johnson 2006, 19.
29. Courtney 1997, 186.
30. Sîan Rees pers. comm.
31. Thomas 2006, 205–206.
32. Hoover and Hoover 1950, 230.
33. Blanchard 1981; 1992, 9.
34. Hare 1985, 156.
35. Johnson 2006, 19.
36. See Bayley 1991.
37. Johnson 2006, 20.
38. Courtney 1989, 115–116.
39. Courtney 1989, 125.
40. James 1997, 184.
41. Doonan 1997, 4.
42. Foreman 1996, 86–87.
43. Rahtz and Hirst 1976, 74.
44. Ellis 1997, 33
45. Foreman 1986, 147.
46. Thomas 2006, 209; Wilson and Hurst 1966, 176; Bull *et al.* 2011, 90; Wilson and Hurst 1962–1963, 314; Walker 1926, 103.
47. Willmott and Bryson 2013, 142; Wright 1843, 291–292.
48. Wright 1843, 278; L. and P. Henry VIII, XII (ii), 432, p.174.
49. Blair and Blair 1991, 82–83.
50. E.g. Greene 1992, 187.
51. Gasquet 1889 II, 428; Hibbert 1910, 257.
52. Dunkin 1878, 50.
53. Walcott 1871, 223.
54. Gasquet 1889 II, 430.
55. Greene 1992, 187.
56. Butler 1976, 12.
57. L. and P. Henry VIII, XVI, 745, p. 351.
58. Hare 1985, 43, 165–166.
59. Doonan 1999, 3.
60. Austin 1987, 147–149.
61. Smith and Gnudi 1942, 281–288.
62. Austin 1987, 149.
63. Lowe 1987, 95.
64. Page 1911b, 129–132.
65. L. and P. Henry VIII, XI, 242, p. 105.
66. L. and P. Henry VIII, XIII (ii), 719, p. 275.

67. Drury 1974, 50–51.
68. Lambrick and Woods 1976, 185.
69. Rylatt and Mason 2003, 26.
70. Beverley 2004.
71. L. and P. Henry VIII XIII (i), 554, p. 204.
72. Trans. Hope 1906, 77–78.
73. Lyne 1987, 31.
74. L. and P. Henry VIII, XII (i), 311, p.143.
75. Brakspear 1907, 495–496.
76. Brakspear 1907, 502.
77. Fergusson and Harrison 1999, 188.
78. Platt 1984, 241; Aston 1973, 241.
79. Cited in Clapham 1926, 69–70.
80. Slade 1975, 51.
81. L. and P. Henry VIII, XIII (i), 590, p. 217.
82. Jenkinson and White 1915, 29.
83. Jenkinson and White 1915, 31–37.
84. L. and P. Henry VIII, XVII, 75, p. 34.
85. Schofield and Lea 2005, 172; Poulton and Woods 1984, 70.
86. Sherlock and Woods 1988, 67, 87.
87. Clapham 1926, 70.
88. Daniels 1986, 272–273.
89. Hope 1901, 14.
90. Dobson and Donaghey 1985, 6.
91. Kemp 1996, 214–216.
92. e.g. Samson 2004.
93. Clapham 1926, 70.
94. Fletcher 1899, 275.
95. Fowler 1903, 102–103.
96. Raine 1828.
97. Nichols 1846, 198.
98. Philp 1968, 15.
99. Gilyard-Beer and Coppack 1986, 162–163.
100. Walbran 1876, 154.
101. Lyne 1997, 31.
102. Willmott and Townend 2017.
103. James 1997, 177.
104. James 1997, 118.
105. Poulton and Woods, 1984, 52.
106. Grainger and Phillpotts 2011, 59–60; Dyson *et al.* 2011, 162.
107. Aston 1973, 239–240.
108. Howsam 2016.
109. Walker 1923, 57.
110. For example, Dickinson 1961, 135–136.
111. Bale 1549, sig. B ir.

112. Howsam 2016, 382–383.
113. Examples of book fittings are being added on an almost daily basis to the Portable Antiquities Scheme database, see www.finds.org.uk. For a summary of those found through excavation see Howsam 2016, 17–18.
114. See Spencer 1998 for a comprehensive overview and discussion of ampullae.
115. Anderson 2010, 198.
116. Mitchiner 1986, 138.
117. Dickens 1959, 123–126.
118. e.g. Gasquet 1889 II, 317–322: Dickinson 1961, 133–134; Platt 1984, 233–234.
119. Dickens 1959 31.
120. Dickens 1959, 99.
121. Dickens 1959, 92.
122. Dickens 1959, 123.
123. L. and P. Henry VII, xiii.(ii), p. 550, no. 25.
124. Dickens 1959, 125.
125. Cook 1965, 226.
126. Dickens 1959, 124.
127. Aveling 1870.
128. L. and P. Henry VIII, XX (i), 717, p. 353.
129. Aveling 1870, 130.
130. L. and P. Henry VIII, XIII (ii), 377, p. 147.
131. L. and P. Henry VIII, XII (ii), 92, p. 32.
132. Gasquet 1889, II 433; Serjeantson and Adkins 1906, 120.
133. Shagan 2003, 162-197.
134. Shagan 2003, 178.
135. Knowles 1930.
136. Shagan 2003, 172; Hamilton 1875, 90.
137. L. and P. Henry VIII XIII (i) 231, p. 79.
138. L. and P. Henry VIII XIII (i) 348, p. 120.
139. Summarized in Hibbert 1910, 258–278.
140. Colvin 1943, 8.
141. Walcott 1871, 221–224.
142. L. and P. Henry VIII, XIX (i), 141, p.77; Colvin 1943, 16–17.
143. Detailed in Walcott 1871
144. Cox 1877b, 253.
145. Colvin 1943, 19.
146. Colvin 1943, 11; L. and P. Henry VIII, XI, 562, p. 223.
147. L. and P. Henry VIII, XVI, 580, p. 273; L. and P. Henry VIII, XV, 613, p. 294.
148. Described and illustrated in detail in Fox 1872, 8–14.
149. Colvin 1939, 131.
150. Ward 1890, 71–72.
151. Hope 1883, 91.
152. Hope 1880, 129-30; Ward 1890, 72.
153. Croft and Mynard 1986.
154. Cox 1879, 327.
155. Cox 1879, 331.
156. Stephenson 1926, 85.

157. Colvin 1943, 19.
158. Fox 1872, 24.
159. Cox 1879, 330.
160. Hope 1879, 105.
161. Drage 1990, 80–81.
162. Ward 1890, 75.
163. Walcot 1871, 222.
164. Ward 1890, 86.
165. Cox 1879, 411.
166. Cox 1877a, 230.
167. Cox 1877b, 308–309.

Chapter 4

1. L. and P. Henry VIII, XI, 1544, p. 505.
2. Merriman 1902, 17.
3. Woodward 1966, 124.
4. Younings 1954, 21.
5. Youings 1971, 117.
6. Youings 1971, 117–8; Woodward 1966, 124.
7. Dugdale 1693; Tanner 1744; Cobbett 1868; Spelman 1853.
8. See Kew 1970.
9. Youings 1971, 129.
10. Hodgett 1951, 93.
11. Rowse 1969, 174–175.
12. Rowse 1969, 178–179.
13. Hodgett 1951, 85.
14. Rowse 1969, 179.
15. L. and P. Henry VIII, XIII (ii), 528, p. 207.
16. Hoggett 1951, 85; Peacock 1883, 58,
17. L. and P. Henry VIII, X, 364, p. 139.
18. Page 1893, xii–xiii.
19. Habakkuk 1958, 362.
20. Youings 1954, 18.
21. Constant 1934, 190.
22. Carew 1769, 110.
23. Fisher 1913, 499.
24. Hodgett 1951, 85.
25. Knowles 1959, 394.
26. Youings 1971, 119.
27. Wyndham 1979, 66; L. and P. Henry VIII, XIV (ii), 780 (35) p. 301.
28. Youings 1971, 122.
29. Knowles 1959, 395.
30. Youings 1954, 24.
31. Habakkuk 1958, 362–363.
32. Habakkuk 1958, 363–364.

33. Habakkuk 1958, 372.
34. Kew 1970, 94–97.
35. Kew 1970, 101.
36. Youings 1971, 119.
37. L. and P. Henry VIII, XIV (ii), 780 (36), p. 301; L. and P. Henry VIII, XVIII (i), 623 (29), p. 362.
38. Habakkuk 1958, 376.
39. Fisher 1913, 499–501.
40. Fisher 1913, 500.
41. L. and P. Henry VIII, XVI, 220, p, 95–96.
42. For example, Bindoff 1950, 115–116.
43. Cameron 1975, 50–53.
44. See Haigh 1969.
45. L. and P. Henry VIII, X, 1256 (5–6), p. 526–527.
46. Betty 1989, 133.
47. Youings 1954, 29.
48. Wyndham 1979, 66.
49. For example, Wyndham 1979, 72–73.
50. Habakkuk 1958, 380.
51. Haigh 1969, 126.
52. Williams 1967, 101–102.
53. Cameron 1975, 54–55.
54. Cameron 1975, 55–56.
55. For example, Habakkak 1958, 380; Youings 1971, 130; Cameron 1975, 57.
56. Walker 1926, 58.
57. Venn and Venn 1922, 172.
58. Willmott and Bryson 2013, 140–401.
59. Willmott and Bryson 2013, 141; Fowler 1903, 102–103.
60. Willmott and Bryson 2013, 142.
61. Knowles 1959, 273; Shaw 2004.
62. Bettey 1968, 296.
63. L. and P. Henry VIII, VI, 578 (10), p. 258.
64. L. and P. Henry VIII, VI, 328, p. 152; Bettey 1968, 298.
65. Rowse 1969, 189.
66. Bettey 1968, 300.
67. L. and P. Henry VIII, XIV (ii), appendix (35), p. 367.
68. L. and P. Henry VIII, XV, 282 (90), p. 90.
69. Shaw 2004.
70. Traskey 1978, 180–182.
71. Prideaux 1907.
72. Shaw 1998.
73. Bettey 1968, 298.
74. For example, Tawney 1926, 140; Bindoff 1950, 116.
75. Habakkuk 1958, 376–379.
76. Youings, 1954, 26; Gray 1987, 136–137.
77. Habukkuk 1958, 378–379.

78. For example, Davies 1994, 194–197.
79. Woodward 1966, 132.
80. Woodward 1964, 778–779.
81. Woodward 1964, 782.
82. Haigh 1969, 132.
83. L. and P. Henry VIII, XVIII (i), 623 (79), p. 366–367; L. and P. Henry VIII, XIX (i), 610 (116), p. 386.
84. Habakkuk 1958, 375–376.
85. Habakkuk 1958, 376.
86. Haigh 1969, 130.
87. Piccope 1857, 107.
88. Swales 1966.
89. Swales 1966, 17.
90. Head 1995, 272–273.
91. Head 1995, 274–275.
92. Swales 1966.
93. Swales 1966, 20–21.
94. L. and P. Henry VIII, XII (i) 1330 (26), p. 604; L. and P. Henry VIII, XII (ii) 1311 (30), p. 471–472; L. and P. Henry VIII, XV, 942 (43), p. 470–471.
95. Head 1995, 276.
96. Swales 1966, 19.
97. Swales 1966, 41.
98. For example, James 1970; Ward 1986; Gunn 1989.
99. L. and P. Henry VIII, XIV (i), 651 (45), p. 258–2561.
100. Everson and Stocker 2003,
101. Everson and Stocker 2003, 151–156.
102. James 1970, 18.
103. James 1970, 29–30; Gunn 1989, 52.
104. L. and P. Henry VIII, XI, 843, p.335–336.
105. Gunn 1988, 143; Gunn 1989, 56.
106. Gunn 1988, 143.
107. Gunn 1988, 158.
108. Gunn 1988, 167.
109. MacCulloch 1987, 69–70.
110. L. and P. Henry VIII, XIII (ii), 1182 (18)–(22), p. 491–495; L. and P. Henry VIII XIV (i), 651 (45), p. 258–261.
111. Nichols and Bruce 1863, 28–41.
112. Tempest 1918, 71.
113. Everson and Stocker 2003.
114. Hodgett 1975, 51.
115. Hodgett 1951, 87.
116. Hodgett 1947, 45.
117. L. and P. Henry VIII, XI, 324, p. 133.
118. Maddison 1888, xxix; Maddison 1903, 481.
119. Hicks 2004.
120. Hofmann 1982b.
121. L. and P. Henry VIII, XV, 942 (118), p. 479–480.
122. Hofmann 1982b.

123. L. and P. Henry VIII, XIV (ii) 264 (5), p. 99.
124. Riordan 2004; Gunn 1989, 57.
125. L. and P. Henry VIII, 651 (49), p. 251.
126. L. and P. Henry VIII, XV, 611 (32), p. 283; L. and P. Henry VIII, XIX (i), 610 (78), p. 379; L. and P. Henry VIII, XIII (i), 1115 (1), p. 408.
127. Maddison 1903, 483.
128. Hofmann 1982; Maddison 1904, 1019.
129. Tyrwhitt 1862, 16.
130. Gunn 1989, 57; Hodgett 1947, 23, L. and P. Henry VIII, 553 and 553, p. 221.
131. Gunn 1989 58; L. and P. Henry VIII XII (i), 392, p. 185.
132. L. and P. Henry VIII XIII (i), 384 (93), p. 142-143.
133. L. and P. Henry VIII, XIV 780 (12), p. 298-299; L. and P. Henry VIII, XVII, 714 (15), p. 322.
134. Maddison 1904, 1020, Tyrwhitt 1862, 17.
135. Fuidge 1981.
136. Dale 1982.
137. Tyrwhitt 1862, 98-100.
138. Maddison 1904, 1021.
139. Hofmann 1982c.
140. Maddison 1904, 1017-1018.
141. Hodgett 1951, 91.
142. Hofmann 1982, 415.
143. L. and P. Henry VIII, 567, p. 225.
144. Hofmann 1982, 415.
145. For example, L. and P. Henry VIII, XXIii, 476 (85), p. 239.
146. Mattison 1888, li and 45; Maddison 1891, xxiv.
147. Hodgett 1975, 59; Maddison 1891, xxiv.
148. Hill 1956, 63.
149. Hodgett 1975, 59; 1951, 92.
150. O'Sullivan 2013, 206.
151. O'Sullivan 2013, 155.

Chapter 5

1. Knowles 1959, 389-392.
2. Knowles 1959, 391.
3. Knowles 1959, 389.
4. Walbran 1862, 304-306.
5. Sodden 2003, 281.
6. Hodgson 1884; 1885, 100-9, 215-245.
7. Heale 2003.
8. Dickinson 1968, 65.
9. Dickinson 1968, 65.
10. E.g. Dickinson 1968, 66; Coppack 1990, 131.
11. Hodgson 1885, 109.
12. Clifton-Taylor 1974, 230-235.
13. For example, St Andrews Sempringham listed here is now known to have been the original parish church, the monastic complex having been identified some distance away (Graham 1940; Cope-Faulkner 2011).

14. Page 1911b, 169–171.
15. Fairweather 1926, 102.
16. Greenslade and Pugh 1970, 340–343.
17. Doubleday and Page 1903, 226–229.
18. Clifton-Taylor 1974, 230–235.
19. Platt 1984, 239.
20. Dickinson 1956, 67.
21. Insall 1985.
22. Heale 2003, 4.
23. Insall 1985, 13.
24. A detailed account of the siege of Crowland can be found in Sweeting 1899.
25. Bulmer 1892, 121.
26. Heale 2003, 11.
27. BL Ms Royal 18/D iii, f 63–63).
28. Heale 2003, 11.
29. Hamilton Thompson 1928, 112.
30. Knowles and St Joseph 1952, 199.
31. Webb 1921, 261–276.
32. Heale 2003, 14.
33. Reddan and Clapham 1924, 19–20.
34. Roth 1966, 295.
35. Holder 2011, 170–171.
36. Ford 2004.
37. Holder 2011, 174.
38. O'Sullivan 2013, 265.
39. Page 1906, 363–369.
40. Page 1973, 56–60.
41. Heale 2003, 7.
42. Sherlock 2008, 115.
43. Heale 2003, 15–6.
44. Clifton-Taylor 1974, 231–235.
45. RCHME 1922, 165–8; RCHME 1916, 320–322.
46. Salzman 1947.
47. Baggs *et al.* 1980, 128–132.
48. Stewart-Brown 1925, 103–104.
49. Robinson 1998, 69.
50. Hope and Brakspear 1906, 139.
51. Hills 1874, 426.
52. Pevsner and Harris 1989, 401.
53. Little 1979, 210–211.
54. E.g. Graves and Heslop 2013, 219.
55. Butler 1984, 134.
56. Stocker 2011, 150.
57. Harbottle 1968, 175–176.
58. L. and P. Henry VIII, XIV (i), 342, p. 133.

59. Ingram 1977, 22.
60. L. and P. Henry VIII, XVI, 1230, p. 578.
61. Summerson 1993; Sodden 2003, 283.
62. L. and P. Henry VIII, XIII (ii), 719, p. 275.
63. Giles 1999, 90.
64. Schofield 1995, 44–45.
65. Tittler 1991, 14–21.
66. Giles 1999, 101.
67. Martin 1937, 57.
68. L. and P. Henry VIII, XIII (ii) 789, p. 297.
69. Harbottle 2001.
70. Palmer 1888, 82.
71. Leighton 1933, 185–186.
72. Leighton 1933, 172–178.
73. Harbottle and Fraser 1987, 23–25.
74. Graves and Heslop 2013, 221–224.
75. Gardner 1754, 60.
76. Palmer 1881, 91–92.
77. Palmer 1883, 144.
78. Martin 1937, 207–209.
79. Johnson 1974; Herbert 1988, 242–245.
80. Gilyard-Beer 1977, 16.
81. Edwards 1949, 193.
82. Alexander 1990, 122.
83. Woodfield 1981, 83; Alexander 1990, 129.
84. Alexander 1990, 142–143.
85. Alexander 1990, 130, 144.
86. Dawley 1955, 25.
87. Jordan 1959, 161-2.
88. Palmer 1994, 229–230.
89. Drury 1974.
90. O'Sullivan 2013, 178.
91. Gilyard-Beer 1977; Blatchly and Wade 1977.
92. Cowie 1976, 467; Martin 1937, 187–188.
93. Holder 2011, 105.
94. James 1997, 10.
95. James 1997, 177.
96. Martin 1937, 93–97.
97. Hayfield 2006.
98. Salzman 1947, 126–131.
99. Palmer 1887, 104.
100. Woodfield 1981, 81-2; Woodfield 2005, 9–10.
101. See Tracy 1997, 77 for a comprehensive description of the stalls.
102. Woodfield 1981, 116–117.
103. Woodfield 1981, 99–100.

104. Woodfield 1981, 125–126.
105. Woodfield 1981, 87, 100.
106. O'Sullivan 2013, 165.
107. Simon 1966, 181.
108. Smith 1966, 133–137.
109. Bull *et al.* 2011, 86.
110. Beier 1983, 20–4.
111. L. and P. Henry VIII XII (2), 1251, p. 518.
112. Whittick 2010, 111–113.
113. Cooper 2004, 91–93.
114. Leech and McWhirr 1982, 191.
115. Fuller 1883, 228.
116. Leech and McWhirr 1982, 191.
117. Gaydon and Pugh 1973, 95.
118. Barber and Thomas 2002, 82.
119. Schofield 1993, 38–39.
120. Rosenfield 1961, 187–8; L. and P. Henry VIII, XIX (ii), 340 (39), p. 188.
121. Schofield 1993, 39.
122. Schofield and Lea 2005, 177–178.
123. Schofield 1993, 39.
124. Blackmore 2005, 256.
125. Holder 2011, 194–195.
126. Willmott 2005, XX
127. Kingsford 1908, 148.
128. Holder 2011, 197–198.
129. Willmott 2005 XX.
130. Martin, 1929, 169–70; Pragnell 2007, 337.
131. L. and P. Henry VIII, XIV (i), 423, p. 170.
132. Pragnell 2007, 337.
133. Martin 1929, 172–173.
134. Palmer 1882, 304.
135. Knowles 1932, 197.
136. Martin 1937, 85; Herbert 1988, 291.
137. Ferris 2001, 116–119.

Chapter 6

1. Howard 1987, 143.
2. Cal. Pat Roll Ed. VI 1924, 153; Cal. Pat Roll Ed. VI 1925, 97.
3. Williams 1983.
4. Gardner 1955, 21.
5. Howard 1987, 156–157.
6. Drury 1982, 97.
7. Drury 1980.
8. Drury 1982, 97–100.
9. Hare 1993, 221.

10. Willmott and Bryson 2013.
11. e.g. Thurley 2013.
12. Willmott and Bryson 2013, 157.
13. Kell 1863, 65.
14. Brown and Howard-Davies 2008; West and Palmer 2014; Willmott and Bryson 2013.
15. Coppack forthcoming; Doggett 2002.
16. Howard 1987, 2003.
17. Howard 2003, 221.
18. Howard 1987, 144.
19. Howard 2003, 221–222.
20. Howard 1987, 139–40; 2003, 226.
21. Summarized in Hope 1906b.
22. Hope 1906b, 232–239.
23. Howard 1987, 153.
24. Hants. Archives 5M53/1444.
25. Summarized in Ward 1989.
26. Hants. Archives 5M53/1556, 1558.
27. Reproduced and briefly discussed in Tamkin 1989.
28. Howard 1987, 152.
29. Howard 2003, 226.
30. Howard 2003, 223.
31. Graves 2004.
32. Clapham 1915, 211.
33. Howard 1987, 149.
34. Clapham 1915, 215.
35. Hare 1993, 216–7.
36. Ford 2004.
37. Kell 1863; Barker *et al.* 2005.
38. Kell 1863, 65 and 74.
39. Kell 1863, 74.
40. Barker *et al.* 2005, 12–3.
41. Kell 1863, 85.
42. Kell 1863, 72.
43. Page 1911, 15–27.
44. Smith 2010, 148.
45. Davies 2004.
46. Smith 2010, 145.
47. Arber 1870, 25.
48. e.g. Howard 1987, 152, Greene 1992, 188.
49. Challis 2004.
50. Brakspear 1900, 1.
51. Hamilton Thompson 1919, 110–111.
52. Black 1982.
53. Thorpe 1982.
54. Thorpe 1982.

55. Toulmin Smith 1907, 78.
56. Frame 2004.
57. Hughes 1898, 42.
58. Miller 1982; Newman 2004.
59. Gilyard-Beer 1960, 10; L. and P. Henry VIII, XIII (i), 190 (42), p. 64.
60. NA E210/9845.
61. L. and P. Henry VIII, XII (i), 976, p. 441.
62. Gilyard-Beer 1960, 15.
63. Howard 2003, 221–222.
64. Howard 2003, 226.
65. L. and P. Henry VIII, XVIII (i), 100 (18), p. 66.
66. Harwood 1844, 498–490.
67. Taylor 1974, 57.
68. Taylor 1974, 60-2.
69. Gaskell Brown 1995, 27.
70. Copeland 1963, 19–21.
71. Loades 2004.
72. Gaskell Brown 1995, 31.
73. Gaskell Brown 1995, 31.
74. Copeland 1963, 29.
75. e.g. Howard 1987, 144.
76. Smith 2009, 123.
77. L. and P. Henry VIII, XX (i), 465 (45), p. 216.
78. Ellis 1997, 49.
79. Coppack *et al.* 2002, 81–3.
80. Tester 1973, 156–157.
81. Swales 1982.
82. McNeil and Turner 1990, 67.
83. Cannon 1991, 23.
84. McNeil and Turner 1990, 67.
85. Brown and Howard-Davies 2008.
86. Helsby 1882, 680.
87. Greene 1989, 150.
88. Brown and Howard-Davies 2008, 199.
89. Brown and Howard-Davies 2008, 203.
90. Marrow 2008, 316–329.
91. Valor Eccl., ii, 113–114.
92. Brakspear 1923, 246.
93. Jackson 1862, 145.
94. Valor Eccl., iv. 221.
95. Brakspear 1903.
96. Parker *et al.* 2007, 76.
97. O'Sullivan 2006.
98. Hodder 1991, 206–207.
99. Mynard *et al.* 1996, 29–30.

100. Christie and Coad 1980, 193–194.
101. Poster and Sherlock 1987, 67.
102. Hare 1978, 192–193.
103. L. and P. Henry VIII, XIX (ii), 527 (13), p. 313.
104. Thorpe 1982b.
105. Cocks 2006.
106. Page 1908, 83.
107. L. and P. Henry VIII, XV 362, p. 143.
108. Hope 1901, 33.
109. Goodall and Kelly 2004.
110. Coad and Coppack 1998.
111. Coad and Coppack 1998.
112. L. and P. Henry VIII, XV, 942 (43), p. 470–471.
113. Wilcox 1987.
114. Page 1906, 367–369.
115. Willmott and Bryson 2013.
116. Caroe 1933, 229.
117. R.C.G. 1981.
118. Caroe 1933, 235.
119. Buckley *et al.* 2006, 104–108.
120. Nichols 1815, 287.
121. Wilson 1905, 184-9; Martindale 1922.
122. Arnold *et al.* 2004.
123. Graham 1940, 78.
124. Cope-Faulkner 2011, 24–26.
125. Page 1906b, 185.
126. McAvoy 1988.
127. Beavitt 1995.
128. Merriman 2004.
129. Johnson 2006, 20.
130. Merriman 2004.
131. Morris 2009.
132. Schofield 1993, 29.
133. Schofield 1993, 30–33; Schofield and Lea 2005.
134. Holder 2011, 160–171.
135. Holder 2011, 171.
136. Barber and Thomas 2002, 73–74.
137. Thomas *et al.* 1997, 131–133.
138. Grainger and Phillpotts 2011, 58–59.
139. Schofield 1993, 29.
140. Schofield 1993, 39.

Chapter 7

1. Bond 2004, 156–170.
2. Coppack 1990, 80.

3. Coppack 1986, 127.
4. Coppack and Aston 2002, 89–92.
5. For example Coppack 1990, 142; Everson and Stocker 2009.
6. For example Knowles 1959, 384; Cook 1965, 138; Aston 1973, 239; Morris 2003, 240, to name just a few.
7. Lower 1845, 3.
8. Everson 2005.
9. King 1983, 472.
10. Everson 2005, 8–13.
11. Smith 2009.
12. Gater 1998.
13. Malden 1967, 89–94.
14. Gater 1998.
15. Campbell *et al.* 1972, 117.
16. Gater 1994.
17. Tester 1973, 131.
18. Burrow 2015.
19. West and Palmer 2014, 379.
20. Archer 2008.
21. West and Palmer 2014, 381.
22. West and Palmer 2014, 45–46.
23. Coppack 1990, 142–143.
24. Dunn and Lax 2001, 12–15.
25. Clarke 2011, 74.
26. Drury 1982, 97.
27. Brown and Howard-Davies 2008, 14.
28. Jecock 1999.
29. Jecock 1999, 20–22.
30. Everson and Stocker 2003.
31. Everson and Stocker 2011, 89–94.
32. Everson and Stocker 2011, 97.
33. Everson and Stocker 2008, 102–104.
34. Coppack and Harrison 2014, 42–43.
35. Everson and Stocker 2008, 102–104; Coppack and Harrison 2014, 43.
36. Oswald *et al.* 2010; Coppack 1991.
37. Page 1906b, 237.
38. Coppack in prep.
39. Cal. Pat. Rolls Ed. VI I 1924, 153.
40. Oswald *et al.* 2010, 37.
41. Cal. Pat. Rolls Ed. VI III 1925, 97.
42. Coppack in prep.
43. Coppack 1991.
44. Tyrwhitt 1869, 97.
45. Rigold 1966.
46. Tyrwhitt 1869, 97. It is important to note that the author of this self-published family history misunderstood the fact that in the 16th century the civil year started on 25th March, so ascribed the date of purchase to

1602. However, this transaction took place in February during the 45th regnal year of Elizabeth I, so 1603. This basic error has been repeated by other authors such as Oswald *et al.* 2010, 15.
47. Oswald *et al.* 2010, 17-18.
48. Oswald *et al.* 2010, 19.
49. Oswald *et al.* 2010, 88.
50. Everson *et al.* 1991, 47, 176; Everson and Stocker 2009, fig. 7.
51. Jackson 1870, 145-146.
52. Roberts 1984.
53. Although known today as the Abbot's lodge, and this building was in fact the documented "New Hall' or guesthouse of the monastery.
54. Jackson 1870, 131.

Chapter 8

1. Although I find the recent review of the monarch's motivations by Bernard 2011 persuasive.
2. Hodgson 1885, 100-9, 215-245; Heale 2003.
3. Holder 2011, 170-171.
4. Heale 2003, 14.
5. Aston 1973, 239-240.
6. For example, Dickinson 1961, 133-134; Platt 1984, 233-234.
7. https://www.english-heritage.org.uk/visit/places/roche-abbey/history/suppression/
8. Williams 1978; Lynne 1987.
9. Howsam 2016.
10. Wright 1951.
11. Swales 1966.
12. Howard 1987, 2003.
13. Everson and Stocker 2003; Jecock 1999; Everson 2005.

BIBLIOGRAPHY

Abington, T. 1723. *The Antiquities of the Cathedral Church of Worcester*. London: W. Mears.

Alexander, M. 1990. *The Growth of English Education 1348-1648. A Social and Cultural History*. London: The Pennsylvania State University Press.

Anderson, W. 2010. "Blessing the field? A study of late-medieval ampullae from England and Wales." *Medieval Archaeology* 54: 182-203.

Arber, E., ed. 1870. *Fragmenta Regalia, or, Observations on the Late Queen Elizabeth, Her Times and Favorites*. London: A. Murray.

Archer, I.W. 2008. "Hill, Sir Rowland (c. 1495-1561)." *Oxford Dictionary of National Biography*. Oxford: Oxford University Press. Online edition, https://doi.org/10.1093/ref:odnb/13296

Arnold, A., R. E. Howard and C. D. Litton. 2004. Tree-Ring Analysis of Timbers from Wetheral Priory Gatehouse, Wetheral, Cumbria. Unpublished English Heritage Centre for Archaeology Report 36/2004.

Aston, M. 1973. "English ruins and English history: the Dissolution and the sense of the past." *Journal of the Warburg Institute* 36: 231-255.

Austin, A. A. 1987. "Appendix E: reverberatory furnace." In B. J. Lowe, "Keynsham Abbey: excavations 1961-1985." *Somerset Archaeology and Natural History* 131: 147-149.

Aveling, J. W. 1870. *The History of Roche Abbey, from its Foundation to its Dissolution*. Worksop: Robert White.

Baggs, A.P., A. J. Kettle, S. J. Lander, A. T. Thacker and D. Wardle. 1980. "Houses of Benedictine monks: The priory of Birkenhead." In *A History of the County of Chester: Volume 3*, edited by C. R. Elrington and B. E. Harris, 128-132. London: Victoria County History.

Baker, S. 1873. "Notice of some excavations made at Muchelney in 1873 and 1874." *Proceedings of the Somerset Archaeological and Natural History Society* 18: 122-126.

Barber, B. and C. Thomas. 2002. *The London Charterhouse*. London: Museum of London Archaeology Service Monograph 10.

Barker, D., T. Sly and K. Strutt. 2005. Netley Abbey Topographic and Geophysical Survey Report. Southampton: Unpublished Archaeological Prospection Services of Southampton Report SREP 13/2005.

Barker, H. R. 1907. *West Suffolk Illustrated*. Bury St Edmunds: Pawsey and Co.

Baskerville, G. 1937. *English Monks and the Suppression of the Monasteries*. London: Jonathan Cape.

Bale, J. 1549. *The laboryouse iourney & serche of Iohan Leylande, for Englandes antiquitees*. London: S. Mierdman.

Bayley, J. 1991. "Processes in precious metal working." In *Archaeological Sciences 1989: Conference on the application of scientific techniques to archaeology*, edited by P. Budd, B. Chapman, C. Jackson, R. Janaway and B. Ottaway, 125-131. Oxbow Monograph 9. Oxford: Oxbow Books.

Beavitt, P. 1995. "Geophysical and building survey at Launde Abbey." *Transactions of the Leicestershire Archaeological and History Society* 69: 22-31.

Beckett, J. V. 2001. *Byron and Newstead: The Aristocrat and the Abbey*. London: Associated Presses.

Beckett, L. 2008. "Smash and grab." *Times Literary Supplement* 5490, June 20 2008, 22.

Beier, A. L. 1983. *The Problem of the Poor in Tudor and Early Stuart England*. London: Methuen.

Bellenger, D. A. 2006. "Gasquet, Francis Neil." *Oxford Dictionary of National Biography*. Oxford: Oxford University Press. Online edition, https://doi.org/10.1093/ref:odnb/33350

Bernard, G. W. 2011. "The Dissolution of the Monasteries." *History* 96(324): 390–409.

Bettey, J. H. 1968. "Sir John Tregonwell of Milton Abbey." *Proceedings of the Dorset Natural History and Archaeology Society* 90: 295–302.

———. 1989. *The Suppression of the Monasteries in the West Country*. Stroud: Alan Sutton.

Beverley, T. 2004. "Portinari, Sir Giovanni." *Oxford Dictionary of National Biography*. Oxford: Oxford University Press. Online edition, https://doi.org/10.1093/ref:odnb/52154

Bindoff, S. T. 1950. *Tudor England*. Harmondsworth: Penguin Books.

Black, C. J. 1982. Byron (Beron), Sir John (1487/88–1567), of Colwick and Newstead, Notts. In *The History of Parliament: the House of Commons 1509-1558,* Volume 1, by S. T. Bindoff, et al.. London: Secker & Warburg.

Blackmore, L. 2005. "The pottery." In *Holy Trinity Priory, Aldgate, City of London. An Archaeological Reconstruction and History*, J. Schofield and R. Lea, 227-247. Museum of London Archaeology Service Monograph 24. London: Museum of London.

Blair, C. and J. Blair. 1991. "Copper Alloys." In *English Medieval Industries: Craftsmen, Techniques, Products,* edited by J. Blair and N. Ramsey, 81-106. London: Hambledon Press.

Blanchard, I. 1981. "Lead mining and smelting in medieval England and Wales." In *Medieval Industry*, edited by D. Crossley, 72-84. Council for British Archaeology Research Report 44. London: Council for British Archaeology.

———. 1992. "Technical implications of the transition from silver to lead smelting in Twelfth-century England." In *Boles and Smeltmills: Report of a Seminar on the History and Archaeology of Lead Smelting Held at Reeth, Yorkshire, 15-17 May 1992,* edited by L. M. Willies and D. Cranstone, 9-11. Historical Metallurgy Society Occasional Publications 3. Matlock Bath: Historical Metallurgy Society.

Blatchly, J. and K. Wade. 1977. "Excavations at Ipswich Blackfriars in 1898 and 1976." *Proceedings of the Suffolk Institute of Archaeology and History* 34(1): 25–34.

Bond, J. 2004. *Monastic Landscapes*. Stroud: Tempus Publishing.

Brakspear, H. 1900. "Lacock Abbey Church." *Archaeological Journal* 57: 1–9.

———. 1903. "Burnham Abbey, Bucks." *Archaeological Journal* 60: 294–317.

———. 1907. "The Cistercian abbey of Stanley, Wiltshire." *Archaeologia* 60(Pt II): 493–516.

———. 1923. "IX- Excavations at some Wiltshire monasteries." *Archaeologia* 73: 225–252.

Breeden, F. 2018. Communal Solitude: The Archaeology of the Carthusian Houses of Great Britain and Ireland, 1178–1569. Unpublished PhD Thesis, University of Sheffield.

Brooke, C.N.L. 2004. "Knowles, Michael Clive (name in religion David) *(1896-1974)*." *Oxford Dictionary of National Biography*. Oxford: Oxford University Press. Online edition, https://doi.org/10.1093/ref:odnb/31322

Brown, F. and C. Howard-Davies. 2008. *Norton Priory: Monastery to Museum Excavations 1970-1997*. Lancaster: Oxford Archaeology North.

Buckley, R., S. Jones, P. Courtney and D. Smith. 2006. "Leicester Abbey after the Dissolution." In *Leicester Abbey. Medieval History: Archaeology and Manuscript Studies,* edited by J. Story, J. Bourne and R. Buckley, 95-118. Leicester: The Leicester Archaeological and Historical Society.

Bull, R., S. Davis, H. Lewis and C. Phillpotts. 2011. *Holywell Priory and the development of Shoreditch to c. 1600. Archaeology from the London Overground East London Line*. Museum of London Archaeology Monograph 53. London: Museum of London.

Bulmer, T. 1892. *History, Topography and Directory of East Yorkshire*. Ashton-on-Ribble: T. Bulmer & Co.

Burrow, C. 2015. "Wyatt, Sir Thomas (c. 1503–1542)." *Oxford Dictionary of National Biography*. Oxford: Oxford University Press. Online edition, https://doi.org/10.1093/ref:odnb/30111

Butler, L.A.S. 1976. *Neath Abbey*. London: HMSO.

———. 1984. "The houses of the mendicant orders in Britain: Recent archaeological work." In *Archaeological Papers from York Presented to M.W. Barley,* edited by P. V. Addyman and V. E. Black, 123-136. York: York Archaeological Trust.

Cameron, A. 1975. "Some social consequences of the Dissolution of the Monasteries in Nottinghamshire." *Transactions of the Thoroton Society* 79: 50–59.

Campbell, C., J. Badeslade, J. Rocque, J. Woolfe and J. Gandon. 1972. *Vitruvius Britannicus or The British Architect*. New York: B. Blom.

Cannon, L. 1991. *Stained Glass in the Burrell Collection*. Edinburgh: Chambers.

Carew, R. 1769. *Survey of Cornwall and an Epistle Concerning the Excellencies of the English Tongue*. New Edition. London: E. Law.

Caroe, W. D. 1933. "Butley Priory, Suffolk. 2. The later history of the priory and gatehouse." *Archaeological Journal* 90: 229–241.

Challis, C. E. 2004. "Sharington, Sir William (c.1495–1553)." *Oxford Dictionary of National Biography*. Oxford: Oxford University Press. Online edition, https://doi.org/10.1093/ref:odnb/25205

Cherry, B. and N. Pevsner. 1989. *The Buildings of England: Devon*. New Haven, CT: Yale University Press.

Christie, P. M. and J. G. Coad. 1980. "Excavations at Denny Abbey." *Archaeological Journal* 137: 138–279.

Clapham, A. W. 1915. "The Augustinian Priory of Little Leez and the mansion of Leez Priory." *Transactions of the Essex Archaeological Society* 13: 200–217.

———. 1926. "The priory of Dartford and the manor house of Henry VIII." *Archaeological Journal* 83: 67–85.

Clarke, H. 1984. *The Archaeology of Medieval England*. London: British Museum Publications.

Clarke, R. 2011. "Tilty Abbey, Essex: Detailed Survey of a Cistercian Abbey and Investigation of its Wider Landscape Setting." Unpublished Oxford Archaeology East Report 1203.

Clifton-Taylor, A. 1974. *English Parish Churches as Works of Art*. London: Batsford.

Coad, J. and C. Coppack. 1998. *Castle Acre Castle and Priory*. London: English Heritage.

Cobbett, W. 1868. *List Of Abbeys, Priories, Nunneries, Hospitals: And Other Religious Foundations In England And Wales And In Ireland, Confiscated, Seized On, Or Alienated, By The Protestant "Reformation" Sovereigns And Parliaments*. Derby: Thomas Richardson and Son.

Cocks, T. Y. 2006. "Wyggeston, William (c.1467–1536)." *Oxford Dictionary of National Biography*. Oxford: Oxford University Press. Online edition, https://doi.org/10.1093/ref:odnb/94979

Colvin, H. M. 1943. "The dissolution of Dale Abbey." *Derbyshire Archaeological and Natural History Society* 64: 1–25.

———. 1999. "Recycling the monasteries: demolition and reuse by the Tudor government, 1536–1547." In *Essays in Architectural History*, by H. M. Colvin, 52–66. New Haven, CT: Yale University Press.

Constant, G. 1934. *The Reformation in England I, The English Schism, Henry VIII (1509–1547)*. Trans. R. E. Scantlebury. New York: Sheed and Ward.

Cook, G. H. 1965. *Letters to Cromwell on the Suppression of the Monasteries*. Aberdeen: The University Press.

Cooper, J. 2004. "History of St Mary Magdalen's hospital." In "Excavations at St Mary Magdalen's hospital, Brook Street, Colchester," by C. Crossan. *Essex History and Archaeology* 24: 91–95.

Cope-Faulkner, P. 2011. *Sempringham: Village to Priory to Mansion*. Lincoln: Heritage Trust for Lincolnshire.

Copeland, G. W. 1963. *Buckland Abbey: An Architectural Survey*. Plymouth: Underhill.

Coppack, G. 1986. "Some descriptions of Rievaulx Abbey in 1538–9: the disposition of a major Cistercian precinct in the early sixteenth century." *Journal of the British Archaeological Association* 139: 100–133.

———. 1990. *English Heritage Book of Abbeys and Priories*. London: Batsford.

———. 1991. "The precinct of Thornton Abbey, South Humberside: The planning of a major Augustinian house." In *Land, People, and Landscapes: Essays on the History of the Lincolnshire Region*, edited by D. Tyszka, K. Miller and G. Bryant, 37–44. Lincoln: Lincolnshire Books.

———. 1993. *English Heritage Book of Fountains Abbey*. London: Batsford.

———. 1998. *The White Monks. The Cistercians in Britain 1128–1540*. Stroud: Tempus Publishing.

———. forthcoming. *Religious Houses in Lincolnshire*. Lincoln: Society for Lincolnshire History and Archaeology.

Coppack, G. and M. Aston. 2002. *Christ's Poor Men: The Carthusians in England*. Stroud: Tempus Publishing Ltd.

Coppack, G. and S. Harrison. 2014. "Reconstructing Kirkstead Abbey, Lincolnshire: The charters, earthworks and architecture of a lost Cistercian house." *Journal of the British Archaeological Association* 167: 1–50.

Coppack, G., C. Hayfield and R.Williams. 2002. "Sawley Abbey: The architecture and archaeology of a smaller Cistercian abbey." *Journal of the British Archaeological Association* 155: 22–114.

Courtney, P. 1989. "Excavations in the outer precinct of Tintern Abbey." *Medieval Archaeology* 33: 99–127.

———. 1997. "Appendix C: Metal working features." In "Excavations at Carmarthen Greyfriars, 1989–1990," by T. James. *Medieval Archaeology* 41: 184–186.

Cowie, L .W. 1976. "The London Greyfriars." *History Today* 26(7): 462–467.

Cox, J. C. 1877a. *Notes on the Churches of Derbyshire. Volume 2: The Hundreds of the High Peak and Wirksworth*. London: Bemrose and Sons.

———. 1877b. *Notes on the Churches of Derbyshire. Volume 3: The Hundreds of Appletree and Repton and Gresley*. London: Bemrose and Sons.

———. 1879. *Notes on the Churches of Derbyshire. Volume 4: The Hundreds of Morleston and Litchurch and general supplement*. London: Bemrose and Sons.

Croft, R. A. and D. C. Mynard. 1986. "A Late 13th-Century Grisaille Window Panel from Bradwell Abbey, Milton Keynes, Buckinghamshire." *Medieval Archaeology* 30: 106–111.

Crossley, D. W. 1990. *Post-Medieval Archaeology in Britain*. Leicester: Leicester University Press.

Cunich, P. 1998. "The Dissolution of the Chantries." In *The Reformation in English Towns, 1500-1640*, edited by P. Collinson and J. Craig, 159–174. London: Palgrave.

Dale, M. K. 1982. "Tyrwhitt, Phillip (c.1510–1558), of Barton upon Humber, Lincs." In *The History of Parliament, The House of Commons, 1509-1558, Volume 3*, edited by S. T. Bindoff, 500-501. London: Secker & Warburg.

Daniels, R. 1986. "The excavation of the church of the Franciscans, Hartlepool, Cleveland." *Archaeological Journal* 143: 260–304.

Davies, C.S.L. 2004. "Fox , Richard (1447/8–1528)." *Oxford Dictionary of National Biography*. Oxford: Oxford University Press. Online edition, https://doi.org/10.1093/ref:odnb/10051

Davies, G. 1994. *A History of Money from Ancient Times to the Present Day*. Cardiff: University of Wales Press.

Dawley, P. M. 1955. *John Whitgift and the Reformation*. London: Adam & Charles Black.

Dickens, A. G. 1959. *Tudor Treatises*. Yorkshire Archaeological Society Record Series 125. Wakefield: Yorkshire Archaeological Society.

———. 1964. *The English Reformation*. London: B.T. Batsford.

Dickinson, J. C. 1956. *The Shrine of Our Lady of Walsingham*. Cambridge: Cambridge University Press.

———. 1961. *Monastic Life in Medieval England*. London: Adam & Charles Black.

———. 1968. "The buildings of the Austin Canons after the dissolution of the monasteries." *Journal of the British Archaeological Association* 31: 60–75.

Dobson, R. B. and S. Donaghey. 1985. *The History of Clementhorpe Nunnery. The Archaeology of York. Historical Sources for York Archaeology After AD1100. Volume 2/1*. York: York Archaeological Trust.

Doggett, N. 2002. *Patterns of Re-use: the Transformation of Former Monastic Buildings in Post-Dissolution Hertfordshire, 1540-1600*. British Archaeological Reports British Series 331. Oxford: Archaeopress.

Doonan, R. C. 1997. "Metallurgical debris from Norwich Greyfriars." Unpublished Ancient Monuments Laboratory Report 114/1997.

———. 1999. "Metallurgical debris from Eynsham Abbey, Oxfordshire." Unpublished Ancient Monuments Laboratory Report 70/1999.

Doubleday, H. A. and W. Page, eds. 1903. *A History of the County of Hampshire. Volume 2*. London: Archibald Constable.

Drage, C. 1990. "Dale Abbey: the south range excavations and survey, 1985–1987." *Derbyshire Archaeological Journal* 110: 60–92.

Drury, P. J. 1974. "Chelmsford Dominican Priory: The excavation of the reredorter, 1973." *Essex Archaeology and History* 6: 40–81.

———. 1980. "No other palace in the kingdom will compare with it: The evolution of Audley End, 1605–1745." *Architectural History* 23: 1–171.

———. 1982. "Walden Abbey into Audley End." In *Saffron Walden: Excavations and Research 1972-1980*, by S. R. Bassett, 94–105. Chelmsford Archaeological Trust Report 2. London: Council for British Archaeology.

Bibliography

Dunn, C. and A. Lax. 2001. "The Medieval and later landscape at Egglestone Abbey, Teesdale, County Durham." Unpublished English Heritage Archaeological Investigation Report Series AI/10/2001.

Duffy, E. 1992. *The Stripping of the Altars: Traditional Religion in England 1400-1580*. New Haven, CT: Yale University Press.

Dugdale, W. 1693. *Monasticon Anglicanum, or the history of the ancient abbies, and other monasteries, hospitals, cathedral and collegiate churches in England and Wales. With divers French, Irish, and Scotch monasteries formerly relating to England*. London: Sam Keble.

Dunkin, E.H.W. 1878. *The Church Bells of Cornwall, Their Archaeology and Present Condition*. London: Privately Printed.

Dunning, G. C. 1952. "A lead ingot at Rievaulx Abbey." *Antiquaries Journal* 32: 199-202.

Dyson, T., M. Samuel, A. Steele and S. M. Wright. 2011. *The Cluniac Priory and Abbey of St Saviour Bermondsey, Surrey. Excavations 1984-1995*. Museum of London Archaeology Monograph 50. London: Museum of London.

Edwards, K. 1949. *The English Secular Cathedrals in the Middle Ages: a Constitutional Study with Special Reference to the Fourteenth Century*. Manchester: Manchester University Press.

Ellis, P. 1997. "Croxden Abbey, Staffordshire: A report on excavations 1956-1957 and 1975-1977." *Staffordshire Archaeological and Historical Society* 36: 29-51.

Elliston Erwood, F. C. 1923. "The Premonstratensian Abbey of Langley, Co. Norfolk." *Norfolk Archaeology* 21: 175-234.

Elton, G.R. 1982. *The Tudor Constitution: Documents and Commentary*. Cambridge: Cambridge University Press.

Everson, P. 2005. "Lewes Priory, Sussex. The Post-Dissolution Mansion and Gardens of Lords Place." Unpublished English Heritage Archaeological Investigation Report AI/7/2005.

Everson, P. and D. Stocker. 2003. "The archaeology of vice-regality: Charles Brandon's brief rule in Lincolnshire." In *The Archaeology of the Reformation 1490-1580*, by D. Gaimster and R. Gilchrist, 145-158. Leeds: Maney Publishing.

———. 2009. "Masters of Kirkstead: Hunting for salvation." In *King's Lynn and the Fenns: Medieval Art, Architecture and Archaeology*, edited by J. McNeill, 83-111. Conference Transaction of the British Archaeological Association 31. Leeds: Maney Publishing.

———. 2009. "The Witham Valley, a landscape with monasteries?." *Church Archaeology* 13: 1-15.

———. 2011. *Custodians of Continuity? The Premonstratensian Abbey at Barlings and the Landscape of Ritual*. Lincoln: Heritage Trust of Lincolnshire.

Fairweather, F. H. 1926. "Excavations on the site of the Augustinian alien priory of Great Bricett, Suffolk." *Proceedings of the Suffolk Institute of Archaeology and Natural History* 19(2): 99-109.

Fergusson, P. and S. A. Harrison. 1999. *Rievaulx Abbey. Community, Architecture, Memory*. New Haven, CT: Yale University Press.

Ferris, I. 2001. "Excavations at Greyfriars, Gloucester, in 1967 and 1974-1975. *Transactions of the Bristol and Gloucestershire Archaeological Society* 119: 95-146.

Fisher, H.A.L. 1913. *The History of England from the Accession of Henry VII to the Death of Henry VIII (1485-1547). The Political History of England Vol. 5*. New edition. London: Longmans, Green and Co.

Fletcher, J. S. 1899. *Picturesque History of Yorkshire. Volume 1*. London: J.M. Dent.

Ford, L. L. 2004. "Paulet, William, first marques of Winchester (1474/1475?-1572)." *Oxford Dictionary of National Biography*. Oxford: Oxford University Press. Online edition, https://doi.org/10.1093/ref:odnb/21622

Foreman, M. 1996. *Further Excavations at the Dominican Priory, Beverley, 1986-1989*. Sheffield: J.R. Collis Publicaitons.

Fowler, J. T., ed. 1903. *Rites of Durham, being a description or brief declaration of all the ancient monuments, rites, & customs belonging or being within the monastical church of Durham before the suppression. Written 1593*. London: Surtees Society 107.

Fox, S. 1872. *The History and Antiquities of the Parish Church of S. Matthew Morley in the County of Derby*. London: Bemrose and Sons.

Frame, R. 2004. "Rokeby, Sir Thomas (d. 1357)." *Oxford Dictionary of National Biography*. Oxford: Oxford University Press. Online edition, https://doi.org/10.1093/ref:odnb/24012

Fuidge, N. M. 1981. "Tyrwhitt, Sir Robert (by 1504-1572), of Leighton Bromswold." In *The History of Parliament, The House of Commons, 1558-1601, Volume 3*, edited by P. W. Hasler, 537-578. London: Secker & Warburg.

Fuller, E. A 1883-1884. "Hospital of St John, Cirencester." *Transactions of the Bristol and Gloucestershire Archaeological Society* 8: 224-228.

Gardner, T. 1754. *An Historical Account of Dunwich*. London: T. Gardner.

Gardner, J. S. 1955. "Coggeshall Abbey and its early brickwork." *Journal of the British Archaeological Association* 18(1): 19-32.

Gaskell Brown, C., ed. 1995. "Buckland Abbey, Devon: Surveys and Excavations, 1983-1995." *Proceedings of the Devon Archaeological Society* 53: 25-82.

Gasquet, F. A. 1889. *Henry VIII and the English Monasteries. Volumes 1 & 2*. London: John Hodges.

Gater, J. A. 1994. "Report on the Geophysical Survey Witham Carthusian Monastery." Unpublished GSB Survey No. 94/21.

———. 1998. "Report on the Geophysical Survey Sheen Charterhouse." Unpublished GSB Survey No. 97/92.

Gaydon, A. T. and R. B. Pugh, eds. 1973. *A History of the County of Shropshire. Volume 2*. London: Oxford University Press for the Institute of Historical Research.

Gilchrist, R. 1995. *Contemplation and Action: The Other Monasticism*. London: Leicester University Press.

Giles, K. 1999. "The familiar fraternity: The appropriation and consumption of medieval guildhalls in early modern York." In *The Familiar Past? Archaeologies of Later Historical Britain*, edited by S. Tarlow and S. West, 87-102. London: Routledge.

Gilyard-Beer, R. 1960. *Cleeve Abbey*. London: HMSO.

———. 1977. "Ipswich Blackfriars." *Proceedings of the Suffolk Institute of Archaeology and History* 34(1): 1-24.

Gilyard-Beer, R. and G. Coppack. 1986. "Excavations at Fountains Abbey, North Yorkshire, 1979-1980: The early development of the monastery." *Archaeologia* 108: 147-188.

Goodall, J. and F. Kelly. 2004. *Muchelney Abbey, Somerset*. London: English Heritage.

Graham, R. 1901. *Saint Gilbert of Sempringham and the Gilbertines: A History of the Only English Monastic Order*. London: Elliot Stock.

———. 1940. "Excavations on the site of Sempringham Priory." *Journal of the British Archaeological Association* 74: 73-101.

Grainger, I. and C. Phillpotts. 2011. *The Cistercian Abbey of St Mary Graces, East Smithfield, London*. Museum of London Archaeology Monograph 44. London: Museum of London.

Graves, C. P. and D. H. Heslop. 2013. *Newcastle upon Tyne: The Eye of the North. An Archaeological Assessment*. Oxford: Oxbow books

Graves, M.A.R. 2004. "Wriothesley, Thomas, first earl of Southampton (1505-1550)." *Oxford Dictionary of National Biography*. Oxford: Oxford University Press. Online edition, https://doi.org/10.1093/ref:odnb/30076

Gray, M. 1987. "Crown property and the land market in south-east Wales in the sixteenth century." *Agricultural History Review* 35(2): 133-150.

Greene, J. P. 1989. *Norton Priory: The Archaeology of a Medieval Religious House*. Cambridge: Cambridge University Press.

———. 1992. *Medieval Monasteries*. London: Leicester University Press.

Greenslade, M. W. and R. B. Pugh, eds. 1970. *A History of the County of Stafford. Volume 3*. London: Oxford University Press for the Institute of Historical Research.

Gunn, S. J. 1988. *Charles Brandon, Duke of Suffolk c.1484-1545*. Oxford: Basil Blackwell Ltd.

———. 1989. "Peers, commons and gentry in the Lincolnshire revolt of 1536." *Past & Present* 123: 52-79.

Habakkuk, H. J. 1958. "The market for monastic property, 1539-1603." *Economic History Review* 10(3): 362-380.

Haigh, C. 1969. *The Last Days of the Lancashire Monasteries and the Pilgrimage of Grace*. Manchester: The Chetham Society.

Haigh, C. 1993. *English Reformations: Religion, Poltics, and Society Under the Tudors*. Oxford: Oxford University Press.

Hamilton, W. D., ed. 1875. *A Chronicle of England During the Reigns of the Tudors, A.D. 1485-1559. By Charles Wriothesley, Windsor Herald. Volume 1*. Camden Society, NS Volume 11. Westminster: J.B. Nichols and Sons.

Handley, S. 2004. "Spelman, Sir Henry." *Oxford Dictionary of National Biography*. Oxford: Oxford University Press. online edition, https://doi.org/10.1093/ref:odnb/26104

Harbottle, B. 1968. "Excavations at the Carmelite Friary, Newcastle upon Tyne, 1965 and 1967." *Archaeologia Aeliana* 4th series 46: 163-223.

———. 2001. "The Augustinian Friary, Newcastle upon Tyne 1970-1971." Unpublished typescript.

Harbottle, B. and R. Fraser. 1987. "Black Friars, Newcastle upon Tyne, after the Dissolution of the Monasteries." *Archaeologia Aeliana* 5th series 15: 23-149.

Hare, J. N. 1978. "The Priory of The Holy Sepulchre, Thetford." *Norfolk Archaeology* 37: 190–201.

Hare, J.N. 1985. *Battle Abbey the Eastern Range and the Excavations of 1978-1980*. London: Historic Buildings and Monuments Commission for England Archaeological Report 2.

———. 1993. "Netley Abbey: Monastery, Mansion and Ruin." *Proceedings of the Hampshire Field Club and Archaeological Society* 49: 207–227.

Harwood, T., ed. 1844. *A Survey of Staffordshire Containing the Antiquities of That County by Sampson Erdeswick, esq.* London: Nichols and Son.

Hayfield, C. 2006. "Conservation Plan for the Greyfriars Building, Broadgate, Lincoln. Pathway." Unpublished Conservation Plan. Lincoln: Colin Hayfield Archaeological Consultancy.

Head, D. M. 1995. *The Ebbs and Flows of Fortune: The Life of Thomas Howard, Third Duke of Norfolk*. Athens: The University of Georgia Press.

Heale, M. 2003. "Monastic-parochial churches in England and Wales, 1066–1540." *Monastic Research Bulletin* 9: 1–19.

Helsby, T., ed. 1882. *History of the County Palatine and City of Chester,* volume 1. London: George Routledge & sons.

Herbert, N. M., ed. 1988. *A History of the County of Gloucester. Volume 4 The City of Gloucester*. London: Oxford University Press for the Institute of Historical Research.

Hibbert, F. A. 1910. *The Dissolution of the Monasteries as Illustrated by the Suppression of the Religious Houses of Staffordshire*. London: Isaac Pitman & Sons.

Hicks, M. 2004. "Heneage, Sir Thomas (b. in or before 1532, d. 1595)." *Oxford Dictionary of National Biography*. Oxford: Oxford University Press. Online edition, https://doi.org/10.1093/ref:odnb/12921

Hill, J.W.F. 1956. *Tudor and Stuart Lincoln*. Cambridge: Cambridge University Press.

Hills, G. M. 1874. "Roche Abbey, Yorkshire; and Beauchief Abbey, Derbyshire." *Journal of the British Archaeological Association* 30(4): 421–429.

Hodder, M. A. 1991. "Excavations at Sandwell Priory and hall 1982-1988." *Transactions of the South Staffordshire Archaeological and Historical Society* 31: 1–229.

Hodgett, G.A.J. 1947. "Dissolution of the Monasteries in Lincolnshire." Unpublished MA Thesis, University of London.

Hodgett, G.A.J. 1951. "The Dissolution of the religious houses in Lincolnshire and the changing structure of society." *Lincolnshire Architectural and Archaeological Society* N.S. 4(1): 83–99.

———. 1975, *Tudor Lincolnshire. History of Lincolnshire VI*. Lincoln: History of Lincolnshire Committee.

Hodgson, J. F. 1884. "On the differences of plan alleged to exist between churches of Austin Canons and those of monks; and the frequency which such churches were parochial." *Archaeological Journal* 41: 374–414.

———. 1885. "On the differences of plan alleged to exist between churches of Austin Canons and those of monks; and the frequency which such churches were parochial." *Archaeological Journal* 42: 96–119, 215–246, 331–369, 440–468.

Hofmann, T. M. 1982. "Bellow, John (by 1513–1559), of Legbourne, Newstead and Grimsby, Lincs." In *The History of Parliament, The House of Commons, 1509-1558, Volume 1,* edited by S. T. Bindoff, 415–416. London: Secker & Warburg.

———. 1982b. "Heneage, John (c.1485–1557) of Benningworth, Lincs." In *The History of Parliament, The House of Commons, 1509-1558, Volume 2,* edited by S. T. Bindoff, 334. London: Secker & Warburg.

———. 1982c. "Tyrwhitt, Marmaduke (1533/34-1600), of Scotter, Lincs." In *The History of Parliament, The House of Commons, 1509-1558, Volume 3,* edited by S. T. Bindoff, 500. London: Secker & Warburg.

Holder, N. 2011. "The Medieval Friaries of London: A Topographic and Archaeological History, Before and After the Dissolution." Unpublished PhD thesis, University of London.

Hoover, H. and L. Hoover, eds. 1950. *Georgius Agricola. De Re Metallica*. New York: Dover Publications.

Hope, W. H. St. J. 1879. "On the recent excavations on the site of Dale Abbey, Derbyshire." *Journal of the Derbyshire Archaeological and Natural History Society* 1: 100–115.

———. 1880. "On the recent excavations on the site of Dale Abbey, Derbyshire." *Journal of the Derbyshire Archaeological and Natural History Society* 2: 128–134.

———. 1883. "The abbots of the monastery of S. Mary de Parco Stanley, or Dale, Derbyshire." *Journal of the Derbyshire Archaeological and Natural History Society* 5: 81–100.

———. 1901. "The Gilbertine Priory of Watton in the East Riding of Yorkshire." *Transactions of the East Riding Antiquarian Society* 8: 1–34.

———. 1906. "The Cluniac Priory of St. Pancras at Lewes." *Sussex Archaeological Collections* 49: 66–88.

———. 1906b. "The making of Place House, Titchfield, near Southampton." *Archaeological Journal* 63: 231–243.

Hope, W. H. St. J. and H. Brakspear. 1906. "The Cistercian abbey of Beaulieu in the County of Southampton." *Archaeological Journal* 63: 129–186.

Howard, M. 1987. *The Early Tudor Country House: Architecture and Politics, 1490-1550*. London: George Philip.

———. 2003. "Recycling the monastic fabric: Beyond the act of dissolution." In *The Archaeology of the Reformation 1490-1580*, edited by D. Gaimster and R. Gilchrist, 221-234. Leeds: Maney Publishing.

Howsam, C. L. 2016. "Book fastenings and Furnishings: an Archaeology of Late Medieval Books." Unpublished PhD thesis, University of Sheffield.

Hoyle, R.W. 2001. *The Pilgrimage of Grace and the Politics of the 1530s*. Oxford: Oxford University Press.

Huggon, M. 2018. "The Archaeology of the Medieval Hospitals of England and Wales 1066-1546." Unpublished PhD thesis, University of Sheffield.

Hughes, A. 1898. *List of Sheriffs for England and Wales from the Earliest Times to A.D. 1831*. London: Eyre & Spottiswoode.

Hughes, P. 1950. *The Reformation in England I. The King's Proceedings*. London: Hollis & Carter.

Ingram, M. 1977. *The Manor of Bridlington and its Lords Feoffees*. Bridlington: The Lords Feoffees.

Insall, D. 1985. *Binam Priory. A Guide to the Priory Church of St Mary and the Holy Cross, Binham, Norfolk*. Hunstanton: Witley Press.

Jackson, C., ed. 1870. *The Diary of Abraham de la Pryme. The Yorkshire Antiquary*. Surtees Society Volume 54. Durham: Andrews & co.

Jackson, J. E., ed. 1862. *Wiltshire: The Geographical Collections of John Aubrey FRS, AD 1659-1670*. Devises: Wiltshire Archaeological and Natural History Society.

James, M. E. 1970. "Obedience and dissent in Henrician England: The Lincolnshire Rebellion, 1536." *Past and Present* 48: 3–78.

James, T. 1997. "Excavations at Carmarthen Greyfriars, 1983–1990." *Medieval Archaeology* 41: 100–194.

Jecock, M. 1999. "Jervaulx Abbey North Yorkshire." Unpublished English Heritage Archaeological Investigation Report AI/4/1999.

Jenkinson, H. and F. P. White. 1915. "Chertsey Abbey after the Dissolution." *Surrey Archaeological Collections* 28: 29–40.

Johnson, E. A. 2006. *Sopwell Priory Excavations 1962-1966*. Supplement to Hertfordshire Archaeology and History 14. St. Albans: Hertfordshire Archaeology Editorial Committee.

Johnson, M. 1974. "The great North Gate of Durham." *Transactions of the Archaeological and Architectural Society of Durham and Northumberland* 4: 105–118, (New Series).

Johnson, M. H. 1996. *An Archaeology of Capitalism*. Oxford: Blackwell Publishers.

Jordan, W. K. 1959. *Philanthropy in England, 1480-1660: A Study of the Changing Patterns of English Social Aspirations*. London: Allen & Unwin.

Kell, E. 1863. "Netley Abbey, with an account of recent excavations and discoveries." *Collectanea Archaeologica, Communications made to the British Archaeological Association* 2(1): 65–92.

Kemp, R.L. 1996. *The Church and Gilbertine Priory of St. Andrew, Fishergate: The Archaeology of York. The Medieval Defences and Suburbs. Volume 11/2*. York: York Archaeological Trust.

Kew, J. 1970. "The disposal of crown lands and the Devon market, 1536-1558." *Agricultural History Review* 18(2): 93–105.

King, C. 1983. *Castellarium Anglicanum*. New York: Kraus.

Kingsford, C. L., ed. 1908. *A Survey of London. Reprinted from the Text of 1603*. Volumes 1 & 2. Oxford: Clarendon Press.

Knowles, D. 1940. *The Monastic Order in England*. Cambridge: Cambridge University Press.

———. 1948. *The Religious Orders in England. Volume I The Old Orders, 1216-1340*. Cambridge: Cambridge University Press.

———. 1955. *The Religious Orders in England. Volume II The End of the Middle Ages*. Cambridge: Cambridge University Press.

———. 1959. *The Religious Orders in England. Volume III The Tudor Age*. Cambridge: Cambridge University Press.

Knowles, D. and R. N. Hadcock. 1953. *Medieval Religious Houses of England and Wales*. London: Longmans.

Knowles, D. and J. K. St Joseph. 1952. *Monastic Sites from the Air*. Cambridge: Cambridge University Press.

Knowles, W. H. 1930. "Teddington Church, Worcestershire, in which are structural fragments from Hayles Abbey." *Transactions of the Bristol and Gloucester Archaeological Society* 52: 93–101.

———. 1932. "The Black Friars at Gloucester." *Transactions of the Bristol and Gloucester Archaeological Society* 54: 67–201.

Lambrick, G. and H. Woods. 1976. "Excavations on the second site of the Dominican Priory, Oxford." *Oxoniensia* 41: 168–231.

Leech, R. H. and A. D. McWhirr. 1982. "Excavations at St John's Hospital, Cirencester, 1971 and 1976." *Transactions of the Bristol and Gloucestershire Archaeological Society* 100: 191–209.

Leighton, W. 1933. "The Black Friars, now Quaker's Friars, Bristol." *Transactions of the Bristol and Gloucestershire Archaeological Society* 55: 151–190.

Little, B. 1979. *Abbeys and Priories in England and Wales*. London: Batsford.

Loades, D. 2004. "Grenville, Sir Richard (1542–1591)." *Oxford Dictionary of National Biography*. Oxford: Oxford University Press. Online edition, https://doi.org/10.1093/ref:odnb/11493

Logan, F. D. 1991. "The first royal visitation of the English universities, 1535." *English Historical Review* 106(421): 861–888.

Lowe, B. J. 1987. "Keynsham Abbey: excavations 1961–1985." *Somerset Archaeology and Natural History* 131: 81–156.

Lowe, B. 2010. *Commonwealth and the English Reformation. Protestantism and the Politics of Religious Change in the Gloucester Vale, 1483-1560*. St Andrews Studies in Reformation History. London: Routledge.

Lower, M. A. 1845. *A Hand-book for Lewes, Historical and Descriptive with Recent Discoveries at the Priory*. London: John Russell Smith.

Lyne, M. 1997. *Lewes Priory: Excavations by Richard Lewis 1969-1982*. Lewes: Lewes Priory Trust.

MacCulloch, D. 1987. *Suffolk and the Tudors: Politics and Religion in an English County, 1500-1600*. Oxford: Oxford University Press.

Maddison, A. R. 1888. *Lincolnshire Wills: First Series A.D. 1500-1600*. Lincoln: Williamson.

———. 1891. *Lincolnshire Wills: Second Series A.D. 1600-1617*. Lincoln: Williamson.

———. 1903. *Lincolnshire Pedigrees*, Volume 2. London: Harleian Society.

———. 1904. *Lincolnshire Pedigrees*, Volume 3. London: Harleian Society.

Malden, H. E., ed. 1911. *A History of the County of Surrey. Volume 2*. London: Archibald Constable.

Mantel, H. 2009. *Wolf Hall*. London: Harper Collins.

Marrow, D. J. 2008. "The statue of St Christopher." In *Norton Priory: Monastery to Museum Excavations 1970-1997*, by F. Brown and C. Howard-Davies, 316–328. Lancaster: Oxford Archaeology North.

Marsh, C. 1998. *Popular Religion in Sixteenth-Century England*. London: Macmillan Press Ltd.

Martin, A. R. 1929. "The Dominican Priory at Canterbury." *Archaeological Journal* 86: 152–177.

———. 1937. *Franciscan Architecture in England*. Manchester: Manchester University Press.

Martindale, J. H. 1922. "Art. XXII The Priory of Wetheral." *Transactions of the Cumberland and Westmorland Antiquarian and Archaeological Society* 22: 239–251.

McAvoy, F. 1988. "Sempringham Priory. Unpublished Central Excavation Unit Fieldwork Summary." HBMC File No. AA31516. Department of the Environment.

McNeil, R. and R. C. Turner. 1990. "An architectural and topographical survey of Vale Royal Abbey." *Journal of the Chester Archaeological Society* 70: 51–79.

Merriman, M. 2004. "Lee, Sir Richard (1501/2–1575)." *Oxford Dictionary of National Biography*. Oxford: Oxford University Press. http://www.oxforddnb.com/view/article/16303

Merriman, R. B. 1902. *Life and Letters of Thomas Cromwell*. Volume 1. Oxford: Clarendon Press.

Miller, H. 1982. "Bowes, Robert (by 1497-1555), of South Cowton, Yorks. and London." In *The History of Parliament, The House of Commons, 1509-1558, Volume 1*, edited by S. T. Bindoff. London: Secker & Warburg. Online edition, http://www.historyofparliamentonline.org/volume/1509-1558/member/bowes-robert-1497-1555

Mitchiner, M. 1986. *Medieval Pilgrim and Secular Badges*. Sanderstead: Hawkins Publications.

Molvarec, S. and D. Yocum, eds. in press. *Carthusian Monasticism: History, Life, World, Texts*. Kalamazoo: Medieval Institute publications.

Morris, R. K. 2003. "Monastic Architecture: Destruction and Reconstruction." In *The Archaeology of Reformation 1480-1580*, edited by D. Gaimster and R. Gilchrist, 235–251. Leeds: Maney.

———. 2009. "'I was never more in love with an olde howse nor never newe worke coulde be better bestowed': The Earl of Leicester's remodelling of Kenilworth Castle for Queen Elizabeth I." *Antiquaries Journal* 89: 241–305.

Mynard, D. C., P. Woodfield and R. J. Zeepvat. 1996. "Bradwell Abbey, Buckinghamshire. Research and excavation, 1968 to 1987." *Records of Buckinghamshire* 36: 1–61.

Newman, C. M. 2004. "Bowes, Sir Robert (1493?–1555)." *Oxford Dictionary of National Biography*. Oxford: Oxford University Press. Online edition, https://doi.org/10.1093/ref:odnb/3058

Nichols, J. 1815. *The History and Antiquities of the County of Leicester: Volume 1 Part 2, Containing a Continuation of the History of the Town of Leicester*. London: Nichols, Son and Bentley.

Nichols, J. G., ed. 1846. *The Chronicle of Calais in the Reigns of Henry VII and Henry VIII*. London: Camden Society 35.

Nichols, J. G. and J. Bruce, eds. 1863. *Wills from Doctors' Commons: A Selection of Wills of Eminent Persons Proved in the Prerogative Court of Canterbury 1495-1695*. London: Camden Society 83.

O'Sullivan, D. 2006. "The little Dissolution of the 1520s." *Post-Medieval Archaeology* 40(2): 227–258.

———. 2013. *In the Company of Preachers: The Archaeology of Medieval Friaries in England and Wales*. Leicester Archaeology Monographs No. 23. Leicester: University of Leicester School of Archaeology and Ancient History.

Oswald, A., J. Goodall, A. Payne and T-J. Sutcliffe. 2010. "Thornton Abbey North Lincolnshire. Historical, Archaeological and Architectural Investigations." Unpublished English Heritage Research Report 100-2010.

Page, W. 1893. *The Chartulary of Brinkburn Priory*. London: Surtees Society 90.

Page, W., ed. 1906. *A History of the County of Norfolk. Volume 2*. London: Archibald Constable.

———. 1906b. *A History of the County of Lincoln: Volume 2*. London: Archibald Constable.

———. 1908. *A History of the County of Warwick. Volume 2*. London: Archibald Constable.

———. 1911. *A History of the County of Hampshire. Volume 4*. London: Archibald Constable.

———. 1911b. *A History of the County of Somerset. Volume 2*. London: Archibald Constable.

———. 1973. *A History of the County of Sussex. Volume 2*. London: Archibald Constable.

———. 1974. *A History of the County of York. Volume 3*. London: Archibald Constable.

Palmer, C.F.R. 1881. "The friar-preachers, or Blackfriars of Boston." *The Reliquary* 22: 87–92.

———. 1882. "The friar-preachers, or Blackfriars of Gloucester." *Archaeological Journal* 39: 296–306.

———. 1883. "The friar-preachers, or Blackfriars of Carlisle." *Transactions of the Cumberland and Westmorland Antiquarian and Archaeological Society* 6: 138–144.

———. 1887. "The friar-preachers, or Blackfriars of Thetford." *The Reliquary* New Series 1: 196–204.

———. 1888. "The friar-preachers, or Blackfriars of Thetford." *The Reliquary* New Series 2: 71–83.

Parker, R. W., T. Ives and J. Allan. 2007. "Excavation and Building Survey at Cleeve Abbey, 1995–2003." *Proceedings of the Somerset Archaeological and Natural History Society* 150: 73–167.

Peacock, E, 1883. "Injunctions of John Longland, Bishop of Lincoln, to certain Monasteries in his Diocese." *Archaeologia* 47: 49–64.

Peers, C.R. 1927. "Two relic-holders from altars in the nave of Rievaulx Abbey, Yorkshire." *Antiquaries Journal* 1: 271–282.

Pevsner, N. and J. Harris. 1989. *The Buildings of England, Lincolnshire*. 2nd ed. London: Penguin Books.

Philp, B. 1968. *Excavations at Faversham. 1965*. First Research Report of the Kent Archaeological Research Group's Council. Crawley: W. & J. Jarvis.

Piccope, G. J., ed. 1857. *Lancashire and Cheshire Wills and Inventories from the Ecclesiastical Court, Chester. Volume 2*. Manchester: The Chetham Society.

Platt, C. 1984. *The Abbeys and Priories of Medieval England*. London: Martin Secker & Warburg.

Poster, J. and D. Sherlock. 1987. "Denny Abbey: the nuns' refectory." *Proceedings of the Cambridge Antiquarian Society* 76: 67–82.

Poulton, R. and H. Woods. 1984. *Excavations on the site of the Dominican Friary at Guildford in 1974 and 1978*. Guildford: Research Volume of the Surrey Archaeological Society No. 9.

Pragnell, H. 2007. "New uses for old friaries: the Greyfriars and Blackfriars in Canterbury." In *The Friars in Medieval Britain: Proceedings of the 2007 Harlaxton Symposium*, edited by N. Roger, 331–339. Donington: Shaun Tyas.

Prescott, H.F.M. 1952. *The Man on the Donkey*. London: Eyre & Spottiswoode.

Prideaux, W. de C. 1907. "The monumental brasses of Dorsetshire." *Journal of the British Archaeological Association* 13(4): 209–226.

R.C.G. 1981. "Forthe, William (aft.1542–99), of Hadleigh, Suff." In *The History of Parliament, The House of Commons, 1558-1601, Volume 2*, edited by P. W. Hasler. London: Secker & Warburg. Online edition, https://www.historyofparliamentonline.org/volume/1558-1603/member/forthe-william-1542-99

Raby, F.J.E. and P. K. Baillie Reynolds. 1952. *Castle Acre Priory*. London: Historic Buildings and Monuments Commission for England.

Rahtz, P. and S. Hirst. 1976. *Bordesley Abbey, Redditch, Hereford-Worcestershire: First Report on Excavations, 1969-1973*. British Archaeological Reports British Series 23. Oxford: British Archaeological Reports.

Raine, J. 1828. *Saint Cuthbert: with an account of the State in which his remains were found upon the opening of his tomb in Durham Cathedral in the year MDCCCXXVII*. Durham: Geo. Andrews.

RCHME 1916. *An Inventory of the Historical Monuments in Essex Volume 1 North West*. London: HSMO.

———. 1922. *An Inventory of the Historical Monuments in Essex Volume 3 North East*. London: HSMO.

Reddan, M. and A. W. Clapham. 1924. *Survey of London: Volume 9, the Parish of St Helen Bishopsgate, Part 1*. London: London County Council.

Rees, S. E. 1987. "Haverfordwest Priory: An Interim Report." *Journal of the Pembrokeshire Historical Society* 2: 19–23.

Rigold, S. E. 1966. "An Elizabethan hoard from Thornton Abbey, Lincolnshire." *British Numismatic Journal* 35: 200–221.

Riordan, M. 2004. "Heneage, Sir Thomas (b. before 1482, d. 1553)." *Oxford Dictionary of National Biography*. Oxford: Oxford University Press. Online edition, https://doi.org/10.1093/ref:odnb/12920

Roberts, D. L. 1984. "John Thorpe's drawings for Thornton College, the house of Sir Vincent Skinner." *Lincolnshire History and Archaeology* 19: 57–64.

Robinson, D., ed. 1998. *The Cistercian Abbeys of Britain. Far from the Concourse of Men*. London: B.T. Batsford.

Rosenfield, M. C. 1961. "The Disposal of the Property of London Monastic Houses, With a Special Study of Holy Trinity, Aldagte." Unpublished PhD thesis, University of London.

Roth, F. 1966. *The English Austin Friars 1249-1538. Volume 1 History*. New York: Augustinian Historical Institute.

Rowse, A. L. 1969. *Tudor Cornwall: Portrait of a Society*. London: Macmillan.

Ryan, J. 1931. *Irish Monasticism, Origins and Early Development*. Dublin: Talbot Press.

Rylatt, M. and P. Mason. 2003. *The Archaeology of the Medieval Cathedral and Priory of St. Mary, Coventry*. Coventry: Coventry City Council.

Salzman, L. F., ed. 1947. *A History of the County of Warwick. Volume 4, Hemlingford Hundred*. London: Oxford University Press for the Institute of Historical Research.

———. 1948. *A History of the County of Cambridge and the Isle of Ely: Volume 2*. London: Oxford University Press for the Institute of Historical Research.

Samson, C. J. 2004. *Dark Fire*. London: Penguin Books.

Savine, A. 1909. *English Monasteries on the Eve of the Dissolution. Oxford Studies in Social and Legal History Vol. 1*. Oxford: Clarendon Press.

Schofield, J. 1993. "Building in religious precincts in London at the Dissolution and after." In *Advances in Monastic Archaeology*, edited by R. Gilchrist and H. Mytum, 29–41. British Archaeological Reports 227. Oxford: Tempus Reparatum.

———. 1995. *Medieval London Houses*. New Haven, CT: Yale University Press.

Schofield, J. and R. Lea. 2005. *Holy Trinity Priory, Aldgate, City of London. An Archaeological Reconstruction and History*. Museum of London Archaeology Service Monograph 24. London: Museum of London.

Serjeantson, R. M. and W.R.D. Adkins, eds. 1906. *A History of the County of Northampton*. Volume 2. London: Archibald Constable.

Shagan, E. H. 2003. *Popular Politics and the English Reformation*. Cambridge: Cambridge University Press.

Shaw, A. N. 1998. "The Northern Visitation of 1535/6: Some New Observations." *Downside Review* 116: 279–299.

———. 2004. "Tregonwell, Sir John (*c.*1498–1565)." *Oxford Dictionary of National Biography*. Oxford: Oxford University Press. Online edition, https://doi.org/10.1093/ref:odnb/27683

Sherlock, D. and H. Woods. 1988. *St. Augustine's Abbey: Report on Excavations, 1960-1978*. Maidstone: Kent Archaeological Society.

Sherlock, P. 2008. *Monuments and Memory in Early Modern England*. Aldershot: Ashgate Publishing.

Simon, J. 1966. *Education and Society in Tudor England*. Cambridge: Cambridge University Press.

Slade, C. F. 1975. "Excavations at Reading Abbey, 1971–1973." *Berkshire Archaeological Journal* 68: 29–70.

Smith, A. 2010. "Netley Abbey: Patronage, preservation and remains." *Journal of the British Archaeological Association* 163: 132–151.

Smith, I. 1966. *Shakespeare's Blackfriars Playhouse. Its History and its Design*. London: Peter Owen.

Smith, P. 2009. "Rufford Abbey and its gardens in the 17th and 18th centuries." *English Heritage Historical Review* 4: 123–153.

Sodden, I. 2003. "The conversion of former monastic buildings to secular use, the case of Coventry." In *The Archaeology of the Reformation 1490-1580*, edited by D. Gaimster and R. Gilchrist, 280–289. Leeds: Maney Publishing.

Spelman, H. 1853. *History and Fate of Sacrilege*. 2nd edition. London: Joseph Masters.

Spencer, B. 1998. *Pilgrim Souvenirs and Secular Badges: Medieval Finds from Excavations in London 7*. London: HMSO.

Steane, J. 1985. *The Archaeology of Medieval England and Wales*. Athens: University of Georgia Press.

Stephenson, M. 1926. *A List of Monumental Brasses in the British Isles*. London: Headley Brothers Limited.

Stewart-Brown, R. 1925. *Birkenhead Priory and the Mersey Ferry*. Liverpool: The State Assurance Company Ltd.

Stocker, D. 2011. "The Grantham conduit-head." In *The Making of Grantham The Medieval Town*, edited by D. Start and D. Stocker, 150. Lincoln: The Heritage Trust of Lincoln.

Styles, P., ed. 1945. *A History of the County of Warwick. Volume 3*, Barlichway Hundred. London: Oxford University Press for the Institute of Historical Research.

Summerson, H. 1993. *Medieval Carlisle: The City and the Borders from the Late Eleventh to the mid-Sixteenth Century, Vol. 1*. Kendal: Cumberland and Westmorland Antiquarian and Archaeological Society.

Sunley, H. and N. Stevens. 1995. *Kenilworth: the Story of the Abbey*. London: The Pleasaunce Press.

Swales, R.J.W. 1982. "Holcroft, Sir Thomas (1505/6-58), of Vale Royal, Cheshire." In *The History of Parliament, The House of Commons, 1509-1558, Volume 2*, edited by S. T. Bindoff. London: Secker & Warburg. Online edition, http://www.historyofparliamentonline.org/volume/1509-1558/member/holcroft-sir-thomas-15056-58

Swales, T. H. 1966. "The redistribution of the monastic lands at the Dissolution." *Norfolk Archaeology* 34: 14–44.

Sweeting, W. D. 1899. "Siege of Crowland." In *Fenland Notes and Queries, a Quarterly Antiquarian Journal for the Fenland* 41: 173.

Talbot, C. 1960. "Cîteaux and Scarborough." *Monastica* 2: 95–158.

Tamkin, A, 1989. "Place House in 1737." In *Titchfield. A Place in History*, edited by R. Wade and G. Watts, 69–73. Southampton: Hampshire Books.

Tanner, T. 1744. *Notitia Monastica: or an account of all the abbies, priories and houses of friers, heretofore in England and Wales; and also of all the colleges and hospitals founded before A.D. MDXL*. London: William Bowyer.

Taunton, E. L. 1897. *The English Black Monks of St. Benedict*. Volume I. London: John C. Nimmo.

Tawney, R. H. 1926. *Religion and the Rise of Capitalism*. London: J. Murray.

Taylor, S. J. 1974. "An excavation on the site of the Augustinian Priory, Canons Ashby, Northamptonshire." *Northamptonshire Archaeology* 9: 57–67.

Tempest, E. B. 1918. "Tattershall." *Lincolnshire Notes and Queries* 15: 71–72.

Tester, P. J. 1973. "Excavations at Boxley Abbey." *Archaeologia Cantiana* 88: 129–158.

Thomas, C., B. Sloane and C. Phillpots. 1997. *Excavations at the Priory and Hospital of St Mary Spital, London*. Museum of London Archaeology Service Monograph 1. London: Museum of London.

Thomas, J. 2006. "Evidence for the Dissolution of Thorney Abbey: Recent excavations and landscape analysis at Thorney, Cambridgeshire." *Medieval Archaeology* 50: 179–241.

Thomson, J. A. 1964. *Kenilworth Church and Abbey Excerpts from Our History*. Kenilworth: J. A. Thomson.

Bibliography

Thompson, A. H. 1919. "The Priory of St. Mary of Newstead in Sherwood Forest with some notes on houses of Regular Canons." *Transactions of the Thoroton Society* 23: 33–141.

———. 1928. *Historical and Architectural Description of the Priory of St. Mary, Bolton-in-Wharfedale*. Leeds: Publications of the Thoresby Society 30.

Thorpe, S. M. 1982. "Strelley, Robert (by 1518-1554), of Great Bowden, Leics." In *The History of Parliament, The House of Commons, 1509-1558, Volume 3*, edited by S. T. Bindoff. London: Secker & Warburg. Online edition, http://www.historyofparliamentonline.org/volume/1509-1558/member/strelley-robert-1518-54

———. 1982b. Wigston, William (by 1509–1577), of Wolston, Warws." *The History of Parliament, The House of Commons, 1509-1558, Volume 3*, edited by S. T. Bindoff. London: Secker & Warburg. Online edition, http://www.historyofparliamentonline.org/volume/1509-1558/member/wigston-william-1509-77

Thurley, S. 2013. *Men from the Ministry: How Britain Saved its Heritage*. New Haven, CT: Yale University Press.

Tittler, R. 1991. *Architecture and Power: The Town Hall and the English Urban Community c.1500-1640*. Oxford: Clarendon Press.

Toulmin Smith, L. 1907. *The Itinerary of John Leland in or About the Years 1535-1543. Parts I to III*. London: George Bell and Sons.

Townend, P. 2017. "The Archaeology of the Monastic Order of the Gilbertines." Unpublished PhD thesis, University of Sheffield.

Tracy, C. 1997. "Choir-stalls from the 14th-century Whitefriars church in Coventry." *Journal of the British Archaeological Association* 150: 76–95.

Traskey, J. P. 1978. *Milton Abbey: A Dorset Monastery in the Middle Ages*. Tisbury: The Compton Press.

Trigge, F. 1589. *An Apologie or Defence of our dayes against the vaine murmurings and complaints of manie. Wherein is plainly proved that our dayes are more happie and blessed than the dayes of our forefathers*. London: John Wolfe.

Tyrwhitt, R. P. 1862. *Notices and Remains of the Family Tyrwhitt*. London: Harrison and Sons.

Venn, J. and J. A. Venn. 1922. *Alumni Cantabrigienses*. Volume 1(1). Cambridge: Cambridge University Press.

Walbran, J. R. 1863. *Memorials of the Abbey of St. Mary of Fountains*. Vol. 1. London: Surtees Society 42.

———. 1876. *Memorials of the Abbey of St. Mary of Fountains*. Vol. 2. London: Surtees Society 67.

Walcott, M.E.C. 1871. "Inventories and valuations of religious houses at the time of the Dissolution from the Public Record Office. With prefatory remarks and illustrative notes." *Archaeologia* 43: 201–249.

Walker, J. W. 1926. *An Historical and Architectural Description of the Priory of St. Mary Magdalene of Monk Bretton in the West Riding of Yorkshire*. Leeds: Yorkshire Archaeological Society.

Ward, A. 1986. *The Lincolnshire Rising, 1536*. Nottingham: Workers Educational Association East Midlands District.

Ward, J. 1890. *Dale and its Abbey*. Derby: Bewley and Roe.

Ward, V. 1989. "A Place House inventory: 1699." In *Titchfield. A Place in History*, edited by R. Wade and G. Watts, 51–55. Southampton: Hampshire Books.

Webb. E. A. 1921. *The Records of St. Bartholomew's Priory and St. Bartholomew the Great, West Smithfield: Volume 1*. London: Oxford University Press.

West, J. J. and N. Palmer. 2014. *Haughmond Abbey. Excavation of a 12th-century Cloister in its Historical and Landscape Context*. Swindon: English Heritage.

Whittick, C. 2010. "The history of the hospital of St Nicholas, Lewes and its successors." *Sussex Archaeological Collections* 148: 111–127.

Wilcox, R. 1987. "Thetford Cluniac Priory Excavations 1971-1974." *Norfolk Archaeology* 40: 1–18.

Williams, D. H. 1983. "Tudor Cistercian Life: Corrodians and Residential Servants." *Cîteaux. Commentarii Cistercienses Achel* 34(3–4): 284–310.

Williams, G. 1967. "The Dissolution of the Monasteries in Glamorgan." In *Welsh Reformation Essays*, edited by G. Williams, 23–43. Cardiff: University of Wales Press.

Williams, J. H. 1978. "Excavations at Greyfriars Northampton 1972." *Northamptonshire Archaeology* 13: 96–160.

Willmott, H. B. 2005. *A History of English Glassmaking, AD43-1800*. Stroud: Tempus Publishing.

Willmott, H. B. and A. Bryson. 2013. "Changing to suit the times, a post-Dissolution history of Monk Bretton Priory, South Yorkshire." *Post-Medieval Archaeology* 47(1): 136–163.

Willmott, H. B. and A. J. Daubney. 2020. "Of saints, sows or smiths? Copper-brazed iron handbells in Early Medieval England." *The Archaeological Journal* 176: 1–20.

Willmott, H. B. and P. L. Townend. 2017. "Richard de Wispeton: A face-to-face encounter with a medieval Lincolnshire priest." *Current Archaeology* 326: 42–46.

Willmott, H. B. and D. W. Wright. In press. "Rethinking early medieval 'productive sites': trade, wealth and worship at little Carlton, East Lindsey." *Antiquaries Journal*.

Wilson, D. M. and D. G. Hurst. 1962–1963. "Medieval Britain in 1961." *Medieval Archaeology* 6–7: 306–368.

———. 1966. "Medieval Britain in 1965." *Medieval Archaeology* 10: 168–219.

Wilson, J., ed. 1905. *A History of the County of Cumberland: Volume 2*. London: Archibald Constable.

Woodfield, C. 1981. "Finds from the Free Grammar School at the Whitefriars, Coventry c. 1545–c. 1557/1558." *Post-Medieval Archaeology* 15: 81–159.

Woodfield, C. 2005. *The Church of Our Lady of Mount Carmel and some conventual buildings at the Whitefriars, Coventry*. British Archaeological Reports British Series 389. Oxford: Archaeopress.

Woodward, G.W.O. 1964. "A speculation in monastic lands." *English Historical Review* 79: 778–783.

———. 1966. *The Dissolution of the Monasteries*. London: Blanford Press.

Wrathmell, S., ed. 2018. *Kirkstall Abbey, Volume II. The Guest House Excavations 1979-1986*. Wakefield: West Yorkshire Archaeology Service.

Wright, T. 1843. *Three Chapters of Letters Relating to the Suppression of Monasteries*. London: Camden Society No 26.

Wyndham, K.S.H. 1979. "In pursuit of Crown Land: The initial recipients of Somerset property in the mid Tudor period." *Somerset Archaeology and Natural History* 123: 65–73.

Youings, J. 1954. "The terms of the disposal of the Devon monastic lands, 1536–1558." *English Historical Review* 69: 18–38.

Youings, J. 1971. *The Dissolution of the Monasteries*. London: George Allen and Unwin.

INDEX

Numbers in *italic* denote pages with figures. Numbers in **bold** denote tables.

A

abbot's lodgings 14, 125, 132, 157, *158*
academic studies
  of abbeys and priories 5–6
  of the Dissolution 1–4
accidents 32
Achard, John 104
Acts
  of Dissolution 18, 19, 86, 91
  of First Fruits and Tenths 19
  for Suppression of the Alien Priories 19
agricultural buildings 14
Alcock, John 17
alien priories 16
almshouses 91–93, *92*
Amesbury Priory, Wiltshire 53
ampullae 38–39
Andries, Jasper 94
archaeology, monastic 5–6
Aston, Margaret 2, 37
Atherstone Blackfriars, Warwickshire 89
Atkins, Caroline 149
Aubrey, John 120
Audley, Sir Thomas 100, 141, 142
Audley End House, Essex 100–101, 142, *142*
Augustinian houses (Austin Friars)
  gardens 136, *136*
  London, division of site 130–131, *130*
  London, Dutch protestant refugees 77–78
  nave conversions 76–77, *76*
  order of **10**, 11, 12
  reuse of 72, 73, 81, 83
  theatre on 91

Aylesbury, Buckinghamshire 82

B

Bagott, Stephen 29
bake house 154, *154*
Bale, John 37
Bales, Edward 68, **68**
Bangor, Gwynedd 87
Bardney Abbey, Lincolnshire 61, 135, 155
Barking Abbey, Essex 32
Barlings Abbey, Lincolnshire 6, 60, 140, *141*, 145, *146*, 147, 148–149
Baskerville, Geoffrey 1
Bassett, William 42
Bathurst, John 95
Battle Abbey, East Sussex 27, 30
Baynton, Sir Edward 32
Beauchief Abbey, South Yorkshire 80
Beaulieu Abbey, Hampshire 79–80, *80*
Beckwith, Leonard 57–58
Bell, Thomas 96
Bellow, John 67–69, **68**, 149
bells 29, 30
belvederes *see* mounds
Benedictine houses
  conversion of 100, 120, 122, 123
  order of 10, **10**, 12
  reuse of 72, 73, 76, 77, 79, 80
beneficiaries of land grants 51–58, **56**, *56*
Bernard, George 4, 18
Beverley Blackfriars, East Yorkshire 28, 29
Binham Priory, Norfolk 32, 75–76, *75*
Birkenhead Priory, Merseyside 79
Blackborough Priory, Norfolk 2

Blanchard, I. 27
blessing ceremonies 38–39
Blithman, William 55, 56, 102
Bodmin, Cornwall
  Greyfriars 85
  Priory 29, 48
Bolton Priory, North Yorkshire 77
book fittings 37–38, *38*, *39*
books 37, 39, 161
Bordesley Abbey, Worcestershire 28
Boston, Lincolnshire 81, 85
Bowes, Sir Ralph 112, *113*
Boxgrove Priory, West Sussex 78
Boxley Abbey, Kent 41–42, 117, 139
Braddyll, John 58
Bradwell Abbey, Buckinghamshire 45, 123
Brandon, Charles, 1st Duke of Suffolk 60–62, *62*, 145, 146, 147
Breedon Priory, Leicestershire 79
brewing 96–97, *97*
bricks, scavenging of 102
Bridgettine house 11
Bridlington Priory, East Yorkshire 41, 76, *76*, 81
Brinkburn, Northumberland 49
Brinklow, Henry 87
Bristol Blackfriars 83–84, *83*
Brocklesby, Robert 68, **68**
Brooke, Sir Richard 118
Brown, Gaskell 116
Broxholme, John 67–69, **68**
Bryson, Alan 6
Buckfast Abbey, Devon 80
Buckland Abbey, Devon 115–116, *116*
building materials
  bricks 102
  floor tiles 45–46, 108
  lead 23–29, 40
  reuse of 43, 161
  stone 31–34, *34*, 102
  timber 40
  window glass 28–29, 44–45, *44*, 109
  woodwork 43, *43*
buildings, monastic 12–16, *13-16*
Burbage, James 91
burials 34–37, *35*, 78–79
Burnham Priory, Buckinghamshire 121, *121*
Burscough Priory, Lancashire 53
Burton Abbey, Staffordshire 42, 72
Bury St Edmunds, Suffolk 22
businesses 93–97, *94-97*
Busterd, Anthony 113
Butler, L. A. S. 81
Butley Priory, Suffolk 126
Butts, William 59
Byng, John 44
Byron, Sir John 111–112

C

Calwick Priory, Staffordshire 115
Cambridge, St Radegund Priory 17
Cammeringham Priory, Lincolnshire 65, *65*, 66–67
candlesticks 42
Canons Ashby, Northamptonshire 115
canons regular 10–11, **10**
Canterbury, Kent
  Blackfriars 95–96, *96*
  St Augustine's Abbey 33, 35
capella extra portas 79
Carew, Richard 49
Carlisle, Cumbria 81, 85
Carmarthen
  Blackfriars 88
  Greyfriars 26, 28, 36
Carmelite houses (White Friars) 11, 81, 89, 90, 93
Carré, Jean 94
Carthusian houses
  buildings 16, *16*
  closure of 40
  gardens 136, 138–139
  order of 10, 11–12
  reuse of 93, 131–132, *132*
Castle Acre Priory, Norfolk 12, 13, *13*, 59–60, *60*, 125
cathedral churches 71–72
Cavendish, Sir William 42
Caversham, Berkshire 22
Chaddesden, Derbyshire 46
Chamber, Jeffrey 41
Champernowne, John 49–50
chantries 19–20
chapels, extramural 79
chapter houses 13, *13*
charterhouses *see* Carthusian houses
Chelmsford, Essex
  Blackfriars 87
  Priory 31
Chertsey Abbey, Surrey 33
Chester, William 83
Chichester, West Sussex 82–83, *82*
choirs 12
Christopher, Saint 119
churches
  cathedral churches 71–72
  chapel, conversion to 107–108, 109
  house, conversion to 115–116, *116*
  monastic churches 12–13, *13-14*
  parish churches 73–80, *74-76*, *78*, *80*, 159–160

Index

Cirencester, St John's Hospital, Gloucestershire 92, *92*
Cistercian houses
  conversion of 117–118, *118*, 124
  order of 10, **10**, 11, 14
  reuse of 72, 79
civic redevelopment 80–85, *82–85*, 162
Civil War 76
Clapham, A. W. 106–107
Clarke, H. 5
Cleeve Abbey, Somerset 113–114, *114*, 122, *122*
Clementhorpe Priory, York 34
Clifford, Henry, 2nd Earl of Cumberland 40
Clifton-Taylor, A. 73, 75
cloister garths 13, *13*
cloisters 13, *13*
  civic reuse of 83–85, *83–85*, 88, 89
  domestic use, conversion to 103–114, *105–106, 108–114*, 162–163
Cluniac houses 10, **10**, 79
Coggeshall Abbey, Essex 79, 100
coinage 21, 23
Colchester, St Mary Magdalen's Hospital, Essex 91–92
colleges 17, 42, 72
Colvin, Sir Howard 1, 43, 45
commissioners 17, 18
company halls 83, 84
Compendium Compertorum 18
Conishead Priory, Cumbria 53
contemporary opinion 2, 4, 19
continuity of ecclesiastical use 159–160
conversi 11, 16
conversions
  agricultural 121–124, *122–123*
  concealed 100–103, *100–101*
  courtyard 103–114, *105–106, 108–114*, 162–163
  landscapes 136–138, *137*, 163
  ranges 114–121, *116, 118–121*
Cope, Sir John 115
Cope-Faulkner, P. 127
Copeland, G. W. 116
Coppack, Glyn 5, 6, 35, 103, 135, 140, 147, 149
copper alloy 29–31, *30*
corrodians 100
Court of Augmentations 3, 47, 50, 86
courtyard conversions 103–114, *105–106, 108–114*, 162–163
Coventry, Warwickshire
  Carmelite Friary 89–90, *89–90*
  Charterhouse 40
  Greyfriars 81
  Priory 31, 72
Crimbleholme, Richard 58
Cromwell, Thomas 17, 31, 47, 49, 55, 59, 127, 130, *130*

crossings 12
Crossley, David 5–6
Crowland Abbey, Lincolnshire 76
Croxden Abbey, Staffordshire 28, 117
Croxford, Norfolk 59–60, *60*
Crutched Friars 94–95
Cuthbert, Saint, shrine of 35

D

Dale Abbey, Derbyshire 29, 42–44, *43–44*, 45–46, *46*, 161
Darcy, Sir Arthur 117, 132
Dartford Priory, Kent 34
de la Pryme, Abraham 156, 157
demolition 31–33
Denny Abbey, Cambridgeshire 123, *123*
Devereux, Sir William 89
Devon land purchases 50–51
Dickens, A. G. 39
disinterment of the dead 34–37, *35*, 40
dispersal of monastic goods 37–39, *38*
Dissolution of the Chantries Act (1547) 86, 91
Dissolution of the Greater Monasteries Act (1539) 19
Dissolution of the Lesser Monasteries Act (1536) 18
Doggett, N. 103
domestic buildings
  conversions to 99, 101, 102, 103–114, *105–106, 108–114*, 162–163
  monastic 14
Dominican houses (Black Friars)
  industry in 95, 96
  order of 11
  reuse of 83–84, *83*, 85, 87, 89, 90–91
Dore Abbey, Herefordshire 79
dormitories 13, 14
dorters 13
double houses 11, 15–16
dramatic arts 90
Draye, Charles 29
Duchy of Lancaster 53
Duffy, Eamon 5
Dunwich, Suffolk 85
Durham Cathedral 35
Dutch protestant refugees 77–78

E

Edmund, Saint, shrine of 22
education 90
  see also colleges; schools
Edwards, Francis 30–31
Egglestone Abbey, County Durham 112–113, *112–113*, 141, *141*
empty graves 36
Erdeswicke, Sampson 115

estates *see* land
Everson, Paul 6, 60, 137, 145, 146, 147
expenses, official 42
extramural chapels 79
Eynsham Abbey, Oxfordshire 30

F

farms 121–124, *122-123*
fatalities 32
faunal remains 90
Faversham Abbey, Kent 35
female houses 10, 11
   see also nunneries
Fiennes, Edward, 1st Earl of Lincoln 127
financial assessment *see* valuations
First Fruits and Tenths Act (1534) 17
Fisher, H. A. L. 51
fixtures and fittings 40, 43
floor tiles 45–46, 108
Foljambe, Godfrey 117
folk rituals 38–39
Forthe, William 126
foundations, reused 127–129, *128*
Fountains Abbey, North Yorkshire 25, 35–36, *35*, 52, 72
Foxe, Charles 93
Foxe, John 39
Foxe, Richard, Bishop of Winchester 109
Franciscan houses (Grey Friars) 11, 81–82, 85, 88, 96–97, *96-97*
Freeman, John 31, 48
friars 10, 11, 19
Fulmerson, Richard 89
funerary monuments 34–35, 79, 112–113, *113*
furnaces 25–26, *26*, 30, *30*

G

gardens
  features 138–143, *140-142*, 145
  medieval 135–136, *136*
  pleasure gardens 143–148, *143-144*, *146-147*
  ruins, as garden features 140–141, *141*, 146, *146*
  Thornton Abbey, Lincolnshire 148–149, *150-151*, 152–156, *153*
  walled gardens 106, *106*, 107, 140, *140*, 153–154, *153*
Gardner, Thomas 85
Gasquet, Francis 2–3, *3*
gatehouses 14–15, *15*, 85, 102, 126–127
Gater, J. A. 138
gentry, land grants to 53–54, 62–67, *63-66*
Gilbertine houses 10, 11, 12, 15–16, 79, 124, 127
Giles, K. 82
Glamorgan 54
glass, window 28–29, 44–45, *44*, 109

glassmaking 94–95, *95*
Glastonbury Abbey, Somerset 22
Gloucester
  Blackfriars 96, *96*
  Greyfriars 96–97, *97*
gold 22, 23
goods, monastic 37–39, *38*
Gowche, Robert 68, **68**
grammar schools 86, 87, 88, 89
Grantham, Lincolnshire 81
grave markers 34–35, 45
Great Bricett Priory, Suffolk 74, *74*
Great Malvern Priory, Worcestershire 75
Greene, Patrick 5, 29
Grene, William 93
Grenville, Sir Richard 115
Gresham, Sir Richard 52
Gresham, Sir Thomas 75
Grimsby, Lincolnshire
  Greyfriars 69
  Wellow Abbey 87
guesthouses 14
Guildford Blackfriars, Surrey 33, 36
guildhalls 82, 83
Gunn, S. J. 65

H

Habakkuk, John 49, 50, 57, 58
Hadcock, R. N. 9
Haigh, Christopher 5, 58
Hailes Abbey, Gloucestershire 41
Hales, Sir Christopher 95
Halls, John 89
Harleston, Clement 100
Harrison, S. 147
Hartlepool Greyfriars, County Durham 34
Hastings, Henry, 3rd Earl of Huntingdon 126
Hathersage, Derbyshire 46
Haughmond Abbey, Shropshire 125, 139–140, *140*
Haverfordwest Priory, Pembrokeshire 24, 26
Hayfield, Colin 88
Heale, M. 72, 79
Hearon, Alexander 49
hearths 27–29, *27-28*
Heneage, Robert 63, *63*
Heneage, Sir Thomas 63–64, *64*, 87
Heneage family in Lincolnshire 62–64, *63-64*
Henry VIII, King of England 17, 47
Hertfordshire 103
Heynings Priory, Lincolnshire 79
Hill, Sir Rowland 140
Hitchin, Hertfordshire 90
Hodgett, G. A. J. 67, 69

Hodgson, J. F. 72, 73
Hogeson, William 49
Holbeach, Henry, Bishop of Lincoln 99-100, 149, 151, *151*, 152-153, 154
Holcroft, Sir Thomas 117, 118
Holder, N. 95, 130, 131
Holgate, Robert 124-125
Hope, W. H. St. J. 44, 45, 104
Hospitallers 11
hospitals 9, 91-92, *92*
houses *see* domestic buildings
houses, monastic *see* monastic orders
Howard, Maurice 103-104, 105, 106, 114
Howard, Thomas, 1st Earl of Suffolk 100-101
Howard, Thomas, 3rd Duke of Norfolk 19, 59-60, *60*, 125-126, 162
Howard, Thomas, 4th Duke of Norfolk 130, 131
Howsam, C. L. 37
Huddlestone, Sir Edmund 132
Hull Austin Friars, East Yorkshire 136, *136*
Hulme Cultram Abbey, Cumbria 79
Hulton Abbey, Staffordshire 29
Humberston Abbey, Lincolnshire 80

I

industries 93-97, *94-97*
infirmaries 14
ingots 23-25, *24*, 26
Ingworth, Richard 19
inkwells 90, *90*
inventories 18-19
Ipswich Blackfriars, Suffolk 85, *86-87*, 87-88
Issak, Edmund 132
Ixworth Priory, Suffolk 24, 25

J

Jansen, Jacob 94
Jennings, John 96
Jervaulx Abbey, North Yorkshire 23, 24, 29, 143-145, *143-144*, 148
jewels 23
John, King of England 35
Johnson, Henry 23
Johnson, Matthew 6

K

Keates, George 32
Kell, E. 108
Kendall, Thomas 132-133
Kenilworth Abbey, Warwickshire 24, *24*
Kersal Priory, Greater Manchester 53
Kerwin, William 93-94
Kettleby, Lincolnshire 66

Kew, J. 51
Keynsham Abbey, Somerset 30-31
Kington Priory, Wiltshire 120, *120*
Kirkstall Abbey, West Yorkshire 14
Kirkstead Abbey, Lincolnshire 60, 146-148, *147*
kitchens 13
Knights Templar 11, 123
Knowles, David 3, *3*, 9, 18

L

Lacock Abbey, Wiltshire 110-111, *110*
Lancashire 53, 54
land 47-69, 162
  beneficiaries 51-58, **56**, *56*
  demand for 49-51
  Lincolnshire case study 60-69, *62-66*, **68**
  pre-Dissolution leasing of 48-49
  topography of acquisition 59-60, *60*
landscapes 136-138, *137*, 163
Langley Abbey, Norfolk 25, *26*
Lapley Priory, Staffordshire 74
latrine blocks 13
Launde Abbey, Leicestershire 127-128
Lawrence, Robert 68, **68**
lay brethren 11, 16
lead 23-29, 40
  ampullae 38-39
  hearths 27-29, *27-28*
  ingots 23-25, *24*, 26
  melting and casting 25-26, *26*
  quantities 23
leases of land 48-49, 50
lecterns 22, *22*, 42
Lee, Sir Richard 128-129
Leez Priory, Essex 106-107, *106*
Leicester Abbey 126
Leland, John 112, 161
Lewes, East Sussex
  Priory 31, 32, 33, 36, 91, 137-138, *137*
  St Nicholas's Hospital 91
lime kilns 33-34, *34*
Lincoln
  Austin Friars 69
  Greyfriars 88
Lincolnshire 60-69, *62-66*, **68**, 103
Lincolnshire Rising 4, 19, 60, 61, 65, 67
Lloyd, Thomas 88
London
  Austin Friars 77-78, 130-131, *130*, 160
  Bermondsey Abbey 36
  Blackfriars 90-91
  Bridgettine House, Syon 11
  Charterhouse 93, 131

Christ's Hospital 88, *88*
Crutched Friars 94–95
Greyfriars 88, *88*
guilds 82
Holy Trinity Priory, Aldgate 33, 93–94, *94*, 130
Holywell Priory, Shoreditch 91
land purchases 51
St Bartholomew's Priory, Smithfield 77, 133, 160
St Helen's, Bishopsgate 77, *78*, 132–133
St Mary Graces, Smithfield 36, 132
St Mary Spital, Spitalfields 132, *133*
urban palaces 129–133, *130-133*
London, Dr. 22, 31, 40–41, 82
Long, Sir Richard 120
looting 36, 37, 40, 41
Lowe, Ben 4
Ludlow, Shropshire 93

M

Maiden Bradley Priory, Wiltshire 53
Mansel, Sir Rice 54
Mantel, Hilary 1
Marksey Abbey, Lincolnshire 62–63
Marsh, C. 1
Martin, A. R. 88, 95–96
McNeil, R. 118
Meaux Abbey, East Yorkshire 33
mendicant orders 11, 19
mercenarii 11, 12
Merevale Abbey, Warwickshire 79
metals
  copper alloy 29–31, *30*
  gold 22, 23
  lead 23–29, *24*, 40
  silver 22, 23, 27, 28
middens 119
military orders **10**, 11
Milton Abbey, Dorset 55–56, *56*
Ministry of Works 102
Mitchiner, M. 38–39
monastic orders 9–12, **10**, 77
Mone, Richard 77
Monk Bretton Priory, South Yorkshire 6–7, *6*
  bells 29
  books 37
  gatehouse 102
  grant of 55
  grave markers 34
  lead 23
  precious metals 22–23
  reuse of materials at 102
Monk Sherborne Priory, Hampshire 74–75
monks 10, **10**

Monson, Thomas 88
Montacute Priory, Somerset 126
Morley, Derbyshire 43–44, *44-45*, *45-46*, 161
Morris, Sir Charles 29
mortar 46, *46*
mounds 137, *137*, 141, *141*, 155
Mount Grace Priory, North Yorkshire 16, *16*, 136
Muchelney Abbey, Somerset 25, 53, 125
Mundy, Thomas 48

N

naves 13, 75–78, *75-76*
Naylor, Brian 94
Neath Abbey, Glamorganshire 29
Netley Abbey, Hampshire 32, 101, *101*, 102–103, 107–110, *108-109*
new builds on old foundations 127–129, *128*
new men, land grants to 54–56
new religious communities 77
Newcastle, Tyne and Wear 81, 83, 84, *84-85*
Newstead Abbey, Nottinghamshire 22, *22*, 54, 111–112, *111*, 140
Newstead upon Ancholme Priory, Lincolnshire 63, *63*
nobility and courtiers, land grants to 52–53, **56**, 59–62, *60*, *62*
Norfolk
  book fittings distribution 38–39, *38*
  land acquisition 59–60, *60*, 162
Normanburgh, Norfolk 59–60, *60*
North, Edward 93, 131
North Ormsby Priory, Lincolnshire 63, *63*
Northampton Greyfriars 25, *26*
Norton Priory, Cheshire 6, 118–119, *119*, 142–143
Norwich, Norfolk 59, *60*
  Blackfriars 78
  Greyfriars 28, 59, *60*
  St Leonard's Priory 59
Nottinghamshire 52–53, 54
Nuncotham Priory, Lincolnshire 48–49, 66
Nunkeeling Priory, East Yorkshire 52
nunneries **10**, 11, 120–121, *120-121*, 124

O

orders, monastic 9–12, **10**, 77
Orford Priory, Lincolnshire 48–49, 65, *65*, 66
organs 42
outcomes of the Dissolution 162
Oxford Blackfriars 31

P

Paget, Sir William 42, 53
Palmer, C. F. R. 85
panelling 43, *43*

parish churches 73–80, *74-76*, *78*, *80*, 159–160
parochial rights of worship 72–73
Paston family in Norfolk 75–76
Paulet, Thomas *130*, 131
Paulet, Sir William
   Austin Friars, London 77–78, *130*, 131, 160
   Netley Abbey, Hampshire 101, 107, 108, 109, 110
Paynell, Thomas 81
Pentney Priory, Norfolk 126
pews 43, *43*
piers 81
Pilgrimage of Grace 4, 19, 48, 55, 76, 142
Pinley, Warwickshire 124
Pipewell Abbey, Northamptonshire 41
plans 12
plate 21, 22–23, *22*
Platt, Colin 5
playhouses 91
plays 90
Pole, Sir Francis 29, 42–43, 44, 46, 161
Pollard, Richard 22, 41
poor people 91
porch 45
Portable Antiquities Scheme (PAS) 37, 38
Porte, Sir John 43
Portinari, Giovanni 31–32, 33
pottery industry 94, *94*
preceptories 11
precincts 84, *84*
precious metals 21–23
pre-Dissolution leases of land 48–49
Premonstratensian (Norbertine) houses **10**, 11, 79
presbyteries 12, 77, 78
Prescott, H. F. M. 1
Prideaux, Nicholas 48
prior's lodgings 14, 124, *124*, 125–126
prisons 85
process of Dissolution 16–20
protestant refugees 77–78
public worship 71–80, *74-76*, *78*, *80*

R

Radbourne, Derbyshire 43, *43*
Radcliffe, Ralph 90
Reading, Berkshire
   Abbey 33
   Greyfriars 40–41
refectories 13–14, 80, *80*, 91, 117
relics 18, 41–42
religious communities, new 77
reredorters 13, 37
resistance to the Dissolution 4
resonance passages 89–90

Reynolds, P. K. Baillie 7, 102
Rich, Richard, 1st Baron 29, 77, 106, 107, 160
Rievaulx Abbey, North Yorkshire 23–24, 26, 32, 136
Ripon, John 35–36, *35*
Risley Hall, Derbyshire 46
rituals 38–39
roads 81
Roberts, David 156
Roche Abbey, South Yorkshire 39–40, 160
Rokeby, Sir Thomas 112
rood screens 13, *14*
Rufford Abbey, Nottinghamshire 54, 117, 138
ruins, as garden features 140–141, *141*, 146, *146*
Rule of Saint Benedict 10
Russell, John, 1st Earl of Bedford 53

S

Sacheverell, Sir Henry 43–44, 45, *45*
Sadler, Sir Ralph 57–58
sale and redistribution 42–46, *43-46*
sanctuaries 12
Sandwell Priory, Staffordshire 122–123
Savine, A. 21, 50, 51
Sawley Abbey, Lancashire 117
scaffolding 33
Scarborough, North Yorkshire 81
Schofield, John 82, 93, 129, 133
schools 86–91, *87-90*, 162
scramble for spoils 49, 160
sea defences 81
Selborne Priory, Hampshire 17
Selby Abbey, North Yorkshire 57–58
Sempringham Priory, Lincolnshire 127
servants 11, 12
Seymour, Edward, 1st Duke of Somerset 53
Seymour, Edward, 1st Earl of Hertford 125
Shagan, Ethan 4, 41
Sharington, Sir William 110, 111
Sharpe, Sir John 100
Sheen Charterhouse, Surrey 138–139
Shelford Priory, Nottinghamshire 54
Sherbrook, Michael 39–40, 160
shrines 21–22, 35
silver 22, 23, 27, 28
Sixhill Priory, Lincolnshire 64, *64*
Skinner, Sir Vincent 152, 156, 157, 158
Skipwith, Edward 66
Smith, A. 109, 138
Smith, I. 91
Somerset 53
Sopwell Priory, Hertfordshire 25, 27, *27*, 128–129, *128*
speculators, land grants to 57–58, 67–69, **68**
Spelman, Sir Henry 2, 75

spoliation of the monasteries 37, 39–42
St Andrew's Priory, York 34
St Augustine's Abbey, Canterbury, Kent 33, 35
St German's Priory, Cornwall 49–50
St Helen's, Bishopsgate, London 77, *78*, 132–133
St John's Hospital, Cirencester, Gloucestershire 92, *92*
St Leonard's Priory, Norwich 59
St Mary Magdalen's Hospital, Colchester, Essex 91–92
St Nicholas's Hospital, Lewes, East Sussex 91
St Radegund Priory, Cambridge 17
Stainfield Priory, Lincolnshire 65, *65*, 66, 155
Stanley Abbey, Wiltshire 32
state care of monastic sites 102
statues 41–42, 119
Steane, J. 5
Stephen, King of England 35
Stewart, Matthew, 4th Earl of Lennox 144
Stocker, David 6, 60, 145, 146, 147
Stogursey Priory, Somerset 74, *74*
Stow, John 94–95
Strelley, Robert 112, 113
Stukeley, William 96, 147, *147*
Suppression of the Alien Priories Act (1414) 16
surrender of the monasteries 18
surveys 17, *17*, 18–19
Sutton, Thomas 93
Swales, T. H. 59, 162
Swine Priory, East Yorkshire 11, 52, 79
Swithun, Saint, shrine of 22
Sydney, Thomas 75
Syon Bridgettines, London 11

T

Talbot, George, 6th Earl of Shrewsbury 138
Talbot family in Nottinghamshire 54, 117
Tattershall Castle, Lincolnshire 61–62
Templars 11, 123
theatres 91
Thetford, Norfolk
  Blackfriars 89
  Priory 19, 59, 123–124, *125–126*, *125*
Thompson, Joan 48–49
Thorney Abbey, Cambridgeshire 27, 35
Thornton Abbey, Lincolnshire
  Abbot's Lodge 157, *158*
  bake house 154, *154*
  burials 36
  clearance of 102
  college 72
  division of 99–100, 149, *150–151*, 151–152
  gardens 152–156, *153*
  gatehouse 15, *15*, 126
  hall 156–158, *156*

lead hearth 28, *28*
lime kiln 34, *34*
Tilty Abbey, Essex 79, 141–142
timber 40
Tintern Abbey, Monmouthshire 27–28, 29
Titchfield Abbey, Hampshire 104–106, *105*
Tittler, R. 82
tomb canopy 45
tomb robbing 34–37, *35*, 40
tomb slab 45, *45*
tombs *see* funerary monuments
topography of land acquisition 59–60, *60*
towers 12, 77, 80
town halls 82, *82*
town walls 81
towns
  palaces 129–133, *130–133*
  property 51, 58
  redevelopment 80–85, *82–85*
transepts 12
translation of the dead 36–37, 40
Tregonwell, John 55–56, *56*
Trigge, Francis 2
Tudor, Edmund 36
Tunstall, William 92
Turner, R. C. 118
Tyldesley, William 121
Tyrell, Henry 40
Tyrwhitt, Sir Robert Sr. 61, 64–66, *65*, 152
Tyrwhitt family in Lincolnshire 64–67, *65–66*, 155

U

undermining 32–33
urban palaces 129–133, *130–133*
urban property 51, 58
urban redevelopment 80–85, *82–85*

V

Vale Royal Abbey, Cheshire 117–118, *118*
Valor Ecclesiasticus (1535) 17, *17*, 21
valuations 21, 42, 50, 51
Vaughn, Stephen 132
Verzelini, Giacomo 94, 95
vestments 40, 42, 77, 161
visitations to the monasteries 17–18
visitors, attraction of 102
votive practices 38–39

W

Walden Abbey, Essex 100–101
Walsingham Priory, Norfolk 75
Waltham Abbey, Essex 19
waste disposal 119

water supplies 81, 88
watercourses 142–143
waterfront developments 81
Watton Priory, East Yorkshire 15, *15*, 34, 124–125, *124*
Waynflete, William 17
weaving 95–96, *96*
Welbeck Abbey, Nottinghamshire 54
Wellow Abbey, Grimsby, Lincolnshire 87
Wenlock Priory, Shropshire 29
west ranges 14, 116–118, *118*
Westwood Priory, Worcestershire 29
Wetheral Priory, Cumbria 126–127
Whalley Abbey, Lancashire 58
Whitereson, Henry 57–58
Whitgift, Robert 87
Whorwood, Robert 122
Wigston, Margaret 124
Wigston, Sir William 124
Williams, Sir John 23
Willmott, Hugh 149
Wilson, William 29
Winchester, Hampshire 22
Winchester House, London 131, *131*
window glass 28–29, 44–45, *44*, 109
window leads 29
windows 44–45, *44*, 109, *109*
Wispington, Richard de 36
Witham Charterhouse, Somerset 139
Wolsey, Ralph 79
Wolsey, Thomas 17
Wood, Robert 99–100, 149, 151, *151*
Woodward, G. W. O. 3, 23, 57
woodwork 43, *43*
Worcester Cathedral 35
Worksop Priory, Nottinghamshire 54
Wormegay Priory, Norfolk 2
worship, public 71–80, *74–76*, *78*, *80*
Wriothesley, Thomas, 1st Earl of Southampton 53, 79, 104, 105–106
writing equipment 90, *90*
Wyatt, Sir Thomas 94, 117, 139

Y

Yetsweirt, Nicase 92
York
  Clementhorpe Priory 34
  guildhalls 82
  St Andrew's Priory 34
Youings, J. 3, 19, 47, 48, 49, 51

www.ingramcontent.com/pod-product-compliance
Lightning Source LLC
Chambersburg PA
CBHW061138230426
43662CB00023B/2461